Early 20th Century
LIGHTING
Electric and Gas

Schiffer Publishing Ltd
4880 Lower Valley Road, Atglen, PA 19310 USA

Library of Congress Control Number: 2002102721

Front matter typeset in Korinna BT

ISBN: 0-7643-1678-8
Printed in China

Published by Schiffer Publishing Ltd.
4880 Lower Valley Road
Atglen, PA 19310
Phone: (610) 593-1777; Fax: (610) 593-2002
E-mail: Schifferbk@aol.com
Please visit our web site catalog at
www.schifferbooks.com
We are always looking for people to write books on new and related subjects. If you have an idea for a book, please contact us at the above address.

This book may be purchased from the publisher.
Include $3.95 for shipping.
Please try your bookstore first.
You may write for a free catalog.

In Europe, Schiffer books are distributed by:
Bushwood Books
6 Marksbury Ave.
Kew Gardens
Surrey TW9 4JF
England
Phone: 44 (0)208 392-8585
Fax: 44 (0)208 392-9876
E-mail: Bushwd@aol.com
Free postage in the UK. Europe: air mail at cost.
Try your bookstore first.

Introduction

The late nineteenth and early twentieth centuries saw the final stage in the transition from gas household lighting to electricty. The conversion had begun in 1879 with Thomas A. Edison's incandescent light bulb. The first overhead electric lighting was installed by Edison at the Madison Square Theater in New York, which opened on February 4, 1890. The real significance of his invention, however, became apparent two years later, when Edison installed a distribution system for electricity in part of New York City. From the Pearl St. generating plant, the world's first permanent central electric-light power plant, to the sockets on the bulbs, Edison created a complete system, proving the practicality of electric power and light for the home, theaters, and businesses. Suddenly longer working hours and "night life" became a possibility.

As the use of electricity spread, so did the demand for lighting devices. In some cases this meant the conversion of existing gas fixtures, but it did not take long for new, more sophisticated designs to emerge. Electricity gave new flexibility to fixture designers, enabling them to experiment with forms that were never possible with the cumbersome and dangerous gas fixtures. Soon they were ushering in an elegant period of household lighting, a golden age of lighting design.

Among the leading American manufacturers of lighting was the Beardslee Chandelier Manufacturing Company, with its factory and showrooms on South Clinton Street in Chicago, Illinois. The pages that follow contain a complete facsimile reproduction of a catalog they produced during the transition from gas to electricity. Although it is undated the styles of fixtures represented, including Victorian, Colonial Revival, Art Nouveau, Prairie School, and early Arts and Crafts designs, would place it in the first few years of the twentieth century. In its pages are illustrations and descriptions of hundreds of gas, electric, and combination lighting fixtures for both indoor and outdoor use. Chandeliers and other hanging lamps, ornately decorated table lamps, desk lamps, glass shades, and lighting accessories are presented with original wholesale prices, measurements, and reference numbers. For today's collectors an estimated value on today's market is included beside each piece.

In the closing line of the letter to the trade that once opened this catalog, the company urged the reader not to "mutilate this Catalog but preserve for future reference." Fortunately someone followed directions, and we have this wonderful reference to a golden age of lighting design.

A Word About Prices

To make this book useful to collectors as well as historians, estimated values for the lighting fixtures have been superimposed next to their illustrations. These figures represent a knowledgable estimate of what a purchaser could expect to pay if they found a similar fixture for sale at a reputable antiques dealer.

Please note:

Although the catalog was originally printed in black and white, many of the shades and fixtures were available in art glass colors. As an aid to the consumer Beardslee pasted in color samples, which we have reproduced on the back cover.

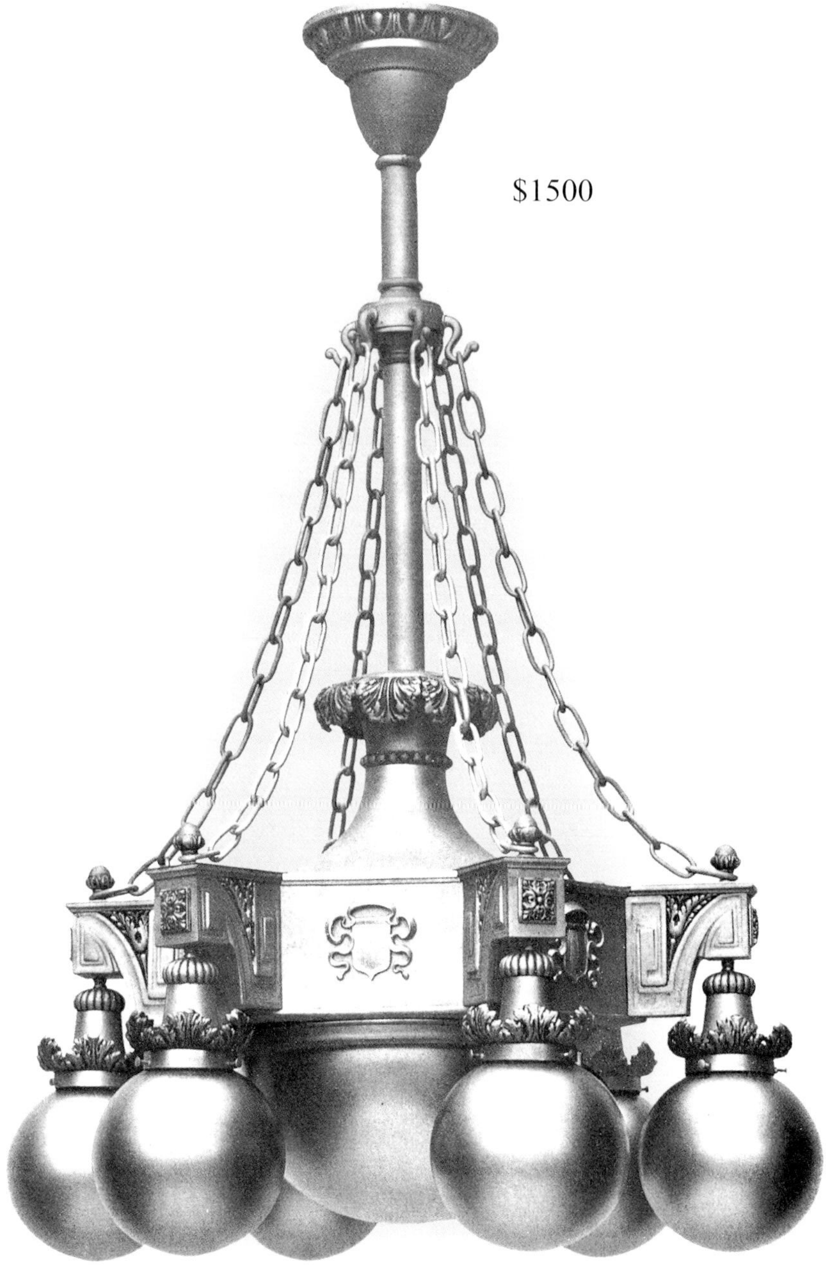

$1500

Number 2647

Length, 48 inches (over all). Spread, 24 inches.

14-inch C. R. I. Bowl and 3¼-inch Holders included.

		Not Wired	Wired	Complete as shown No lamps
9 Electric (3 Lights in Bowl)	Brush Brass and Black	$178.00	$182.50	$190.60

3¼x7-inch Crystal Roughed Inside Balls.

Price in right hand column always includes sockets; also holders and shades if shown but no lamps. Other prices include glassware, sockets, lamps or electric holders only where mentioned.

$1600

Number 2648

Length, 50 inches (over all). Spread, 24 inches.

14-inch C. R. I. Bowl, C. R. I. Flame and 3¼-inch Holders included.

	Not Wired	Wired	Complete as shown No lamps
10 Electric (3 Lights in Bowl, 1 Light in Flame) Brush Brass and Black......	$183.00	$188.00	$196.50

3¼x7-inch Crystal Roughed Inside Balls.

Price in right hand column always includes sockets; also holders and shades if shown but no lamps. Other prices include glassware, sockets, lamps or electric holders only where mentioned.

Number 2421

Length, 48 inches (over all). Spread, 38 inches.

16-inch C. R. I. Bowl and 3¼-inch Holders included.

		Not Wired	Wired	Complete as shown No lamps
8 Electric (4 Lights in Bowl)	Brush Brass and Black	$96.50	$99.50	$105.70
9 " (4 " ")	" " " "	110.00	113.50	120.85
10 " (4 " ")	" " " "	123.50	127.50	136.00
12 " (4 " ")	" " " "	150.50	155.50	166.30

3¼x7-inch Crystal Roughed Inside Balls.

Price in right hand column always includes sockets; also holders and shades if shown but no lamps. Other prices include glassware, sockets, lamps or electric holders only where mentioned.

$1200

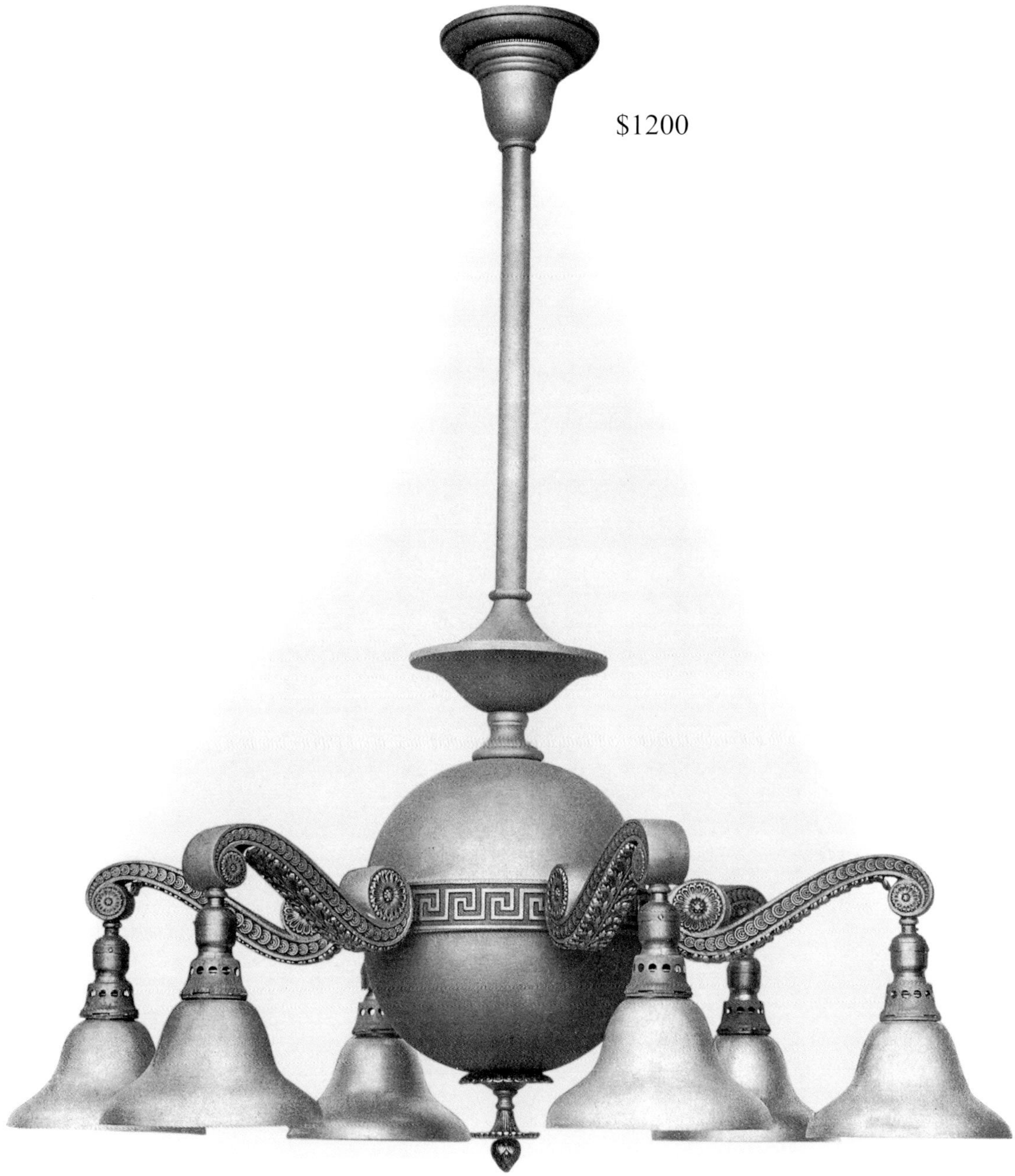

Number 2413

Length, 48 inches (over all). Spread, 31 inches.

		Not Wired	Wired	Complete as shown No lamps
4	Electric Brush Brass and Black....	$76.00	$78.00	$82.80
5	" " " " "	88.50	91.00	97.00
6	" " ' " "	101.00	104.00	111.20
8	" " " " "	126.00	130.00	139.60

Shades No. B 250 Crystal Roughed Inside. Diameter, 8 inches.

Price in right hand column always includes sockets; also holders and shades if shown but no lamps. Other prices include glassware, sockets, lamps or electric holders only where mentioned.

$1100

Number 2415

Length, 48 inches (over all). Spread, 31 inches.

6 Light Clusters included.

				Not Wired	Wired	Complete as shown No lamps
24	Electric	(4 Arms)	Brush Brass and Black	$96.00	$98.00	$98.00
30	"	(5 ")	" " " "	113.50	116.00	116.00
36	"	(6 ")	" " " "	131.00	134.00	134.00
42	"	(7 ")	" " " "	148.50	152.00	152.00
48	"	(8 ")	" " " "	166.00	170.00	170.00

Price in right hand column always includes sockets; also holders and shades if shown but no lamps.
Other prices include glassware, sockets, lamps or electric holders only where mentioned.

Number 2420

Length, 18 inches (over all). Spread, 30 inches.

16-inch C. R. I. Bowl and 6 Light Clusters included.

			Not Wired	Wired	Complete as shown No lamps
28	Electric (4 Lights in Bowl)	Brush Brass and Black	$139.50	$142.50	$144.10
34	" (4 " ")	" " " "	163.75	167.25	168.85
40	" (4 " ")	" " " "	188.00	192.00	193.60
52	" (4 " ")	" " " "	236.50	241.50	243.10

Price in right hand column always includes sockets; also holders and shades if shown but no lamps.
Other prices include glassware, sockets, lamps or electric holders only where mentioned.

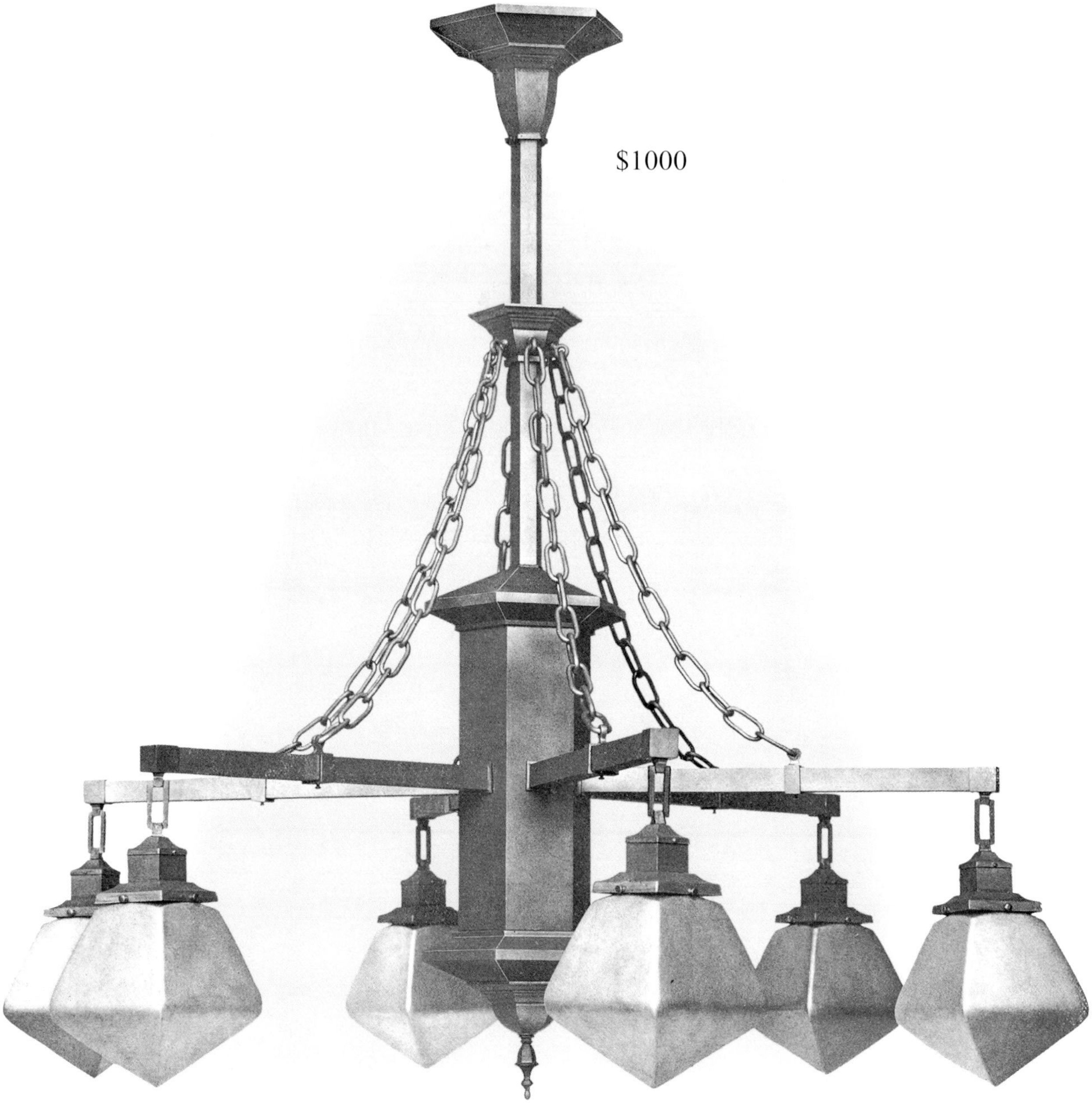

Number 2417
Length, 48 inches (over all). Spread, 40 inches.
3¼-inch Socket Cover Holders included.

		Not Wired	Wired	Complete as shown No lamps
2 Electric	Brush Brass	$47.00	$48.00	$51.80
3 "	" "	53.75	55.25	60.95
6 "	" "	74.00	77.00	88.40

No. B 180 3¼x8-inch Crystal Roughed Inside Square Balls.
Extra lengthening per foot 80 cents not wired, 90 cents wired.
Without 3¼-inch Socket Cover Holders deduct $1.25 each list.

Price in right hand column always includes sockets; also holders and shades if shown but no lamps. Other prices include glassware, sockets, lamps or electric holders only where mentioned.

$1000

Number 2418

Length, 48 inches (over all). Spread, 40 inches.

	Not Wired	Wired	Complete as shown No lamps
2 Electric Brush Brass	$40.00	$41.00	$43.40
3 " " "	43.75	45.25	48.85
6 " " "	55.00	58.00	65.20

Shades No. B 250 Crystal Roughed Inside. Diameter, 8 inches.
Extra lengthening per foot 80 cents not wired, 90 cents wired.

Price in right hand column always includes sockets; also holders and shades if shown but no lamps. Other prices include glassware, sockets, lamps or electric holders only where mentioned.

$1000

Number 2656

Length, 48 inches (over all). Spread, 22 inches.

14-inch C. R. I. Bowl, C .R. I. Flame and 3¼-inch Holders included.

	Not Wired	Wired	Complete as shown No lamps
10 Electric (3 Lights in Bowl, 1 Light in Flame) Brush Brass and Black......	$143.75	$148.75	$157.25

3¼x7-inch Crystal Roughed Inside Balls.

Price in right hand column always includes sockets; also holders and shades if shown but no lamps. Other prices include glassware, sockets, lamps or electric holders only where mentioned.

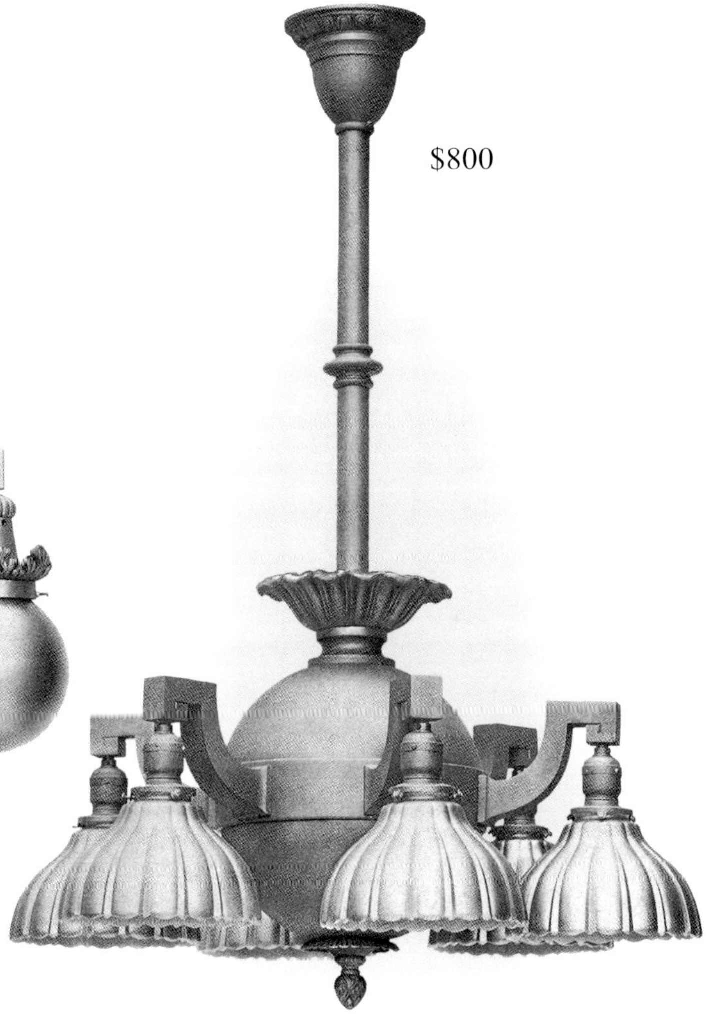

Number 2630

Length, 40 inches (over all). Spread, 19 inches.

3¼-inch Holders included.

	Not Wired	Wired	Complete as shown No lamps
3 Electric Brush Brass and Black....	$54.75	$56.25	$59.25
4 " " " " "	63.00	65.00	69.00
5 " " " " "	71.25	73.75	78.75
6 " " " " "	79.50	[illegible]	[illegible]

3¼x6-inch Crystal Roughed Inside Balls.

Number 2629

Length, 40 inches. Spread, 19 inches.

	Not Wired	Wired	Complete as shown No lamps
3 Electric Brush Brass and Black....	$42.75	$44.25	$50.25
4 " " " " "	47.00	[illegible]	[illegible]
5 " " " " "	[illegible]	[illegible]	[illegible]
6 " " " " "	55.50	58.50	70.50

Shades No. B 3424 Alba.

Price in right hand column always includes sockets; also holders and shades if shown but no lamps.
Other prices include glassware, sockets, lamps or electric holders only where mentioned.

$500

$800

Number 2672

Length, 40 inches (over all).

10-inch Iridescent Prisms included.

		Not Wired	Wired	Complete as shown No lamps
1 Electric	Brush Brass and Black....	$43.60	$44.85	$45.25
2 "	" " " "	43.85	45.35	46.15
3 "	" " " "	44.10	45.85	47.05
4 "	" " " "	44.35	46.35	47.95

Extra lengthening per foot, $2.00.

Number 2594

Length, 40 inches (over all). Spread, 21 inches.

		Not Wired	Wired	Complete as shown No lamps
2 Electric	Brush Brass and Black....	$37.00	$38.00	$42.30
3 "	" " " "	41.50	43.00	49.45
4 "	" " " "	46.00	48.00	56.60
5 "	" " " "	50.50	53.00	63.75
6 "	" " " "	55.00	58.00	70.90

Shades No. B 3424 Alba.

Price in right hand column always includes sockets; also holders and shades if shown but no lamps.
Other prices include glassware, sockets, lamps or electric holders only where mentioned.

$500

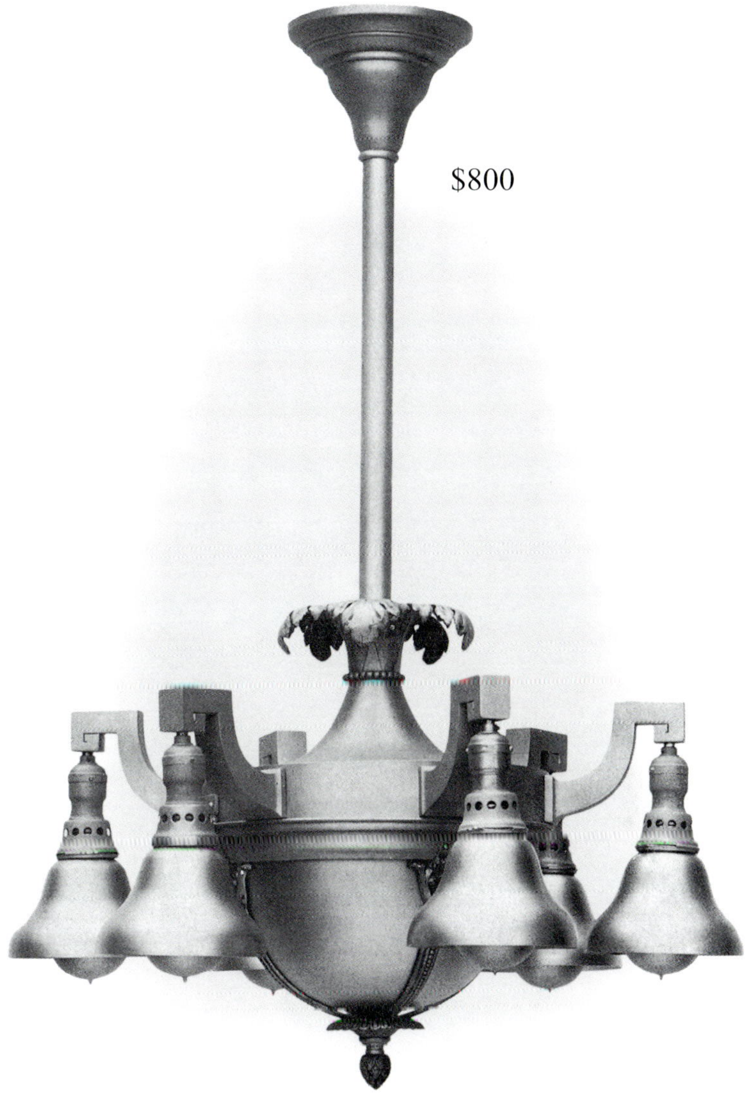

$800

Number 2614

Length, 36 inches. Spread, 12 inches.

		Not Wired	Wired	Complete as shown No lamps
2 Electric	Brush Brass	$22.50	$23.50	$25.80
4 "	" "	31.00	33.00	36.60

2¼x7-inch Crystal Roughed Inside Domes.

Number [illegible]

Length, 40 inches. Spread, 22 inches.

12-inch C. R. I. Bowl included.

		Not Wired	Wired	Complete as shown No lamps
5 Electric (2 Lights in Bowl)	Brush Brass and Black	$46.25	$49.75	[illegible]
6 " (2 " ")		50.50	53.50	63.30
7 " (2 " ")		54.75	58.25	64.05
8 " (2 " ")		59.00	63.00	69.80

Shades No. B 249 Crystal Roughed Inside. Diameter, 6 inches.

Price in right hand column always includes sockets; also holders and shades if shown but no lamps.
Other prices include glassware, sockets, lamps or electric holders only where mentioned.

Number 2283

Length, 55 inches (over all). Spread, 28 inches.

4x10-inch C. R. I. Bottom Ball and Holders included.

		Not Wired	Wired	Complete as shown No lamps
4	Electric Brush Brass and Black....	$75.05	$77.80	$81.65
5	" " " " "	84.55	87.80	92.80
6	" " " " "	94.05	97.80	103.95
7	" " " " "	103.55	107.80	115.10
8	" " " " "	113.05	117.80	126.25
9	" " " " "	122.55	127.80	137.40

3¼x7-inch Crystal Roughed Inside Balls.

Beardslee Patent Chandelier Stem used in Stem. Extra lengthening per foot, $7.50.

Price in right hand column always includes sockets; also holders and shades if shown but no lamps.
Other prices include glassware, sockets, lamps or electric holders only where mentioned.

Number 2639

Number 2639½

Number 2639

Length, 36 inches (over all). Spread, 18 inches.

			Not Wired	Wired	Complete as shown No lamps
2	Electric	Brush Brass	$6.55	$7.35	$9.45
[illegible]	"	" "	[illegible]	[illegible]	[illegible]
4	"	" "	7.85	9.45	13.65
6	"	" "	9.15	11.55	[illegible]

Number 2639½

Spread, 24 inches.

			Not Wired	Wired	Complete as shown No lamps
2	Electric	Brush Brass	$6.75	$7.55	$9.65
0	"	" "	7.50	8.70	11.85
4	"	" "	8.25	9.85	14.05
6	"	" "	9.75	12.15	18.45

2¼x7-inch Crystal Roughed Inside Domes.

Number [illegible]

Length, 48 inches (over all). Spread, 20 inches.

3¼-inch Holders included.

			Not Wired	Wired	Complete as shown No lamps
2	Electric	Brush Brass and Black	$25.50	$26.50	$28.80
3	"	" " " "	31.75	33.25	36.70
4	"	" " " "	38.00	40.00	44.60
5	"	" " " "	44.25	46.75	52.50

3¼x7-inch Crystal Roughed Inside Balls.

Price in right hand column always includes sockets; also holders and shades if shown but no lamps.
Other prices include glassware, sockets, lamps or electric holders only where mentioned.

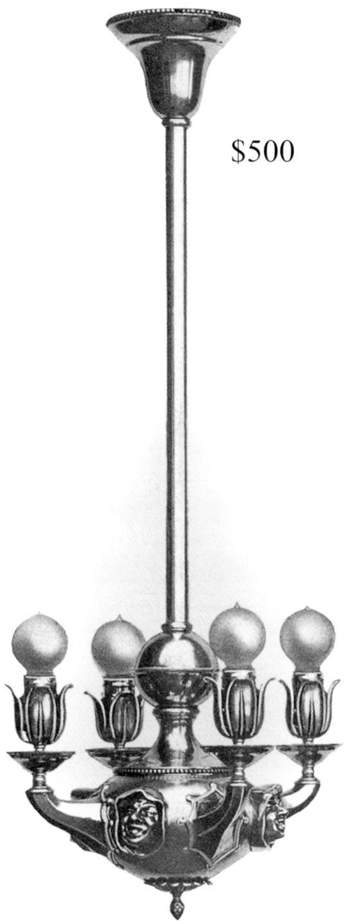

$500

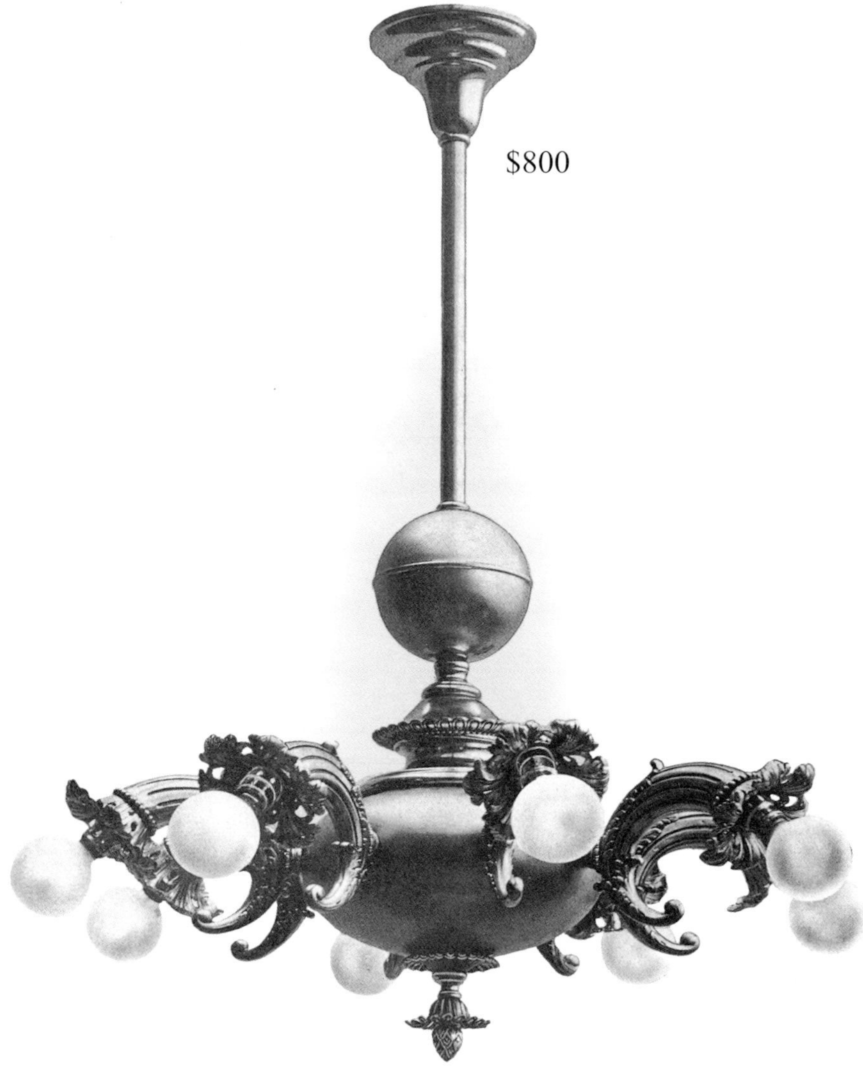

$800

Number 2156

Length, 36 inches. Spread, 11 inches.

Socket Husks included.

		Not Wired	Wired	Complete as shown No lamps
2 Electric	Brush Brass	$17.75	$18.75	$19.55
3 "	" "	23.00	24.50	25.70
4 "	" "	28.25	30.25	31.85

If wanted with Chain Pull Sockets add 30 cents for each light to prices in right hand column.

Number 2158

Length, 40 inches. Spread, 32 inches.

		Not Wired	Wired	Complete as shown No lamps
3 Electric	Polished Brass and Black..	$54.75	$56.25	$57.45
4 "	" " " " ..	65.00	67.00	68.60
5 "	" " " " ..	75.25	77.75	79.75
6 "	" " " " ..	85.50	88.50	90.90
8 "	" " " " ..	106.00	110.00	113.20

Price in right hand column always includes sockets; also holders and shades if shown but no lamps.
Other prices include glassware, sockets, lamps or electric holders only where mentioned.

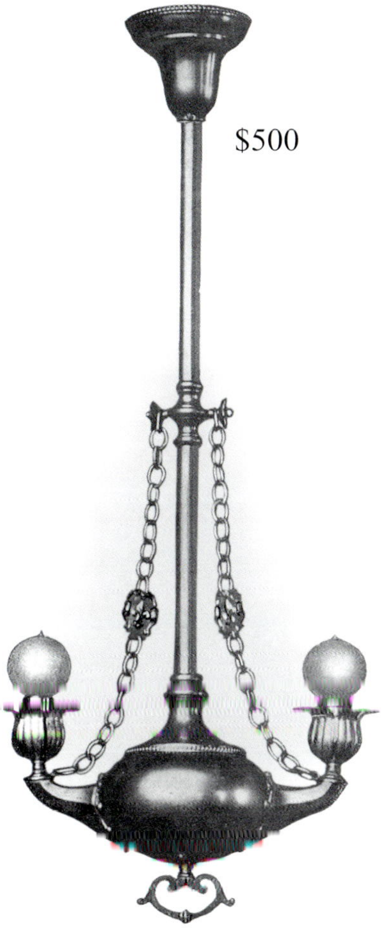

[illegible]

Length, 36 inches. Spread, 11 inches.
Socket Husks included.

		Not Wired	Wired	Complete as shown No lamps
2 Electric	Brush Brass and Black....	$15.25	$16.25	$17.05
3 "	" " " "	23.25	24.75	25.95
4 "	" " " "	31.25	33.25	34.85

If wanted with Chain Pull Sockets add 30 cents for each light to prices in right hand column.

Number 2102

Length, 10 inches. Spread, 34 inches.
12-inch C. R. I. Bowl included.

		Not Wired	Wired	Complete as shown No lamps
7 Electric (4 Lights in Bowl)	Polished Brass and Black	$60.85	$64.35	$67.15
8 " (4 " ")		71.10	75.10	78.30
9 " (4 " ")		81.35	85.85	89.45
10 " (4 " ")		91.60	96.60	100.60
12 " (4 " ")		112.10	118.10	122.90

Price in right hand column always includes sockets; also holders and shades if shown but no lamps.
Other prices include glassware, sockets, lamps or electric holders only where mentioned.

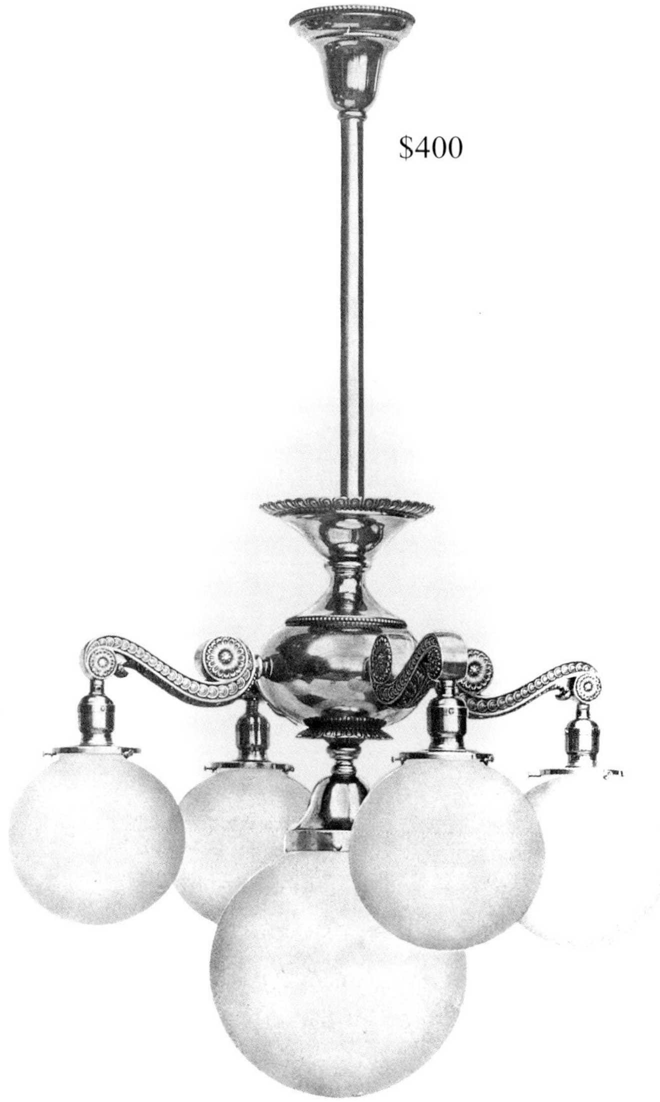

Number 2164

Length, 42 inches (over all). Spread, 19 inches.

4x8-inch C. R. I. Bottom Ball included.

		Not Wired	Wired	Complete as shown No lamps
3 Electric	Polished Brass and Black..	$26.00	$28.25	$30.45
4 "	" " " " ..	32.00	34.75	37.85
5 "	" " " " ..	38.00	41.25	45.25
6 "	" " " " ..	44.00	47.75	52.65
7 "	" " " " ..	50.00	54.25	60.05

2¼x7-inch Crystal Roughed Inside Domes.

Extra lengthening per foot, $2.00.

Number 1944

Length, 42 inches (over all). Spread, 19 inches.

4x10-inch C. R. I. Bottom Ball included.

		Not Wired	Wired	Complete as shown No lamps
3 Electric	Polished Brass and Black..	$26.00	$27.50	$30.60
4 "	" " " " ..	32.00	34.00	38.45
5 "	" " " " ..	38.00	40.50	46.30
6 "	" " " " ..	44.00	47.00	54.15
7 "	" " " " ..	50.00	53.50	62.00

3¼x7-inch Crystal Roughed Inside Balls.

Price in right hand column always includes sockets; also holders and shades if shown but no lamps.
Other prices include glassware, sockets, lamps or electric holders only where mentioned.

Number 1554

Length, 42 inches (over all). Spread, 22 inches.

3¼-inch Holders and Husks included.

			Not Wired	Wired	Complete as shown No lamps
3	Electric	Rich Gilt	$61.50	$63.00	$68.70
4	"	" "	72.00	74.00	81.60
5	"	" "	82.50	85.00	94.50
6	"	" "	93.00	96.00	107.40
8	"	" "	114.00	118.00	133.20

No. B 5121 3¼x6-inch Ground and Cut Star Balls.

Number 1796

Length, 42 inches (over all). Spread, 22 inches.

			Not Wired	Wired	Complete as shown No lamps
3	Electric	Rich Gilt	$54.00	$56.25	$59.85
4	"	" "	63.00	65.75	70.55
5	"	" "	72.00	75.25	81.25
6	"	" "	81.00	84.75	91.95
8	"	" "	99.00	103.75	113.35

3¼x6-inch Crystal Roughed Inside Balls.

Extra lengthening per foot, $2.00.

Price in right hand column always includes sockets; also holders and shades if shown but no lamps.
Other prices include glassware, sockets, lamps or electric holders only where mentioned.

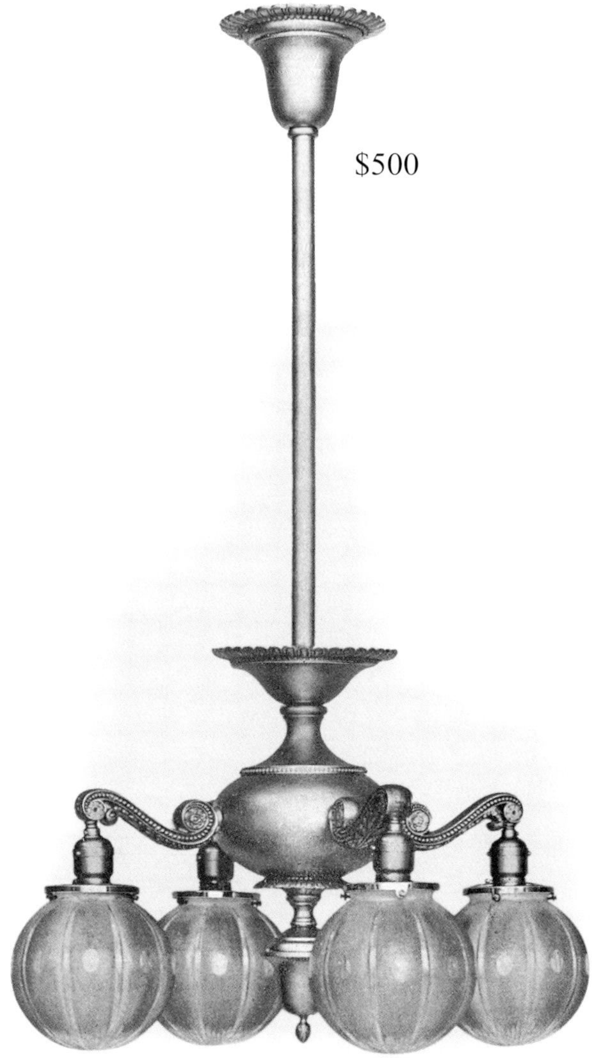

Number 2124

Length, 36 inches (over all). Spread, 15 inches.

		Not Wired	Wired	Complete as shown No lamps
2 Electric	Polished Brass and Black..	$14.25	$15.25	$17.65
3 "	" " " " ..	16.50	18.00	21.60
4 "	" " " " ..	18.75	20.75	26.15
5 "	" " " " ..	21.00	23.50	29.50

3¼x6-inch Crystal Roughed Inside Balls.

Number 1560

Length, 36 inches (over all). Spread, 16 inches.

		Not Wired	Wired	Complete as shown No lamps
2 Electric	Rich Gilt	$21.25	$22.25	$29.45
3 "	" "	25.00	26.50	37.30
4 "	" "	28.75	30.75	45.15
5 "	" "	32.50	35.00	53.00

No. B 906 3¼x6-inch Etched and Cut Balls.

Price in right hand column always includes sockets; also holders and shades if shown but no lamps.
Other prices include glassware, sockets, lamps or electric holders only where mentioned.

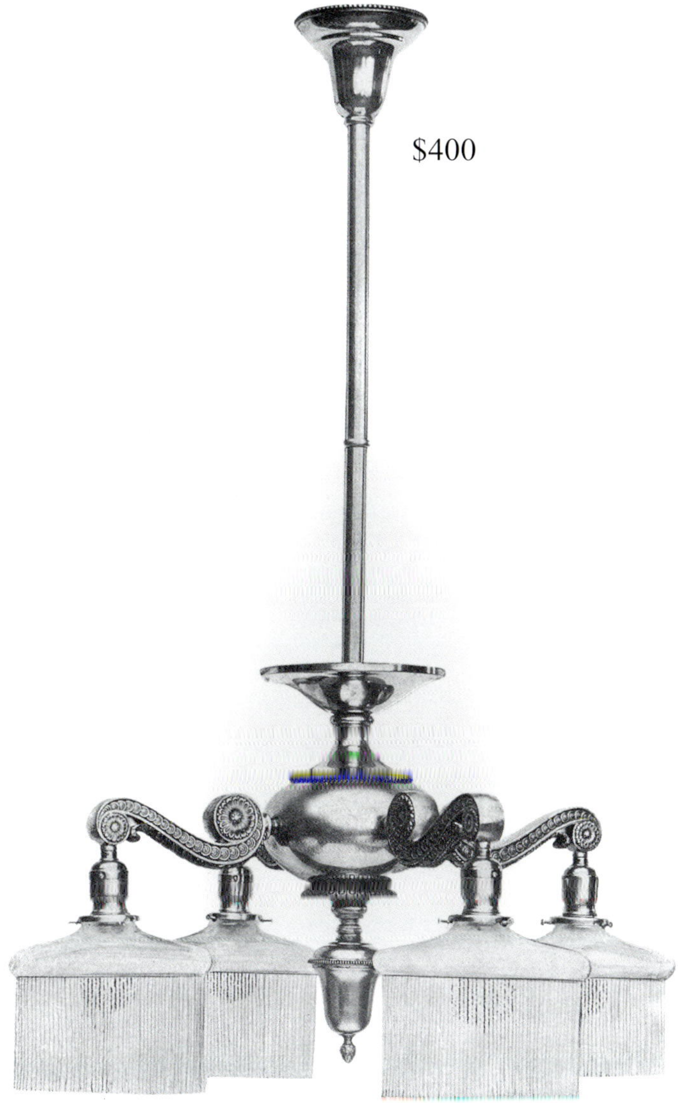

Number 1940

Length, 36 inches (over all), Spread, 16 inches

Brass Shades and Prisms included.

		Not Wired	Wired	Complete as shown No lamps
2 Electric	Antique Brush Brass	$25.00	$26.00	$26.80
3 "	" " "	31.50	33.00	34.20
4 "	" " "	38.00	40.00	41.60
5 "	" " "	44.50	47.00	49.00
6 "	" " "	51.00	54.00	56.40

Number 1972

Length, [illegible] inches (over all). Spread, 15 inches.

		Not Wired	Wired	Complete as shown No lamps
2 Electric	Antique Brush Brass	$22.00	$23.00	$27.00
3 "	" " "	28.00	29.50	35.50
4 "	" " "	34.00	36.00	44.00
5 "	" " "	40.00	42.50	52.50
6 "	" " "	46.00	49.00	61.00

Shades No. G 448 Crystal Roughed Inside with Glass Bead Fringe.

If wanted with Chain Pull Sockets add 30 cents for each light to prices in right hand column.

Price in right hand column always includes sockets; also holders and shades if shown but no lamps.
Other prices include glassware, sockets, lamps or electric holders only where mentioned.

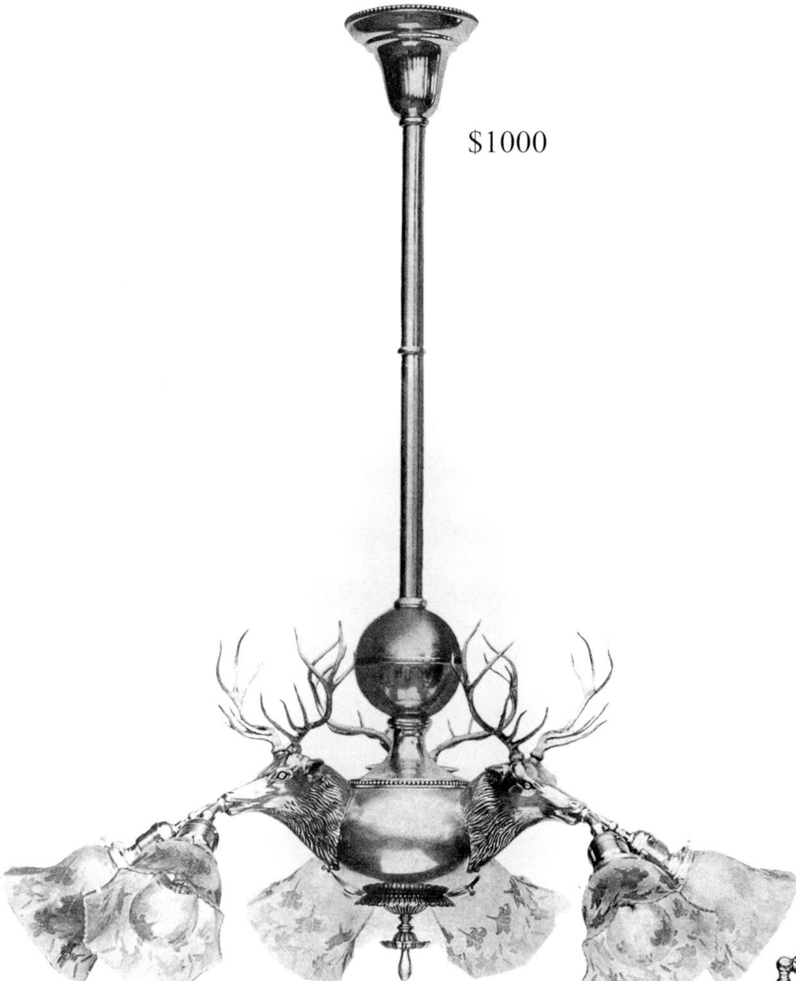

Number 2086

Length, 36 inches (over all). Spread, 24 inches.

		Not Wired	Wired	Complete as shown No lamps
2 Electric (1 Light on Each Head)	Brush Brass and Black	$27.25	$28.25	$30.95
3 " (1 " " " ")		36.25	37.75	41.80
4 " (2 " " " ")		27.75	29.75	35.15
6 " (2 " " " ")		37.00	40.00	48.10

Shades No. B 1532½ Metallic Etched.

Number 1874

Length, 40 inches (over all). Spread, 20 inches.

		Not Wired	Wired	Complete as shown No lamps
2 Electric	Brush Brass and Black....	$43.50	$44.50	$46.90
3 "	" " " "	52.50	54.00	57.60
4 "	" " " "	61.50	63.50	68.30

3¼x6-inch Crystal Roughed Inside Balls.

Price in right hand column always includes sockets; also holders and shades if shown but no lamps.
Other prices include glassware, sockets, lamps or electric holders only where mentioned.

Number 1879

Length, 40 inches (over all). Spread, 36 inches.

		Not Wired	Wired	Complete as shown No lamps
4 Electric	Brush Brass and Black.....	$45.50	$47.50	$51.10
6 "	" " " "	55.50	58.50	63.90
8 "	" " " "	65.50	69.50	76.70

Shades No. B 1906½ White Acid.

Price in right hand column always includes sockets; also holders and shades if shown but no lamps. Other prices include glassware, sockets, lamps or electric holders only where mentioned.

Number 2189
Length, 36 inches (over all). Spread, 19 inches.
No. B 2032½ 3¼x8-inch Silver Etched Bottom Ball included.

		Not Wired	Wired	Complete as shown No lamps
3 Electric	Rich Gilt	$24.25	$25.75	$30.35
4 "	" "	26.50	28.50	35.20
5 "	" "	28.75	31.25	40.05
6 "	" "	31.00	34.00	44.90

No. B 2032½ 3¼x6-inch Silver Etched Balls.

Number 1431
Length, 42 inches (over all). Spread, 22 inches.
3¼-inch Holders included.

		Not Wired	Wired	Complete as shown No lamps
2 Electric	Rich Gilt	$32.00	$33.00	$35.00
3 "	" "	37.00	38.50	41.50
4 "	" "	42.00	44.00	48.00
5 "	" "	47.00	49.50	54.50
6 "	" "	52.00	55.00	61.00

3¼x6-inch Crystal Roughed Inside Balls.

Price in right hand column always includes sockets; also holders and shades if shown but no lamps.
Other prices include glassware, sockets, lamps or electric holders only where mentioned.

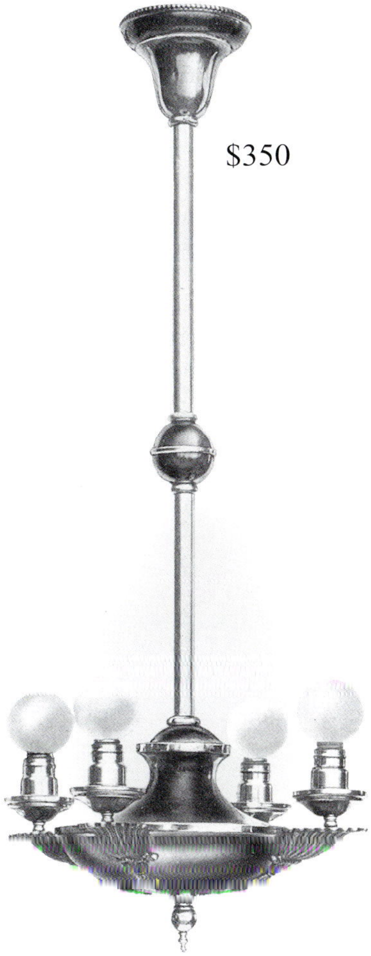

Number 1983
Length, 36 inches. Spread, 12 inches.

		Not Wired	Wired	Complete as shown No lamps
2	Electric Rich Gilt	$11.50	$12.50	$13.30
3	" " "	13.50	15.00	16.20
4	" " "	15.50	17.50	19.10
5	" " "	17.50	20.00	22.00
6	" " "	19.50	22.50	24.90

Number 1623
Length, 42 inches. Spread, 23 inches.
Socket Husks included.

		Not Wired	Wired	Complete as shown No lamps
3	Electric Antique Brush Brass	$55.50	$57.00	$58.20
4	" " " "	61.00	63.00	64.60
5	" " " "	66.50	69.00	71.00
6	" " " "	72.00	75.00	77.40
8	" " " "	83.00	87.00	90.20

Price in right hand column always includes sockets; also holders and shades if shown but no lamps.
Other prices include glassware, sockets, lamps or electric holders only where mentioned.

$400

$750

Number 2671

Length, 36 inches (over all). Diameter, 8 inches.

Crystal Prisms included.

		Not Wired	Wired	Complete as shown No lamps
1 Electric	Brush Brass and Black.....	$15.80	$17.05	$17.80

Chain Pull Socket included in right hand column only.

Extra lengthening per foot, $1.00.

Number 2635

Length, 42 inches (over all). Spread, 25 inches.

		Not Wired	Wired	Complete as shown No lamps
6 Electric (2 Lights in Bowl)	Brush Brass and Black	$104.00	$107.00	$109.40
7 " (2 " ")		109.90	113.40	116.20
8 " (2 " ")		115.80	119.80	123.00

Price in right hand column always includes sockets; also holders and shades if shown but no lamps.
Other prices include glassware, sockets, lamps or electric holders only where mentioned.

$1000

$1200

Number 2536

Length, 34 inches. Spread, 18 inches (over all).

		Not Wired	Wired	Complete as shown No lamps
6 Electric	Brush Brass and Black.....	**$114.00**	**$117.00**	**$119.40**

Number 2552

Length, 40 inches (over all). Spread, 27 inches.

		Not Wired	Wired	Complete as shown No lamps
6 Electric (2 Lights in Bowl)	Brush Brass and Black	**$93.10**	**$96.10**	**$98.50**
8 " (2 " ")		**110.10**	**114.10**	**117.30**

Price in right hand column always includes sockets; also holders and shades if shown but no lamps.
Other prices include glassware, sockets, lamps or electric holders only where mentioned.

Number 2498

Length, 36 inches. Spread, 10 inches.

Art Glass Shade and Socket Husks included.

		Not Wired	Wired	Complete as shown No lamps
5 Electric	Brush Brass	$53.00	$56.25	$58.25

Number 2465

Length, 36 inches (over all). Spread, 18 inches.

Brass Shades and 6-inch Iridescent Prisms included.

		Not Wired	Wired	Complete as shown No lamps
2 Electric	Brush Brass	$37.50	$38.50	$39.30
4 "	" "	61.50	63.50	65.10

Price in right hand column always includes sockets; also holders and shades if shown but no lamps.
Other prices include glassware, sockets, lamps or electric holders only where mentioned.

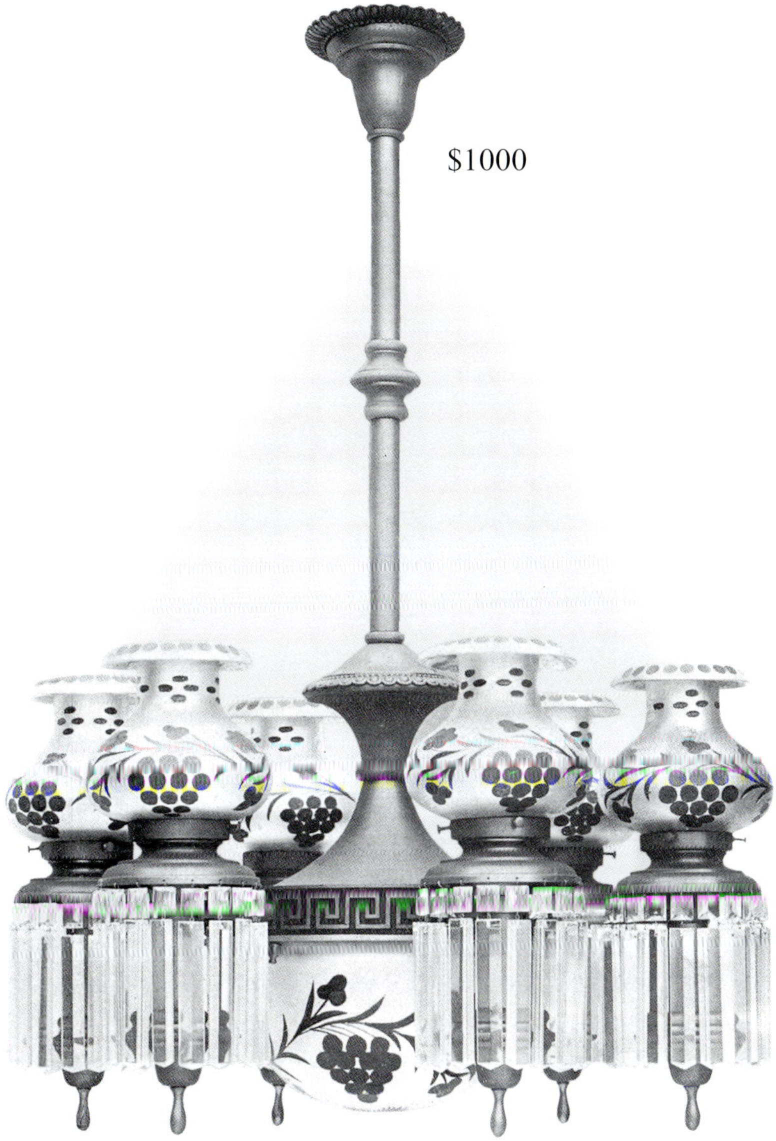

Number 1576

Length, 36 inches (over all). Spread, 12 inches.

		Not Wired	Wired	Complete as shown No lamps
2 Electric	Rich Gilt	$20.00	$21.00	$25.30
3 "	" "	23.75	25.25	31.70
4 "	" "	27.50	29.50	38.10

Shades No. B 2906½ Etched and Cut.

Number 2371

Length, 40 inches (over all). Spread, 23 inches.

12-inch Colonial Cut Bowl, Colonial Cut Shades and Prisms included.

		Not Wired	Wired	Complete as shown No lamps
6 Electric (2 Lights in Bowl)	Brush Brass and Black	$91.65	$94.65	$97.05
7 " (2 " ")		104.00	107.50	110.30
8 " (2 " ")		116.35	120.35	123.55

Price in right hand column always includes sockets; also holders and shades if shown but no lamps.
Other prices include glassware, sockets, lamps or electric holders only where mentioned.

$350

$600

Number 2624

Length, 32 inches (over all).

12-inch Colonial Cut Bowl included.

		Not Wired	Wired	Complete as shown No lamps
2 Electric	Brush Brass	$28.25	$29.50	$30.30
3 "	" "	28.50	30.00	31.20
4 "	" "	28.75	30.50	32.10

Extra lengthening, ¾-inch Casing from Canopy, per foot 50 cents.

Number 2625

Length, 40 inches (over all). Spread, 23 inches.

12-inch Colonial Cut Bowl and 4-inch Holders included.

		Not Wired	Wired	Complete as shown No lamps
6 Electric (2 Lights in Bowl)	Brush Brass	$46.25	$49.75	$67.15

No. B 1039 4x7-inch Colonial Cut Squat Balls.

Extra lengthening, Single Chain from Canopy, per foot $2.00.

Price in right hand column always includes sockets; also holders and shades if shown but no lamps.
Other prices include glassware, sockets, lamps or electric holders only where mentioned.

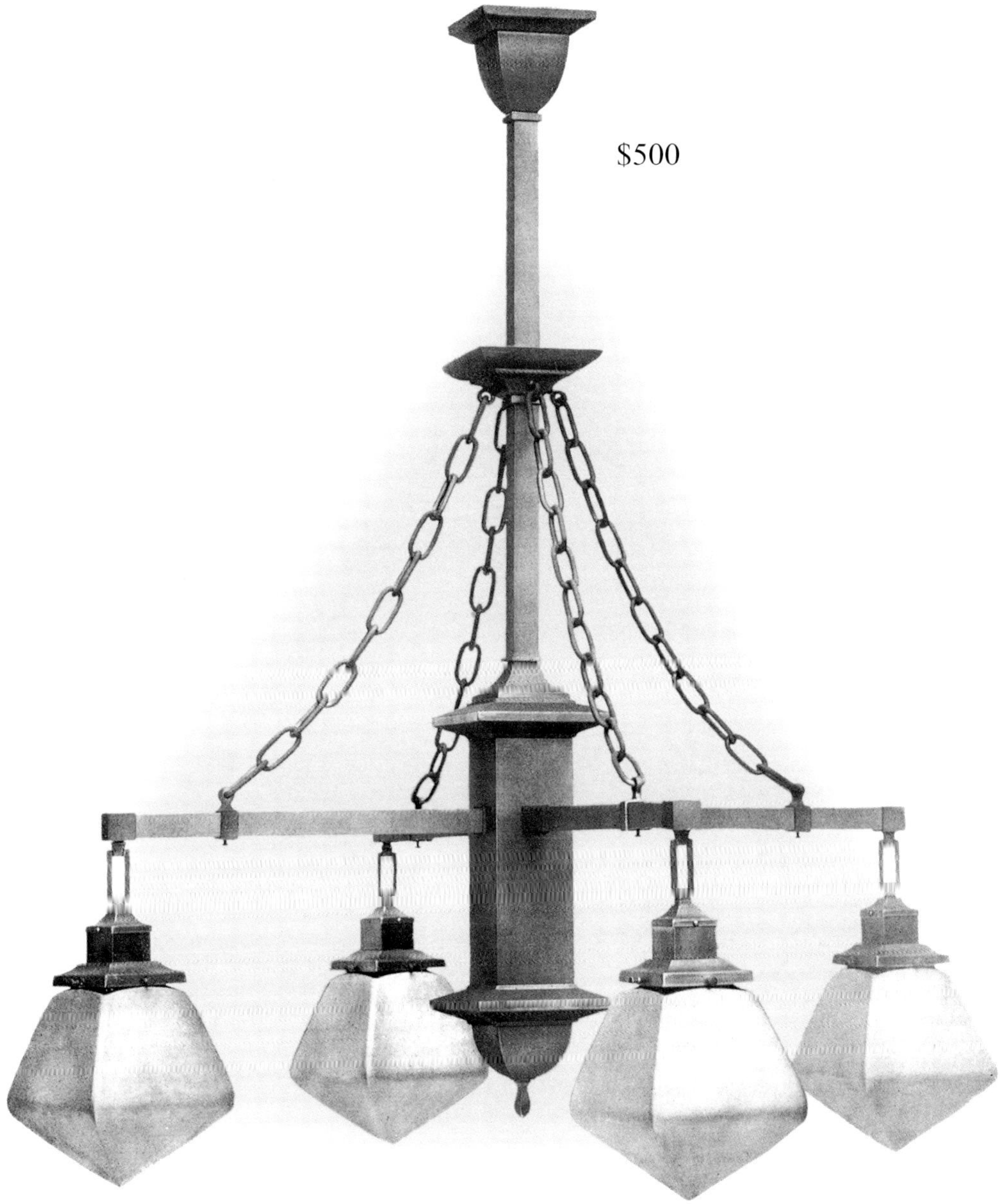

$500

Number 2289

Length, 42 inches (over all). Spread, 30 inches.

3¼ inch Socket Cover Holders included.

		Not Wired	Wired	Complete as shown No lamps
2 Electric	Brush Brass	$28.00	$29.00	$32.80
4 "	" "	41.00	43.00	50.60

No. B 180 3¼x8-inch Crystal Roughed Inside Square Balls.

Extra lengthening per foot 80 cents not wired, 90 cents wired.

Without 3¼-inch Socket Cover Holders deduct $1.25 each list.

Price in right hand column always includes sockets; also holders and shades if shown but no lamps. Other prices include glassware, sockets, lamps or electric holders only where mentioned.

Number 2249

Length, 40 inches (over all). Spread, 30 inches.

3¼-inch Socket Cover Holders included.

		Not Wired	Wired	Complete as shown No lamps
2 Electric	Brush Brass	$22.00	$23.00	$26.80
4 "	" "	30.00	32.00	39.60

No. B 180 3¼x8-inch Crystal Roughed Inside Square Balls.

Without 3¼-inch Socket Cover Holders deduct $1.25 each list.

Price in right hand column always includes sockets; also holders and shades if shown but no lamps.
Other prices include glassware, sockets, lamps or electric holders only where mentioned.

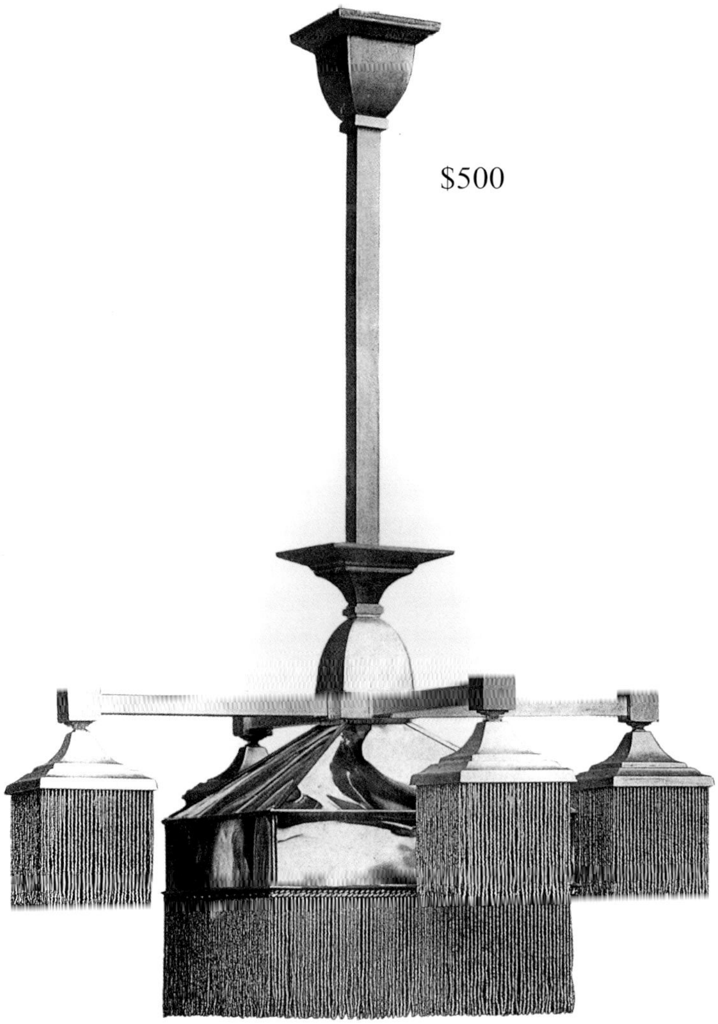

$500

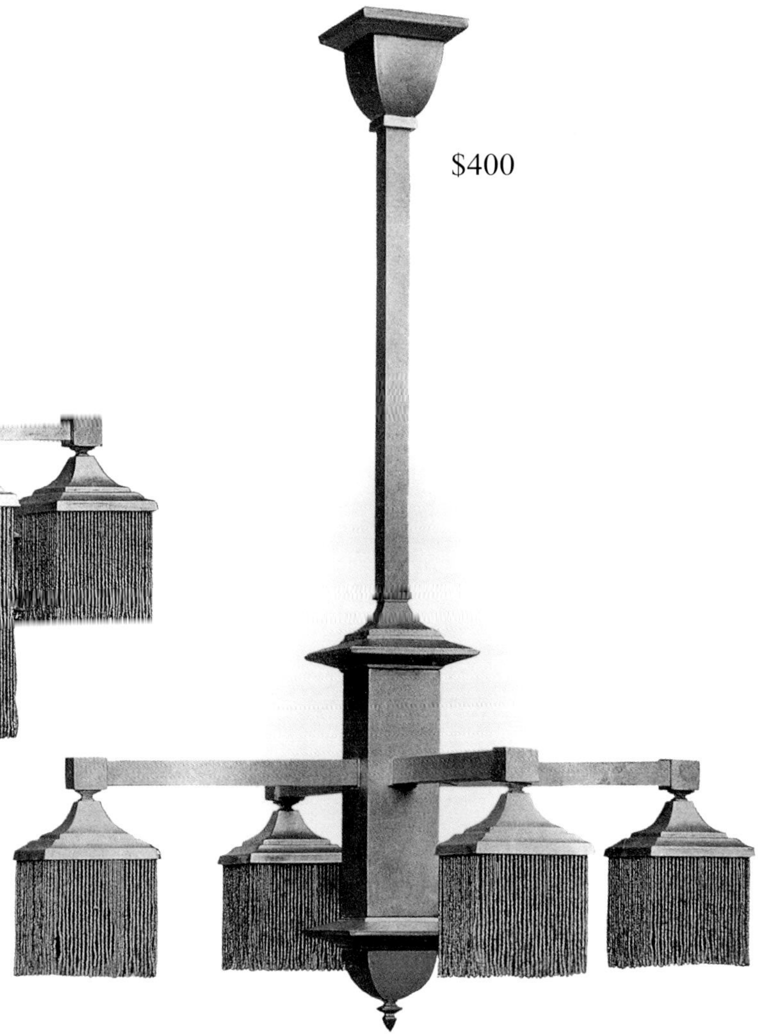

$400

Number 1692

Length, 40 inches (over all). Spread, 23 inches.
Art Glass Center Shade, Brass Shades and Glass Bead Fringe included.
Select Glass Colors by Number. See last page.

		Not Wired	Wired	Complete as shown No lamps
3 Electric	Brush Brass	$35.00	$36.50	$37.70
5 "	" "	45.00	47.50	49.50

Number 1690

Length, 40 inches. Spread, 24 inches.
Brass Shades and Glass Bead Fringe included.

		Not Wired	Wired	Complete as shown No lamps
2 Electric	Brush Brass	$26.30	$27.20	$28.00
4 "	" "	35.10	37.10	38.70

If wanted with Chain Pull Sockets add 30 cents per light to prices in right hand column.

Price in right hand column always includes sockets; also holders and shades if shown but no lamps.
Other prices include glassware, sockets, lamps or electric holders only where mentioned.

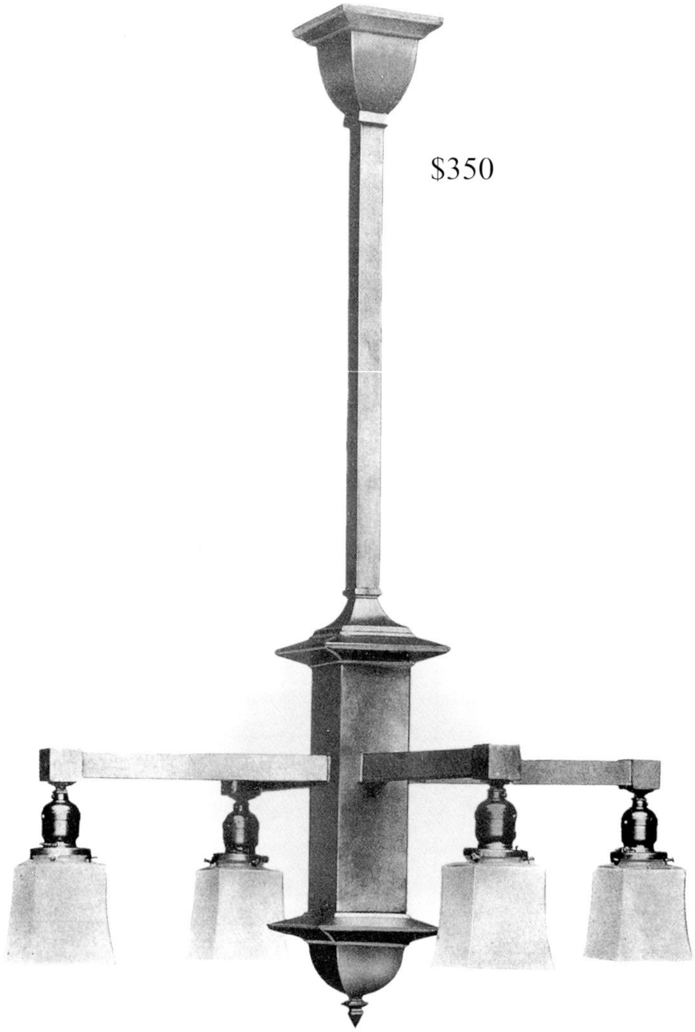

Number 1691
Length, 40 inches. Spread, 24 inches.

		Not Wired	Wired	Complete as shown No lamps
2 Electric	Brush Brass	$16.00	$17.00	$19.00
4 "	" "	19.00	21.00	25.00

Shades No. B 9321½ Crystal Roughed Inside.

Number 1719
Length, 40 inches. Spread, 18 inches.
Socket Husks included.

		Not Wired	Wired	Complete as shown No lamps
4 Electric (2 Arms)	Brush Brass and Black	$58.00	$60.00	$63.20
8 " (4 ")		78.00	82.00	88.40

3¼x6-inch Crystal Roughed Inside Balls.

Price in right hand column always includes sockets; also holders and shades if shown but no lamps.
Other prices include glassware, sockets, lamps or electric holders only where mentioned.

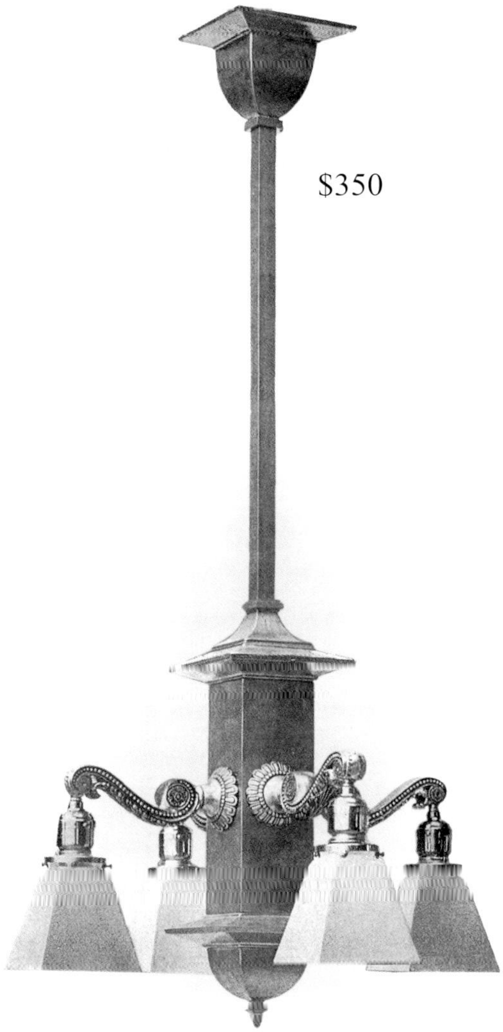

Number 1720
Length, 36 inches. Spread, 15 inches.

		Not Wired	Wired	Complete as shown No lamps
2 Electric	Brush Brass and Black.....	$26.00	$27.00	$29.00
4 "	" " " "	34.50	36.50	40.50

Shades No. B 9547½ Crystal Roughed Inside.

Number 2384
Length, 36 inches (over all). Spread, 20 inches.
Art Glass included.
Select Glass Colors by Numbers. See last page.

		Not Wired	Wired	Complete as shown No lamps
2 Electric	Brush Brass	$25.00	$26.00	$27.40
4 "	" "	43.50	45.50	48.30

Chain Pull Sockets included in right hand column only.

Price in right hand column always includes sockets; also holders and shades if shown but no lamps.
Other prices include glassware, sockets, lamps or electric holders only where mentioned.

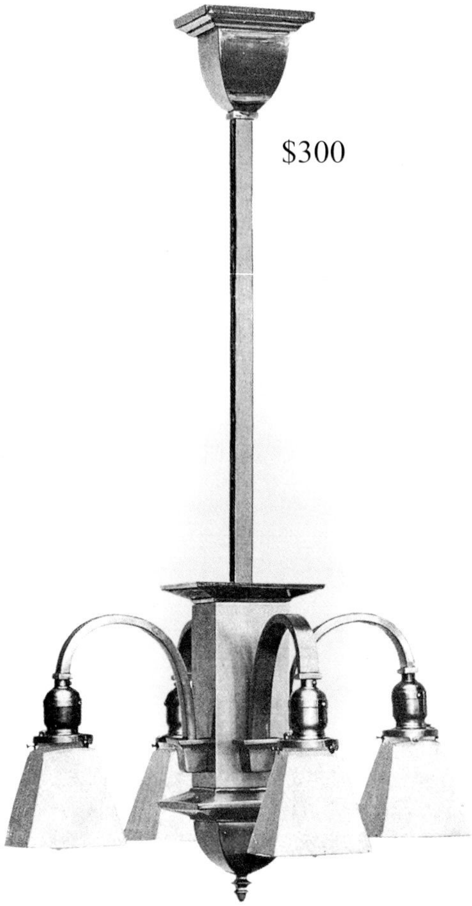

Number 1923

Length, 36 inches. Spread, 17 inches.

		Not Wired	Wired	Complete as shown No lamps
2 Electric	Brush Brass	$15.00	$16.00	$18.00
4 "	" "	19.00	21.00	25.00

Shades No. B 9547½ Crystal Roughed Inside.

Number 2270

Length, 36 inches (over all). Spread, 20 inches.

		Not Wired	Wired	Complete as shown No lamps
2 Electric	Brush Brass	$10.00	$11.00	$13.70
4 "	" "	13.50	15.50	20.90

No. B 180 3¼x6-inch Crystal Roughed Inside Square Balls.

Price in right hand column always includes sockets; also holders and shades if shown but no lamps.
Other prices include glassware, sockets, lamps or electric holders only where mentioned.

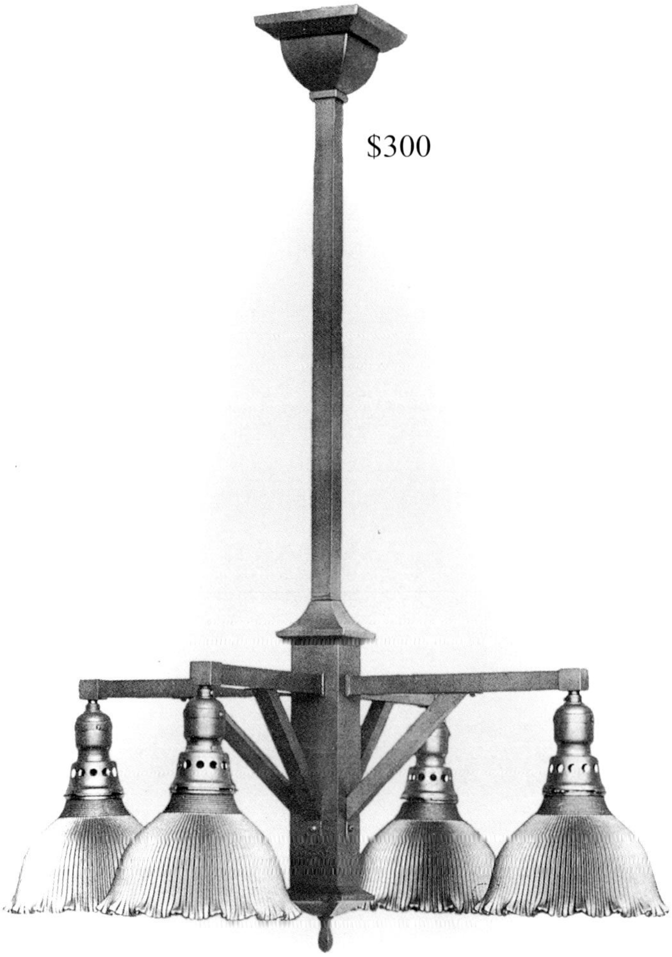

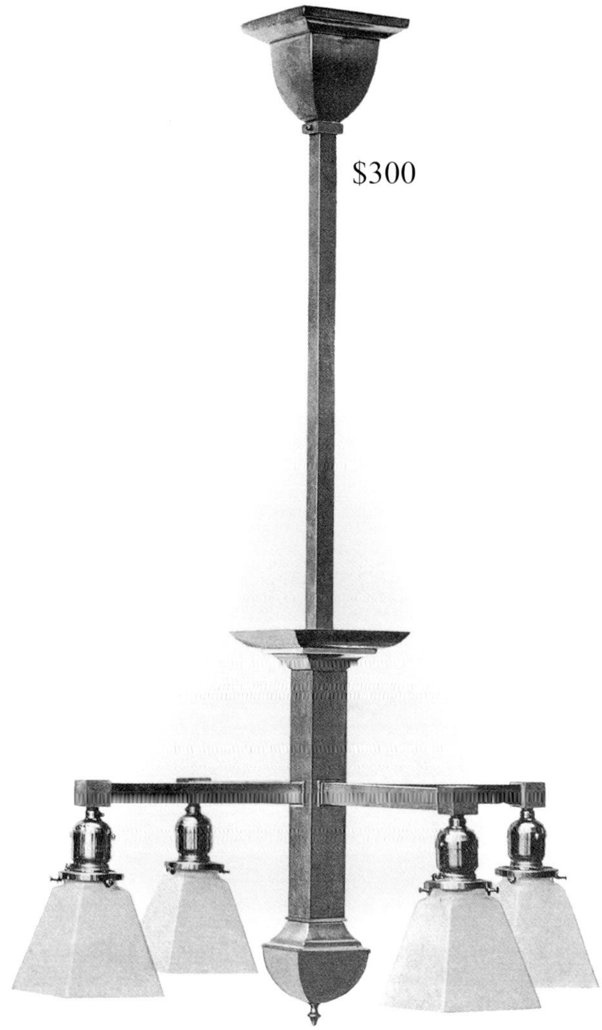

Number 2367

Length, 36 inches (over all). Spread, 20 inches.

		Not Wired	Wired	Complete as shown No lamps
2 Electric	Brush Brass	$10.00	$11.00	$15.00
4 "	" "	13.50	15.50	23.50

Holophane Shades No. 2 B. C.

Number 1781

Length, 36 inches (over all). Spread, 18 inches.

		Not Wired	Wired	Complete as shown No lamps
2 Electric	Brush Brass	$12.00	$13.00	$15.00
4 "	" "	15.50	17.50	21.50

Shades No. B 9547½ Crystal Roughed Inside.

Price in right hand column always includes sockets; also holders and shades if shown but no lamps.
Other prices include glassware, sockets, lamps or electric holders only where mentioned.

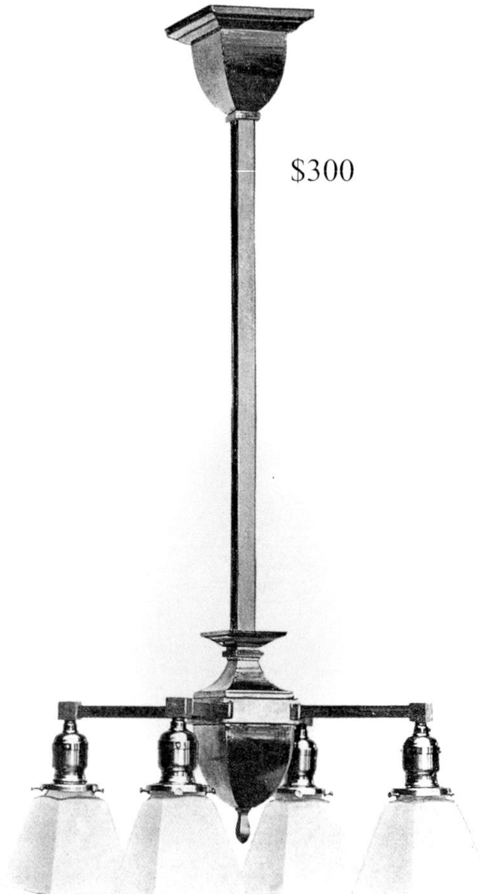

Number 1938

Length, 36 inches (over all). Shade, 18 inches.
Art Glass Shade and Glass Bead Fringe included.
Select Glass Colors by Number. See last page.

		Not Wired	Wired	Complete as shown No lamps
4 Electric (2 under shade)	Brush Brass	$23.20	$24.70	$26.30
8 " (4 " ")	" "	24.90	27.90	31.10

Number 1924

Length, 36 inches (over all). Spread, 14 inches.

		Not Wired	Wired	Complete as shown No lamps
2 Electric	Brush Brass	$7.75	$8.75	$10.75
4 "	" "	9.25	11.25	15.25

Shades No. B 9547½ Crystal Roughed Inside.

Price in right hand column always includes sockets; also holders and shades if shown but no lamps.
Other prices include glassware, sockets, lamps or electric holders only where mentioned.

$300

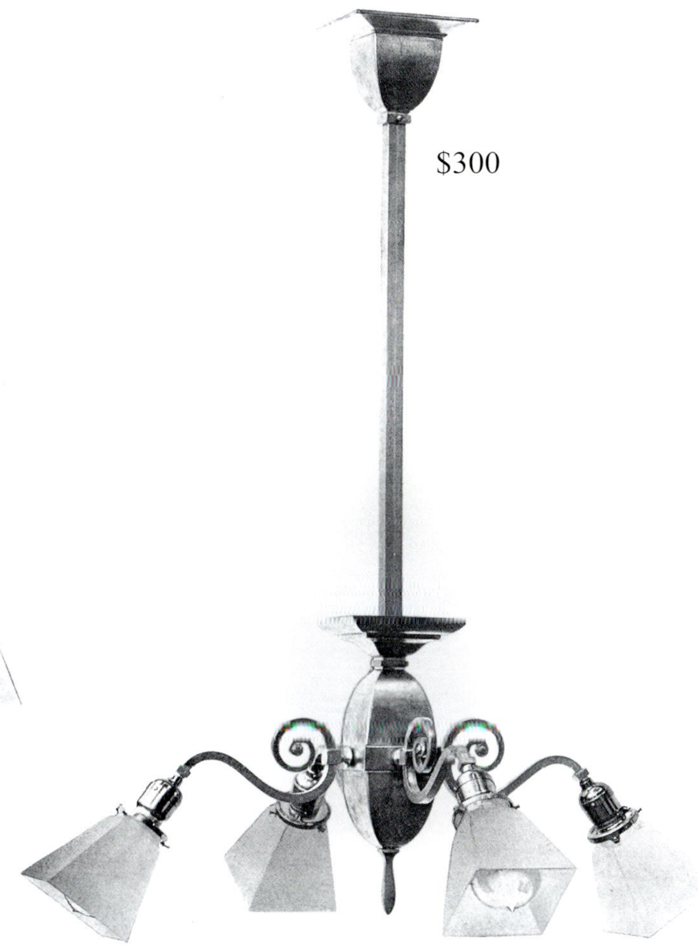

$300

Number 1799
Length, 36 inches (over all). Spread, 18 inches.

		Not Wired	Wired	Complete as shown No lamps
2 Electric	Brush Brass	$12.50	$13.50	$15.50
4 "	" "	16.00	18.00	22.00

Shades No. B 9547½ Crystal Roughed Inside.
Extra lengthening per foot, $2.60.

Number 1712
Length, 36 inches (over all). Spread, 27 inches.

		Not Wired	Wired	Complete as show No lamps
2 Electric	Brush Brass	$12.50	$13.50	$15.50
4 "	" "	15.75	17.75	21.75

Shades No. B 9547½ Crystal Roughed Inside.

Price in right hand column always includes sockets; also holders and shades if shown but no lamps.
Other prices include glassware, sockets, lamps or electric holders only where mentioned.

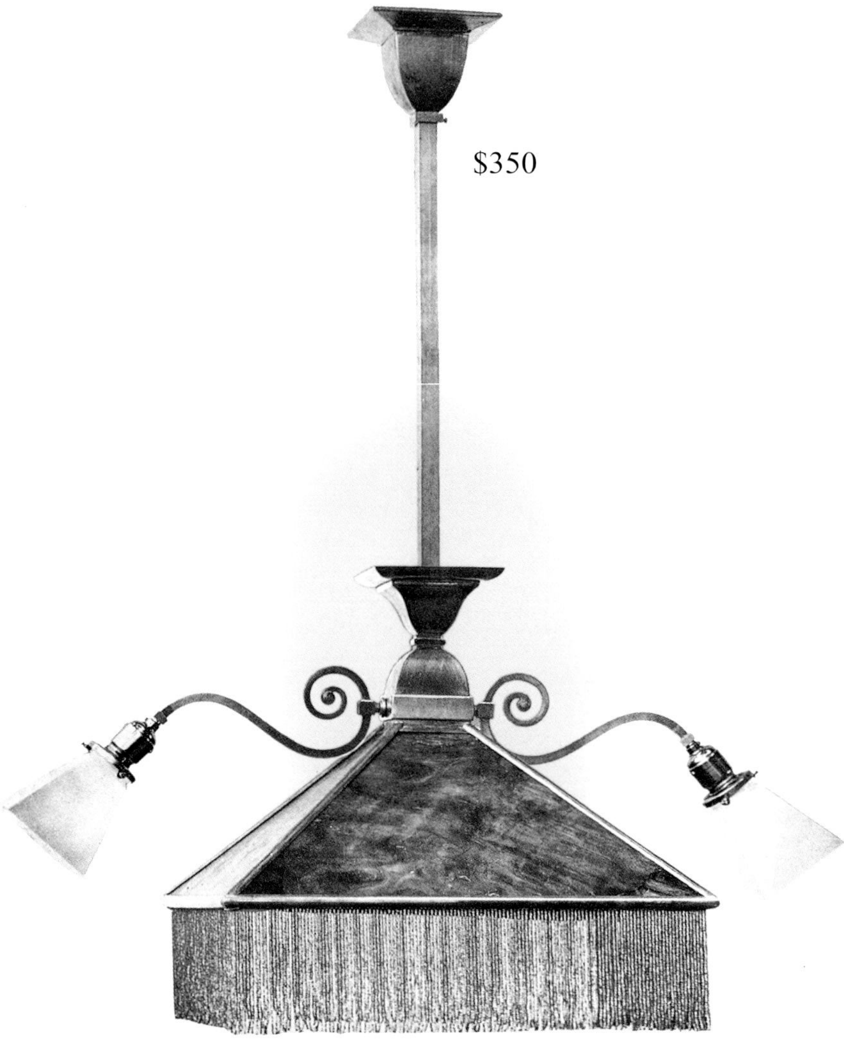

$350

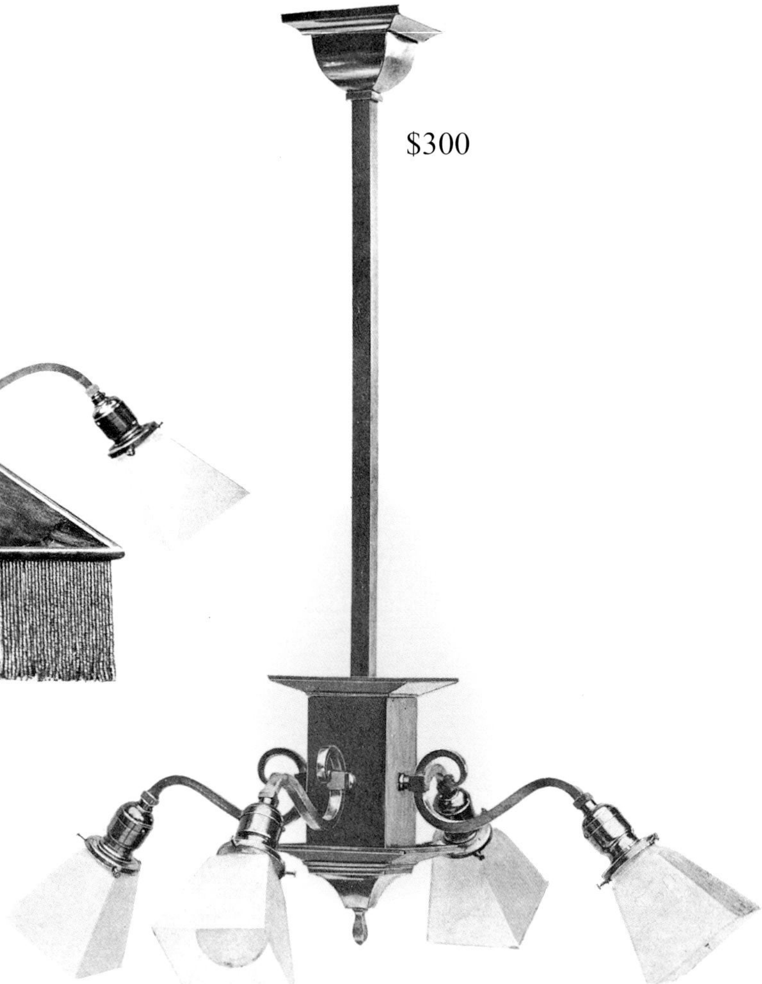

$300

Number 1723

Length, 42 inches (over all). Spread, 31 inches.
18-inch Art Glass Shade and Glass Bead Fringe included.
Select Glass Colors by Number. See last page.

		Not Wired	Wired	Complete as shown No lamps
4 Electric (2 under shade)	Brush Brass	$29.00	$31.00	$33.80
8 " (4 " ")	" "	33.00	37.00	42.60

Shades No. B 9547½ Crystal Roughed Inside.

Number 1918

Length, 36 inches (over all). Spread, 27 inches.

		Not Wired	Wired	Complete as shown No lamps
2 Electric	Brush Brass	$11.50	$12.50	$14.50
4 "	" "	14.50	16.50	20.50

Shades No. B 9547½ Crystal Roughed Inside.

Price in right hand column always includes sockets; also holders and shades if shown but no lamps.
Other prices include glassware sockets, lamps or electric holders only where mentioned.

Number 2150
Length, 36 inches (over all). Spread, 18 inches.

		Not Wired	Wired	Complete as shown No lamps
2 Electric	Polished Brass	$5.75	$6.75	$8.35
3 "	" "	6.50	8.00	10.40
4 "	" "	7.25	9.25	12.45

Shades No. B 8983½ Crystal Roughed Inside.

Number 2151
Length, 40 inches (over all). Spread, 28 inches.
3¼x16-inch Art Glass Shade and Glass Bead Fringe included.
Select Glass Colors by Number. See last page.

		Not Wired	Wired	Complete as shown No lamps
3 Electric	Polished Brass	$18.75	$20.25	$22.25
5 "	" "	20.25	22.75	26.35

Shades No. B 8983½ Crystal Roughed Inside.

Price in right hand column always includes sockets; also holders and shades if shown but no lamps.
Other prices include glassware, sockets, lamps or electric holders only where mentioned.

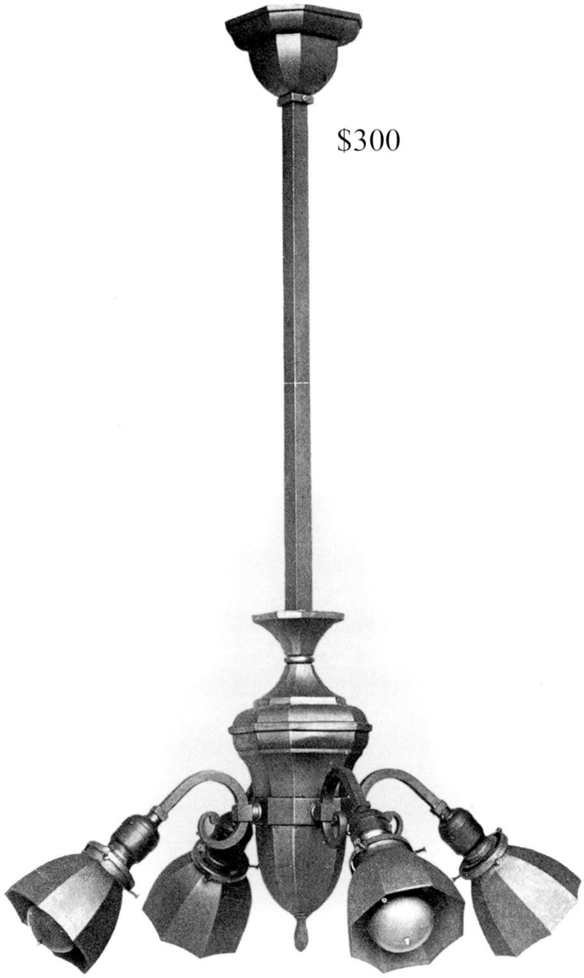

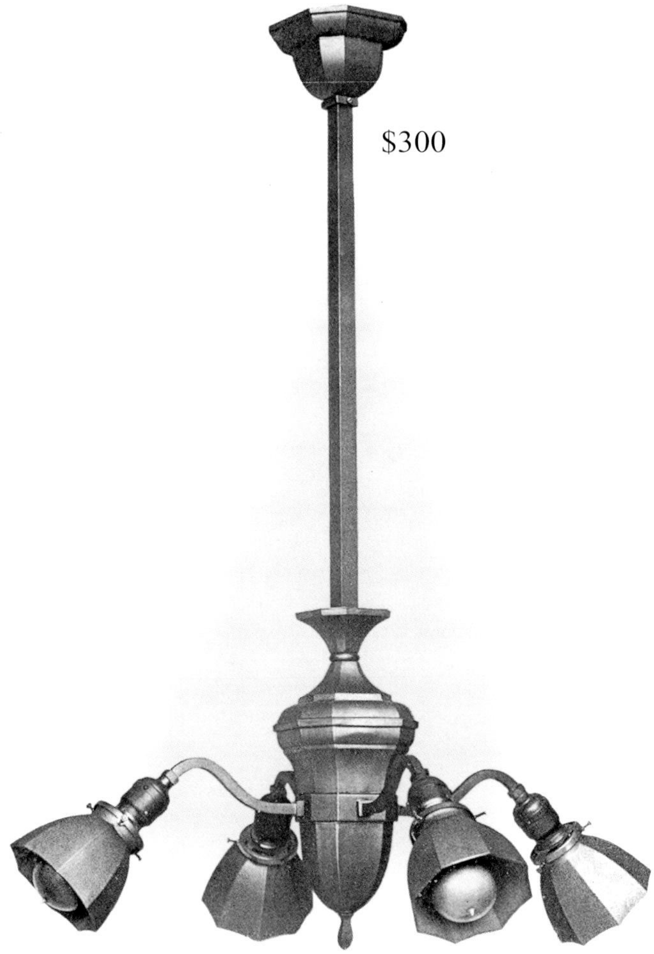

Number 2385

Length, 36 inches (over all). Spread, 21 inches.

		Not Wired	Wired	Complete as shown No lamps
2 Electric	Brush Brass	$8.75	$9.75	$11.95
4 "	" "	10.75	12.75	17.15
8 "	" "	14.75	18.75	27.55

Shades No. B 4134½ Crystal Roughed Inside.

Number 2386

Length, 36 inches (over all). Spread, 24 inches.

		Not Wired	Wired	Complete as shown No lamps
2 Electric	Brush Brass	$8.25	$9.25	$11.45
4 "	" "	9.75	11.75	16.15
8 "	" "	12.75	16.75	25.55

Shades No. B 4134½ Crystal Roughed Inside.

Price in right hand column always includes sockets; also holders and shades if shown but no lamps.
Other prices include glassware, sockets, lamps or electric holders only where mentioned.

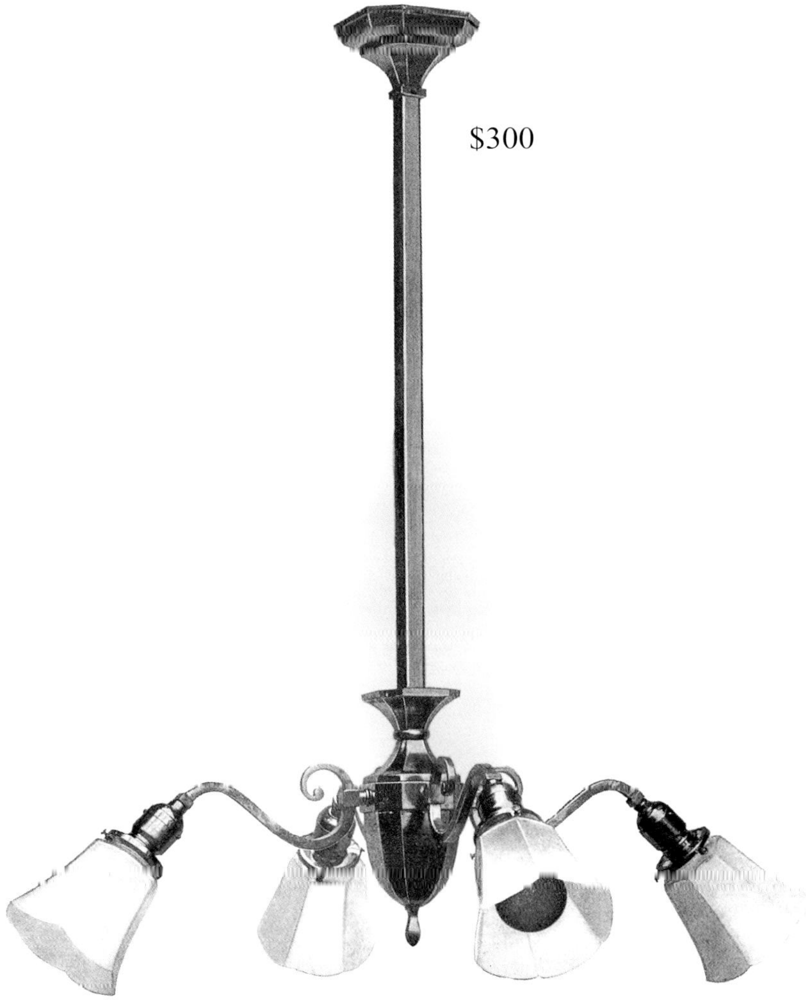

$300

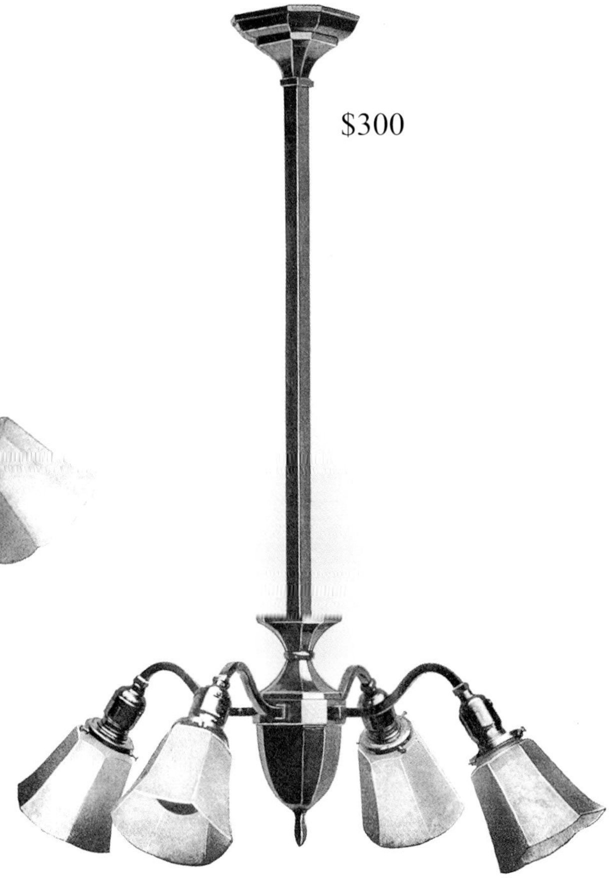

$300

Number 2175

Length, 36 inches (over all). Spread, 30 inches.

		Not Wired	Wired	Complete as shown No lamps
2 Electric	Brush Brass	$8.25	$9.25	$11.05
4 "	" "	11.25	13.25	16.85
8 "	" "	17.25	21.25	28.45

Shades No. B 68½ Crystal Roughed Inside.

Number 2159

Length, 36 inches (over all). Spread, 24 inches.

		Not Wired	Wired	Complete as shown No lamps
2 Electric	Brush Brass	$6.75	$7.75	$9.55
4 "	" "	8.25	10.25	13.85
8 "	" "	11.25	15.25	22.45

Shades No. B 68½ Crystal Roughed Inside.

Price in right hand column always includes sockets; also holders and shades if shown but no lamps.
Other prices include glassware, sockets, lamps or electric holders only where mentioned.

Number 1725

Length, 36 inches. Spread, 25 inches.

			Not Wired	Wired	Complete as shown No lamps
2	Electric	Rich Gilt	$6.50	$7.50	$9.30
3	"	" "	7.50	9.00	11.70
4	"	" "	8.50	10.50	14.10
5	"	" "	9.50	12.00	16.50
6	"	" "	10.50	13.50	18.90

Shades No. B 68½ Crystal Roughed Inside.

Number 1726

Length, 36 inches. Spread, 27 inches.

			Not Wired	Wired	Complete as shown No lamps
2	Electric	Rich Gilt	$6.50	$7.50	$9.30
3	"	" "	7.75	9.25	11.95
4	"	" "	9.00	11.00	14.60
5	"	" "	10.25	12.75	17.25
6	"	" "	11.50	14.50	19.90

Shades No. B 68½ Crystal Roughed Inside.

Price in right hand column always includes sockets; also holders and shades if shown but no lamps.
Other prices include glassware, sockets, lamps or electric holders only where mentioned.

Number 1727
Length, 36 inches. Spread, 27 inches.

		Not Wired	Wired	Complete as shown No lamps
2 Electric	Rich Gilt	$5.25	$6.25	$8.35
3 "	" "	5.75	7.25	10.40
4 "	" "	6.25	8.25	12.45
5 "	" "	6.75	9.25	14.50
6 "	" "	7.25	10.25	16.55

Shades No. B 615½ Etched.

Number 1724
Length, 36 inches. Spread, 27 inches.

		Not Wired	Wired	Complete as shown No lamps
2 Electric	Rich Gilt	$5.00	$6.00	$8.10
3 "	" "	5.50	7.00	10.15
4 "	" "	6.00	8.00	12.20
5 "	" "	6.50	9.00	14.25
6 "	" "	7.00	10.00	16.30

Shades No. B 615½ Etched.

Price in right hand column always includes sockets; also holders and shades if shown but no lamps.
Other prices include glassware, sockets, lamps or electric holders only where mentioned.

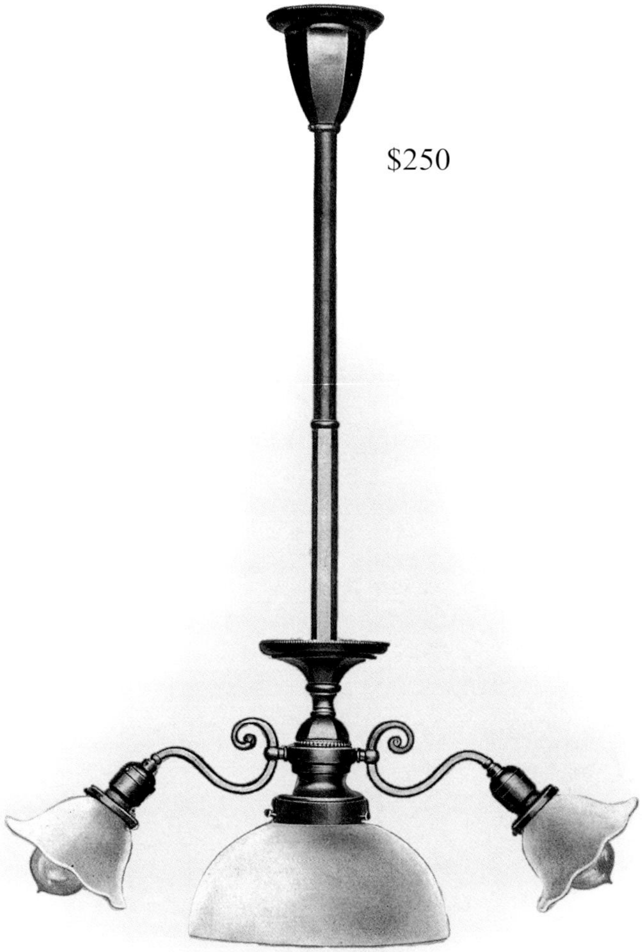

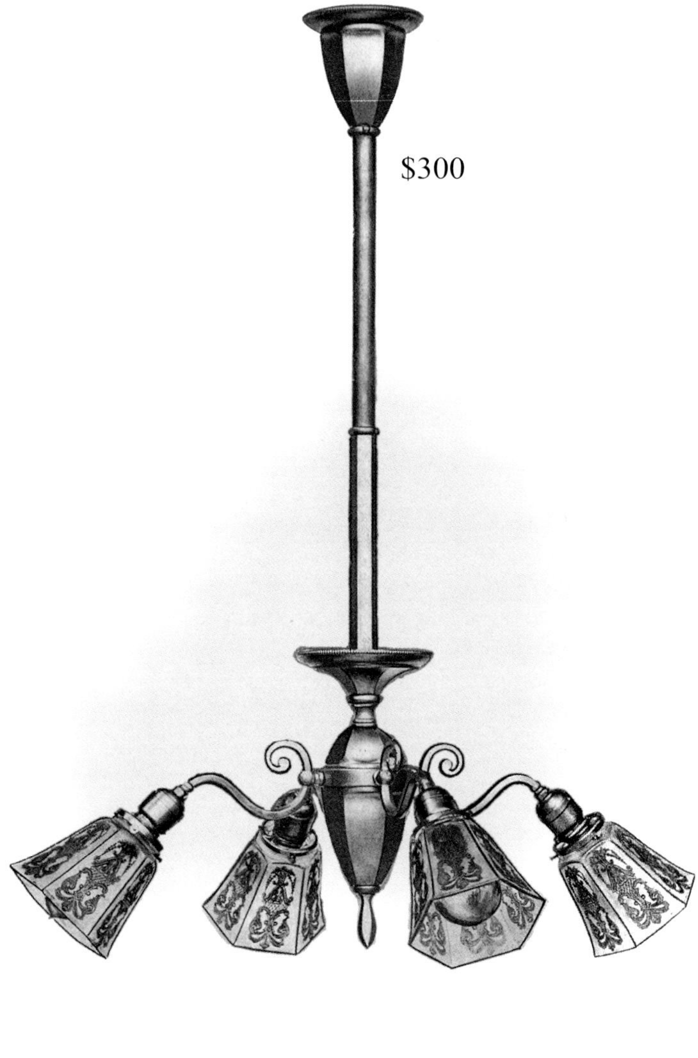

Number 2203

Length, 36 inches (over all). Spread, 23 inches.

3¼x10-inch C. R. I. Dome included.

		Not Wired	Wired	Complete as shown No lamps
3 Electric	Rich Gilt	$7.75	$9.25	$11.45
4 "	" "	8.75	10.75	13.85
5 "	" "	9.75	12.25	16.25

Shades No. B 2013½ Crystal Roughed Inside.

Number 1540

Length, 36 inches (over all). Spread, 24 inches.

		Not Wired	Wired	Complete as shown No lamps
2 Electric	Rich Gilt	$6.50	$7.50	$9.60
3 "	" "	7.50	9.00	12.15
4 "	" "	8.50	10.50	14.70
5 "	" "	9.50	12.00	17.25
6 "	" "	10.50	13.50	19.80

Shades No. B 615½ Etched.

Price in right hand column always includes sockets; also holders and shades if shown but no lamps. Other prices include glassware, sockets, lamps or electric holders only where mentioned.

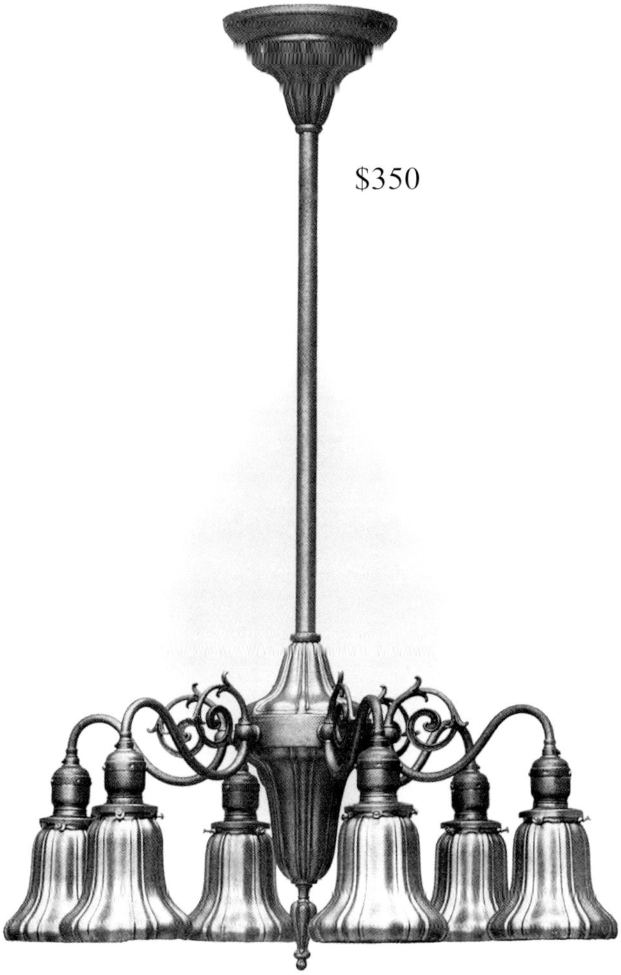

$350

$300

Number 2549
Length, 36 inches. Spread, 18 inches.

		Not Wired	Wired	Complete as shown No lamps
2 Electric	Brush Brass	$9.00	$10.00	$12.10
3 "	" "	10.25	11.75	14.90
4 "	" "	11.50	13.50	17.70
5 "	" "	12.75	15.25	20.50
6 "	" "	14.00	17.00	23.30

Shades No. B 5014½ Crystal Roughed Inside.

Number 2548
Length, 36 inches. Spread, 18 inches.

		Not Wired	Wired	Complete as shown No lamps
2 Electric	Brush Brass	$7.20	$8.20	$10.60
3 "	" "	8.05	9.55	13.15
4 "	" "	8.90	10.90	15.70

Shades No. B 250 Crystal Roughed Inside. Diameter, 8 inches.

Price in right hand column always includes sockets; also holders and shades if shown but no lamps.
Other prices include glassware, sockets, lamps or electric holders only where mentioned.

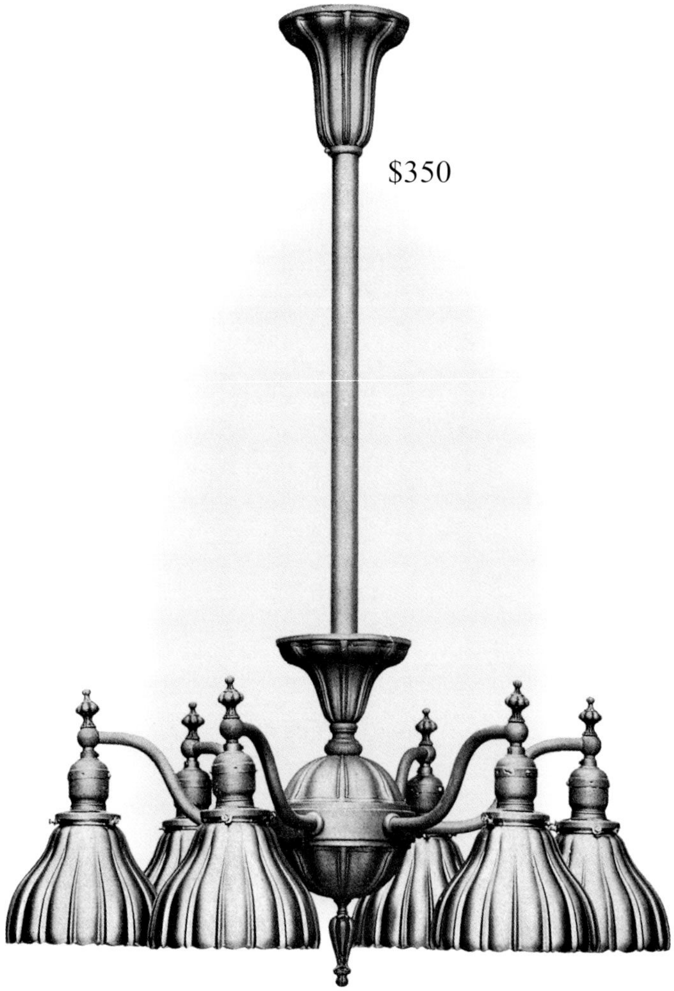

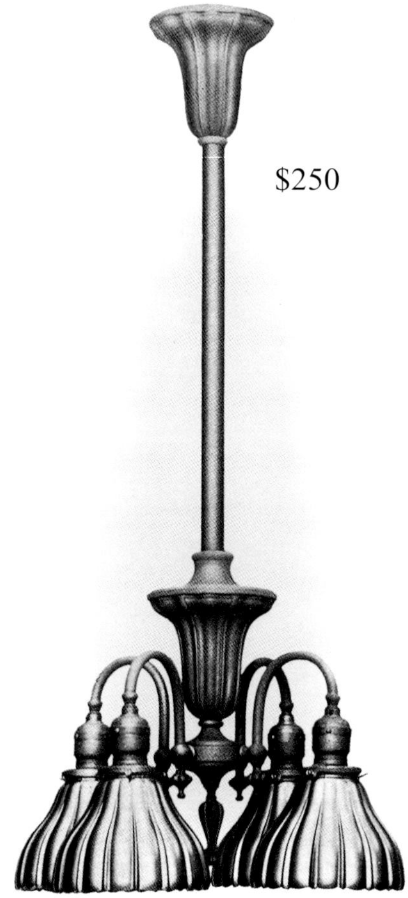

Number 2619

Length, 36 inches. Spread, 18 inches.

		Not Wired	Wired	Complete as shown No lamps
2	Electric Brush Brass	$9.50	$10.50	$14.00
3	" " "	10.50	12.00	17.25
4	" " "	11.50	13.50	20.50
5	" " "	12.50	15.00	23.75
6	" " "	13.50	16.50	27.00

Shades No. B 3420 Alba.

Number 2617

Length, 36 inches (over all). Spread, 10 inches.

		Not Wired	Wired	Complete as shown No lamps
2	Electric Brush Brass	$7.75	$8.75	$12.25
3	" " "	8.50	10.00	15.25
4	" " "	9.25	11.25	18.25

Shades No. B 3420 Alba.

Price in right hand column always includes sockets; also holders and shades if shown but no lamps.
Other prices include glassware, sockets, lamps or electric holders only where mentioned.

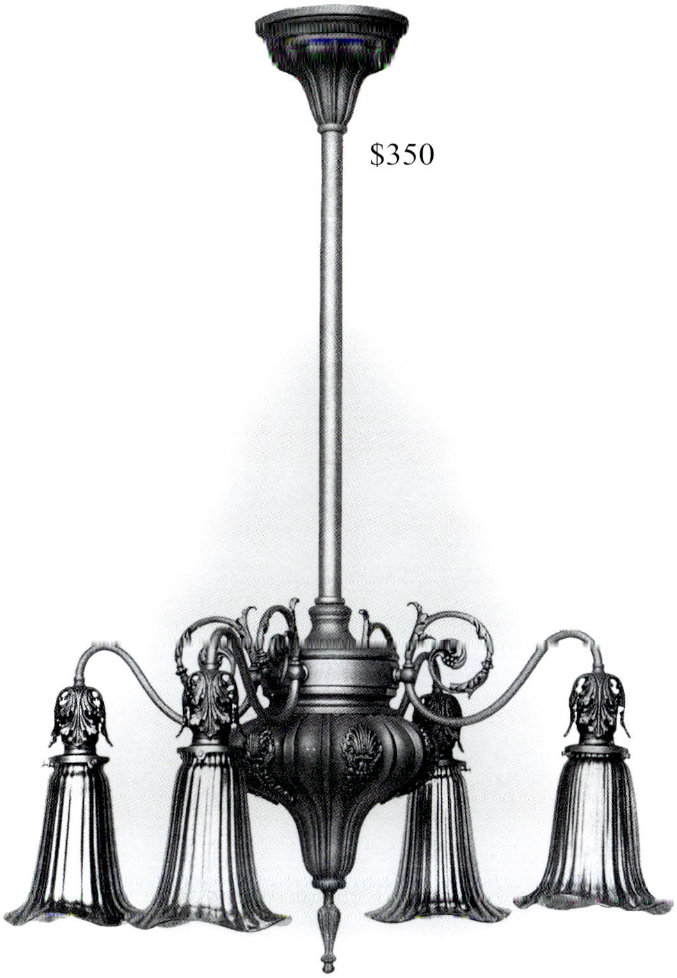

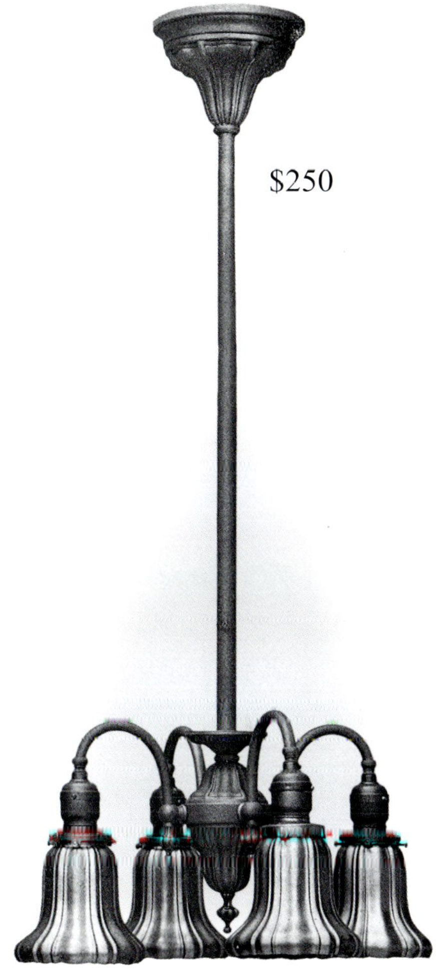

Number 2584
Length, 36 inches. Spread, 21 inches.
Cast Socket Husks included.

		Not Wired	Wired	Complete as shown No lamps
2 Electric	Brush Brass	$23.75	$24.75	$43.75
3 "	" "	27.00	28.50	57.00
4 "	" "	30.25	32.25	70.25
5 "	" "	33.50	36.00	83.50
6 "	" "	36.75	39.75	96.75

Shades No. B 831 Amber Lustre.

Number 2575
Length, 36 inches (over all). Spread, 12 inches.

		Not Wired	Wired	Complete as shown No lamps
2 Electric	Brush Brass	$6.25	$7.25	$9.35
3 "	" "	7.00	8.50	11.65
4 "	" "	7.75	9.75	13.95

Shades No. B 5014½ Crystal Roughed Inside.

Price in right hand column always includes sockets; also holders and shades if shown but no lamps.
Other prices include glassware, sockets, lamps or electric holders only where mentioned.

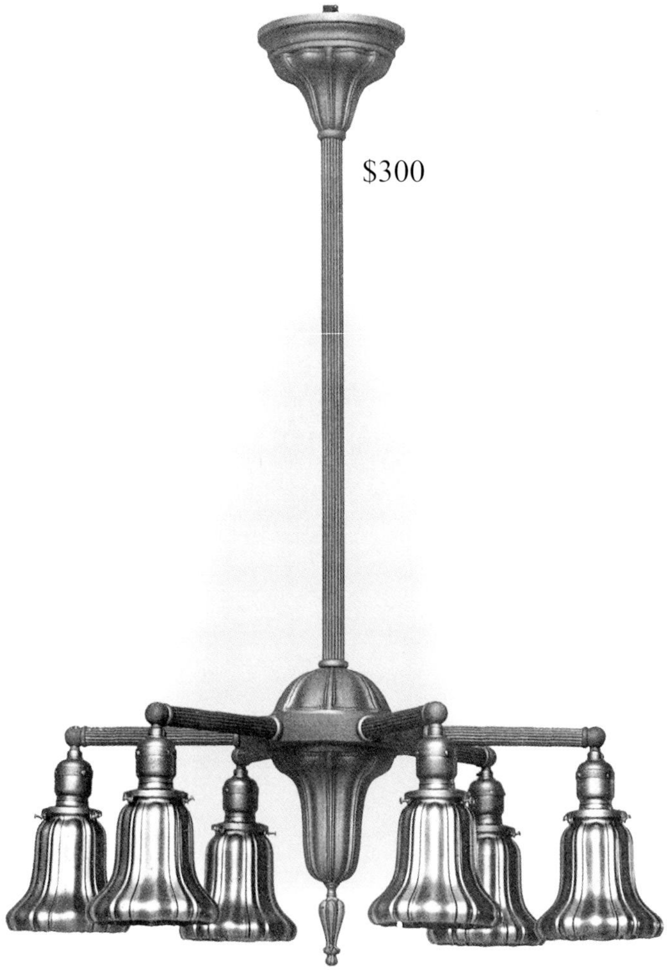

$300

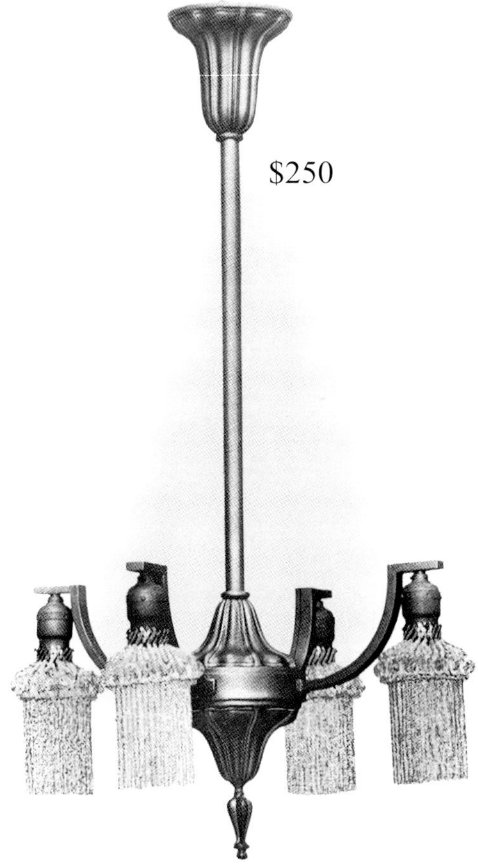

$250

Number 2572

Length, 36 inches. Spread, 20 inches.

		Not Wired	Wired	Complete as shown No lamps
2 Electric	Brush Brass	$10.00	$11.00	$13.10
3 "	" "	11.00	12.50	15.65
4 "	" "	12.00	14.00	18.20
5 "	" "	13.00	15.50	20.75
6 "	" "	14.00	17.00	23.30
8 "	" "	16.00	20.00	28.40

Shades No. B 5014½ Crystal Roughed Inside.

Number 2618

Length, 36 inches. Spread, 15 inches.

		Not Wired	Wired	Complete as shown No lamps
2 Electric	Brush Brass	$8.75	$9.75	$17.15
3 "	" "	10.00	11.50	22.60
4 "	" "	11.25	13.25	28.05
5 "	" "	12.50	15.00	33.50
6 "	" "	13.75	16.75	38.95

Shades No. B 1226½ Crystal Bead.

Price in right hand column always includes sockets; also holders and shades if shown but no lamps.
Other prices include glassware, sockets lamps or electric holders only where mentioned.

Number 1950
Length, 36 inches (over all). Spread, 20 inches.
Metal Shades and Glass Bead Fringe included.

		Not Wired	Wired	Complete as shown No lamps
2 Electric	Brush Brass and Black.....	$19.00	$20.00	$20.80
3 "	" " " "	23.25	24.75	25.95
4 "	" " " "	27.50	29.50	31.10
5 "	" " " "	31.75	34.25	36.25
6 "	" " " "	36.00	39.00	41.40

If wanted with Chain Pull Sockets, add 30 cents for each light to prices in right hand column.

Number 2650
Length, 36 inches (over all). Spread, 18 inches.

		Not Wired	Wired	Complete as shown No lamps
2 Electric	Brush Brass	$9.00	$10.00	$12.40
3 "	" "	10.50	12.00	15.60
4 "	" "	12.00	14.00	18.80
5 "	" "	13.50	16.00	22.00
6 "	" "	15.00	18.00	25.20

3¼x6-inch Crystal Roughed Inside Balls.
Extra lengthening, per foot, $2.00.

Price in right hand column always includes sockets; also holders and shades if shown but no lamps.
Other prices include glassware, sockets, lamps or electric holders only where mentioned.

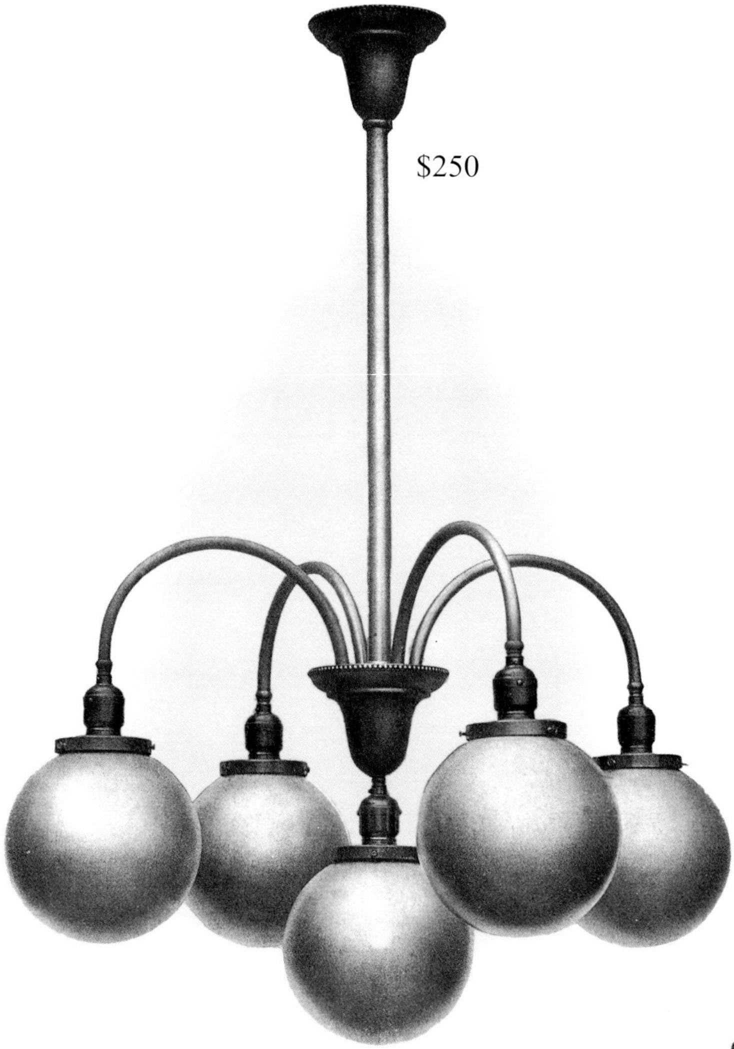

Number 2260

Length, 38 inches (over all). Spread, 21 inches.

		Not Wired	Wired	Complete as shown No lamps
3 Electric	Rich Gilt	$3.75	$4.75	$8.80
4 "	" "	4.50	6.00	11.40
5 "	" "	5.25	7.25	14.00
6 "	" "	6.00	8.50	16.60

3¼x7-inch Crystal Roughed Inside Balls.

Number 2275

Length, 40 inches (over all). Spread, 18 inches.

		Not Wired	Wired	Complete as shown No lamps
3 Electric	Brush Brass	$3.40	$4.40	$7.70
4 "	" "	4.00	5.50	9.90
5 "	" "	4.60	6.60	12.10

Shades No. B 250 Crystal Roughed Inside. Diameter, 8 inches.
Extra lengthening, Brass Plated Steel Chain, per foot, 50 cents.

Price in right hand column always includes sockets; also holders and shades if shown but no lamps.
Other prices include glassware, sockets, lamps or electric holders only where mentioned.

Number 1832
Length, 42 inches (over all). Spread, 23 inches.
3¼x8-inch C. R. I. Bottom Ball included.

		Not Wired	Wired	Complete as shown No lamps
3 Electric	Polished Brass and Black	$8.00	$9.50	$12.30
4 "	" " " "	8.75	10.75	14.75
5 "	" " " "	9.50	12.00	17.20
6 "	" " " "	10.25	13.25	19.65
7 "	" " " "	11.00	14.50	22.10

3¼x6-inch Crystal Roughed Inside Balls.

Number 2649
Length, 36 inches (over all). Spread, 18 inches.

		Not Wired	Wired	Complete as shown No lamps
2 Electric	Brush Brass	$8.50	$9.50	$13.50
3 "	" "	9.50	11.00	17.00
4 "	" "	10.50	12.50	20.50
5 "	" "	11.50	14.00	24.00

Holophane Shades No. 2 B.
Extra lengthening, per foot, $2.00.

Price in right hand column always includes sockets; also holders and shades if shown, but no lamps.
Other prices include glassware, sockets, lamps or electric holders only where mentioned.

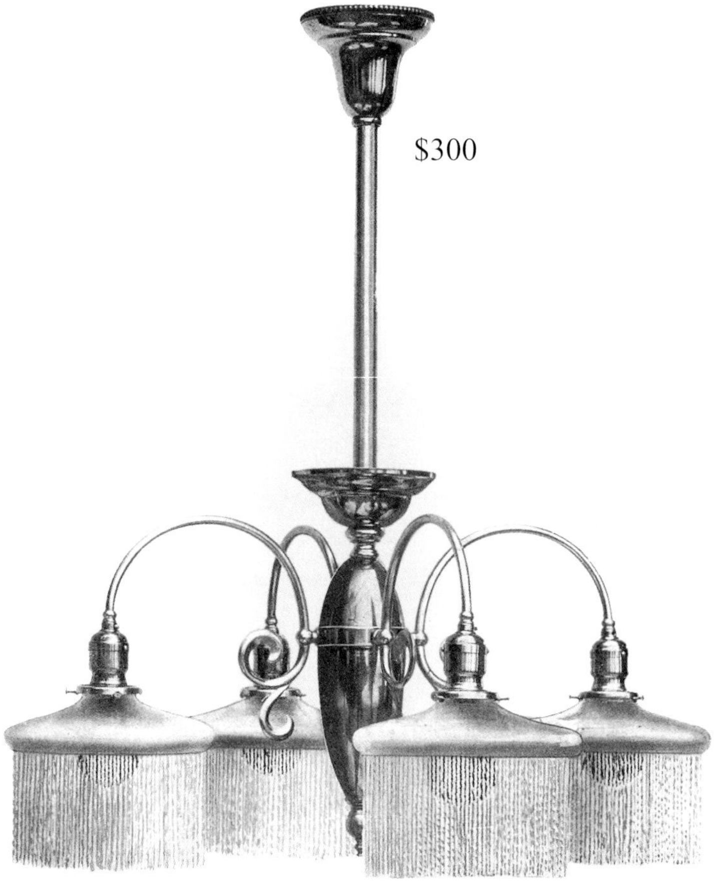

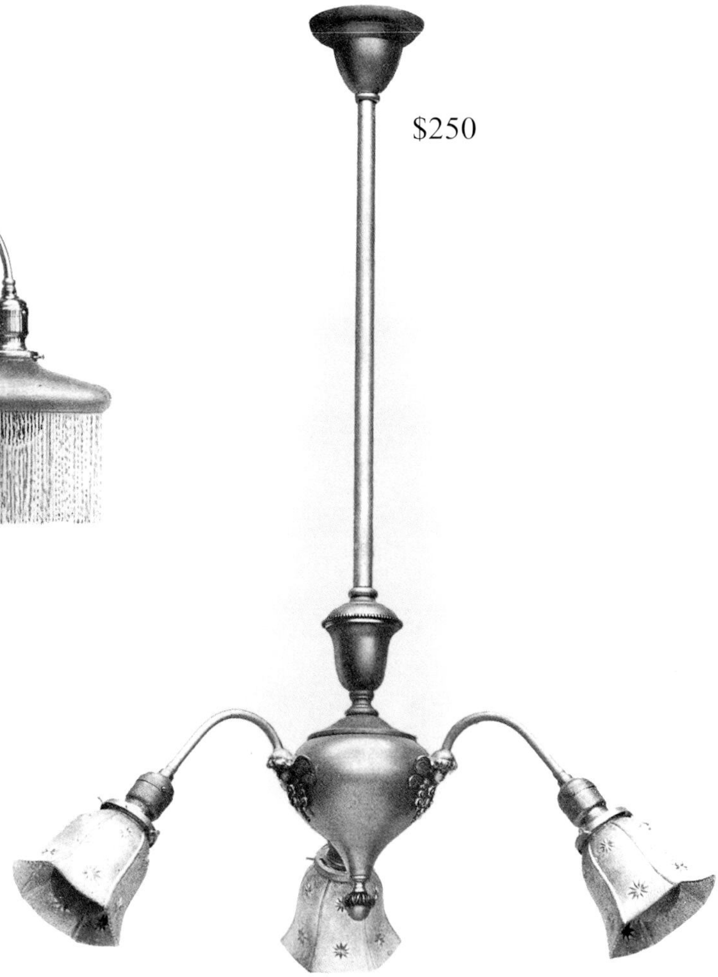

Number 1921
Length, 36 inches (over all). Spread, 19 inches.

			Not Wired	Wired	Complete as shown No lamps
2	Electric	Polished Brass	$8.50	$9.50	$13.50
3	"	" "	10.00	11.50	17.50
4	"	" "	11.50	13.50	21.50
5	"	" "	13.00	15.50	25.50

Shades No. G 448 Crystal Roughed Inside and Opal Glass Bead Fringe.

Number 2301
Length, 36 inches (over all). Spread, 25 inches.

			Not Wired	Wired	Complete as shown No lamps
2	Electric	Rich Gilt	$7.05	$8.05	$9.55
3	"	" "	8.20	9.70	11.95
4	"	" "	9.35	11.35	14.35

Shades No. B 41½ Crystal.

Price in right hand column always includes sockets; also holders and shades if shown but no lamps.
Other prices include glassware, sockets, lamps or electric holders only where mentioned.

Number 1831

Length, 36 inches (over all). Spread, 25 inches.

3¼x8-inch C. R. I. Bottom Ball included.

		Not Wired	Wired	Complete as shown No lamps
3 Electric	Polished Brass and Black	$6.00	$7.00	$9.00
4 "	" " " "	6.50	7.75	10.55
5 "	" " " "	7.00	8.50	12.10
6 "	" " " "	7.50	9.25	13.65
7 "	" " " "	8.00	10.00	15.20

Shades No. B 8983½ Crystal Roughed Inside.

Number 2651

Length, 42 inches (over all). Spread, 25 inches.

4x10-inch C. R. I. Bottom Ball included.

		Not Wired	Wired	Complete as shown No lamps
3 Electric	Polished Brass	$11.50	$13.00	$15.80
4 "	" "	12.25	14.25	18.25
5 "	" "	13.00	15.50	20.70
6 "	" "	13.75	16.75	23.15
7 "	" "	14.50	18.00	25.60

3¼x6-inch Crystal Roughed Inside Balls.

Price in right hand column always includes sockets; also holders and shades if shown but no lamps.
Other prices include glassware, sockets, lamps or electric holders only where mentioned.

$350

$400

Number 1859

Length, 36 inches (over all). Spread, 15 inches.

		Not Wired	Wired	Complete as shown No lamps
2 Electric	Rich Gilt and Satin.........	$19.00	$20.00	$22.40
3 "	" " " "	21.00	22.50	26.10
4 "	" " " "	23.00	25.00	29.80
5 "	" " " "	25.00	27.50	33.50

3¼x6-inch Crystal Roughed Inside Balls.

Number 1607

Length, 42 inches (over all). Spread, 22 inches.

		Not Wired	Wired	Complete as shown No lamps
2 Electric	Rich Gilt and Satin.........	$35.75	$36.75	$40.95
3 "	" " " "	38.50	40.00	46.30
4 "	" " " "	41.25	43.25	51.65
5 "	" " " "	44.00	46.50	57.00

No. B 5122 3¼x8-inch Ground and Cut Star Stalactites.

Price in right hand column always includes sockets; also holders and shades if shown but no lamps.
Other prices include glassware, sockets, lamps or electric holders only where mentioned.

$350

$400

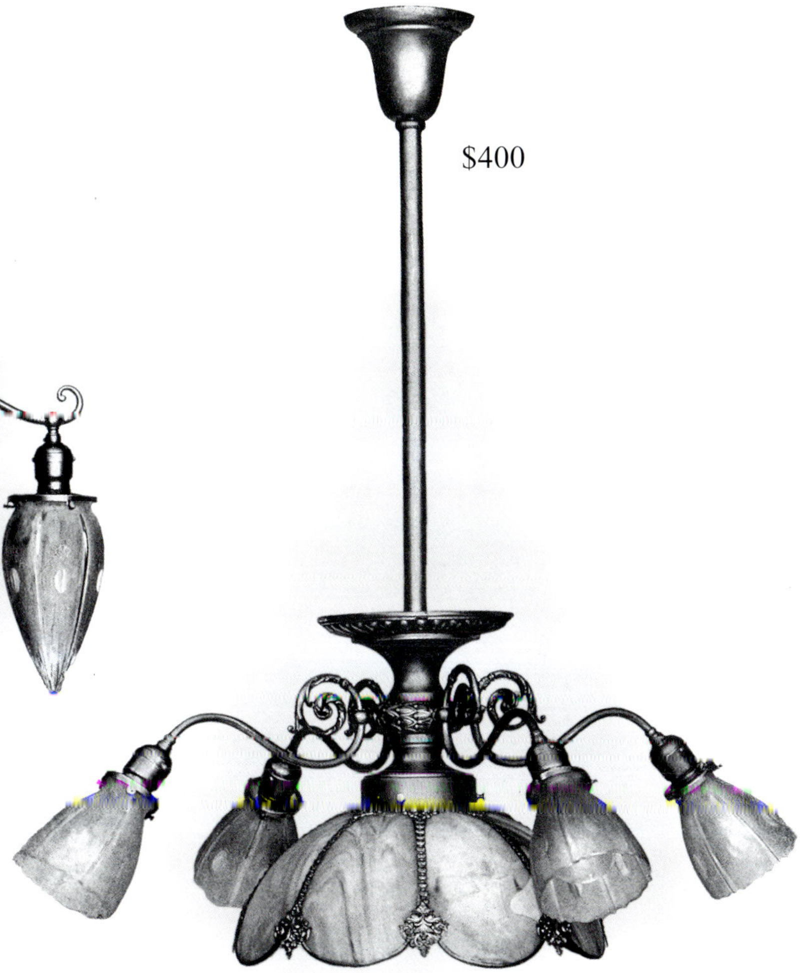

Number 1579

Length, 36 inches. Spread, 19 inches.

		Not Wired	Wired	Complete as shown No lamps
2 Electric	Rich Gilt	$14.25	$15.25	$21.95
3 "	" "	17.50	19.00	29.05
4 "	" "	20.75	22.75	36.15
5 "	" "	24.00	26.50	43.25
6 "	" "	27.25	30.25	50.35

No. B 906½ 3¼x8-inch Etched and Cut Stalactites.

Number 1563

Length, 40 inches (over all). Spread, 30 inches.

4x14-inch Art Glass Dome included.

Select Glass Colors by Number. See last page.

		Not Wired	Wired	Complete as shown No lamps
3 Electric	Rich Gilt	$23.50	$25.00	$29.70
4 "	" "	25.00	27.00	33.85
5 "	" "	26.50	29.00	38.00
6 "	" "	28.00	31.00	42.15

Shades No. B 2906½ Etched and Cut.

Price in right hand column always includes sockets; also holders and shades if shown but no lamps.
Other prices include glassware, sockets, lamps or electric holders only where mentioned.

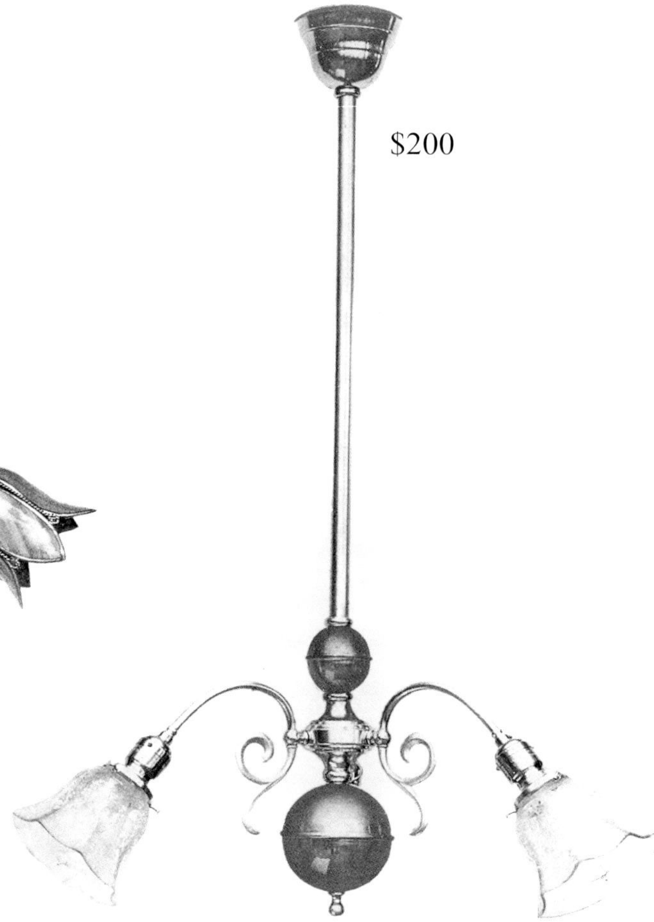

Number 2654

Length, 36 inches (over all). Spread, 23 inches.

4x14-inch Art Glass Dome included.

Select Glass Colors by Number. See last page.

		Not Wired	Wired	Complete as shown No lamps
3 Electric	Old Brass	$16.00	$17.50	$26.90
4 "	" "	17.00	19.00	32.90
5 "	" "	18.00	20.50	38.90
6 "	" "	19.00	22.00	44.90

Shades No. G 436 Art Glass.

Number 2087

Length, 36 inches (over all). Spread, 24 inches.

		Not Wired	Wired	Complete as shown No lamps
2 Electric	Old Brass	$5.50	$6.50	$8.30
3 "	" "	6.50	8.00	10.70
4 "	" "	7.50	9.50	13.10
5 "	" "	8.50	11.00	15.50
6 "	" "	9.50	12.50	17.90

Shades No. B 1412½ White Acid.

Price in right hand column always includes sockets; also holders and shades if shown but no lamps.
Other prices include glassware, sockets, lamps or electric holders only where mentioned.

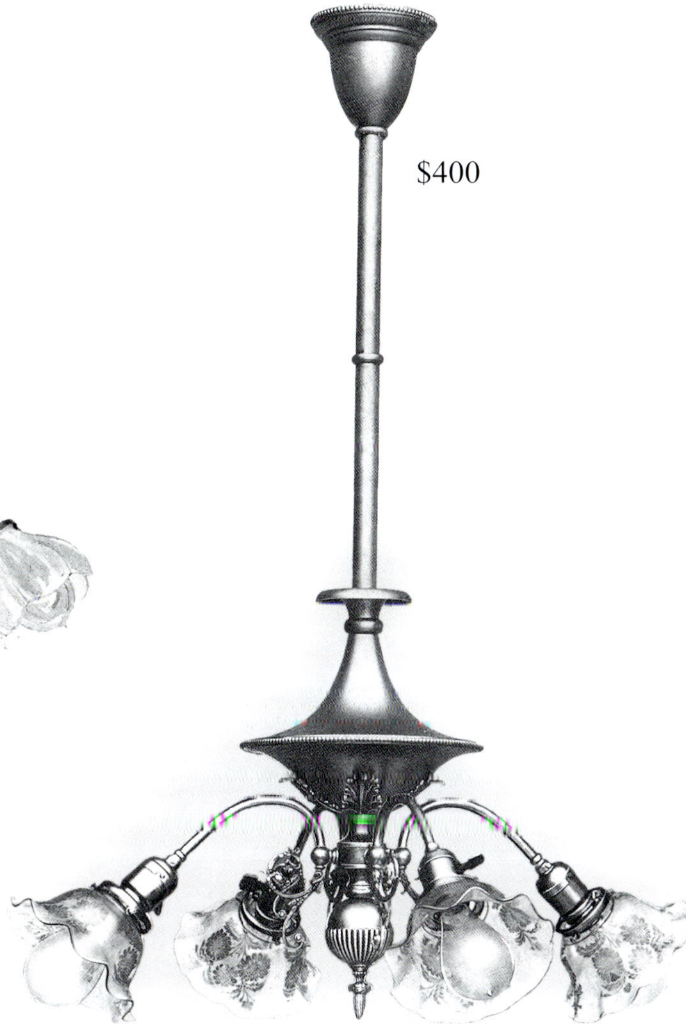

Number 1863
Length, 36 inches. Spread, 22 inches.

		Not Wired	Wired	Complete as shown No lamps
2 Electric	Rich Gilt and Satin.........	$19.00	$20.00	$21.90
3 "	" " " "	21.00	22.50	25.35
4 "	" " " "	23.00	25.00	28.80
5 "	" " " "	25.00	27.50	32.25

Shades No. B 539½ Crystal Roughed Inside.

Number 1464
Length, 36 inches (over all). Spread, 24 inches.

		Not Wired	Wired	Complete as shown No lamps
2 Electric	Rich Gilt and Satin.........	$10.50	$11.50	$13.30
3 "	" " " "	11.50	13.00	15.70
4 "	" " " "	12.50	14.50	18.10
5 "	" " " "	13.50	16.00	20.50

Shades No. B 1906½ White Acid.

Price in right hand column always includes sockets; also holders and shades if shown but no lamps.
Other prices include glassware, sockets lamps or electric holders only where mentioned.

$350

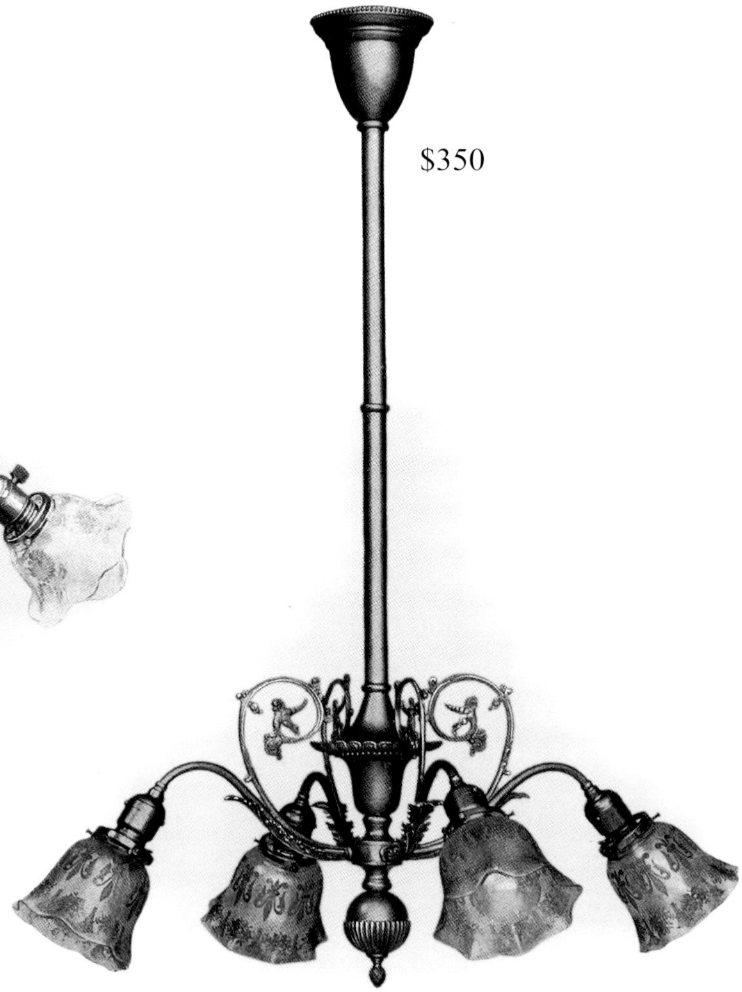

$350

Number 1460
Length, 36 inches. Spread, 28 inches.

		Not Wired	Wired	Complete as shown No lamps
2 Electric	Rich Gilt and Satin	$12.25	$13.25	$15.05
3 "	" " " "	13.75	15.25	17.95
4 "	" " " "	15.25	17.25	20.85
5 "	" " " "	16.75	19.25	23.75
6 "	" " " "	18.25	21.25	26.65

Shades No. B 1906½ White Acid.

Number 1577
Length, 36 inches (over all). Spread, 27 inches.

		Not Wired	Wired	Complete as shown No lamps
2 Electric	Rich Gilt	$9.75	$10.75	$13.15
3 "	" "	11.50	13.00	16.60
4 "	" "	13.25	15.25	20.05
5 "	" "	15.00	17.50	23.50

Shades No. B 1345½ Silver Etched.

Price in right hand column always includes sockets; also holders and shades if shown but no lamps.
Other prices include glassware, sockets, lamps or electric holders only where mentioned.

$350

$350

Number 1943

Length, 36 inches (over all). Spread, 25 inches.

			Not Wired	Wired	Complete as shown No lamps
2	Electric	Brush Brass and Black.....	**$20.50**	**$21.50**	**$23.40**
3	"	" " " "	**25.25**	**26.75**	**29.60**
4	"	" " " "	**30.00**	**32.00**	**35.80**
5	"	" " " "	**34.75**	**37.25**	**42.00**

Shades No. B 539½ Crystal Roughed Inside.

Number 1569

Length, 36 inches (over all). Spread, 27 inches.

			Not Wired	Wired	Complete as shown No lamps
2	Electric	Rich Gilt	**$11.50**	**$12.50**	**$14.40**
3	"	" "	**13.25**	**14.75**	**17.60**
4	"	" "	**15.00**	**17.00**	**20.80**
5	"	" "	**16.75**	**19.25**	**24.00**

Shades No. B 5990½ White Acid.

Price in right hand column always includes sockets; also holders and shades if shown but no lamps.
Other prices include glassware, sockets, lamps or electric holders only where mentioned.

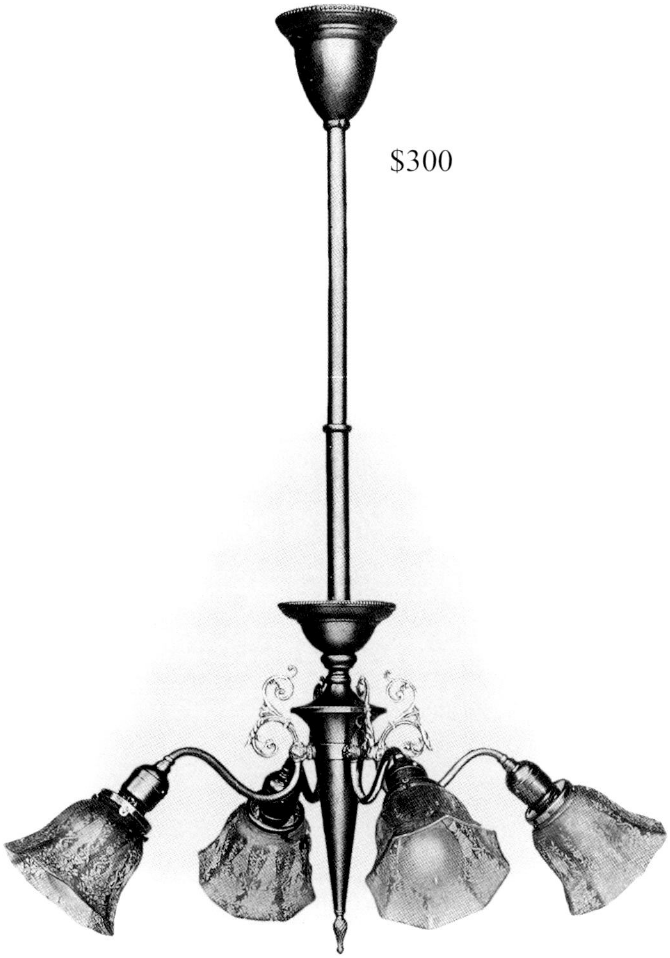

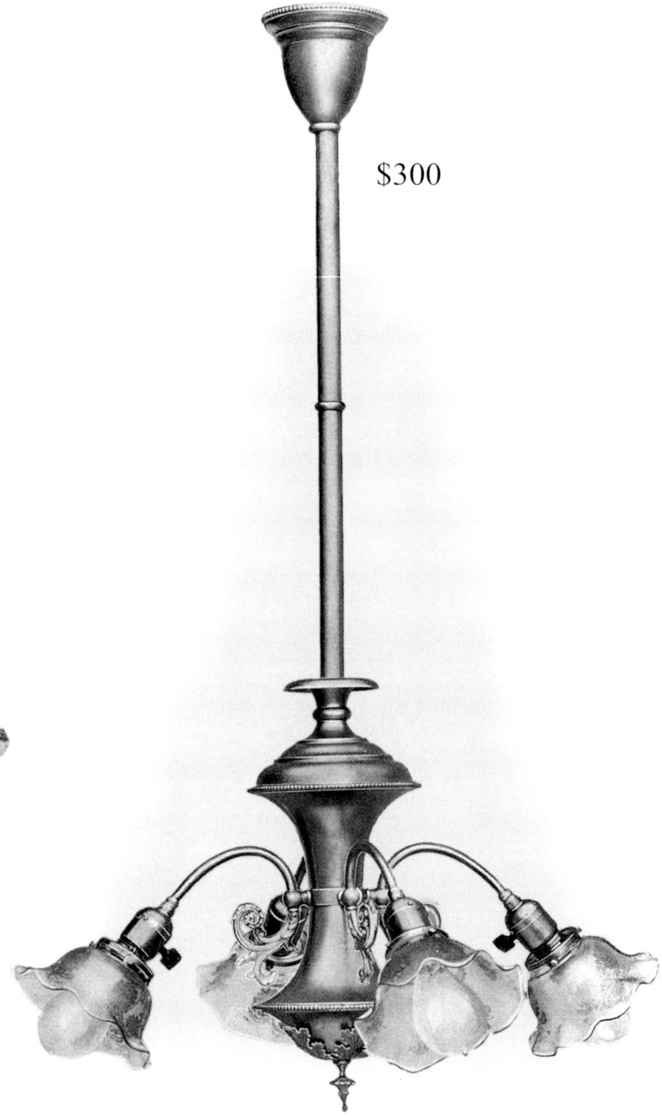

Number 1565
Length, 36 inches. Spread, 21 inches.

			Not Wired	Wired	Complete as shown No lamps
2	Electric	Rich Gilt	$6.50	$7.50	$9.30
3	"	" "	7.50	9.00	11.70
4	"	" "	8.50	10.50	14.10
5	"	" "	9.50	12.00	16.50
6	"	" "	10.50	13.50	18.90

Shades No. B 1412½ White Acid.

Number 1461
Length, 36 inches. Spread, 22 inches.

			Not Wired	Wired	Complete as shown No lamps
2	Electric	Rich Gilt and Satin	$10.50	$11.50	$13.30
3	"	" " " "	11.75	13.25	15.95
4	"	" " " "	13.00	15.00	18.60
5	"	" " " "	14.25	16.75	21.25

Shades No. B 1906½ White Acid.

Price in right hand column always includes sockets; also holders and shades if shown but no lamps.
Other prices include glassware, sockets, lamps or electric holders only where mentioned.

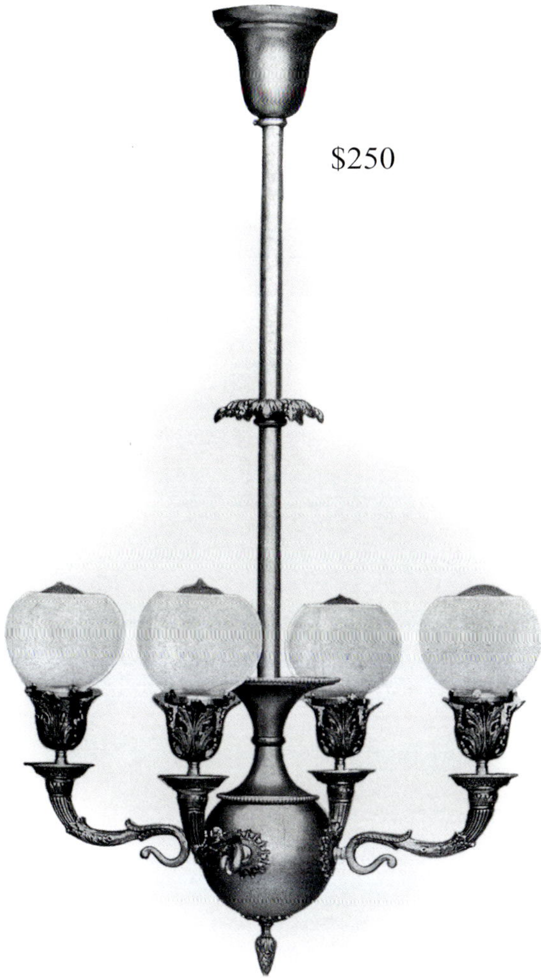

$250

$250

Number 1510
Length, 36 inches. Spread, 17 inches.
Socket Husks included.

			Not Wired	Wired	Complete as shown No lamps
2	Electric	Rich Gilt and Satin	$19.75	$20.75	$22.55
3	"	" " " "	25.00	26.50	29.20
4	"	" " " "	30.25	32.25	35.85
5	"	" " " "	35.50	38.00	42.50
6	"	" " " "	40.75	43.75	49.15

Shades No. B 4149 Crystal Roughed Inside.

Number 2160
Length, 36 inches. Spread, 19 inches.
Socket Husks included.

			Not Wired	Wired	Complete as shown No lamps
2	Electric	Brush Brass	$23.00	$24.00	$24.80
4	"	" "	31.00	33.00	34.60

Price in right hand column always includes sockets; also holders and shades if shown but no lamps.
Other prices include glassware, sockets, lamps or electric holders only where mentioned.

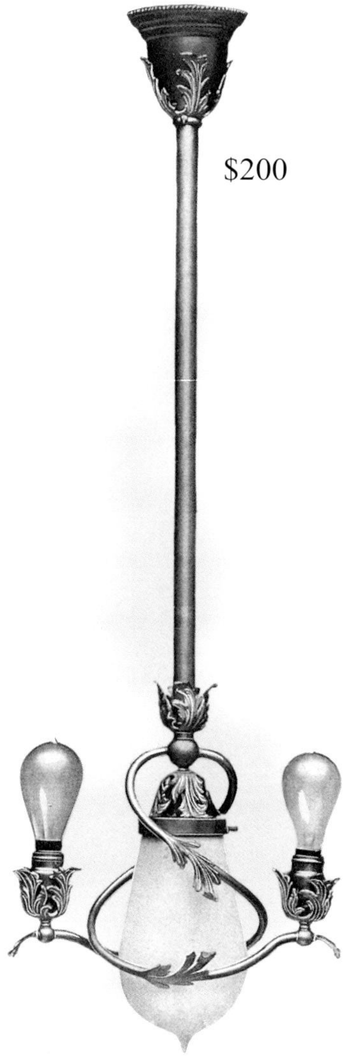

$200

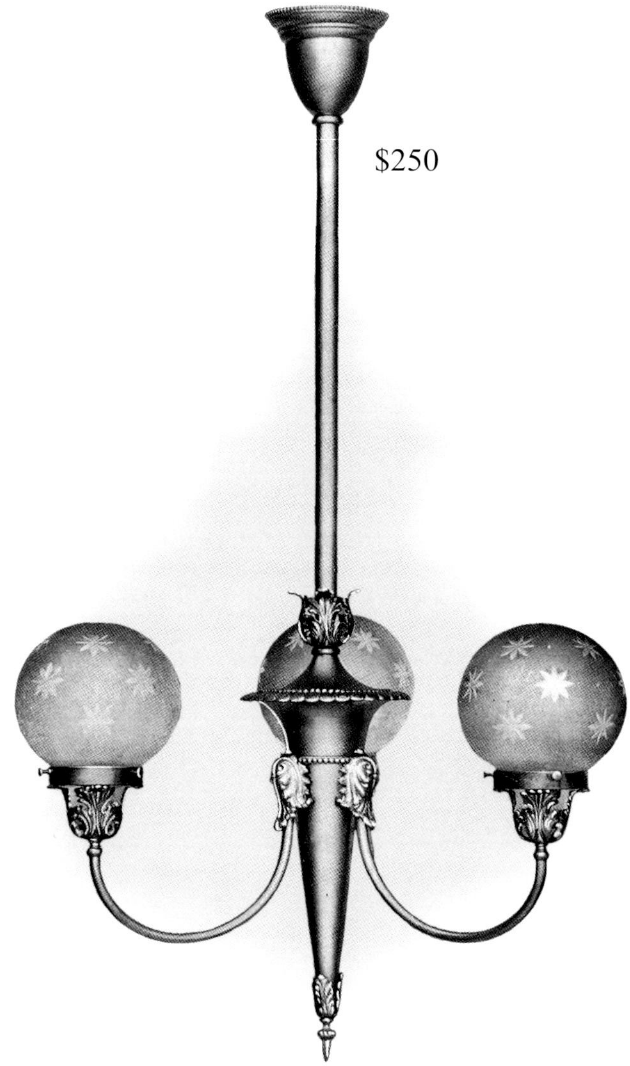

$250

Number 1457
Length, 36 inches (over all). Spread, 10 inches.
Socket Husks and P. S. O. Stalactite included.

		Not Wired	Wired	Complete as shown No lamps
3 Electric	Rich Gilt and Satin........	$10.00	$11.50	$12.70

Number 1558
Length, 42 inches. Spread, 18 inches.
Socket Husks and Holders included.

		Not Wired	Wired	Complete as shown No lamps
2 Electric	Rich Gilt and Satin.........	$16.75	$17.75	$21.55
3 "	" " " "	20.00	21.50	27.20
4 "	" " " "	23.25	25.25	32.85
5 "	" " " "	26.50	29.00	38.50

No. B 5121 3¼x6-inch Ground and Cut Star Balls.

Price in right hand column always includes sockets; also holders and shades if shown but no lamps.
Other prices include glassware. sockets, lamps or electric holders only where mentioned.

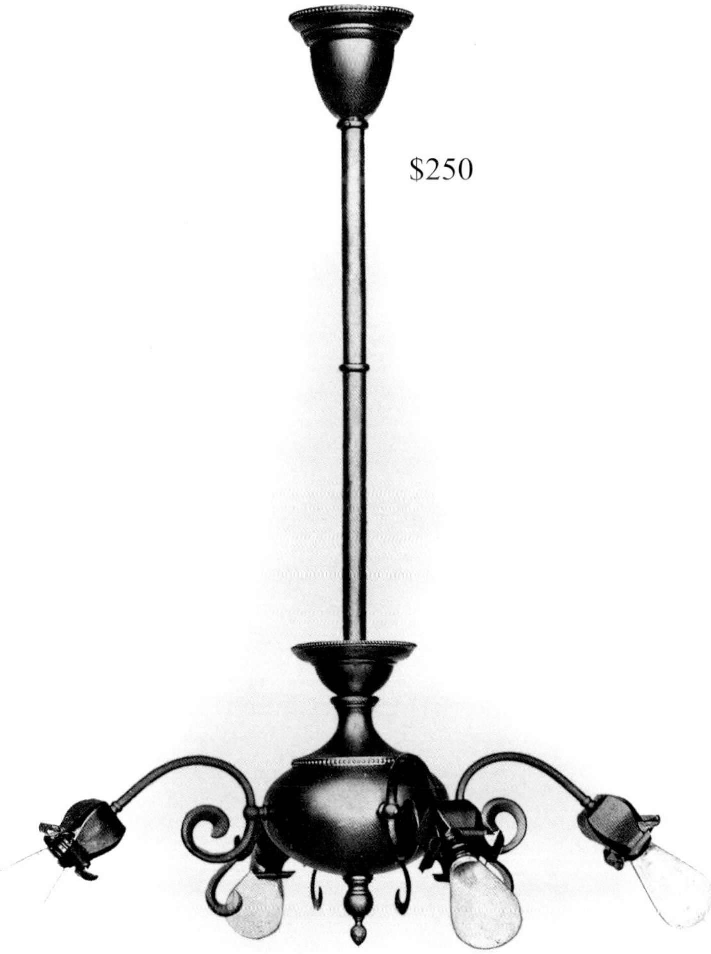

$250

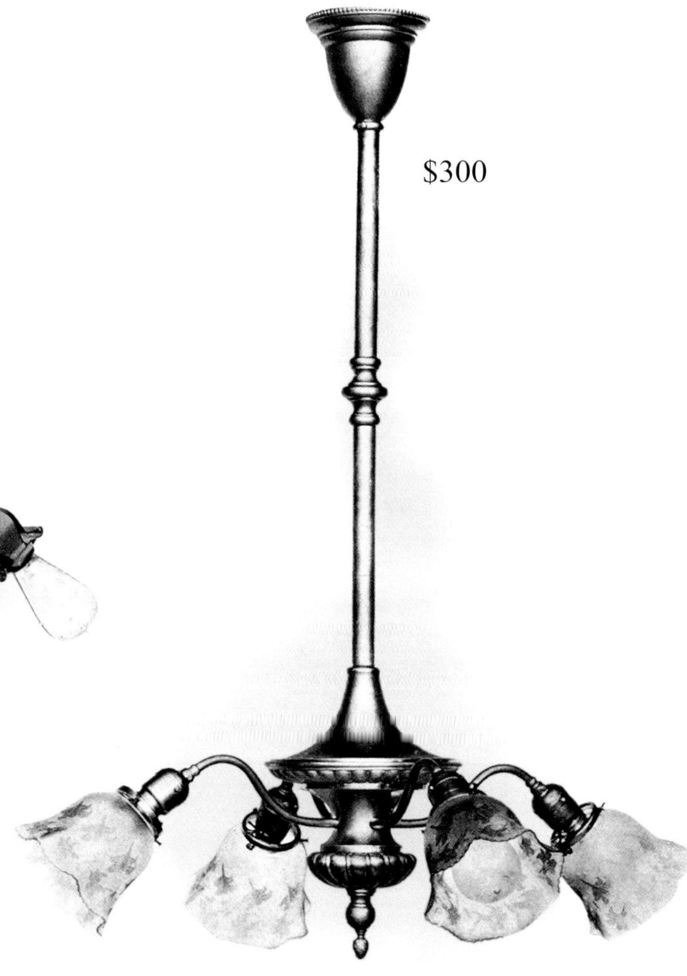

$300

Number 1568

Length, 36 inches (over all). Spread, 28 inches.

Socket Husks included.

		Not Wired	Wired	Complete as shown No lamps
2 Electric	Old Brass	$10.50	$11.50	$12.30
3 "	" "	13.00	14.50	15.70
4 "	" "	15.50	17.50	19.10
5 "	" "	18.00	20.50	22.50
6 "	" "	20.50	23.50	25.90

Without Socket Husks deduct $1.00 per light.

Number 1578

Length, 36 inches. Spread, 24 inches.

		Not Wired	Wired	Complete as shown No lamps
2 Electric	Rich Gilt	$13.00	$14.00	$16.70
3 "	" "	13.50	15.00	19.05
4 "	" "	14.00	16.00	21.40
5 "	" "	14.50	17.00	23.75
6 "	" "	15.00	18.00	26.10

Shades No. B 1532½ Metallic Etched.

Price in right hand column always includes sockets; also holders and shades if shown but no lamps.
Other prices include glassware, sockets, lamps or electric holders only where mentioned.

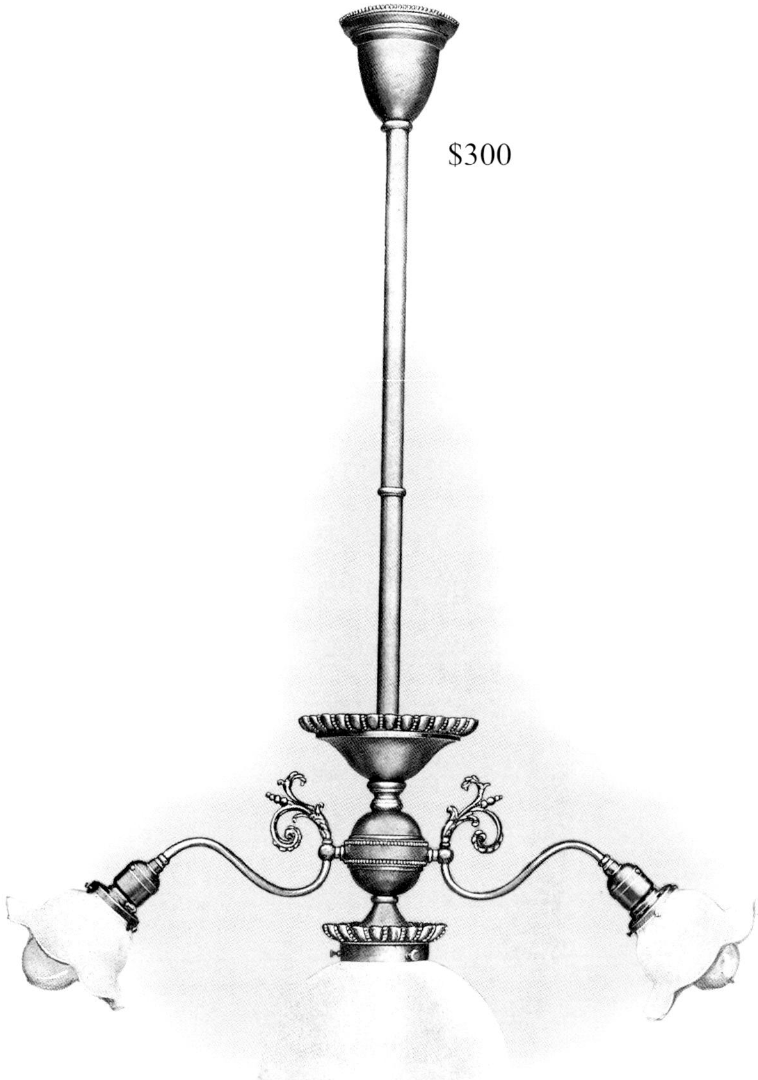

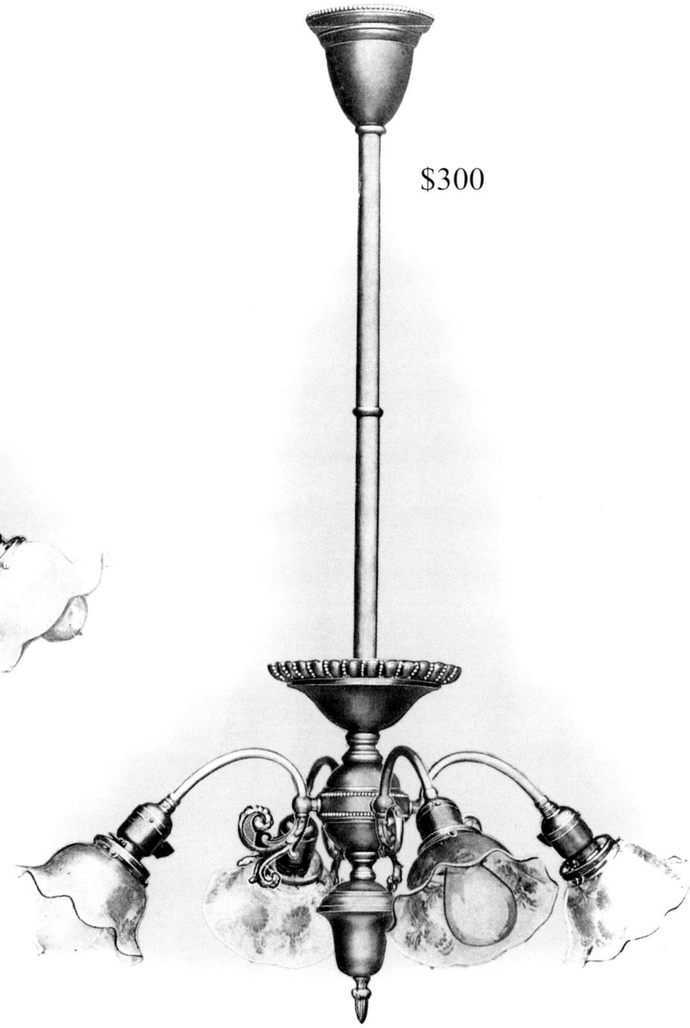

Number 1477

Length, 36 inches (over all). Spread, 27 inches.

3¼x10-inch P. S. O. Dome included.

		Not Wired	Wired	Complete as shown No lamps
3 Electric	Rich Gilt	$10.75	$12.25	$14.65
4 "	" "	12.25	14.25	17.65
5 "	" "	13.75	16.25	20.65
6 "	" "	15.25	18.25	23.65

Shades No. B 5213½ Plain Straw Opalescent.

Number 1465

Length, 36 inches. Spread, 24 inches.

		Not Wired	Wired	Complete as shown No lamps
2 Electric	Rich Gilt	$8.50	$9.50	$11.30
3 "	" "	9.75	11.25	13.95
4 "	" "	11.00	13.00	16.60
5 "	" "	12.25	14.75	19.25
6 "	" "	13.50	16.50	21.90

Shades No. B 1906½ White Acid.

Price in right hand column always includes sockets; also holders and shades if shown but no lamps.
Other prices include glassware, sockets, lamps or electric holders only where mentioned.

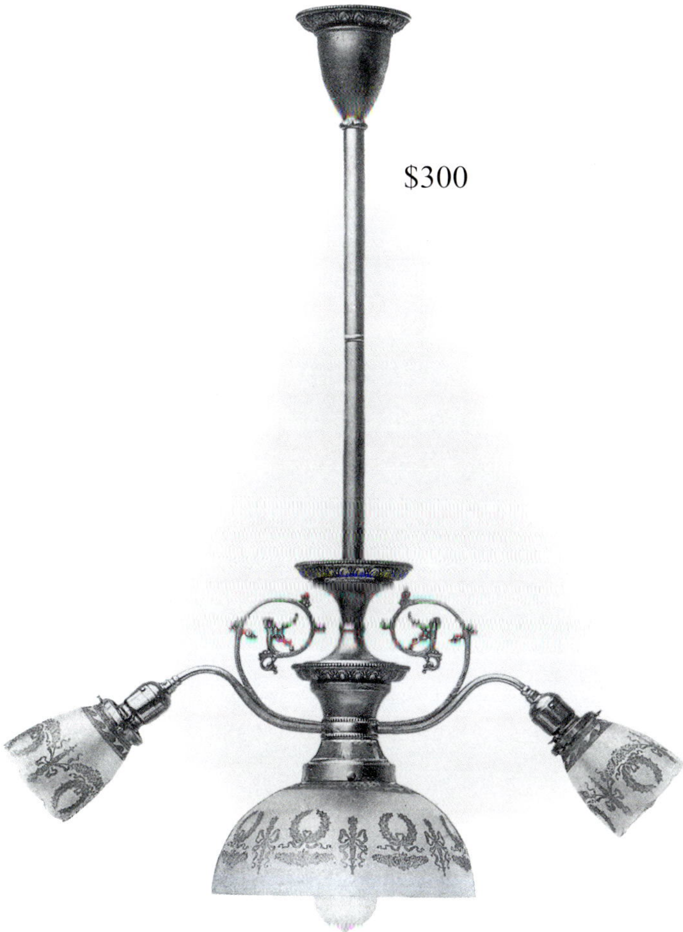

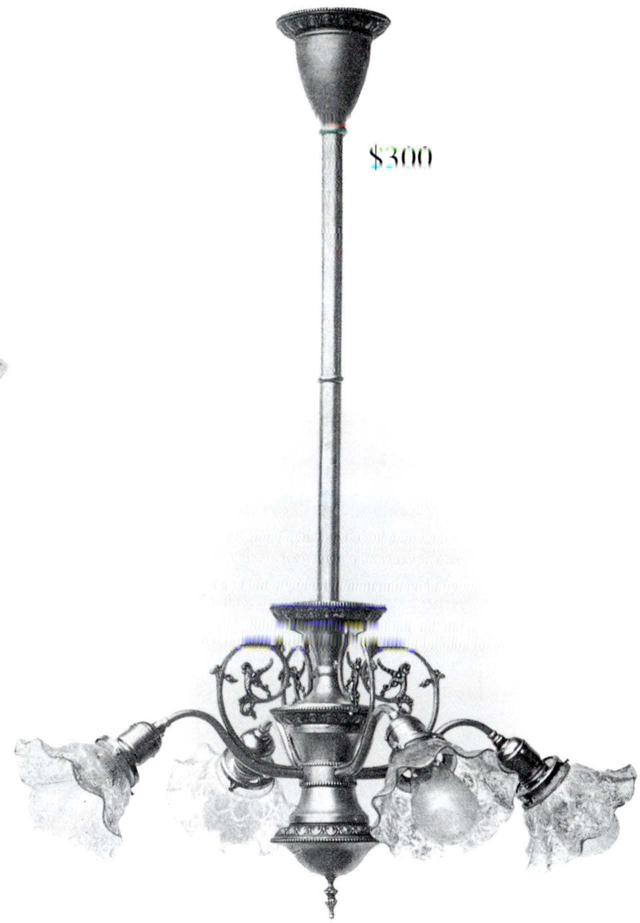

Number 1710
Length, 36 inches (over all). Spread, 23 inches.
3¼x10-inch Etched Dome included.

		Not Wired	Wired	Complete as shown No lamps
3 Electric	Polished Brass and Black..	$8.15	$9.65	$12.55
4 "	" " " " ..	9.35	11.35	15.50
5 "	" " " " ..	10.55	13.05	18.45

Shades No. B 6568½ Etched.

Number 1709
Length, 36 inches Spread, 23 inches.

		Not Wired	Wired	Complete as shown No lamps
2 Electric	Polished Brass and Black..	$6.65	$7.65	$9.45
3 "	" " " " ..	7.85	9.35	12.05
4 "	" " " " ..	9.05	11.05	14.65

Shades No. B 1538½ White Acid.

Price in right hand column always includes sockets; also holders and shades if shown but no lamps.
Other prices include glassware, sockets, lamps or electric holders only where mentioned.

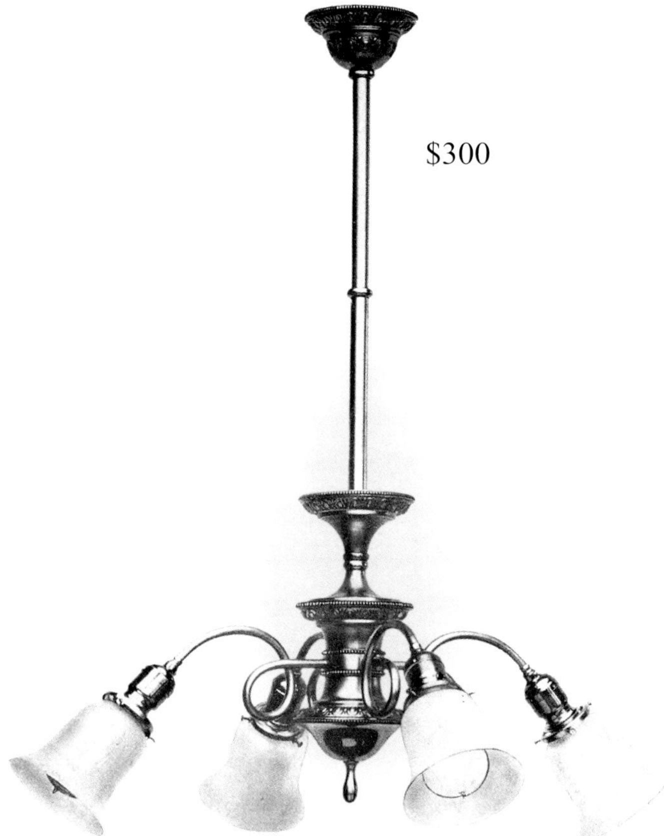

Number 1901
Length, 36 inches (over all). Spread, 23 inches.
4x8-inch C. R. I. Ball included.

		Not Wired	Wired	Complete as shown No lamps
3 Electric	Rich Gilt	$6.20	$7.70	$9.70
4 "	" "	6.80	8.80	11.60
5 "	" "	7.40	9.90	13.50

Shades No. B 8983½ Crystal Roughed Inside.

Number 1875
Length, 36 inches (over all). Spread, 23 inches.

		Not Wired	Wired	Complete as shown No lamps
2 Electric	Rich Gilt	$5.45	$6.45	$8.05
3 "	" "	6.05	7.55	9.95
4 "	" "	6.65	8.65	11.85

Shades No. B 8983½ Crystal Roughed Inside.

Price in right hand column always includes sockets; also holders and shades if shown but no lamps.
Other prices include glassware, sockets, lamps or electric holders only where mentioned.

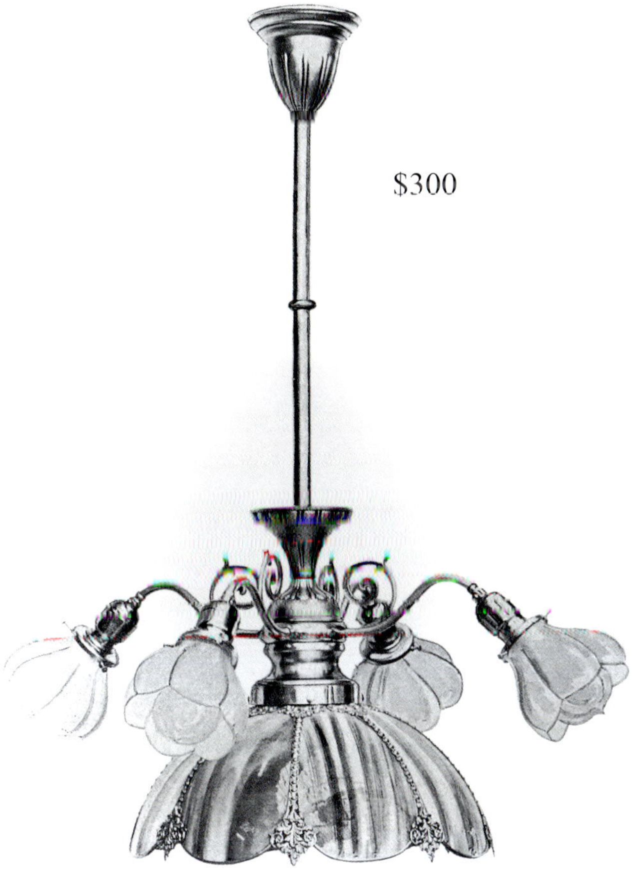

$300

$300

Number 1903

Length, 36 inches. (over all). Spread, 25 inches.

4x14-inch Art Glass Dome included.

Select Glass Colors by Number. See last page.

		Not Wired	Wired	Complete as shown No lamps
3 Electric	Brush Brass and Black.....	$14.50	$16.00	$18.30
4 "	" " " "	15.25	17.25	20.50
5 "	" " " "	16.00	18.50	22.70
6 "	" " " "	16.75	19.75	24.90

Shades No. B 539½ Crystal Roughed Inside.

Number 1794

Length, 36 inches (over all). Spread, 25 inches.

		Not Wired	Wired	Complete as shown No lamps
2 Electric	Brush Brass and Black.....	$5.75	$6.75	$8.25
3 "	" " " "	6.75	8.25	10.50
4 "	" " " "	7.75	9.75	12.75
5 "	" " " "	8.75	11.25	15.00
6 "	" " " "	9.75	12.75	17.25

Shades No. B 41½ Crystal.

Price in right hand column always includes sockets; also holders and shades if shown but no lamps.
Other prices include glassware, sockets, lamps or electric holders only where mentioned.

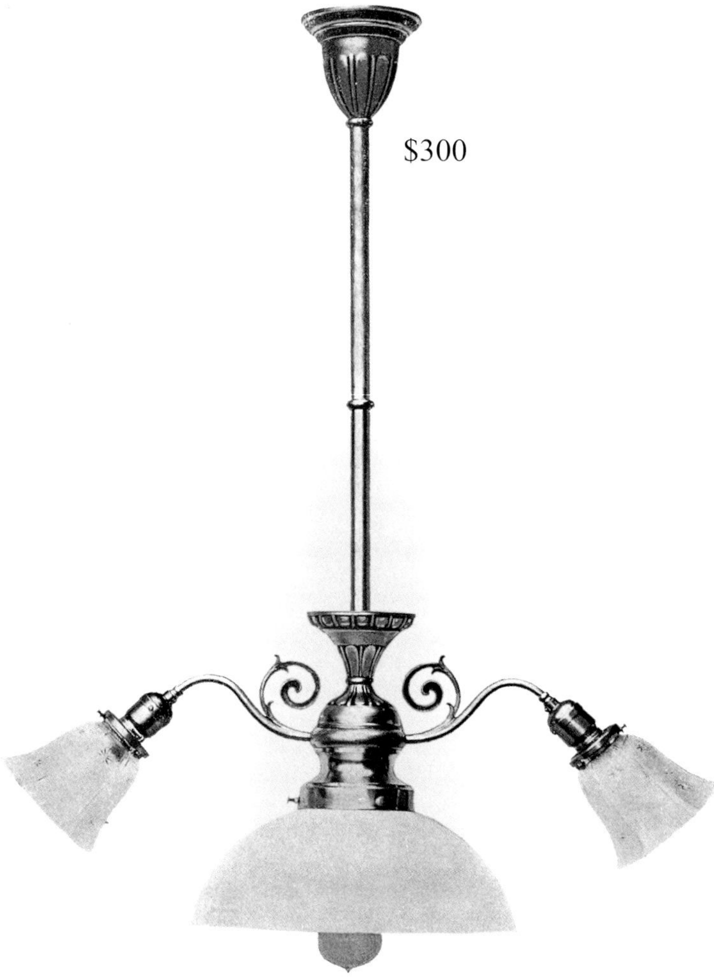

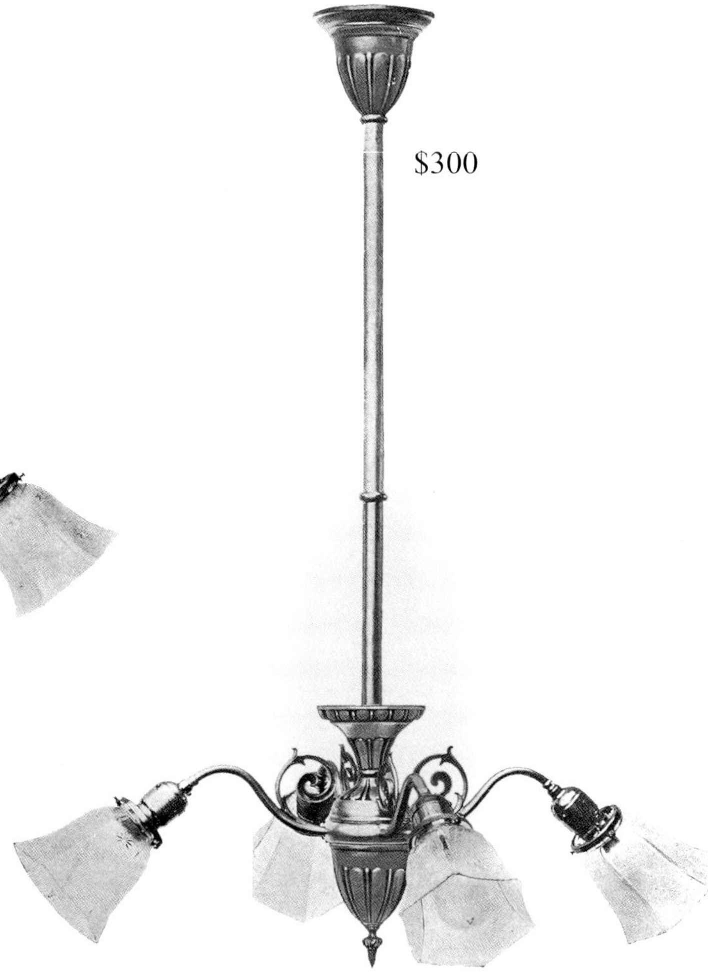

Number 1793

Length, 36 inches (over all). Spread, 24 inches.

4x12-inch C. R. I. Dome included.

		Not Wired	Wired	Complete as shown No lamps
3 Electric	Brush Brass and Black.....	$7.00	$8.00	$9.90
4 "	" " " "	7.75	9.25	11.90
5 "	" " " "	8.50	10.50	13.90

Shades No. B 41½ Crystal.

Number 1795

Length, 36 inches Spread, 24 inches.

		Not Wired	Wired	Complete as shown No lamps
2 Electric	Brush Brass and Black.....	$5.25	$6.25	$7.75
3 "	" " " "	6.00	7.50	9.75
4 "	" " " "	6.75	8.75	11.75
5 "	" " " "	7.50	10.00	13.75
6 "	" " " "	8.25	11.25	15.75

Shades No. B 41½ Crystal.

Price in right hand column always includes sockets; also holders and shades if shown but no lamps.
Other prices include glassware, sockets, lamps or electric holders only where mentioned.

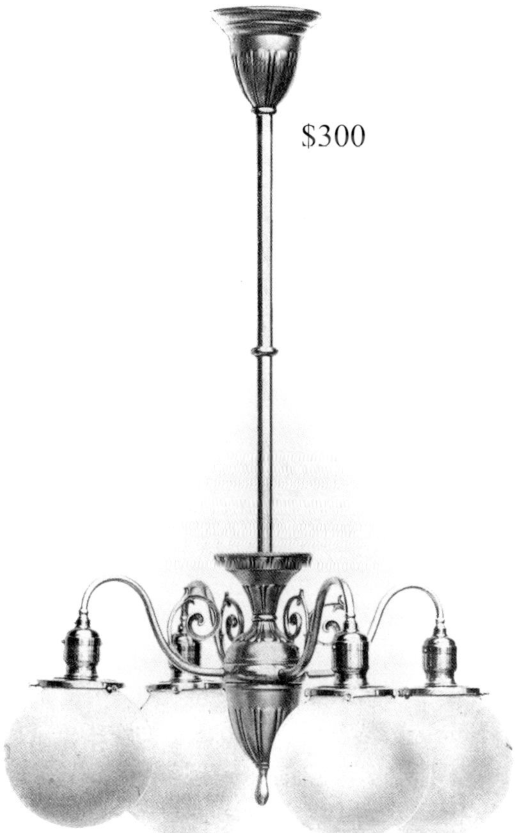

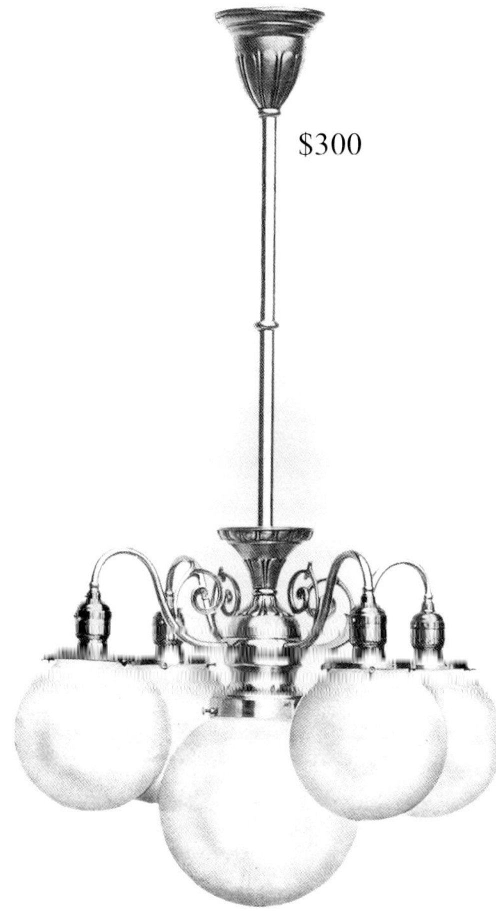

Number 1870

Length, 36 inches (over all). Spread, 15 inches.

		Not Wired	Wired	Complete as shown No lamps
2 Electric	Brush Brass and Black.....	$5.25	$6.25	$8.65
3 "	" " " "	6.00	7.50	11.10
4 "	" " " "	6.75	8.75	13.55

3¼x6-inch Crystal Roughed Inside Balls.

Number 1882

Length, 36 inches (over all). Spread, 15 inches.

4x8-inch C. R. I. Bottom Ball included.

		Not Wired	Wired	Complete as shown No lamps
3 Electric	Brush Brass and Black.....	$6.50	$8.00	$10.80
4 "	" " " "	7.25	9.25	13.25
5 "	" " " "	8.00	10.50	15.70

3¼x6-inch Crystal Roughed Inside Balls.

Price in right hand column always includes sockets; also holders and shades if shown but no lamps.
Other prices include glassware, sockets, lamps or electric holders only where mentioned.

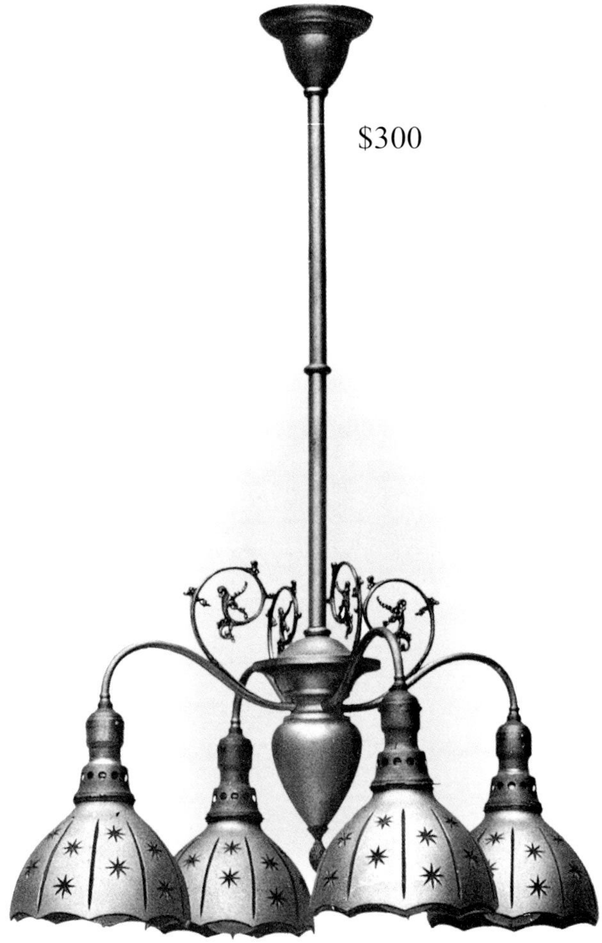

Number 2540

Length, 36 inches (over all). Spread, 14 inches.

			Not Wired	Wired	Complete as shown No lamps
2	Electric	Brush Brass	$5.25	$6.25	$8.25
3	"	" "	5.75	7.25	10.25
4	"	" "	6.25	8.25	12.25

Shades No. B 249 Crystal Roughed Inside. Diameter, 6 inches.

Number 2533

Length, 36 inches (over all). Spread, 17 inches.

			Not Wired	Wired	Complete as shown No lamps
2	Electric	Brush Brass	$6.75	$7.75	$10.25
3	"	" "	8.00	9.50	13.25
4	"	" "	9.25	11.25	16.25

Shades No. B 007½ Frosted, with Crystal Stars and Bars. Diameter, 7 inches.

Price in right hand column always includes sockets; also holders and shades if shown but no lamps.
Other prices include glassware, sockets, lamps or electric holders only where mentioned.

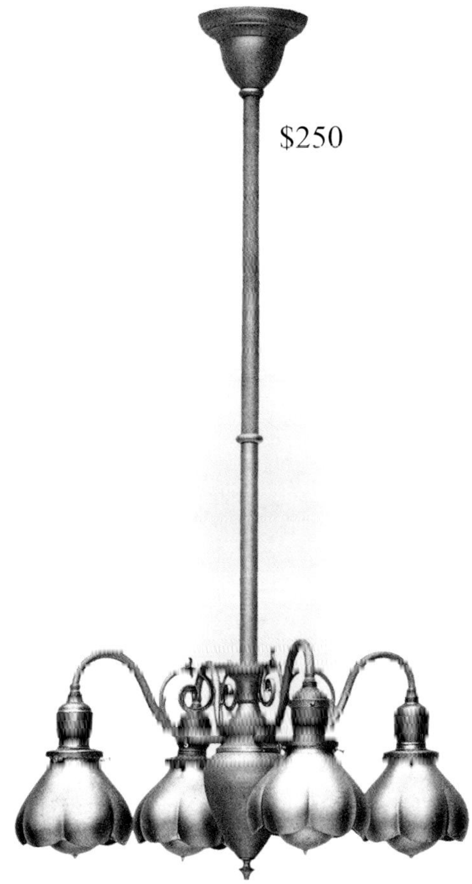

Number 2542

Length, 36 inches (over all). Spread, 23 inches.

				Not Wired	Wired	Complete as shown No lamps
2	Electric	Brush	Brass	$5.25	$6.25	$7.75
3	"	"	"	5.75	7.25	9.50
4	"	"	"	6.25	8.25	11.25
5	"	"	"	6.75	9.25	13.00
6	"	"	"	7.25	10.25	14.75

Shades No. B 41½ Crystal.

Number 2532

Length, 36 inches. Spread, 14 inches.

				Not Wired	Wired	Complete as shown No lamps
2	Electric	Brush	Brass	$5.25	$6.25	$8.25
3	"	"	"	6.00	7.50	10.50
4	"	"	"	6.75	8.75	12.75

Shades No. B 539½ Crystal Roughed Inside.

Price in right hand column always includes sockets; also holders and shades if shown but no lamps. Other prices include glassware, sockets, lamps or electric holders only where mentioned.

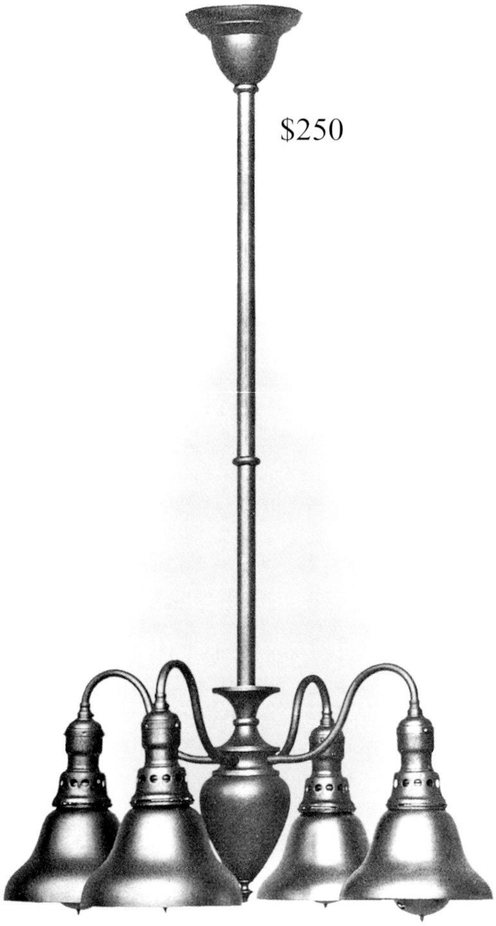

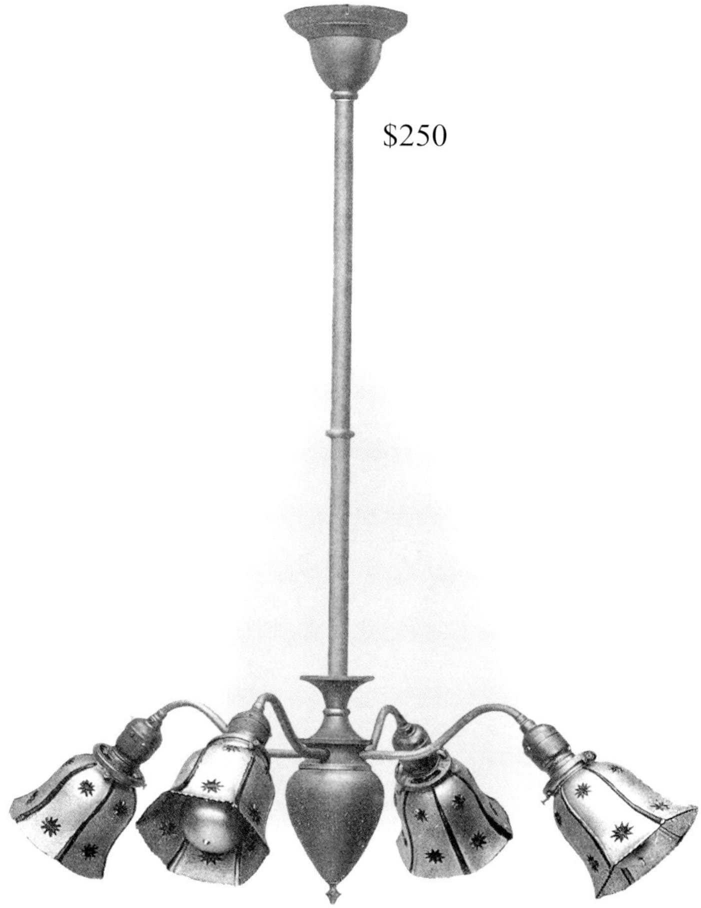

Number 2543
Length, 36 inches (over all). Spread, 14 inches.

			Not Wired	Wired	Complete as shown No lamps
2	Electric	Brush Brass	$4.75	$5.75	$7.75
3	"	" "	5.25	6.75	9.75
4	"	" "	5.75	7.75	11.75

Shades No. B 249 Crystal Roughed Inside. Diameter, 6 inches.

Number 2541
Length, 36 inches (over all). Spread, 23 inches.

			Not Wired	Wired	Complete as shown No lamps
2	Electric	Brush Brass	$4.75	$5.75	$7.25
3	"	" "	5.25	6.75	9.00
4	"	" "	5.75	7.75	10.75
5	"	" "	6.25	8.75	12.50
6	"	" "	6.75	9.75	14.25

Shades No. B 41½ Crystal.

Price in right hand column always includes sockets; also holders and shades if shown but no lamps.
Other prices include glassware, sockets, lamps or electric holders only where mentioned.

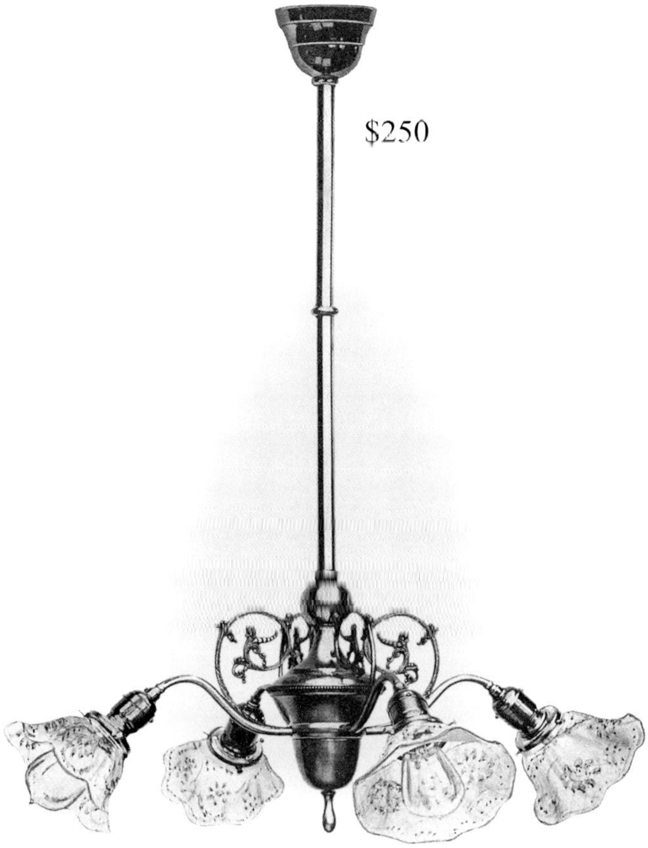

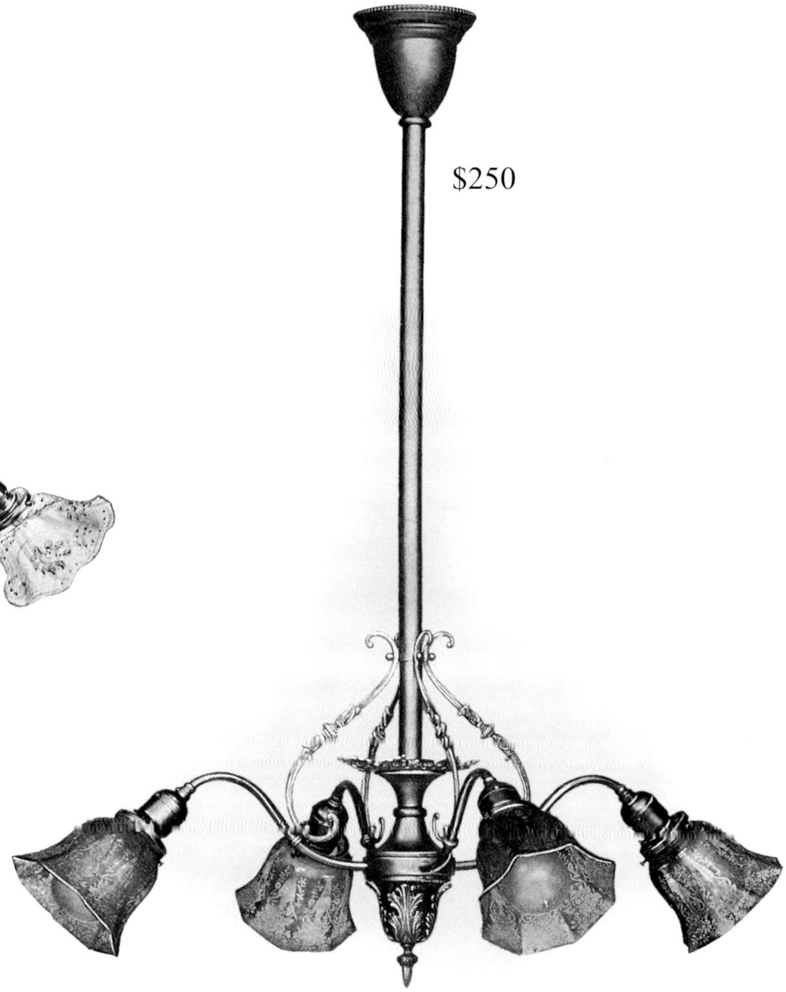

Number 1926

Length, 36 inches (over all). Spread, 23 inches.

			Not Wired	Wired	Complete as shown No lamps
2	Electric	Rich Gilt	$5.40	$6.40	$8.20
3	"	" "	6.60	8.10	10.80
4	"	" "	7.80	9.80	13.40

Shades No. B 1906½ White Acid.

Number 1573

Length, 36 inches (over all). Spread, 27 inches.

			Not Wired	Wired	Complete as shown No lamps
2	Electric	Rich Gilt	$7.75	$8.75	$10.55
3	"	" "	8.75	10.25	12.95
4	"	" "	9.75	11.75	15.35
5	"	" "	10.75	13.25	17.75
6	"	" "	11.75	14.75	20.15

Shades No. B 1412½ White Acid.

Price in right hand column always includes sockets; also holders and shades if shown but no lamps.
Other prices include glassware, sockets, lamps or electric holders only where mentioned.

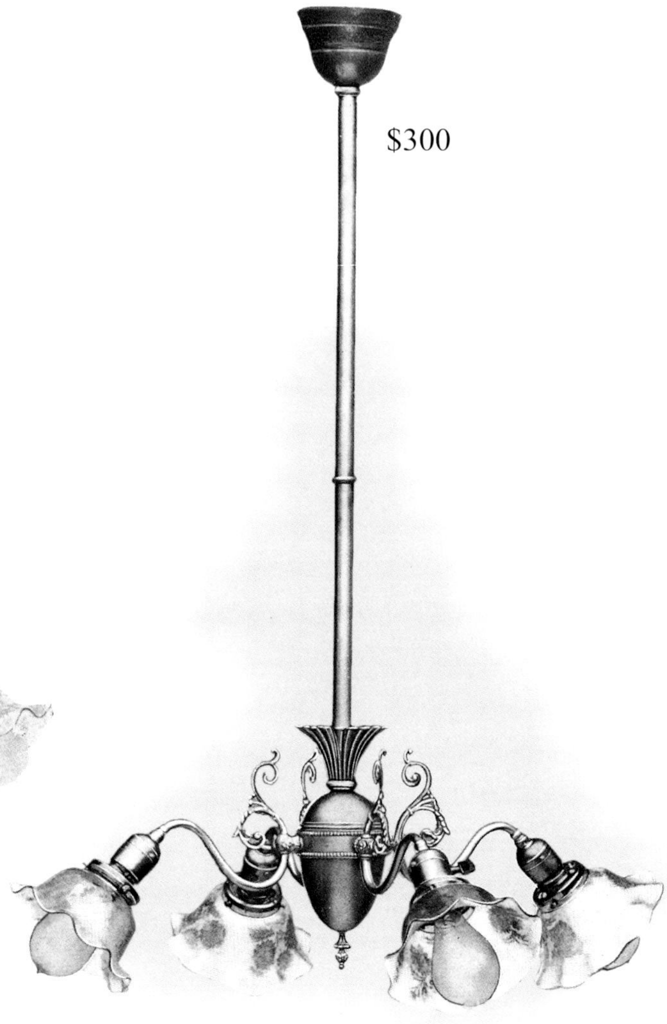

Number 1708
Length, 36 inches (over all). Spread, 23 inches.

		Not Wired	Wired	Complete as shown No lamps
2 Electric	Polished Brass and Black..	$5.75	$6.75	$8.55
3 "	" " " " ..	6.75	8.25	10.95
4 "	" " " " ..	7.75	9.75	13.35

Shades No. B 1538½ White Acid.

Number 1467
Length, 36 inches (over all). Spread, 23 inches.

		Not Wired	Wired	Complete as shown No lamps
2 Electric	Rich Gilt	$4.75	$5.75	$7.55
3 "	" "	5.75	7.25	9.95
4 "	" "	6.75	8.75	12.35
5 "	" "	7.75	10.25	14.75
6 "	" "	8.75	11.75	17.15

Shades No. B 1906½ White Acid.

Price in right hand column always includes sockets; also holders and shades if shown but no lamps.
Other prices include glassware, sockets, lamps or electric holders only where mentioned.

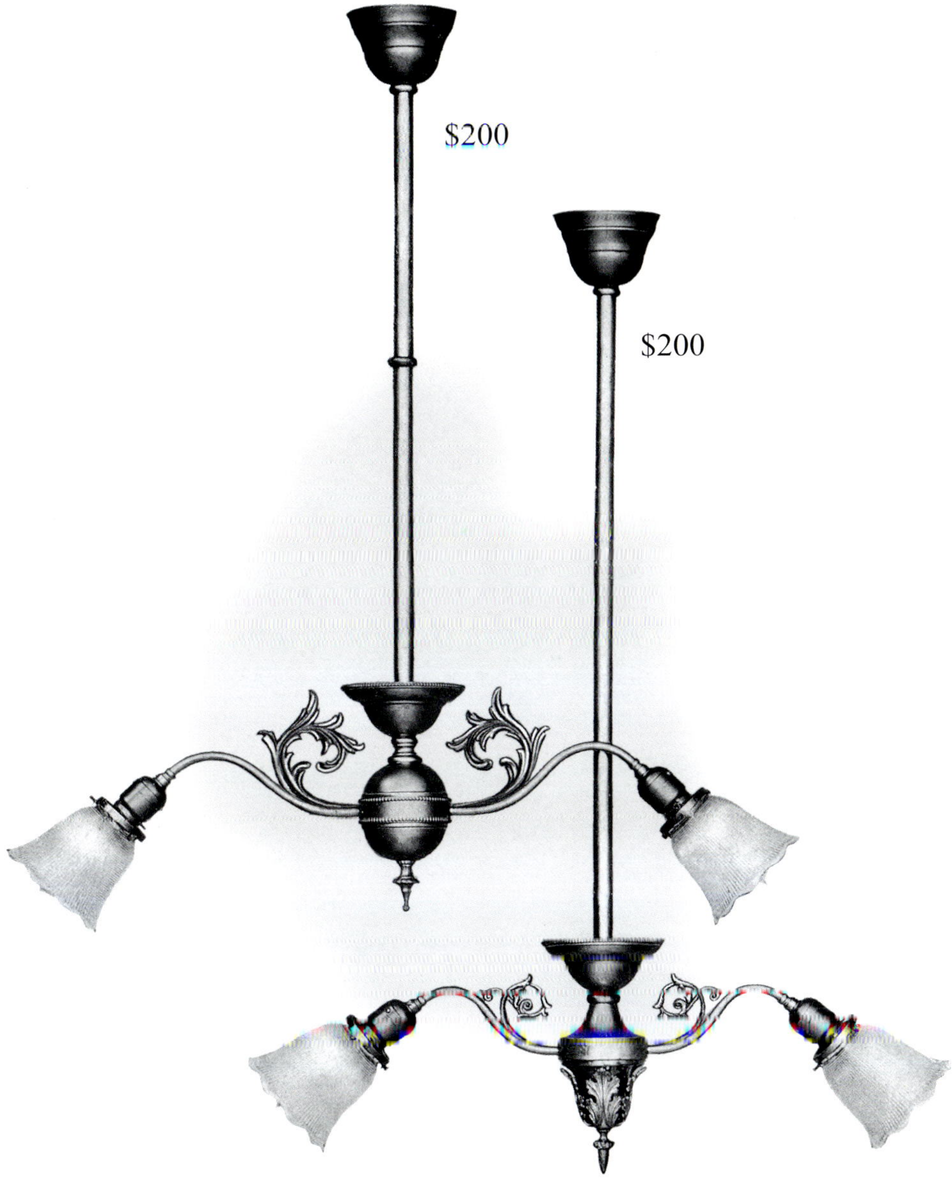

Number 1574

Length, 36 inches (over all). Spread, 27 inches.

		Not Wired	Wired	Complete as shown No lamps
2 Electric	Rich Gilt	$5.00	$5.75	$7.25
3 "	" "	6.10	7.10	9.35
4 "	" "	7.20	8.45	11.45
5 "	" "	8.30	9.80	13.55
6 "	" "	9.40	11.15	15.65

Shades No. B 33½ Crystal Prism.

Number 1575

Length, 36 inches (over all). Spread, 24 inches.

		Not Wired	Wired	Complete as shown No lamps
2 Electric	Rich Gilt	$6.00	$6.75	$8.25
3 "	" "	6.75	7.75	10.00
4 "	" "	7.50	8.75	11.75
5 "	" "	8.25	9.75	13.50
6 "	" "	9.00	10.75	15.25

Shades No. B 33½ Crystal Prism.

Price in right hand column always includes sockets; also holders and shades if shown but no lamps.
Other prices include glassware, sockets, lamps or electric holders only where mentioned.

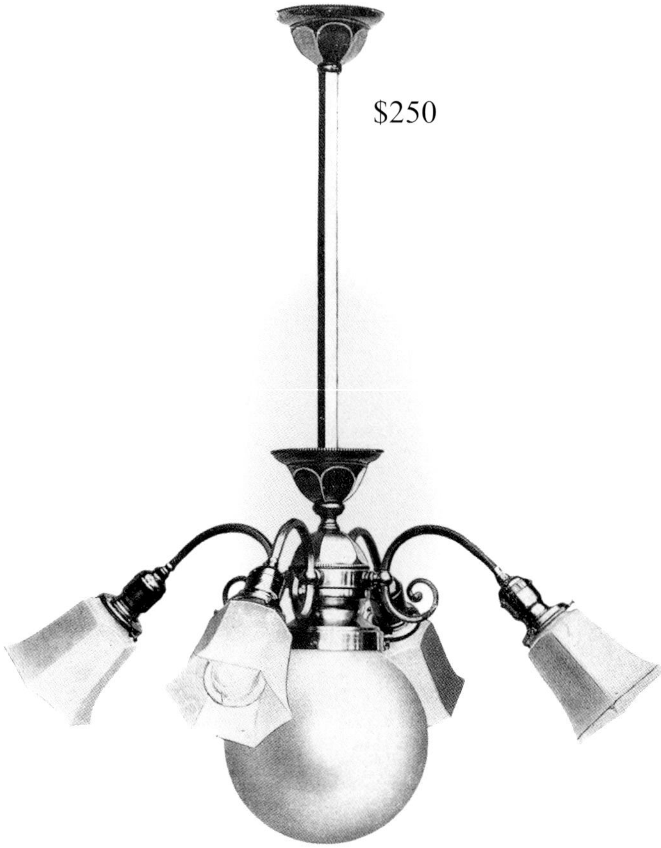

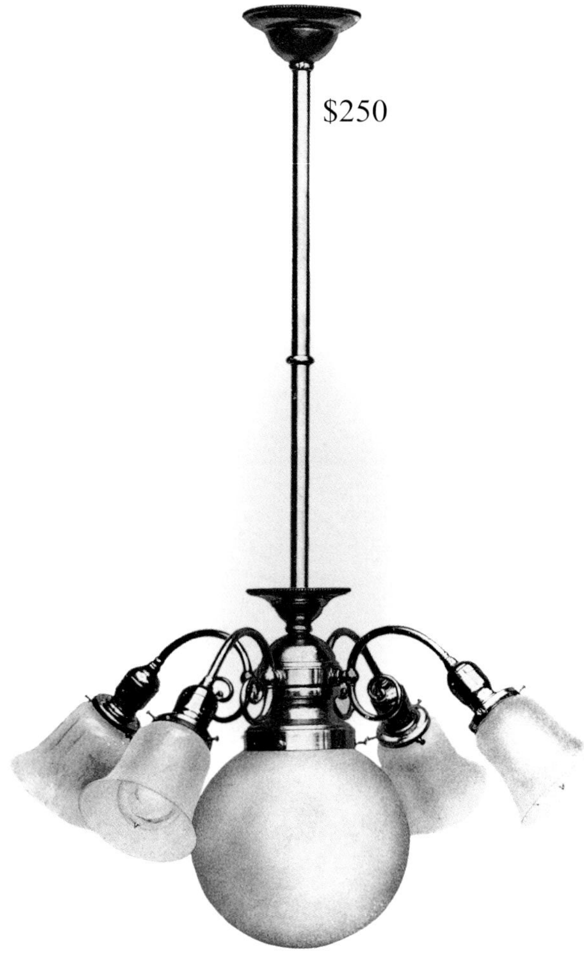

Number 1878
Length, 36 inches (over all). Spread, 24 inches.
4x8-inch C. R. I. Ball included.

		Not Wired	Wired	Complete as shown No lamps
3 Electric	Rich Gilt	$7.25	$8.75	$10.95
4 "	" "	8.25	10.25	13.35
5 "	" "	9.25	11.75	15.75
6 "	" "	10.25	13.25	18.15

Shades No. B 68½ Crystal Roughed Inside.

Number 1877
Length, 36 inches (over all). Spread, 23 inches.
4x8-inch C. R. I. Ball included.

		Not Wired	Wired	Complete as shown No lamps
3 Electric	Rich Gilt	$6.50	$8.00	$10.00
4 "	" "	7.50	9.50	12.30
5 "	" "	8.50	11.00	14.60
6 "	" "	9.50	12.50	16.90

Shades No. B 8983½ Crystal Roughed Inside.

Price in right hand column always includes sockets; also holders and shades if shown but no lamps.
Other prices include glassware, sockets, lamps or electric holders only where mentioned.

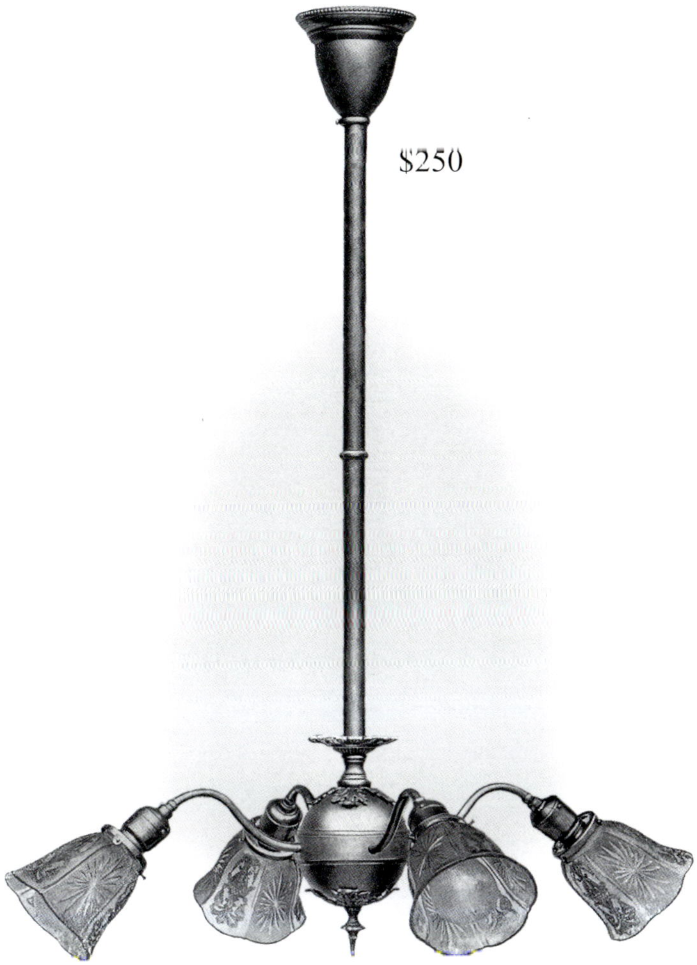

Number 1543
Length, 36 inches (over all). Spread, 23 inches.

		Not Wired	Wired	Complete as shown No lamps
2 Electric	Rich Gilt	$5.00	$5.75	$8.15
3 "	" "	5.50	6.50	10.10
4 "	" "	6.00	7.25	12.05
5 "	" "	6.50	8.00	14.00
6 "	" "	7.00	8.75	15.95

Shades No. B 602½ Etched and Imitation Cut.

Number 1846
Length, 36 inches (over all). Spread, 24 inches.

		Not Wired	Wired	Complete as shown No lamps
2 Electric	Rich Gilt	$3.95	$4.95	$6.45
3 "	" "	4.55	6.05	8.30
4 "	" "	5.15	7.15	10.15

Shades No. B 41½ Crystal.

Price in right hand column always includes sockets; also holders and shades if shown but no lamps.
Other prices include glassware, sockets, lamps or electric holders only where mentioned.

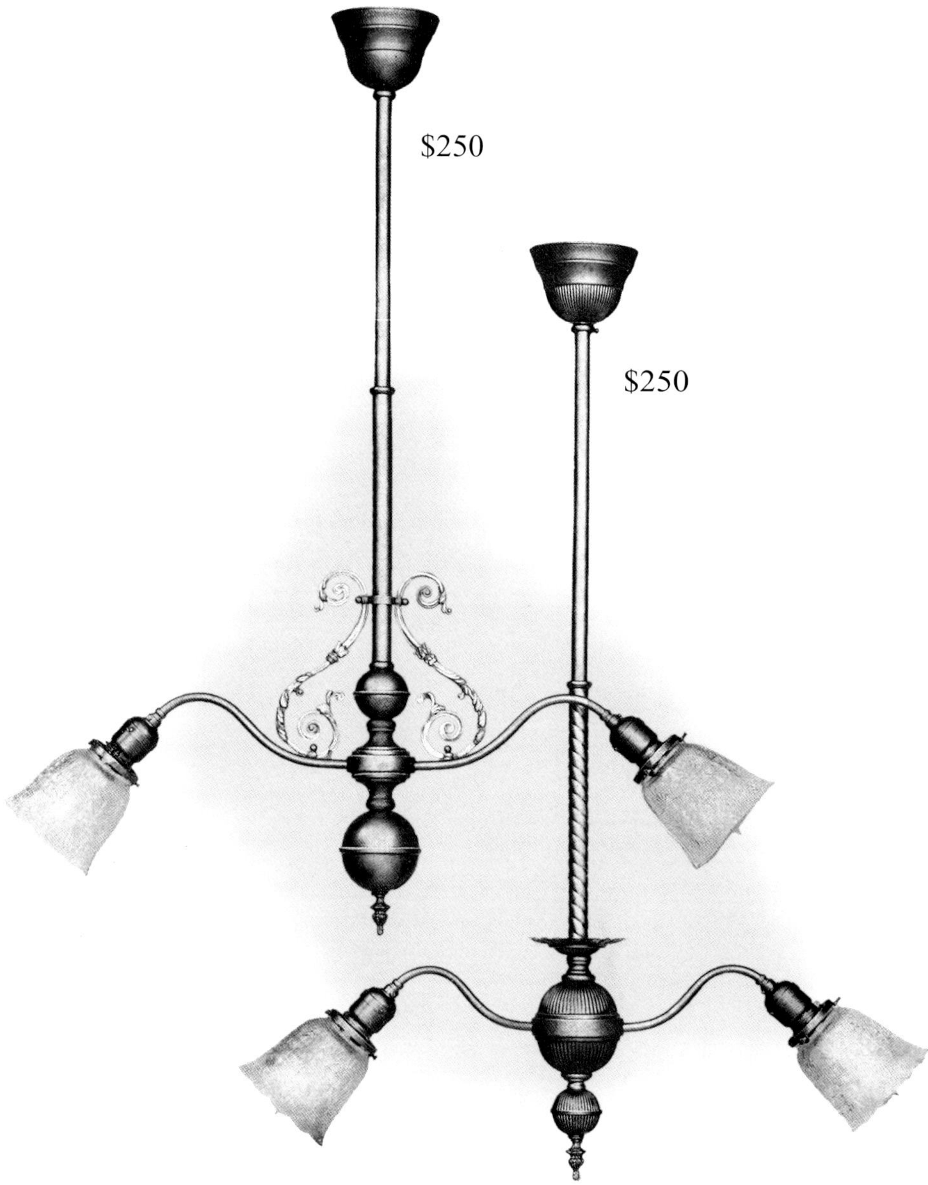

Number 1580
Length, 36 inches. Spread, 27 inches.

		Not Wired	Wired	Complete as shown No lamps
2 Electric	Rich Gilt	$6.00	$6.75	$8.35
3 "	" "	7.25	8.25	10.65
4 "	" "	8.50	9.75	12.95
5 "	" "	9.75	11.25	15.25

Shades No. B 140½ Crystal.

Number 1581
Length, 36 inches. Spread, 24 inches.

		Not Wired	Wired	Complete as shown No lamps
2 Electric	Rich Gilt	$3.50	$4.25	$5.85
3 "	" "	4.00	5.00	7.40
4 "	" "	4.50	5.75	8.95
5 "	" "	5.00	6.50	10.50

Shades No. B 140½ Crystal.

Price in right hand column always includes sockets; also holders and shades if shown but no lamps.
Other prices include glassware, sockets, lamps or electric holders only where mentioned.

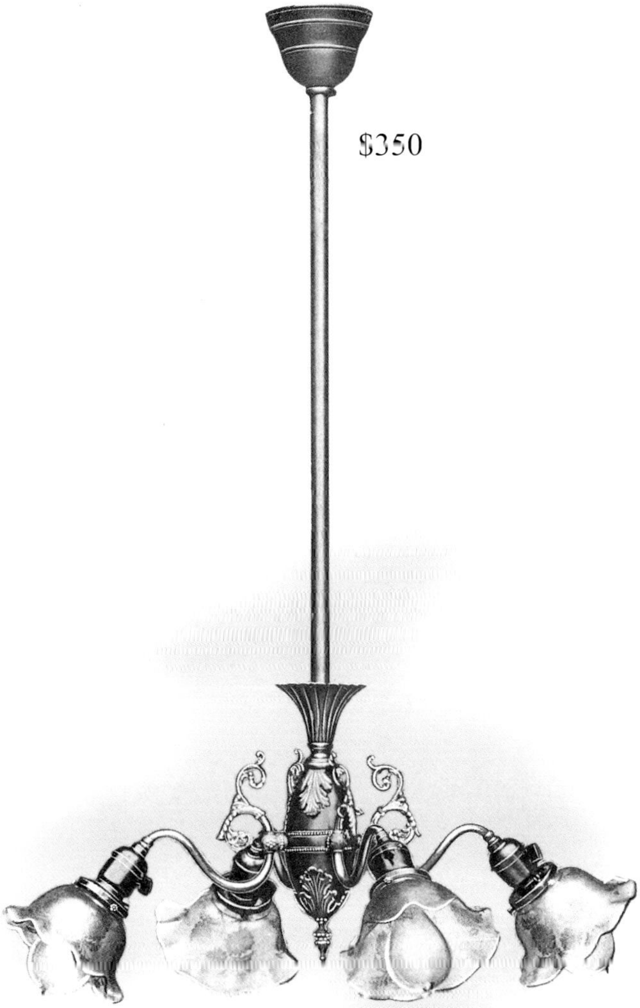

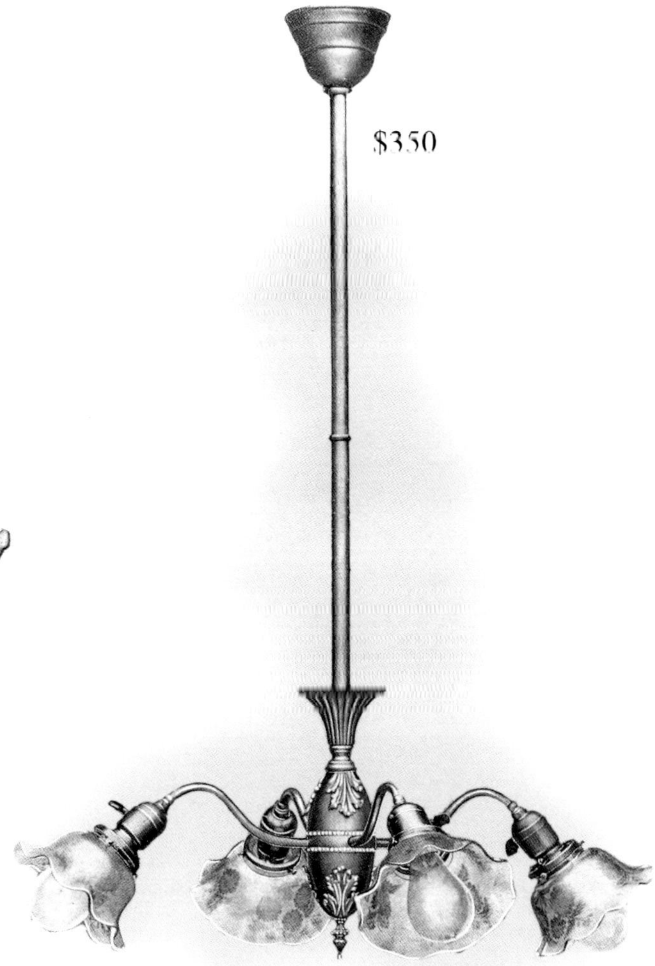

Number 1458

Length, 36 inches (over all). Spread, 23 inches.

		Not Wired	Wired	Complete as shown No lamps
2	Electric Rich Gilt and Satin.........	$6.00	$7.00	$8.80
3	" " " " "	7.00	8.50	11.20
4	" " " " "	8.00	10.00	13.60
5	" " " " "	9.00	11.50	16.00
6	" " " " "	10.00	13.00	18.40

Shades No. B 1906½ White Acid.

Number 1463

Length, 36 inches (over all). Spread, 24 inches.

		Not Wired	Wired	Complete as shown No lamps
2	Electric Rich Gilt and Satin.........	$5.00	$6.00	$7.80
3	" " " " "	5.50	7.00	9.70
4	" " " " "	6.00	8.00	11.60
5	" " " " "	6.50	9.00	13.50
6	" " " " "	7.00	10.00	15.40

Shades No. B 1906½ White Acid.

Price in right hand column always includes sockets; also holders and shades if shown but no lamps.
Other prices include glassware, sockets, lamps or electric holders only where mentioned.

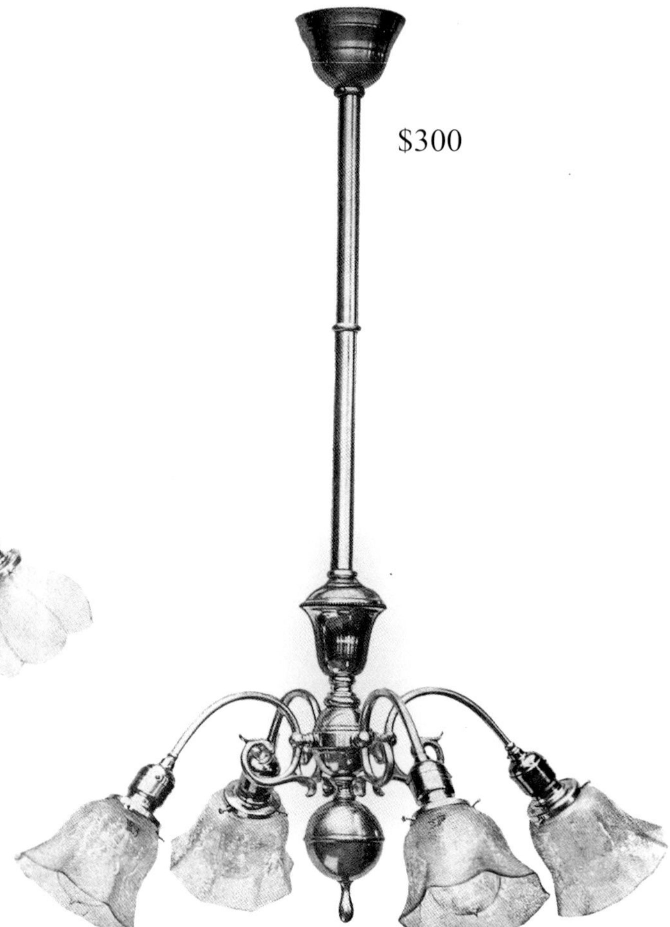

Number 1967

Length, 36 inches (over all). Spread, 23 inches.

		Not Wired	Wired	Complete as shown No lamps
2 Electric	Brush Brass	$10.50	$11.50	$13.40
3 "	" "	11.75	13.25	16.10
4 "	" "	13.00	15.00	18.80
5 "	" "	14.25	16.75	21.50
6 "	" "	15.50	18.50	24.20

Shades No. B 539½ Crystal Roughed Inside.

Number 2085

Length, 36 inches (over all). Spread, 23 inches.

		Not Wired	Wired	Complete as shown No lamps
2 Electric	Brush Brass	$5.75	$6.75	$8.55
3 "	" "	7.00	8.50	11.20
4 "	" "	8.25	10.25	13.85
5 "	" "	9.50	12.00	16.50
6 "	" "	10.75	13.75	19.15

Shades No. B 1412½ White Acid.

Price in right hand column always includes sockets; also holders and shades if shown but no lamps.
Other prices include glassware, sockets, lamps or electric holders only where mentioned.

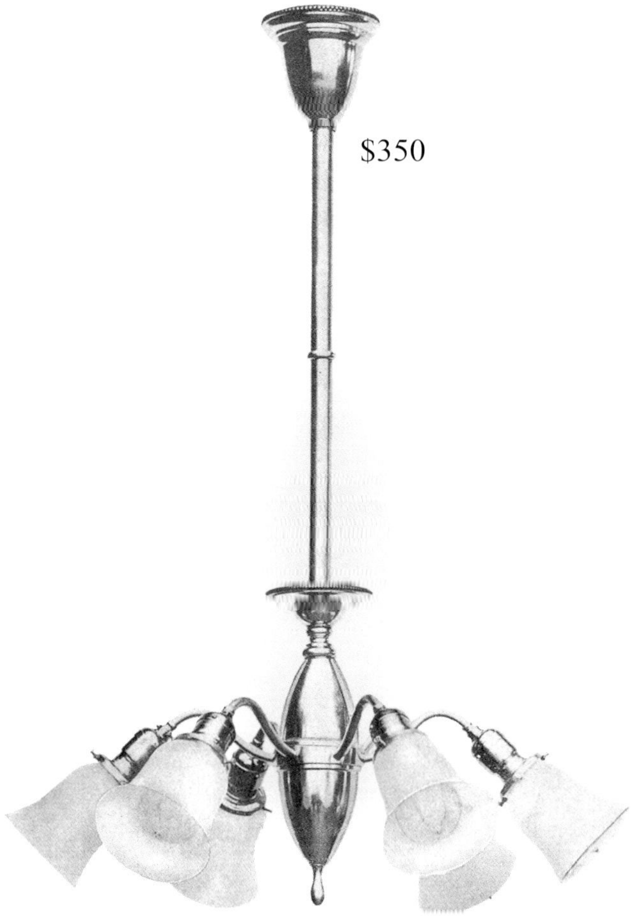

$350

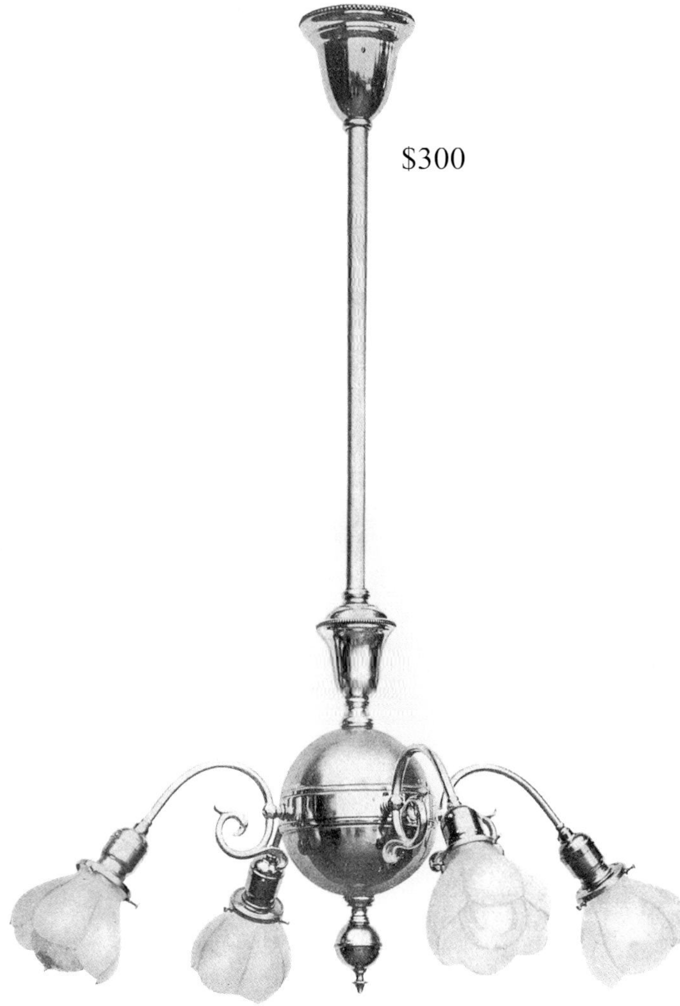

$300

Number 1984

Length, 36 inches. Spread, 24 inches.

		Not Wired	Wired	Complete as shown No lamps
2 Electric	Polished Brass	$4.50	$5.25	$6.85
3 "	" "	5.00	6.00	8.40
4 "	" "	5.50	6.75	9.95
5 "	" "	6.00	7.50	11.50
6 "	" "	6.50	8.25	13.05

Shades No. B 8983½ Crystal Roughed Inside.

Number 1985

Length, 36 inches (over all). Spread, 23 inches.

		Not Wired	Wired	Complete as shown No lamps
2 Electric	Brush Brass	$8.25	$9.25	$11.15
3 "	" "	9.50	11.00	13.85
4 "	" "	10.75	12.75	16.55
5 "	" "	12.00	14.50	19.25
6 "	" "	13.25	16.25	21.95

Shades No. B 539½ Crystal Roughed Inside.

Price in right hand column always includes sockets; also holders and shades if shown but no lamps.
Other prices include glassware, sockets, lamps or electric holders only where mentioned.

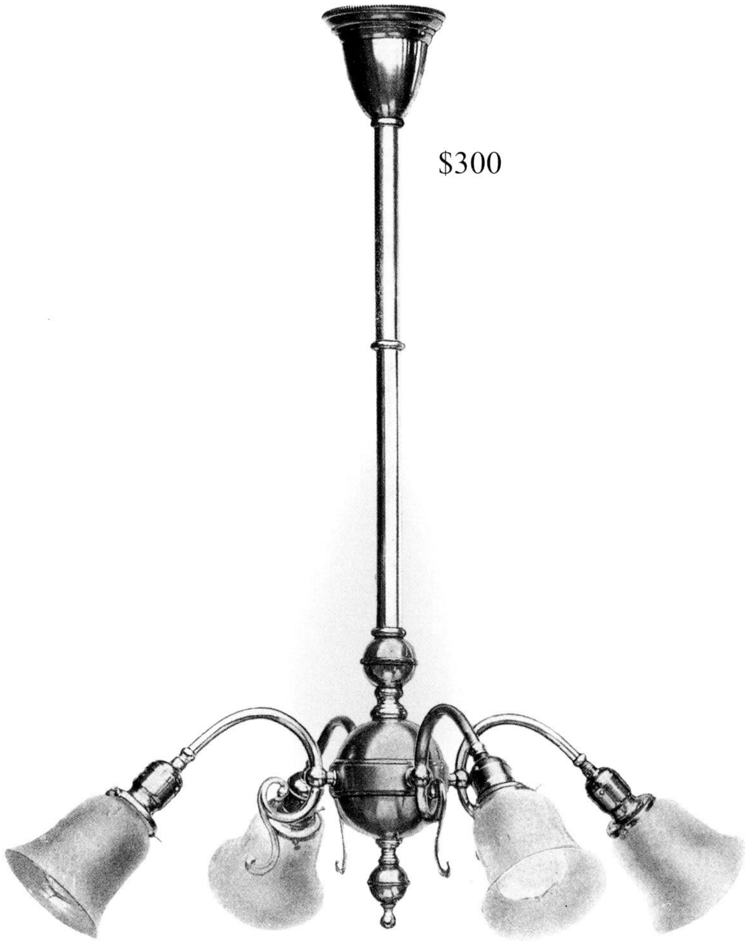

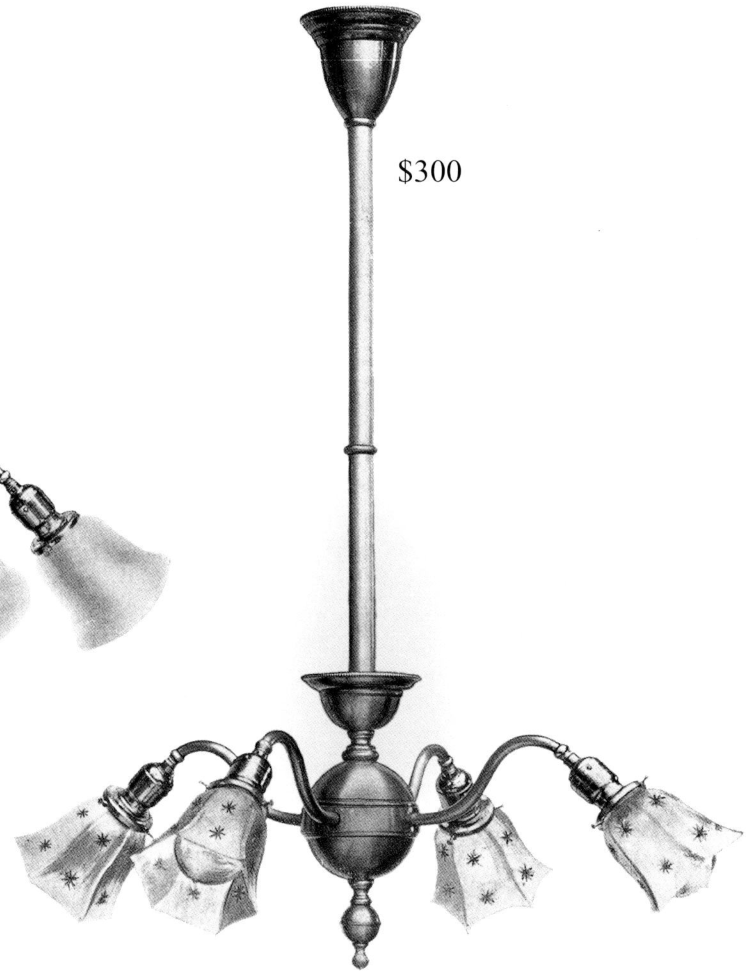

Number 1851

Length, 36 inches (over all). Spread, 26 inches.

		Not Wired	Wired	Complete as shown No lamps
2 Electric	Polished Brass	$6.50	$7.50	$9.10
3 "	" "	7.75	9.25	11.65
4 "	" "	9.00	11.00	14.20
5 "	" "	10.25	12.75	16.75
6 "	" "	11.50	14.50	19.30

Shades No. B 8983½ Crystal Roughed Inside.

Number 1852

Length, 36 inches. Spread, 27 inches.

		Not Wired	Wired	Complete as shown No lamps
2 Electric	Polished Brass	$5.00	$5.75	$7.25
3 "	" "	5.50	6.50	8.75
4 "	" "	6.00	7.25	10.25
5 "	" "	6.50	8.00	11.75
6 "	" "	7.00	8.75	13.25

Shades No. B 41½ Crystal.

Price in right hand column always includes sockets; also holders and shades if shown but no lamps.
Other prices include glassware, sockets, lamps or electric holders only where mentioned.

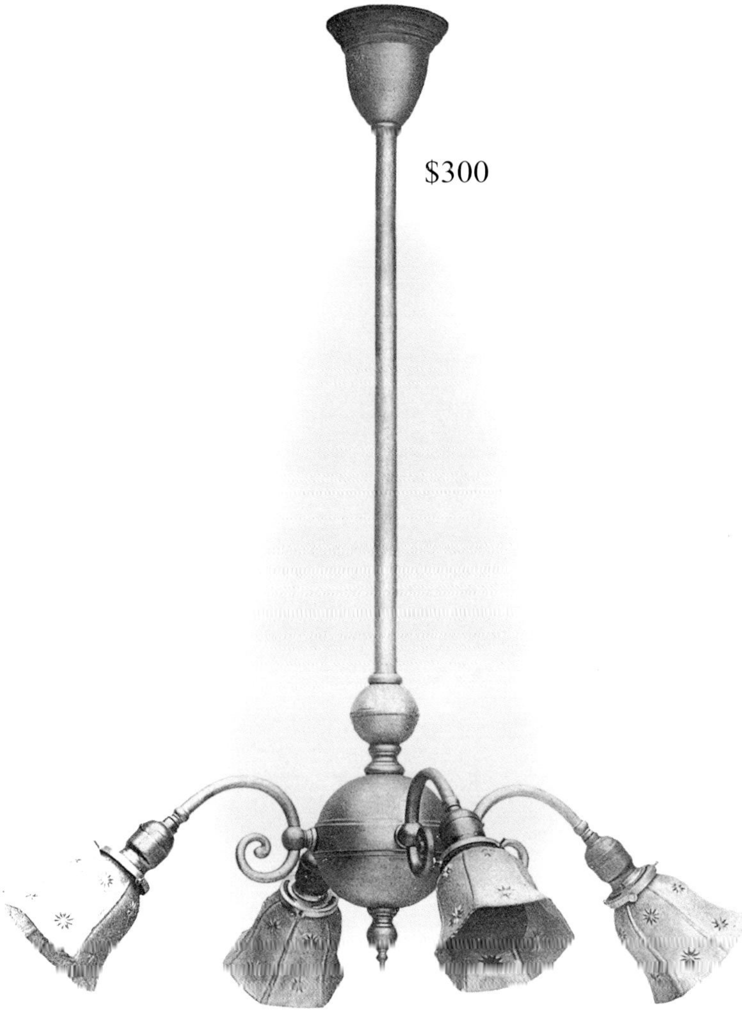

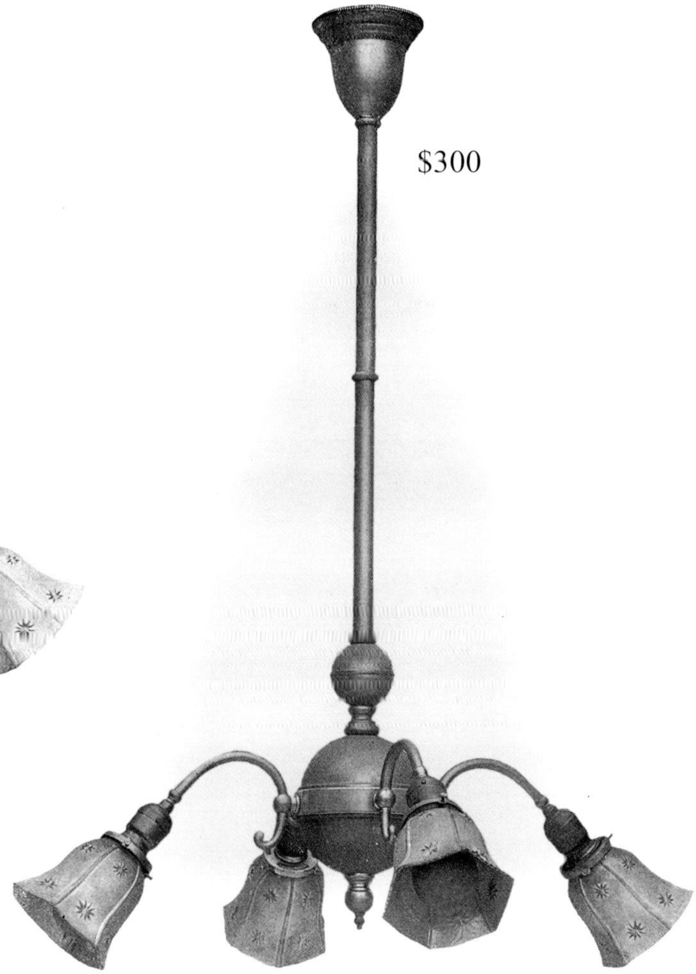

Number 2307

Length, 36 inches (over all). Spread, 26 inches.

		Not Wired	Wired	Complete as shown No lamps
2 Electric	Polished Brass	$6.50	$7.50	$9.00
3 "	" "	7.75	9.25	11.50
4 "	" "	9.00	11.00	14.00
5 "	" "	10.25	12.75	16.50
6 "	" "	11.50	14.50	19.00
8 "	" "	14.00	18.00	24.00

Shades No. B 41½ Crystal.

Number 2306

Length, 36 inches (over all). Spread, 25 inches.

		Not Wired	Wired	Complete as shown No lamps
2 Electric	Polished Brass	$5.60	$6.60	$8.10
3 "	" "	6.40	7.90	10.15
4 "	" "	7.20	9.20	12.20
5 "	" "	8.00	10.50	14.25
6 "	" "	8.80	11.80	16.30
8 "	" "	10.40	14.40	20.40

Shades No. B 41½ Crystal.

Price in right hand column always includes sockets; also holders and shades if shown but no lamps.
Other prices include glassware, sockets, lamps or electric holders only where mentioned.

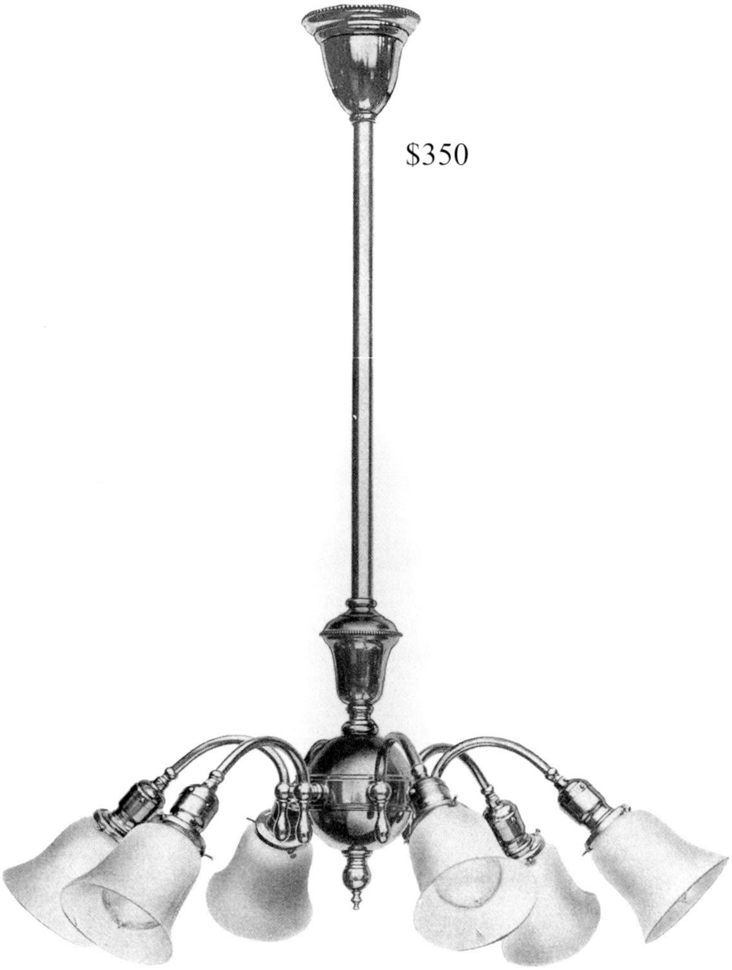

Number 1966

Length, 36 inches (over all). Spread, 25 inches.

			Not Wired	Wired	Complete as shown No lamps
2	Electric	Polished Brass	$5.60	$6.60	$8.20
3	"	" "	6.40	7.90	10.30
4	"	" "	7.20	9.20	12.40
5	"	" "	8.00	10.50	14.50
6	"	" "	8.80	11.80	16.60

Shades No. B 8983½ Crystal Roughed Inside.

Number 1968

Length, 40 inches (over all). Spread, 32 inches.

			Not Wired	Wired	Complete as shown No lamps
3	Electric	Polished Brass	$10.50	$12.00	$14.40
4	"	" "	12.00	14.00	17.20
5	"	" "	13.50	16.00	20.00
6	"	" "	15.00	18.00	22.80
8	"	" "	18.00	22.00	28.40

Shades No. B 8983½ Crystal Roughed Inside.

Price in right hand column always includes sockets; also holders and shades if shown but no lamps.
Other prices include glassware, sockets, lamps or electric holders only where mentioned.

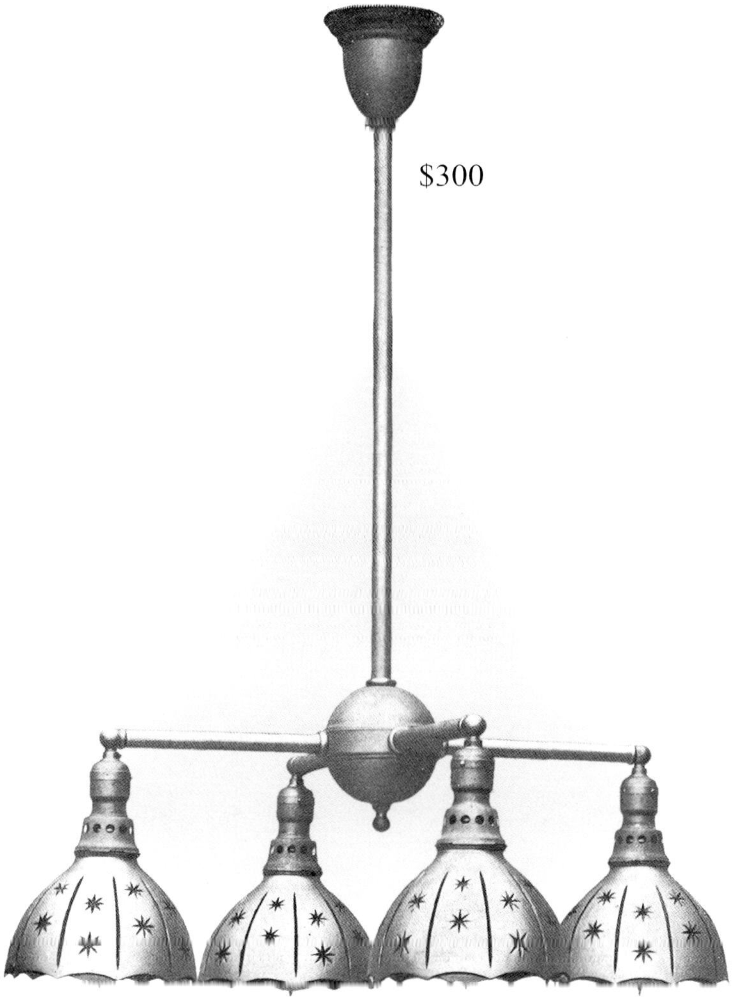

Number 2472
Number 2472½

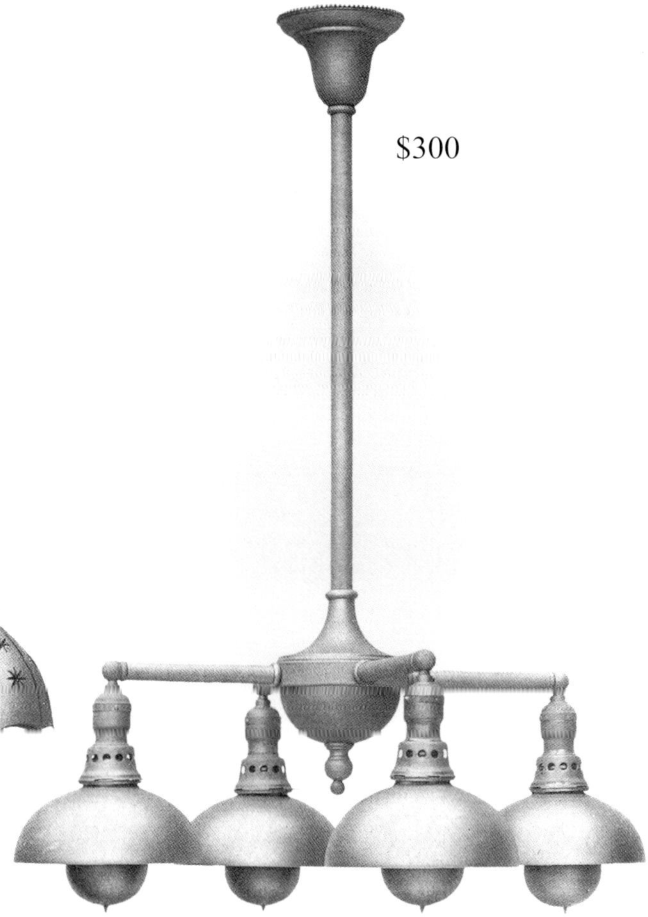

Number 2638
Number 2638½

Number 2472
Length, 36 inches (over all). Spread, 24 inches.

		Not Wired	Wired	Complete as shown No lamps
2 Electric	Brush Brass	$3.65	$4.45	$6.95
3 "	" "	4.40	5.60	9.35
4 "	" "	5.15	6.75	11.75
6 "	" "	6.65	9.05	16.55

Number 2472½
Spread, 36 inches.

		Not Wired	Wired	Complete as shown No lamps
2 Electric	Brush Brass	$4.05	$4.85	$7.35
3 "	" "	5.00	6.20	9.95
4 "	" "	5.95	7.55	12.55
6 "	" "	7.85	10.25	17.75

Shades No. B 007½ Frosted, with Crystal Stars and Bars. Diameter, 7 inches.

Number 2638
Length, 36 inches (over all). Spread, 18 inches.

		Not Wired	Wired	Complete as shown No lamps
2 Electric	Brush Brass	$5.05	$5.85	$7.95
3 "	" "	5.70	6.90	10.05
4 "	" "	6.35	7.95	12.15
6 "	" "	7.65	10.05	16.35

Number 2638½
Spread, 24 inches.

		Not Wired	Wired	Complete as shown No lamps
2 Electric	Brush Brass	$5.25	$6.05	$8.15
3 "	" "	6.00	7.20	10.35
4 "	" "	6.75	8.35	12.55
6 "	" "	8.25	10.65	16.95

2¼x7-inch Crystal Roughed Inside Domes.

Price in right hand column always includes sockets; also holders and shades if shown but no lamps.
Other prices include glassware, sockets, lamps or electric holders only where mentioned.

Number 2092
Number 2092½
Length, 36 inches (over all).
Spread given below.

Number 2091
Number 2091½
Length, 36 inches (over all).
Spread given below.

Number 2093
Number 2093½
Length, 36 inches (over all).
Spread given below.

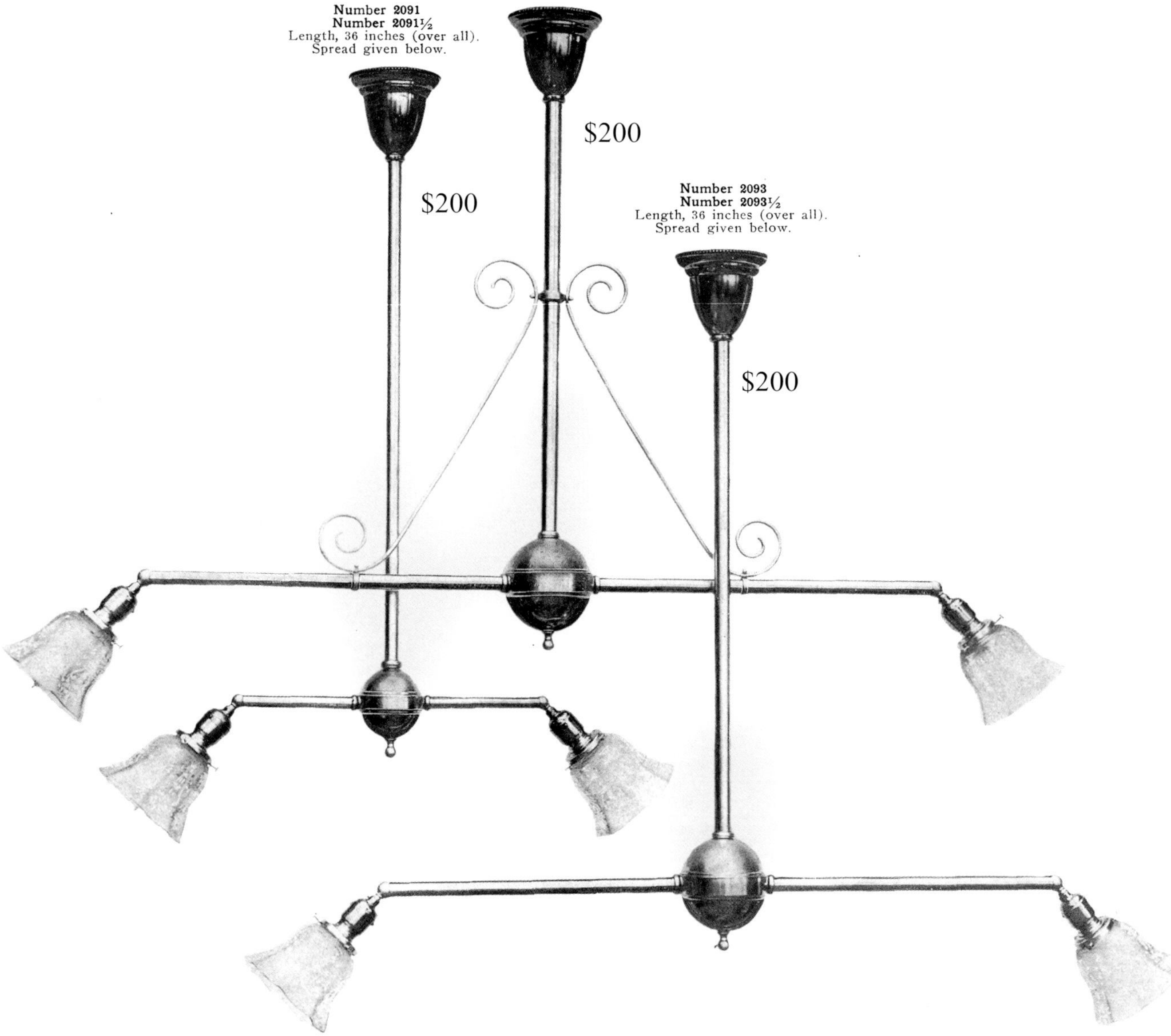

Number 2093
Spread, 36 inches.

			Not Wired	Wired	Complete as shown No lamps
2	Electric	Polished Brass	$3.80	$4.80	$6.60
4	"	" "	5.10	7.10	10.70
6	"	" "	6.40	9.40	14.80

Number 2093½
Spread, 42 inches.

			Not Wired	Wired	Complete as shown No lamps
2	Electric	Polished Brass	$4.00	$5.00	$6.80
4	"	" "	5.50	7.50	11.10
6	"	" "	7.00	10.00	15.40

Shades No. B 1412½ White Acid.

Number 2091
Spread, 24 inches.

			Not Wired	Wired	Complete as shown No lamps
2	Electric	Polished Brass	$2.80	$3.55	$5.35
3	"	" "	3.30	4.30	7.00
4	"	" "	3.80	5.05	8.65

Number 2091½
Spread, 30 inches.

			Not Wired	Wired	Complete as shown No lamps
2	Electric	Polished Brass	$3.00	$3.75	$5.55
3	"	" "	3.60	4.60	7.30
4	"	" "	4.20	5.45	9.05

Shades No. B 1412½ White Acid.

Number 2092
Spread, 42 inches.

			Not Wired	Wired	Complete as shown No lamps
2	Electric	Polished Brass	$5.50	$6.50	$8.30
4	"	" "	8.50	10.00	13.60
6	"	" "	11.50	14.50	19.90

Number 2092½
Spread, 48 inches.

			Not Wired	Wired	Complete as shown No lamps
2	Electric	Polished Brass	$5.70	$6.70	$8.50
4	"	" "	8.90	10.90	14.50
6	"	" "	12.10	15.10	20.50

Shades No. B 1412½ White Acid.

Price in right hand column always includes sockets; also holders and shades if shown but no lamps.
Other prices include glassware, sockets, lamps or electric nolders only where mentioned.

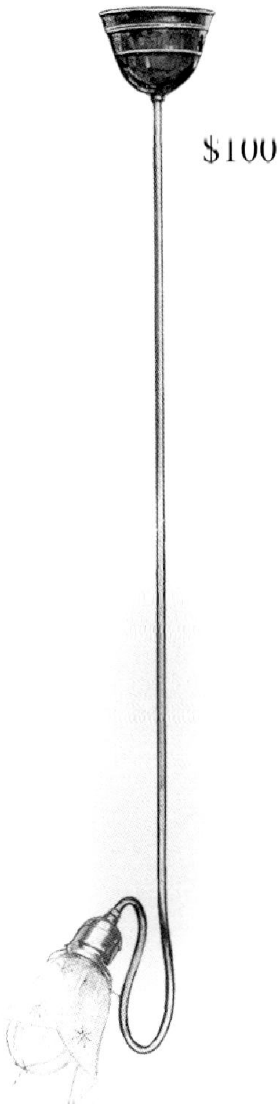

Number 1914

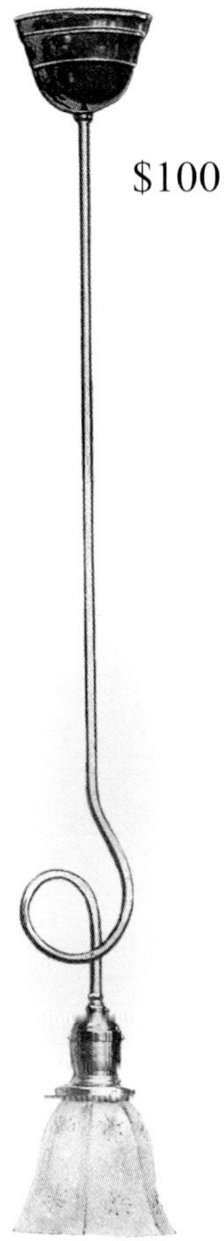

Number 1916

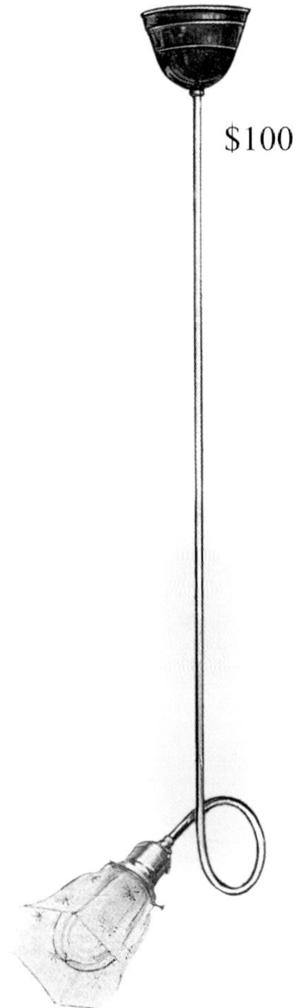

Number 1915

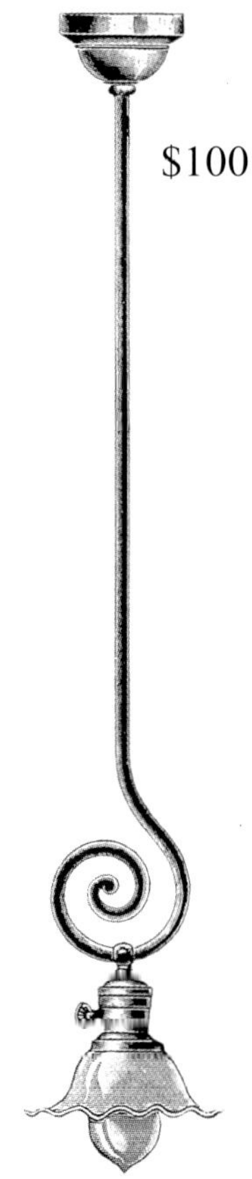

Number 1815
Number 1815½

Number 1914
Length, 36 inches (over all).
Made of ⅜-inch Brass Tubing.

	Not Wired	Wired	Complete as shown No lamps
Polished Brass	**$1.50**	**$1.80**	**$2.55**

Shade No. B 41½ Crystal.

Number 1916
Length, 36 inches (over all).
Made of ⅜-inch Brass Tubing.

	Not Wired	Wired	Complete as shown No lamps
Polished Brass	**$1.50**	**$1.80**	**$2.55**

Shade No. B 41½ Crystal.

Number 1915
Length, 36 inches (over all).
Made of ⅜-inch Brass Tubing.

	Not Wired	Wired	Complete as shown No lamps
Polished Brass	**$1.50**	**$1.80**	**$2.55**

Shade No. B 41½ Crystal.

Number 1815 Made of ⅜-inch Brass Tubing.
Number 1815½ " 7/16-inch " "
Length, 36 inches (over all).

	Not Wired	Wired	Complete as shown No lamps
Number 1815 Polished Brass	**$1.80**	**$2.10**	**$2.80**
" 1815½ " "	**2.10**	**2.40**	**3.10**

Shade No. B 256½ Opal.

Price in right hand column always includes sockets; also holders and shades if shown but no lamps.
Other prices include glassware, sockets, lamps or electric holders only where mentioned.

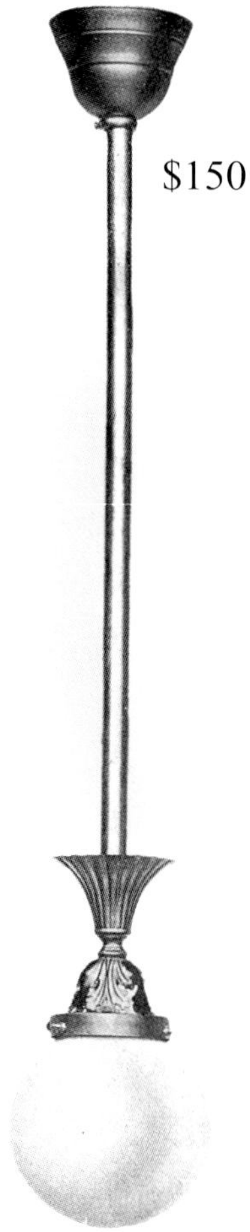

Number 1545

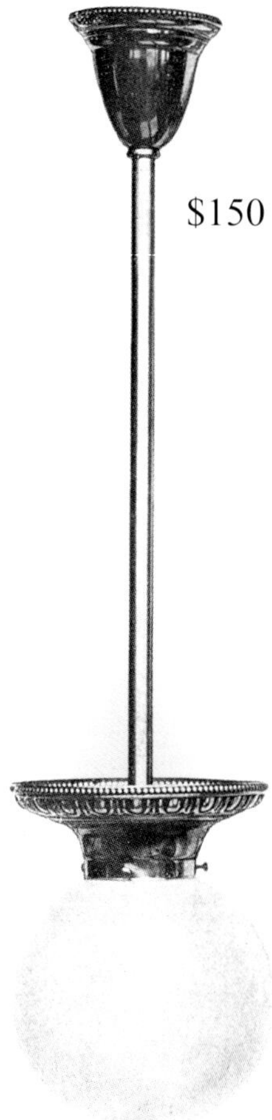

Number 1836

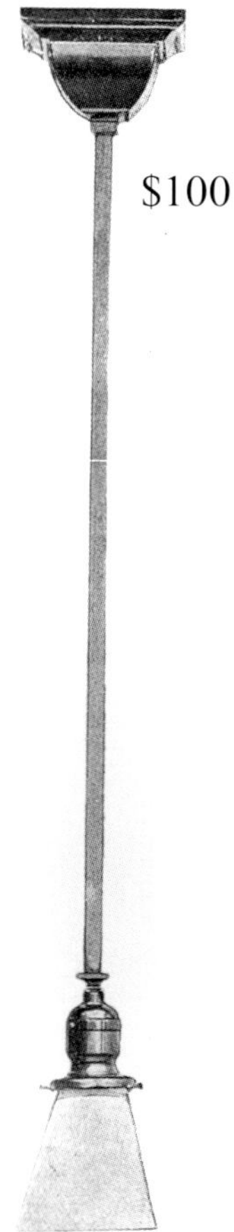

Number 1911

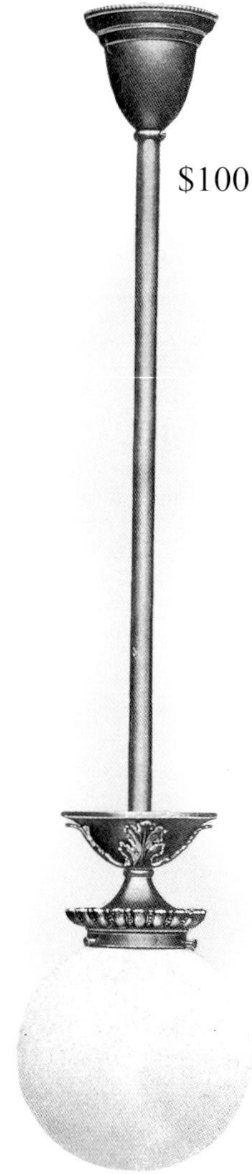

Number 1456

Number 1545
Length, 36 inches (over all).
3¼x6-inch C. R. I. Ball and Holder included

	Not Wired	Wired	Complete as shown No lamps
Rich Gilt	**$3.75**	**$4.05**	**$4.45**

Number 1836
Length, 36 inches (over all).
3¼x8-inch C. R. I. Ball and Holder included.

	Not Wired	Wired	Complete as shown No lamps
Rich Gilt	**$4.25**	**$4.55**	**$4.95**

Number 1911
Length, 36 inches (over all).

	Not Wired	Wired	Complete as shown No lamps
Brush Brass	**$2.35**	**$2.65**	**$3.65**

Shade No. B 9321½ C. R. I.

Number 1456
Length, 36 inches (over all).
3¼x8-inch C. R. I. Ball and Holder included.

	Not Wired	Wired	Complete as shown No lamps
Rich Gilt	**$6.40**	**$6.70**	**$7.10**

Price in right hand column always includes sockets; also holders and shades if shown but no lamps.
Other prices include glassware, sockets, lamps or electric holders only where mentioned.

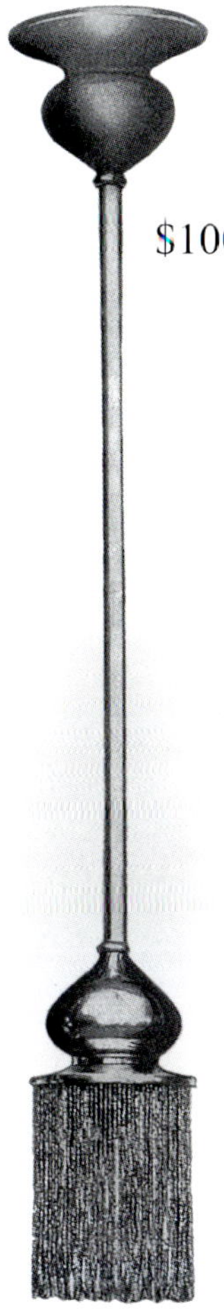

Number 1954

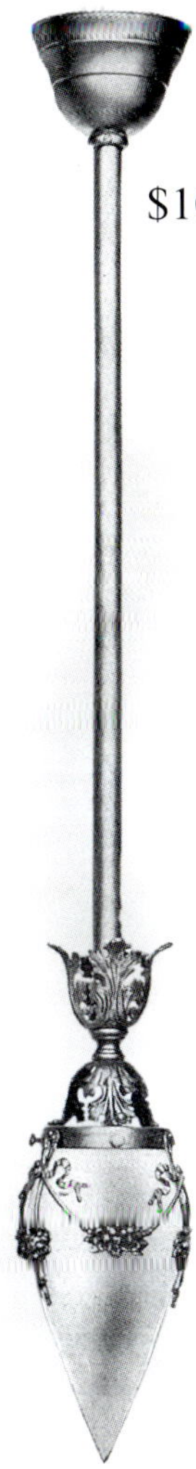

Number 1550

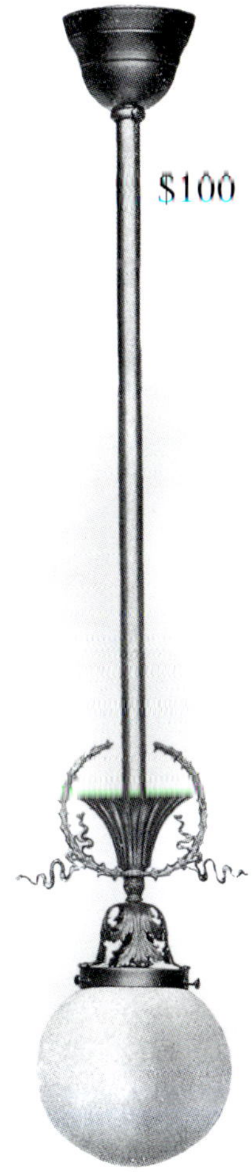

Number 1548

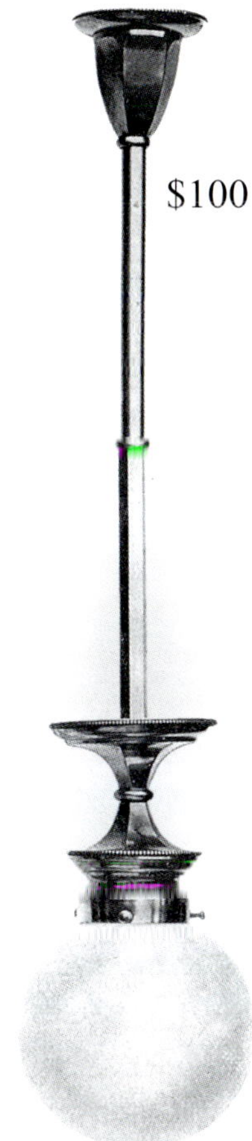

Number 1839

Number 1954
Length, 36 inches (over all).
Brass Shade and Glass Bead Fringe included.

	Not Wired	Wired	Complete as shown No lamps
Brush Brass	**$6.15**	**$6.45**	**$6.85**

If wanted with Chain Pull Socket, add 30 cents to price in right hand column.

Number 1550
Length, 36 inches (over all).
C. R. I. Stalactite and Holder included.

	Not Wired	Wired	Complete as shown No lamps
Rich Gilt	**$7.00**	**$7.30**	**$7.70**

Number 1548
Length, 36 inches (over all).
3¼x6-inch C. R. I. Ball and Holder included.

	Not Wired	Wired	Complete as shown No lamps
Rich Gilt	**$5.10**	**$5.40**	**5.80**

Number 1839
Length, 36 inches (over all).
3¼x7-inch C. R. I. Ball and Holder included.

	Not Wired	Wired	Complete as shown No lamps
Rich Gilt	**$4.25**	**$4.55**	**$4.95**

Price in right hand column always includes sockets; also holders and shades if shown but no lamps.
Other prices include glassware, sockets, lamps or electric holders only where mentioned.

Number 2663

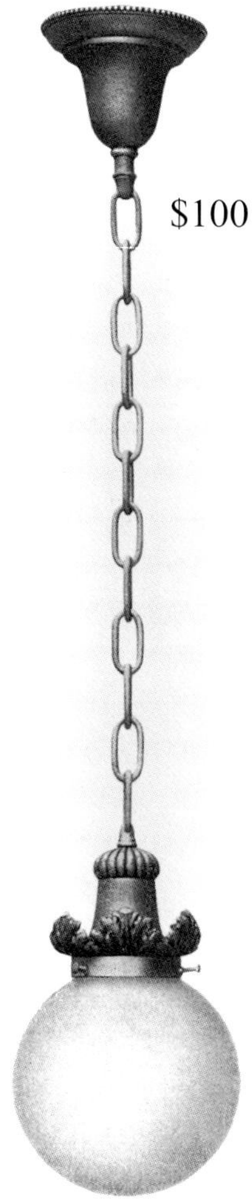

Number 2662

Number 1957

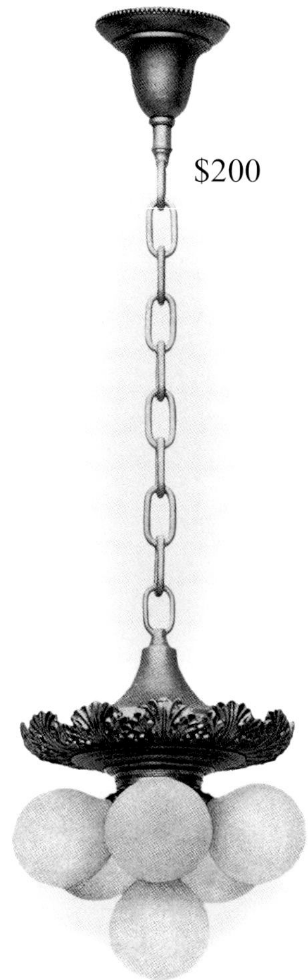

Number 2623

Number 2663
Length, 36 inches (over all).
6x12-inch C. R. I. Ball included.

		Not Wired	Wired	Complete as shown No lamps
1 Electric	Brush Brass	$13.50	$14.50	$14.90
2 "	" "	14.00	15.25	16.05
3 "	" "	14.50	16.00	17.20

Extra lengthening per foot, $2.00.

Number 2662
Length, 36 inches (over all).
3¼x7-inch C. R. I. Ball and Holder included.

	Not Wired	Wired	Complete as shown No lamps
Brush Brass	$7.50	$8.50	$8.90

Extra lengthening per foot, $1.00.

Number 1957
Length, 40 inches (over all).
Brass Shade and Glass Bead Fringe included.

	Not Wired	Wired	Complete as shown No lamps
Brush Brass	$11.50	$12.50	$12.90

Extra lengthening per foot, $1.00.

Number 2623
Length, 36 inches (over all).
6-Light Cluster included.

	Not Wired	Wired	Complete as shown No lamps
Brush Brass	$23.75	$24.75	$24.75

Extra lengthening per foot, $2.00.

Price in right hand column always includes sockets; also holders and shades if shown but no lamps.
Other prices include glassware, sockets, lamps or electric holders only where mentioned.

Number 2107

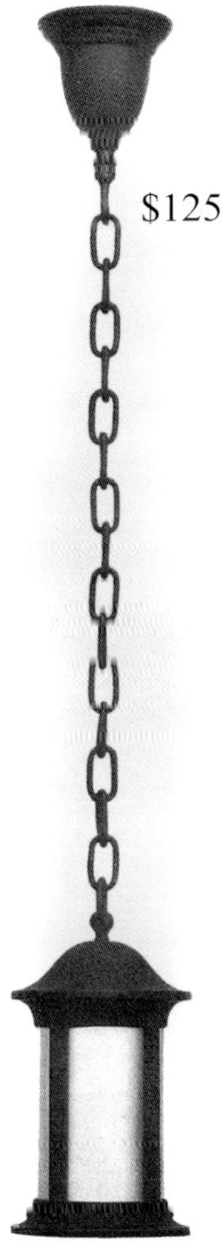

Number 2286
Number 2286½

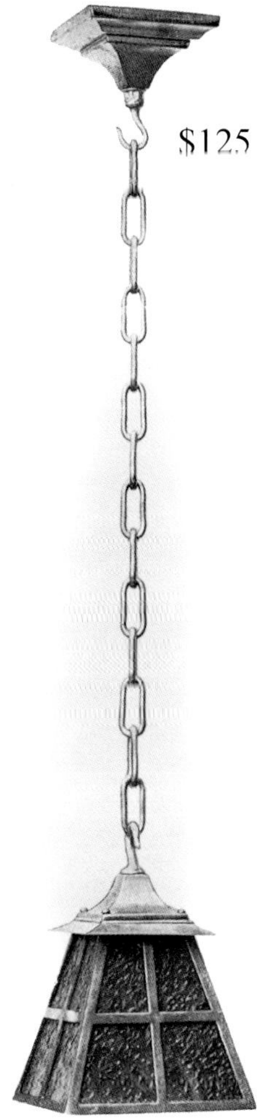

Number 1780

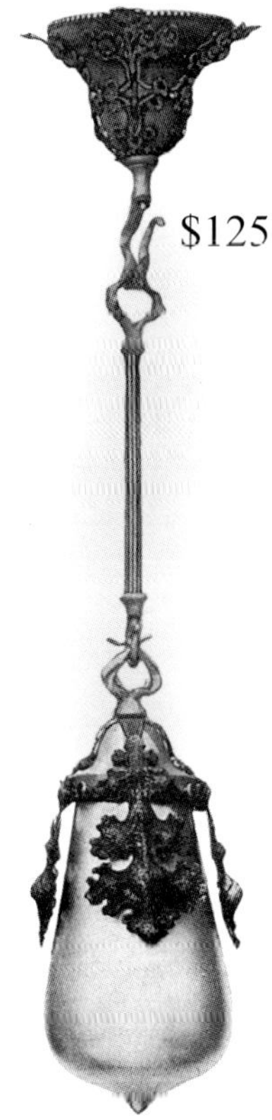

Number 2326

Number 2107
Length, 36 inches.
Art Glass included.
Select Glass Colors by Number. See last page.

	Not Wired	Wired	Complete as shown No lamps
Black Iron only	**$10.00**	**$11.25**	**$11.95**

Chain Pull Socket included in right hand column only.
Extra lengthening per foot, 35 cents.

Number 2286 Black Iron only.
Number 2286½ Brush Brass.
Length, 36 inches (over all).
4x6-inch C. R. I. Cylinder included.

	Not Wired	Wired	Complete as shown No lamps
Number 2286 Black Iron only	**$5.30**	**$6.05**	**$6.75**
" 2286½ Brush Brass	6.55	7.30	8.00

Chain Pull Socket included in right hand column only.
Extra lengthening for No. 2286 per foot, 35 cents.
Extra lengthening for No. 2286½ per foot, $1.00.

Number 1780
Length, 36 inches (over all).
Art Glass included.
Select Glass Colors by Number. See last page.

	Not Wired	Wired	Complete as shown No lamps
Brush Brass	**$13.25**	**$14.00**	**$14.40**

If wanted with Chain Pull Socket, add 30 cents to price in right hand column.
Extra lengthening per foot, $1.00.

Number 2326
Length, 30 inches (over all).
3¼x9-inch C. R. I. "D." Stalactite and Holder included.

	Not Wired	Wired	Complete as shown No lamps
Antique Brush Brass	**$14.75**	**$15.25**	**$15.65**

If wanted with Chain Pull Socket, add 30 cents to price in right hand column.

Price in right hand column always includes sockets; also holders and shades if shown but no lamps.
Other prices include glassware, sockets, lamps or electric holders only where mentioned.

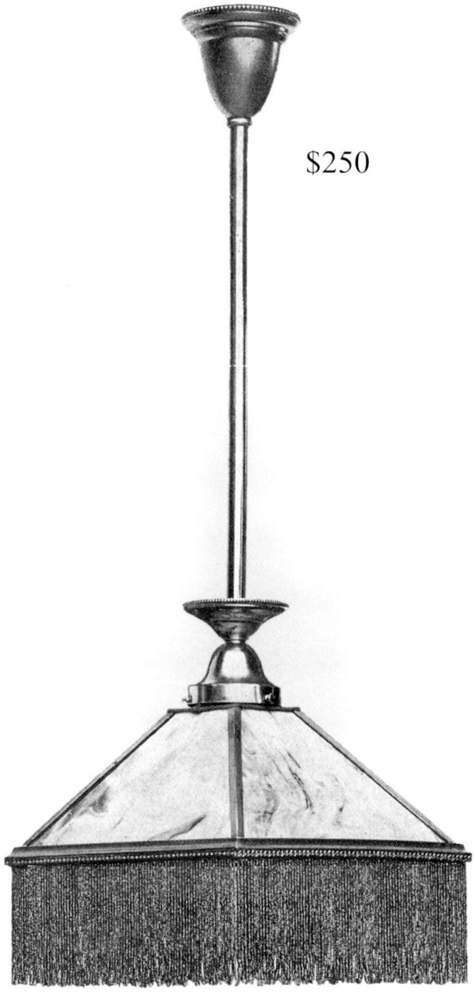

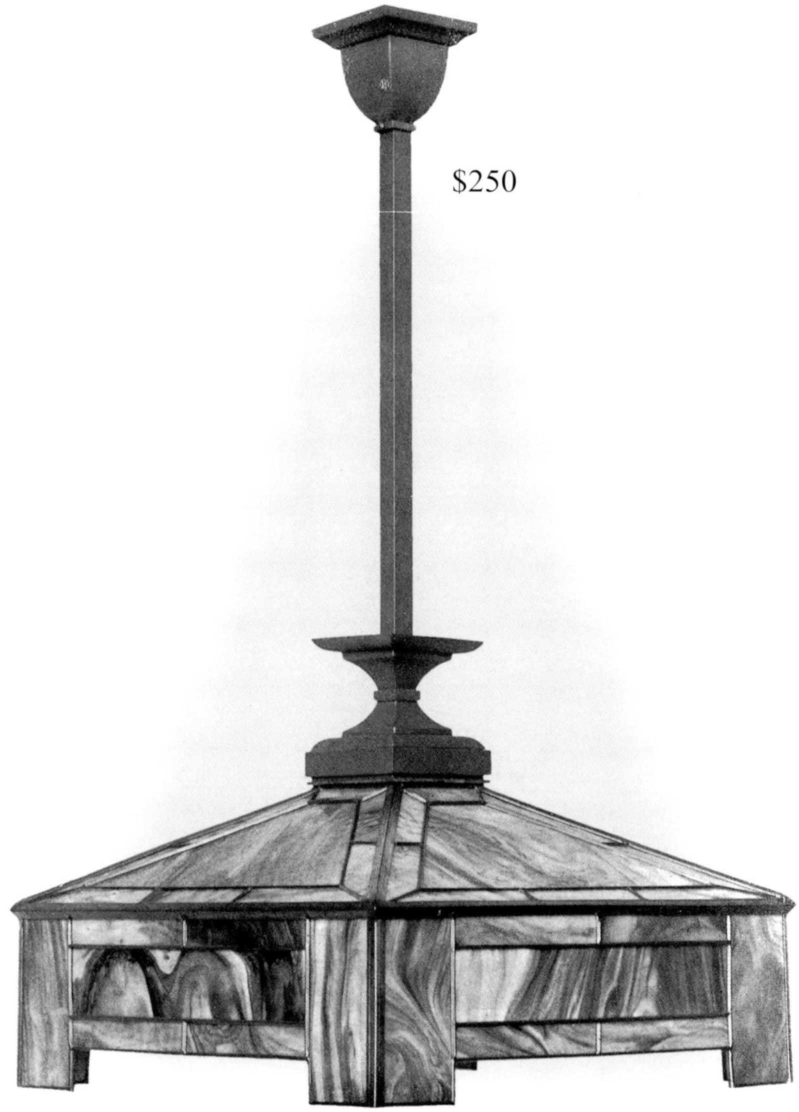

Number 1936

Length, 36 inches (over all).

3¼x14-inch Art Glass Shade and Glass Bead Fringe included.

Select Glass Colors by Number. See last page.

		Not Wired	Wired	Complete as shown No lamps
1 Electric	Brush Brass	$10.50	$11.00	$11.40
2 "	" "	11.00	11.75	12.55
3 "	" "	11.25	12.25	13.45
4 "	" "	11.50	12.75	14.35

Number 2411

Length, 40 inches (over all).

20-inch Art Glass Shade included.

Select Glass Colors by Number. See last page.

		Not Wired	Wired	Complete as shown No lamps
1 Electric	Brush Brass	$34.00	$34.75	$35.15
2 "	" "	34.25	35.25	36.05
3 "	" "	34.50	35.75	36.95
4 "	" "	34.75	36.25	37.85

Price in right hand column always includes sockets; also holders and shades if shown but no lamps.
Other prices include glassware, sockets, lamps or electric holders only where mentioned.

$250

$250

Number 2669
Length, 40 inches (over all).
20-inch Art Glass Shade and Glass Bead Fringe included.
Select Glass Colors by Number. See last page.

			Not Wired	Wired	Complete as shown No lamps
1	Electric	Brush Brass	$32.75	$33.75	$34.15
2	"	" "	33.00	34.25	35.05
3	"	" "	33.25	34.75	35.95
4	"	" "	33.50	35.25	36.85
5	"	" "	33.75	35.75	37.75

Extra lengthening per foot, $2.00.

Number 1977
Length, 42 inches (over all).
20-inch Art Glass Shade and Glass Bead Fringe included.
Select Glass Colors by Number. See last page.

			Not Wired	Wired	Complete as shown No lamps
1	Electric	Rich Gilt	$50.50	$51.50	$51.90
2	"	" "	51.00	52.25	53.05
3	"	" "	51.25	52.75	53.95
4	"	" "	51.50	53.25	54.85
6	"	" "	52.00	54.25	56.65

Extra lengthening per foot, $2.00.

Price in right hand column always includes sockets; also holders and shades if shown but no lamps.
Other prices include glassware, sockets, lamps or electric holders only where mentioned.

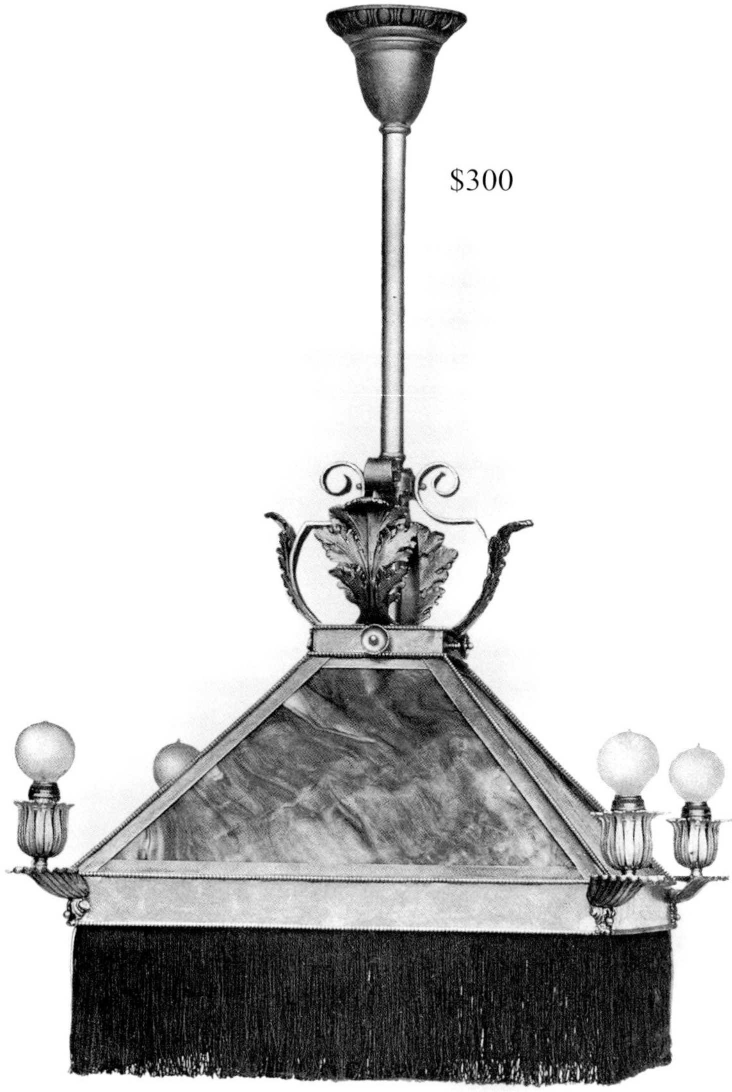

Number 2171

Length, 42 inches (over all). Spread, 31 inches.
20-inch Art Glass Shade and Glass Bead Fringe included.
Select Glass Colors by Number. See last page.

	Finish	Not Wired	Wired	Complete as shown No lamps
8 Electric (4 under Shade)	Brush	$88.50	$92.50	$95.70
10 " (6 " ")	Brass	89.00	94.00	98.00

Number 2670

Length, 42 inches (over all).
18-inch Art Glass Shade and Glass Bead Fringe included.
Select Glass Colors by Number. See last page.

	Not Wired	Wired	Complete as shown No lamps
1 Electric Brush Brass	$20.00	$20.50	$20.90
2 " " "	20.25	21.00	21.80
3 " " "	20.50	21.50	22.70
4 " " "	20.75	22.00	23.60

Price in right hand column always includes sockets; also holders and shades if shown but no lamps.
Other prices include glassware, sockets, lamps or electric holders only where mentioned.

$350

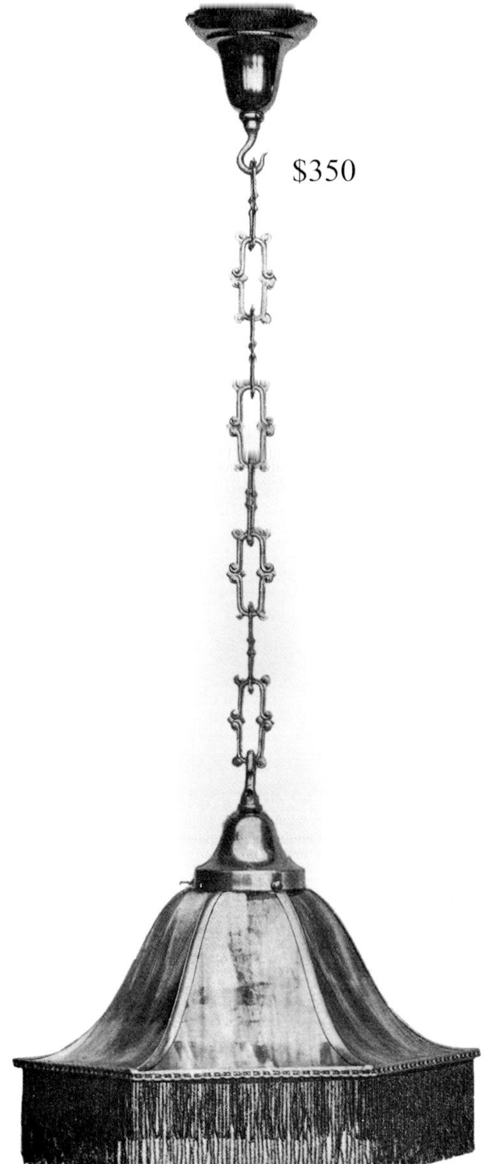

$350

Number 2214
Length, 48 inches (over all).
24-inch Art Glass Shade included.
Select Glass Colors by Number. See last page.

		Not Wired	Wired	Complete as shown No lamps
1 Electric	Brush Brass	$76.25	$77.50	$77.90
2 "	" "	76.50	78.00	78.80
3 "	" "	76.75	78.50	79.70
4 "	" "	77.00	79.00	80.60
6 "	" "	77.50	80.00	82.40

Extra lengthening per foot, $3.00.

Number 1973
Length, 42 inches (over all).
4x18-inch Art Glass Shade and Glass Bead Fringe included.
Select Glass Colors by Number. See last page.

		Not Wired	Wired	Complete as shown No lamps
1 Electric	Polished Brass and Black	$26.60	$27.60	$28.00
2 "	" " " "	27.10	28.35	29.15
3 "	" " " "	27.35	28.85	30.05
4 "	" " " "	27.60	29.35	30.95

Extra lengthening per foot, $2.00.

Price in right hand column always includes sockets; also holders and shades if shown but no lamps.
Other prices include glassware, sockets, lamps or electric holders only where mentioned.

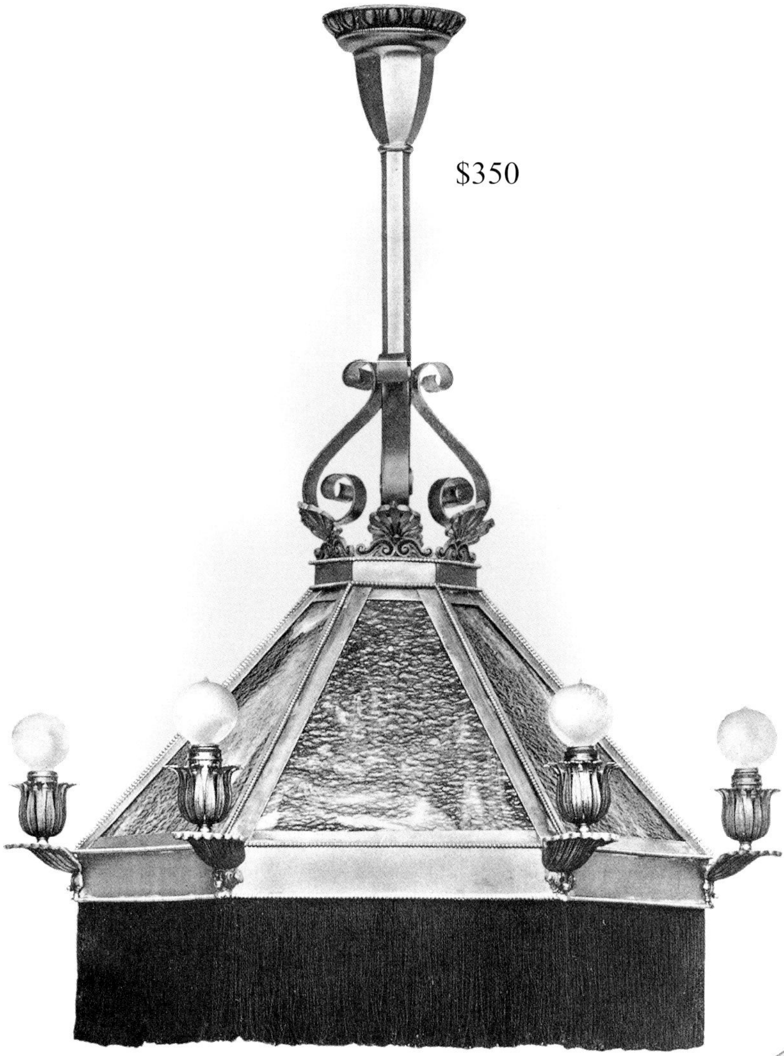

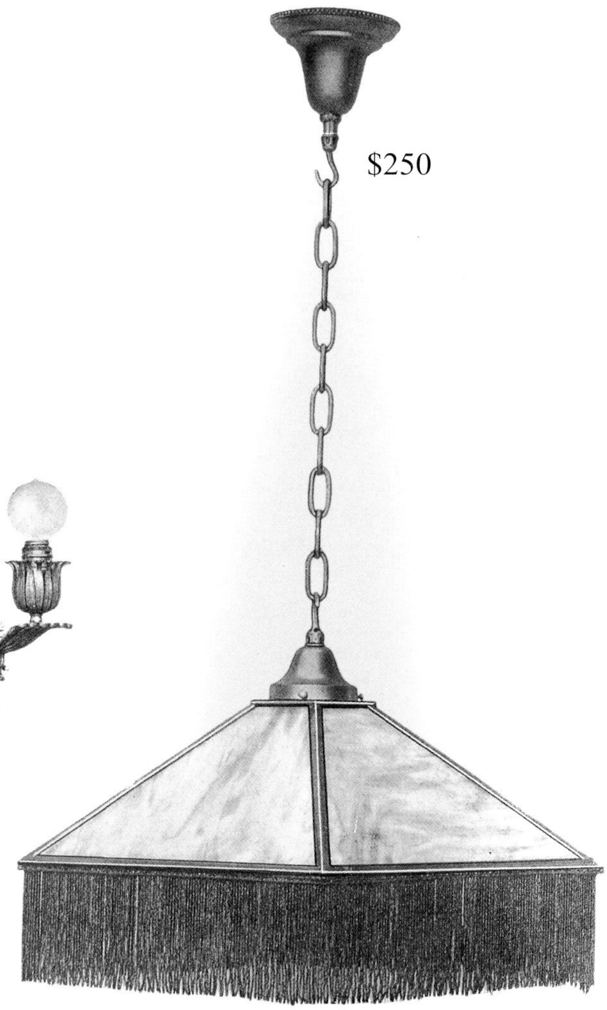

Number 2172

Length, 42 inches (over all). Spread, 27 inches.
Socket Husks, 24-inch Art Glass Shade and Glass Bead Fringe included.
Select Glass Colors by Number. See last page.

		Not Wired	Wired	Complete as shown No lamps
9 Electric (3 under Shade)	Brush Brass and Black	$91.00	$95.50	$99.10
12 " (6 " ")		93.50	99.50	104.30

Number 2668

Length, 40 inches (over all).
3¼x14-inch Art Glass Shade and Glass Bead Fringe included.
Select Glass Colors by Number. See last page.

		Not Wired	Wired	Complete as shown No lamps
1 Electric	Brush Brass	$13.00	$14.00	$14.40
2 "	" "	13.25	14.25	15.05
3 "	" "	13.50	15.00	16.20
4 "	" "	13.75	15.50	17.10

Extra lengthening per foot, $1.00.

Price in right hand column always includes sockets; also holders and shades if shown but no lamps.
Other prices include glassware, sockets, lamps or electric holders only where mentioned.

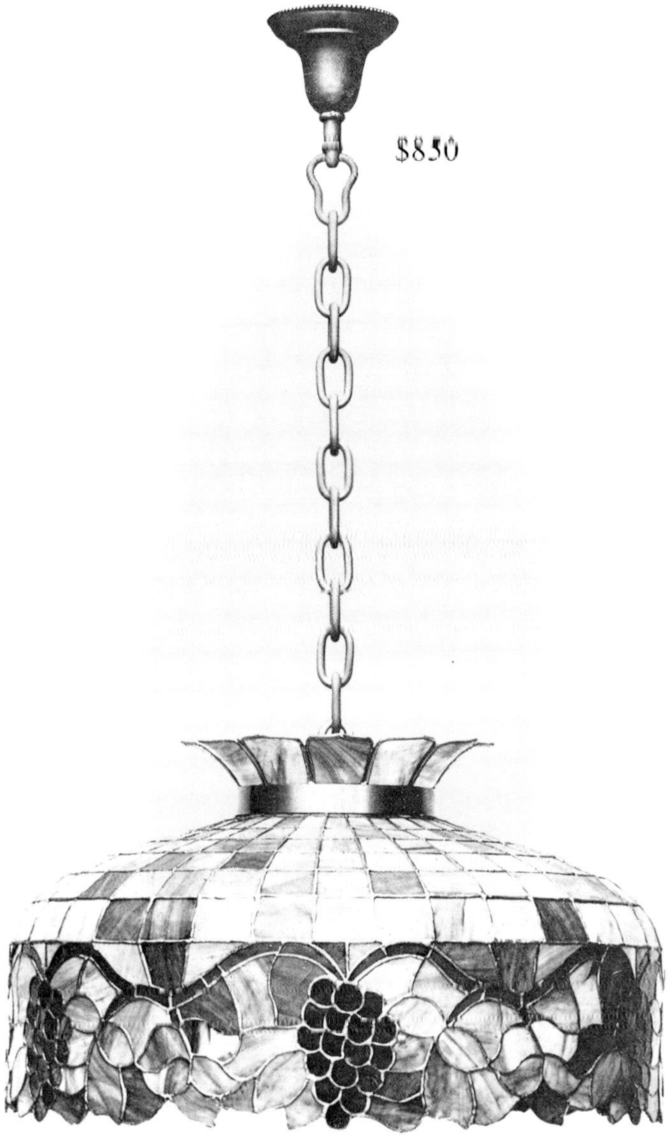

$850

$650

Number 2634
Length, 42 inches (over all).
24-inch Art Glass Shade included.
Select Glass Colors by Number. See last page.

		Not Wired	Wired	Complete as shown No lamps
1 Electric	Brush Brass	$79.50	$80.75	$81.15
2 "	" "	79.75	81.25	82.05
3 "	" "	80.00	81.75	82.95
4 "	" "	80.25	82.25	83.85
5 "	" "	80.50	82.75	84.75
6 "	" "	80.75	83.25	85.65

Extra lengthening per foot, $2.00.

Number 2422
Length, 36 inches (over all).
18-inch Art Glass Shade included.
Select Glass Colors by Number. See last page.

		Not Wired	Wired	Complete as shown No lamps
1 Electric	Brush Brass	$45.35	$46.60	$47.00
2 "	" "	45.60	47.10	47.90
3 "	" "	45.85	47.60	48.80
4 "	" "	46.10	48.10	49.70

Extra lengthening per foot, $2.00.

Price in right hand column always includes sockets; also holders and shades if shown but no lamps.
Other prices include glassware, sockets, lamps or electric holders only where mentioned.

$600

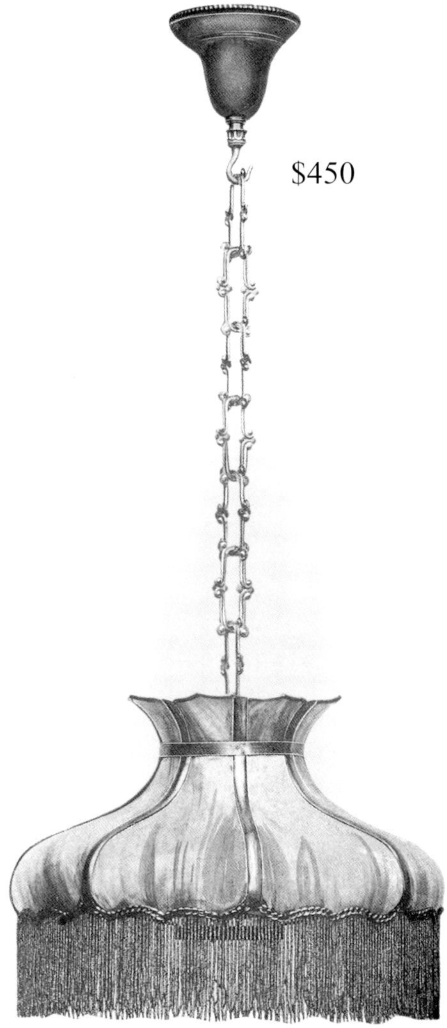

$450

Number 2463

Length, 42 inches (over all).

24-inch Art Glass Shade included.

Select Glass Colors by Number. See last page.

		Not Wired	Wired	Complete as shown No lamps
1 Electric	Brush Brass	$31.50	$32.75	$33.15
2 "	" "	31.75	33.25	34.05
3 "	" "	32.00	33.75	34.95
4 "	" "	32.25	34.25	35.85
5 "	" "	32.50	34.75	36.75
6 "	" "	32.75	35.25	37.65

Extra lengthening per foot, $2.00.

Number 1948

Length, 36 inches (over all).

16-inch Art Glass Shade and Glass Bead Fringe included.

Select Glass Colors by Number. See last page.

		Not Wired	Wired	Complete as shown No lamps
1 Electric	Polished Brass and Black	$23.25	$24.25	$24.65
2 "	" " " "	23.75	25.00	25.80
3 "	" " " "	24.00	25.50	26.70
4 "	" " " "	24.25	26.00	27.60

Extra lengthening per foot, $2.00.

Price in right hand column always includes sockets; also holders and shades if shown but no lamps.
Other prices include glassware, sockets, lamps or electric holders only where mentioned.

$400

$300

Number 2288
Length, 46 inches (over all). Spread, 18 inches.

	Not Wired	Wired	Complete as shown No lamps
2 Electric (1 Bar) Black Iron only....	$6.25	$7.75	$10.15
3 " (3 Bars) " " "	8.25	10.50	14.10
4 " (4 ") " " "	10.25	13.25	18.05

Shades No. B 250 Crystal Roughed Inside. Diameter, 8 inches.
Extra lengthening per foot, 50 cents.

Number 2106
Length, 40 inches (over all).
Made of Iron.
6x12-inch C. R. I. Ball included.

	Not Wired	Wired	Complete as shown No lamps
1 Electric Antique Brush Brass only..	$16.00	$17.25	$17.65
2 " " " " " ..	16.50	18.00	18.80
3 " " " " " ..	17.00	18.75	19.95
4 " " " " " ..	17.50	19.50	21.10

Extra lengthening per foot, 50 cents.

Price in right hand column always includes sockets; also holders and shades if shown but no lamps.
Other prices include glassware, sockets, lamps or electric holders only where mentioned.

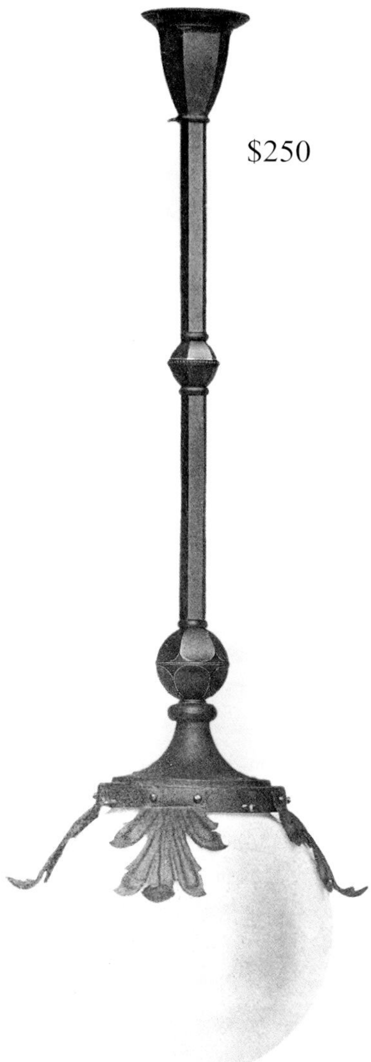

$250

$450

Number 2190

Length, 42 inches (over all).

6x12-inch C. R. I. Ball included.

		Not Wired	Wired	Complete as shown No lamps
1	Electric Black Iron only	$12.00	$12.50	$12.90
2	" " " "	12.50	13.50	14.30
3	" " " "	13.00	14.50	15.70
4	" " " "	13.50	15.50	17.10

Number 2294

Length, 54 inches (over all). Spread, 18 inches.

Lanterns and 4x6-inch C. R. I. Cylinders included.

		Not Wired	Wired	Complete as shown No lamps
4	Electric (No Center Light) Black Iron only....	$23.45	$26.45	$28.05
5	" (With " ") Black Iron only....	28.00	31.75	33.75

Extra lengthening per foot, 50 cents.

Without Lanterns and Cylinders deduct $3.30 per light.

Price in right hand column always includes sockets; also holders and shades if shown but no lamps.
Other prices include glassware, sockets, lamps or electric holders only where mentioned.

$650

$300

Number 2302
Length, 40 inches (over all). Spread, 21 inches.
3¼-inch Holders included.

		Not Wired	Wired	Complete as shown No lamps
4 Electric	Brush Brass and Black.....	$45.60	$48.60	$57.40
5 "	" " " "	50.80	54.55	65.55
6 "	" " " "	56.00	60.50	73.70

No. B 5213 3¼x6-inch Grecian Etched and Cut Star Balls.
Extra lengthening per foot, $2.00.

Number 2163
Length, 42 inches (over all).
6x12-inch C. R. I. Ball included.

		Not Wired	Wired	Complete as shown No lamps
2 Electric	Antique Brush Brass......	$43.00	$44.50	$45.30
3 "	" " "	43.50	45.50	46.70
4 "	" " "	44.00	46.50	48.10

Extra lengthening per foot, $2.00.

Price in right hand column always includes sockets; also holders and shades if shown but no lamps.
Other prices include glassware, sockets, lamps or electric holders only where mentioned.

$300

$400

Number 1553
Length, 42 inches.
Art Glass included.
Select Glass Colors by Number. See last page.

		Not Wired	Wired	Complete as shown No lamps
1 Electric	Old Brass	$75.00	$75.50	$75.90
2 "	" "	76.00	77.00	77.80
3 "	" "	76.50	78.00	79.20

Number 2304
Length, 55 inches (over all). Spread, 21 inches.
Lanterns and 4x6-inch C. R. I. Cylinders included.

		Not Wired	Wired	Complete as shown No lamps
4 Electric	Brush Brass and Black	$55.15	$58.15	$59.75
5 "	" " " "	62.85	66.60	68.60
6 "	" " " "	70.55	75.05	77.45
7 "	" " " "	78.25	83.50	86.30

Extra lengthening per foot, $2.00.

Price in right hand column always includes sockets; also holders and shades if shown but no lamps.
Other prices include glassware, sockets, lamps or electric holders only where mentioned.

$450

$450

Number 2263

Length, 30 inches (over all). Spread, 19 inches.

3¼-inch Socket Cover Holders included.

		Not Wired	Wired	Complete as shown No lamps
3 Electric	Brush Brass	$45.60	$47.85	$53.55
5 "	" "	70.20	73.95	83.45

No. B 180 3¼x8-inch Crystal Roughed Inside Square Balls.

Number 2284

Length, 34 inches (over all). Spread, 13 inches.

Holders and 3¼x8-inch C. R. I. Square Balls included.

		Not Wired	Wired	Complete as shown No lamps
3 Electric	Antique Brush Brass......	$52.75	$55.00	$56.20
5 "	" " "	84.50	88.25	90.25

Price in right hand column always includes sockets; also holders and shades if shown but no lamps.
Other prices include glassware, sockets, lamps or electric holders only where mentioned.

$750

$650

Number 2578
Length, 40 inches (over all). Spread, 19 inches.

		Not Wired	Wired	Complete as shown No lamps
6 Electric	Brush Brass and Black.....	$78.00	$82.50	$89.10

Shades No. B 007½ Frosted, with Crystal Stars and Bars. Diameter, 7 inches.
Extra lengthening per foot, $2.00.

Number 2522
Length, 44 inches (over all). Spread, 17 inches.

		Not Wired	Wired	Complete as shown No lamps
6 Electric	Brush Brass and Black.....	$66.00	$70.50	$127.50

Shades No. B 831 Amber Lustre.
Extra lengthening per foot, $4.25.

Price in right hand column always includes sockets; also holders and shades if shown but no lamps.
Other prices include glassware, sockets, lamps or electric holders only where mentioned.

$600

$600

Number 2530

Length, 36 inches (over all). Spread, 18 inches.

Cast Socket Husks included.

			Not Wired	Wired	Complete as shown No lamps
4	Electric	Brush Brass and Black.....	$38.75	$41.75	$79.75
5	"	" " " "	46.00	49.75	97.25
6	"	" " " "	53.25	57.75	114.75
7	"	" " " "	60.50	65.75	132.25

Shades No. B 831 Amber Lustre.

Number 2531

Length, 38 inches (over all). Spread, 18 inches.

Cast Socket Husks included.

			Not Wired	Wired	Complete as shown No lamps
4	Electric	Brush Brass and Black.....	$35.65	$38.65	$76.65
5	"	" " " "	42.20	45.95	93.45
6	"	" " " "	48.75	53.25	110.25
7	"	" " " "	55.30	60.55	127.15

Shades No. B 831 Amber Lustre.

Price in right hand column always includes sockets; also holders and shades if shown but no lamps.
Other prices include glassware, sockets, lamps or electric holders only where mentioned.

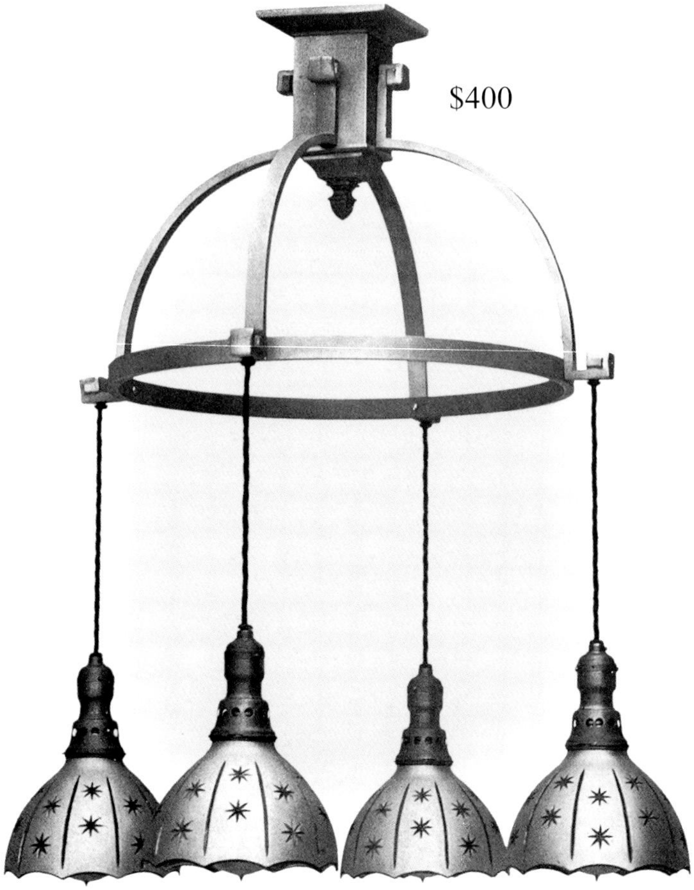

Number 2510
Length, 36 inches (over all). Spread, 20 inches.

	Not Wired	Wired	Complete as shown No lamps
2 Electric Antique Brush Brass......	$15.20	$16.70	$19.20
4 " " " "	21.40	24.40	29.40

Shades No. B 007½ Frosted, with Crystal Stars and Bars. Diameter, 7 inches.

Number 2515
Length, 42 inches (over all). Spread, 18 inches.

	Not Wired	Wired	Complete as shown No lamps
3 Electric Antique Brush Brass......	$35.25	$37.50	$51.75
4 " " " "	40.25	43.25	62.25

Shades No. B 820 Ivory, with Gold Lustre and Green decoration.

Price in right hand column always includes sockets; also holders and shades if shown but no lamps.
Other prices include glassware, sockets, lamps or electric holders only where mentioned.

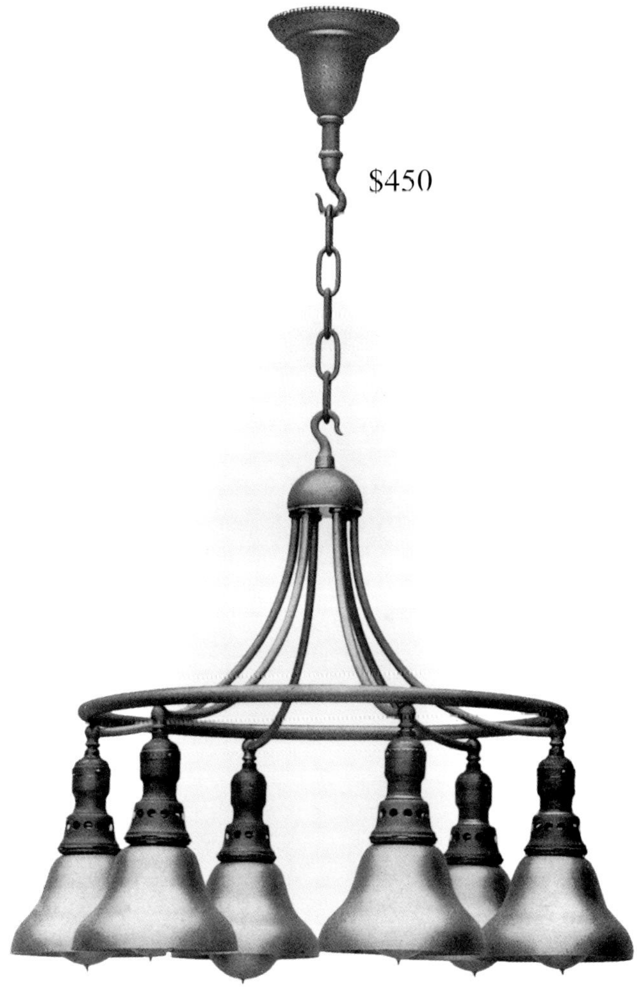

Number 2503

Length, 36 inches (over all). Spread, 17 inches.

	Not Wired	Wired	Complete as shown No lamps
3 Electric Brush Brass	$11.50	$13.75	$16.75
4 " " "	12.50	15.50	19.50
5 " " "	13.50	17.25	22.25
6 " " "	14.50	19.00	25.00

Shades No. B 249 Crystal Roughed Inside. Diameter, 6 inches.

Extra lengthening per foot, 85 cents.

Number 2513

Length, 36 inches (over all). Spread, 18 inches.

	Not Wired	Wired	Complete as shown No lamps
3 Electric Brush Brass	$9.25	$11.25	$14.25
4 " " "	10.00	12.50	16.50
5 " " "	10.75	13.75	18.75
6 " " "	11.50	15.00	21.00

Shades No. B 249 Crystal Roughed Inside. Diameter, 6 inches.

Extra lengthening per foot, $1.00.

Price in right hand column always includes sockets; also holders and shades if shown but no lamps.
Other prices include glassware, sockets, lamps or electric holders only where mentioned.

Number 2538
Length, 42 inches (over all). Spread, 14 inches.
Cast Socket Husks included.

		Not Wired	Wired	Complete as shown No lamps
4 Electric (No center light)	Brush Brass	$41.00	$44.00	$63.00
5 " (With " ")	and Black	42.75	46.50	70.25

Shades No. B 820 Ivory, with Gold Lustre and Green decoration.

Number 2507
Length, 42 inches (over all). Spread, 14 inches.

		Not Wired	Wired	Complete as shown No lamps
4 Electric (No center light)	Brush Brass	$34.00	$37.00	$43.00
5 " (With " ")	and Black	34.00	37.75	45.25

Shades No. B 939½ Rose Tint.

Price in right hand column always includes sockets; also holders and shades if shown but no lamps.
Other prices include glassware, sockets, lamps or electric holders only where mentioned.

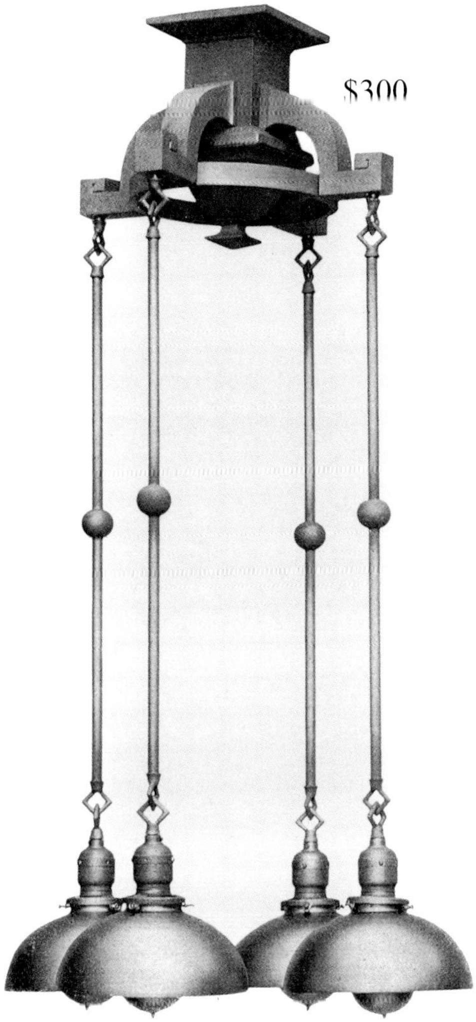

Number 2611

Length, 36 inches (over all). Spread, 12 inches.

		Not Wired	Wired	Complete as shown No lamps
2 Electric	Brush Brass	$21.25	$22.75	$24.55
4 "	" "	33.25	36.25	39.85

$2\frac{1}{4}$x7-inch Crystal Roughed Inside Domes.

Number 2609

Length, 33 inches (over all). Spread, 16 inches.

			Not Wired	Wired	Complete as shown No lamps
2 Electric	(No center light)	Brush Brass ...	$12.25	$13.75	$20.75
3 "	(With " ")	" " ...	13.25	15.50	26.00
4 "	(No " ")	" " ...	18.25	21.25	35.25
5 "	(With " ")	" " ...	19.25	23.00	40.50

Shade No. B 10168 Roughed and Cut. Diameter, 8 inches.

Price in right hand column always includes sockets; also holders and shades if shown but no lamps.
Other prices include glassware, sockets, lamps or electric holders only where mentioned.

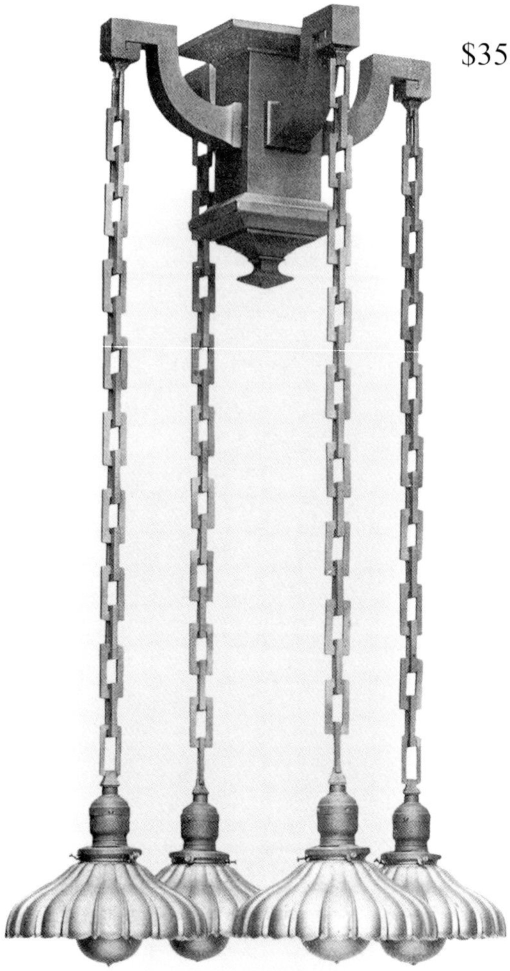

$350

$300

Number 2613

Length, 36 inches (over all). Spread, 12 inches.

			Not Wired	Wired	Complete as shown No lamps
2	Electric	Brush Brass	$26.50	$28.00	$31.50
4	"	" "	45.50	48.50	55.50

Shades No. B 3431 Alba.

Number 2512

Length, 33 inches (over all). Spread, 14 inches.

			Not Wired	Wired	Complete as shown No lamps
3	Electric	Brush Brass	$13.00	$15.25	$18.25
4	"	" "	15.00	18.00	22.00
5	"	" "	17.00	20.75	25.75
6	"	" "	19.00	23.50	29.50

Shades No. B 539½ Crystal Roughed Inside.

Price in right hand column always includes sockets; also holders and shades if shown but no lamps.
Other prices include glassware, sockets, lamps or electric holders only where mentioned.

$500

$500

Number 2529

Length, 34 inches (over all). Spread, 16 inches.

		Not Wired	Wired	Complete as shown No lamps
3 Electric	Brush Brass and Black.....	$15.20	$17.45	$21.65
4 "	" " " "	19.10	22.10	27.70
5 "	" " " "	23.00	26.75	33.75

Shades No. B 118½ Satin Finish Pink.

Number 2539

Length, 35 inches (over all). Spread, 14 inches.

No. B 397 3¼x6-inch Roughed and Cut Ball only included.

		Not Wired	Wired	Complete as shown No lamps
3 Electric	Brush Brass	$16.00	$18.25	$23.45
4 "	" "	18.00	21.00	28.50
5 "	" "	20.00	23.75	33.55
6 "	" "	22.00	26.50	38.60

Shades No. B 398½ Roughed and Cut.

Price in right hand column always includes sockets; also holders and shades if shown but no lamps.
Other prices include glassware, sockets, lamps or electric holders only where mentioned.

Number 2562

Length, 36 inches (over all). Spread, 14 inches.

	Not Wired	Wired	Complete as shown No lamps
3 Electric Brush Brass	$7.50	$9.75	$12.90
4 " " "	8.75	11.75	15.95
5 " " "	10.00	13.75	19.00
6 " " "	11.25	15.75	22.05

Shades No. B 5014½ Crystal Roughed Inside.

Number 2520

Length, 36 inches (over all). Spread, 18 inches.

	Not Wired	Wired	Complete as shown No lamps
4 Electric Brush Brass	$7.50	$10.50	$14.50
5 " " "	8.25	12.00	17.00
6 " " "	9.00	13.50	19.50
7 " " "	9.75	15.00	22.00

Shades No. B 539½ Crystal Roughed Inside.

Price in right hand column always includes sockets; also holders and shades if shown but no lamps.
Other prices include glassware, sockets, lamps or electric holders only where mentioned.

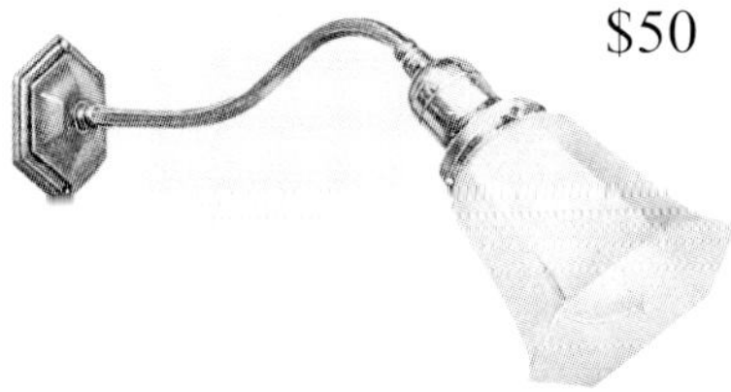

$50

Number 1754

	Not Wired	Wired	Complete as shown No lamp
Rich Gilt	$1.00	$1.10	$2.00

Shade No. B 68½ C. R. I.

$50

Number 1743

	Not Wired	Wired	Complete as shown No lamp
Rich Gilt	$1.60	$1.90	$2.80

Shade No. B 68½ C. R. I.

$50

Number 1742

	Not Wired	Wired	Complete as shown No lamp
Rich Gilt	$1.60	$1.90	$2.80

Shade No. B 68½ C. R. I.

$50

Number 2192

	Not Wired	Wired	Complete as shown No lamp
Polished Brass	$0.45	$0.55	$1.30

Shade No. B 41½ Crystal.

$50

Number 2196

	Not Wired	Wired	Complete as shown No lamp
Polished Brass	$0.60	$0.75	$1.50

Shade No. B 41½ Crystal.

$50

Number 2191

	Not Wired	Wired	Complete as shown No lamp
Polished Brass	$0.40	$0.50	$1.25

Shade No. B 41½ Crystal.

$50

Number 2193

	Not Wired	Wired	Complete as shown No lamp
Polished Brass	$0.50	$0.60	$1.35

Shade No. B 41½ Crystal.

$50

Number 2197

	Not Wired	Wired	Complete as shown No lamp
Polished Brass	$0.75	$1.05	$1.80

Shade No. B 4284½ Crystal.

$50

Number 2057

	Not Wired	Wired	Complete as shown No lamp
Rich Gilt	$0.80	$1.10	$1.85

Shade No. B 41½ Crystal.

$50

Number 2066

	Not Wired	Wired	Complete as shown No lamp
Rich Gilt	$0.50	$0.60	$1.35

Shade No. B 41½ Crystal.

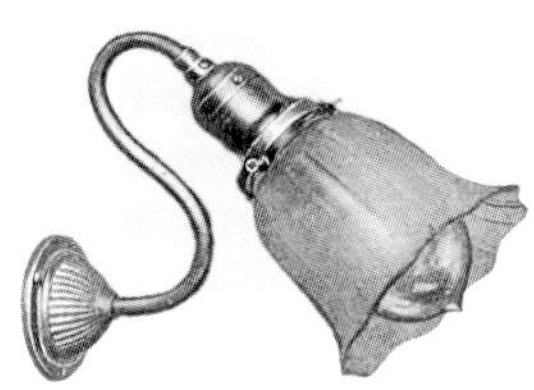

$50

Number 2194

	Not Wired	Wired	Complete as shown No lamp
Polished Brass	$0.60	$0.75	$1.50

Shade No. B 4284½ Crystal.

$50

Number 1519

	Not Wired	Wired	Complete as shown No lamp
Polished Brass	$0.65	$0.75	$1.95

Shade No. B 602½ Etched and Imitation Cut.

Price in right hand column always includes sockets; also holders and shades if shown but no lamps.
Other prices include glassware, sockets, lamps or electric holders only where mentioned.

Number 1765
Single Swing.

	Not Wired	Wired	Complete as shown No lamp
Rich Gilt	$1.30	$1.60	$2.50

Shade No. 1412½ White Acid.

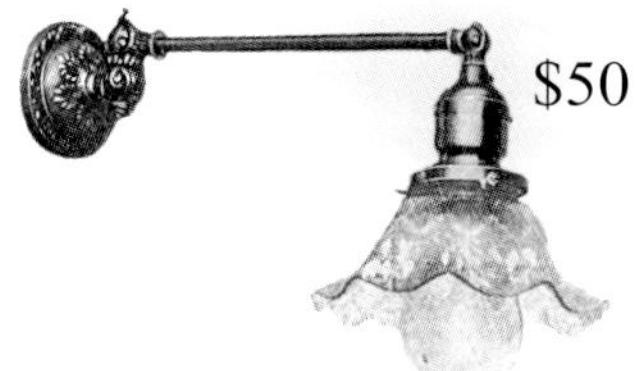

Number 1761
Single Swing.

	Not Wired	Wired	Complete as shown No lamp
Rich Gilt	$1.10	$1.40	$2.30

Shade No. B 1538½ White Acid.

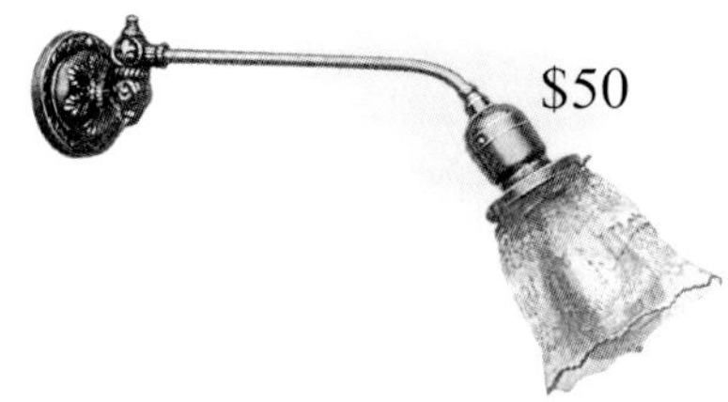

Number 1767
Single Swing.

	Not Wired	Wired	Complete as shown No lamp
Rich Gilt	$1.10	$1.40	$2.30

Shade No. B 1319½ White Acid.

Number 1766
Double Swing.

	Not Wired	Wired	Complete as shown No lamp
Rich Gilt	$2.00	$2.40	$3.30

Shade No. B 1412½ White Acid.

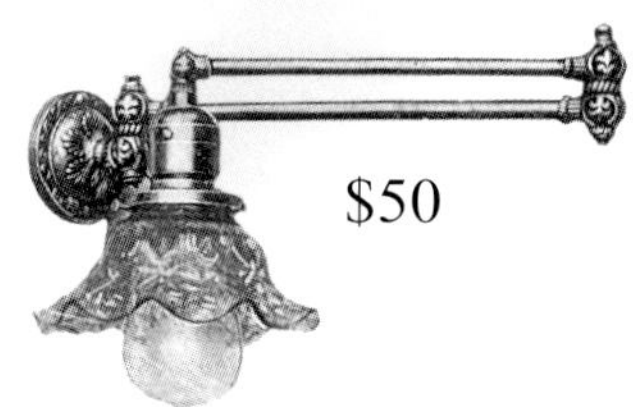

Number 1762
Double Swing.

	Not Wired	Wired	Complete as shown No lamp
Rich Gilt	$1.70	$2.10	$3.00

Shade No. B 1538½ White Acid.

Number 1768
Double Swing.

	Not Wired	Wired	Complete as shown No lamp
Rich Gilt	$1.70	$2.10	$3.00

Shade No. B 1319½ White Acid.

Number 1770
Single Swing.

	Not Wired	Wired	Complete as shown No lamp
Rich Gilt	$1.25	$1.55	$2.30

Shade No. B 33½ Crystal Prism.

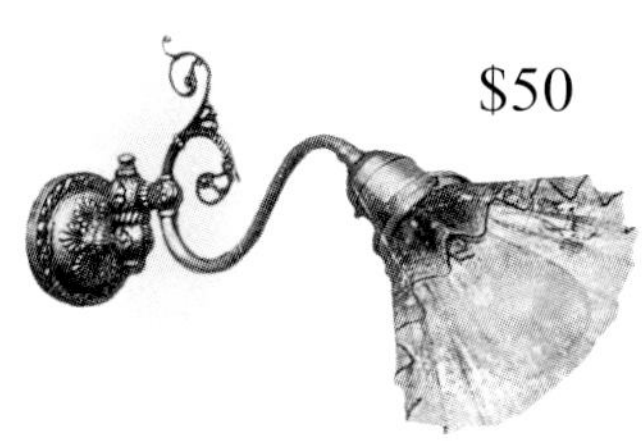

Number 1747
Single Swing.

	Not Wired	Wired	Complete as shown No lamp
Rich Gilt	$2.25	$2.55	$3.45

Shade No. B 2986½ White Acid.

Number 1764
Single Swing.

	Not Wired	Wired	Complete as shown No lamp
Rich Gilt	$1.20	$1.50	$2.25

Shade No. B 33½ Crystal Prism.

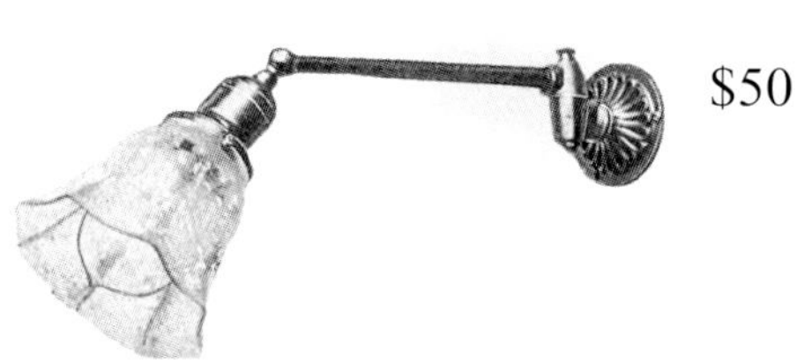

Number 1759 Single Swing.
Number 1759½ Double Swing.
Made of ½-inch Tubing.

		Not Wired	Wired	Complete as shown No lamp
1759	Rich Gilt	$1.75	$2.05	$2.95
1759½	" "	2.75	3.15	4.05

Shade No. B 1412½ White Acid.

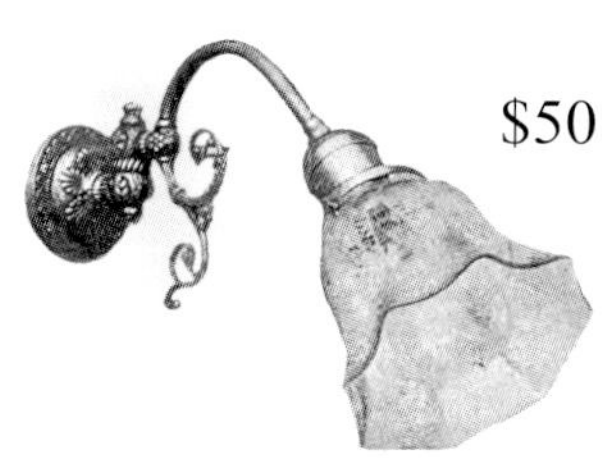

Number 1746
Single Swing.

	Not Wired	Wired	Complete as shown No lamp
Rich Gilt	$2.25	$2.55	$3.45

Shade No. B 1412½ White Acid.

Number 1760 Single Swing.
Number 1760½ Double Swing.
Made of ½-inch Tubing.

		Not Wired	Wired	Complete as shown No lamp
1760	Rich Gilt	$1.75	$2.05	$2.95
1760½	" "	2.75	3.15	4.05

Shade No. B 1412½ White Acid.

Price in right hand column always includes sockets; also holders and shades if shown but no lamps.
Other prices include glassware, sockets, lamps or electric holders only where mentioned.

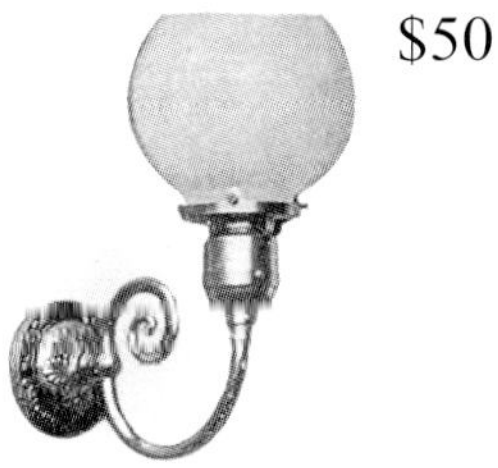

Number 1745

	Not Wired	Wired	Complete as shown No lamp
Rich Gilt	$1.50	$1.80	$2.70

Shade No. B 4149 C. R. I.

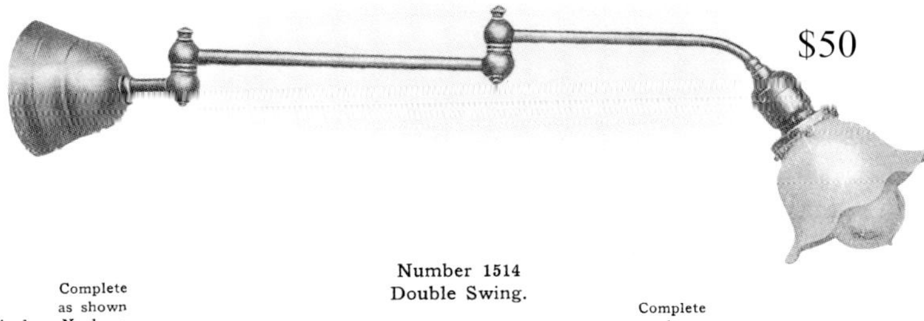

Number 1514
Double Swing.

	Not Wired	Wired	Complete as shown No lamp
Polished Brass	$2.20	$2.60	$3.60

Shade No. B 5213½ P. S. O.

Number 1525
Socket Husk included.

	Not Wired	Wired	Complete as shown No lamp
Rich Gilt	$2.40	$2.70	$3.10

Number 1748

	Not Wired	Wired	Complete as shown No lamp
Rich Gilt	$1.60	$1.90	$2.80

Shade No. B 1412½ White Acid.

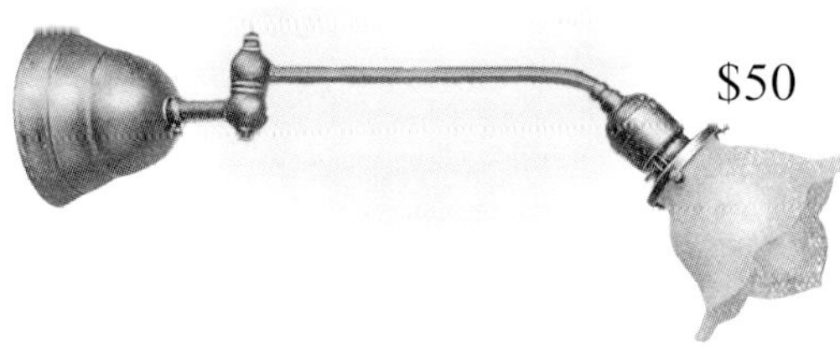

Number 1513
Single Swing.

	Not Wired	Wired	Complete as shown No lamp
Polished Brass	$1.50	$1.80	$2.80

Shade No. B 5213½ P. S. O.

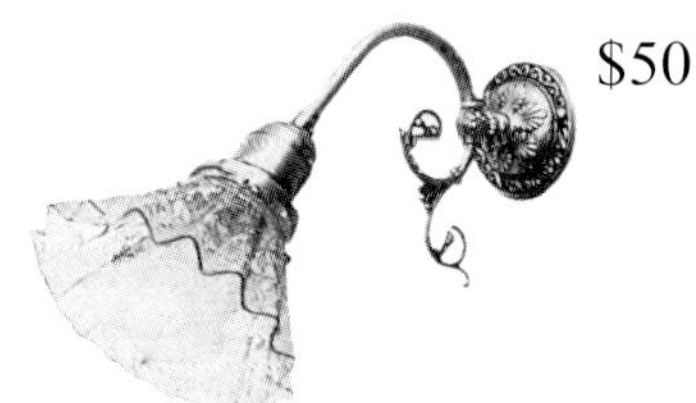

Number 1729

	Not Wired	Wired	Complete as shown No lamp
Rich Gilt	$1.50	$1.80	$2.70

Shade No. B 2986½ White Acid.

Number 1736

	Not Wired	Wired	Complete as shown No lamp
Rich Gilt	$1.50	$1.80	$2.70

Shade No. B 1412½ White Acid.

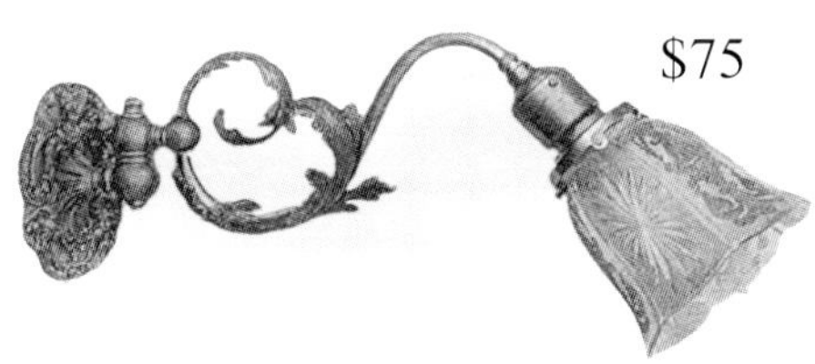

Number 1527
Single Swing.

	Not Wired	Wired	Complete as shown No lamp
Rich Gilt and Satin....	$4.50	$5.00	$6.20

Shade No. B 602½ Etched and Imitation Cut.

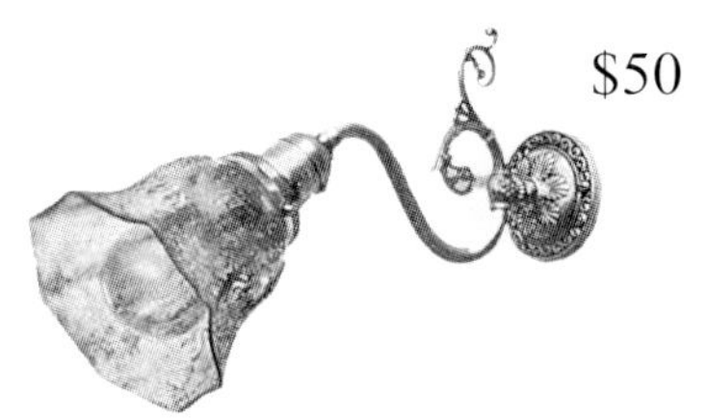

Number 1730

	Not Wired	Wired	Complete as shown No lamp
Rich Gilt	$1.50	$1.80	$2.70

Shade No. B 1412½ White Acid.

Number 1769
Single Swing.

	Not Wired	Wired	Complete as shown No lamp
Rich Gilt	$2.25	$2.55	$3.45

Shade No. B 2986½ White Acid.

Number 1735

	Not Wired	Wired	Complete as shown No lamp
Rich Gilt	$1.60	$1.90	$2.80

Shade No. B 2986½ White Acid.

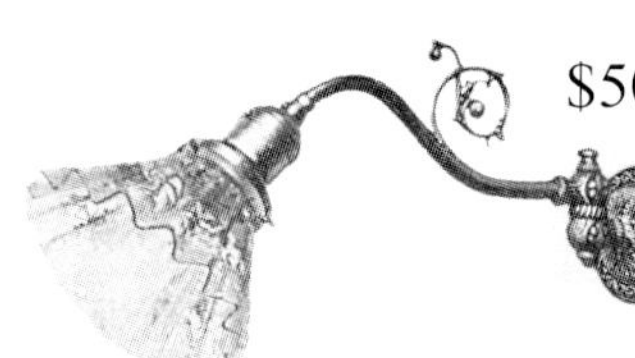

Number 1763
Single Swing.

	Not Wired	Wired	Complete as shown No lamp
Rich Gilt	$1.75	$2.05	$2.95

Shade No. B 2986½ White Acid.

Price in right hand column always includes sockets; also holders and shades if shown but no lamps.
Other prices include glassware, sockets, lamps or electric holders only where mentioned.

Number 1737

	Not Wired	Wired	Complete as shown No lamp
Rich Gilt	$1.00	$1.30	$2.20

Shade No. B 1319½ White Acid.

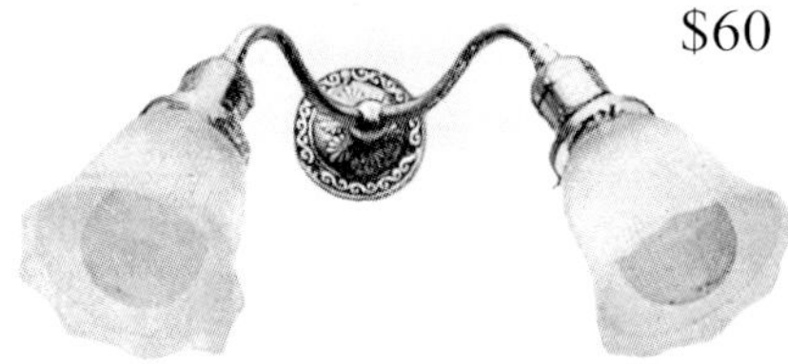

Number 1750

	Not Wired	Wired	Complete as shown No lamps
Polished Brass	$1.50	$2.10	$3.60

Shades No. B 33½ Crystal Prism.

Number 1732

	Not Wired	Wired	Complete as shown No lamp
Rich Gilt	$0.70	$0.80	$1.55

Shade No. B 33½ Crystal Prism.

Number 1749

	Not Wired	Wired	Complete as shown No lamp
Rich Gilt	$1.50	$1.80	$2.70

Shade No. B 1538½ White Acid.

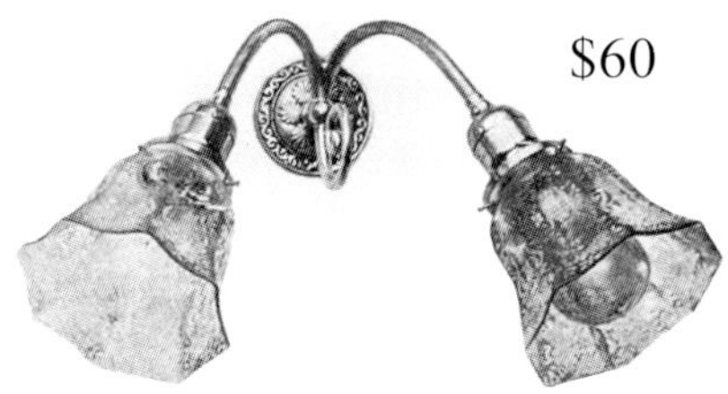

Number 1772

	Not Wired	Wired	Complete as shown No lamps
Polished Brass	$2.00	$2.75	$4.55

Shades No. B 1412½ White Acid.

Number 1744

	Not Wired	Wired	Complete as shown No lamp
Rich Gilt	$1.10	$1.40	$2.15

Shade No. B 33½ Crystal Prism.

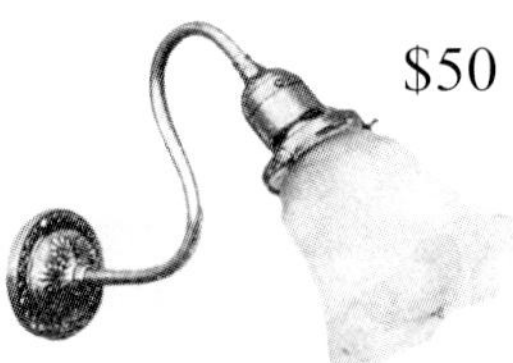

Number 1738

	Not Wired	Wired	Complete as shown No lamp
Rich Gilt	$0.85	$1.00	$1.75

Shade No. B 33½ Crystal Prism.

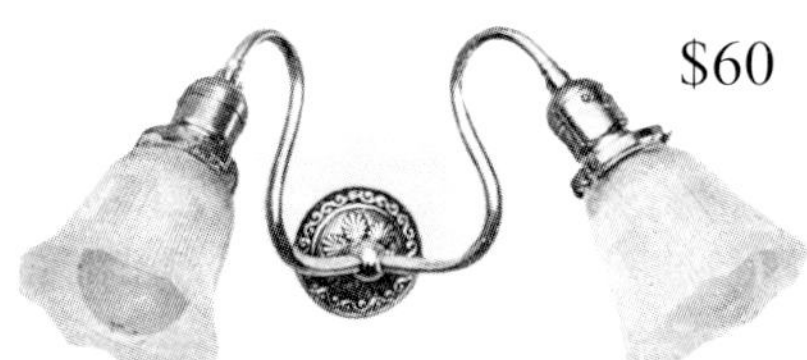

Number 1775

	Not Wired	Wired	Complete as shown No lamps
Polished Brass	$1.75	$2.50	$4.00

Shades No. B 33½ Crystal Prism.

Number 1731

	Not Wired	Wired	Complete as shown No lamp
Rich Gilt	$1.15	$1.25	$2.15

Shade No. B 1319½ White Acid.

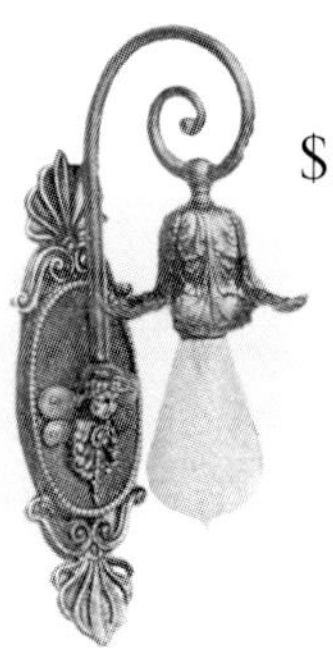

Number 1591
Socket Husk included.

	Not Wired	Wired	Complete as shown No lamp
Rich Gilt	$6.75	$7.25	$7.65

Number 1771

	Not Wired	Wired	Complete as shown No lamps
Rich Gilt	$4.50	$5.25	$7.75

Shades No. B 6568½ Etched.

Number 1740

	Not Wired	Wired	Complete as shown No lamp
Rich Gilt	$3.75	$4.05	$5.30

Shade No. B 6568½ Etched.

Price in right hand column always includes sockets; also holders and shades if shown, but no lamps.
Other prices include glassware, sockets, lamps or electric holders only where mentioned.

Number 2047

	Not Wired	Wired	Complete as shown No lamp
Rich Gilt	$1.25	$1.55	$2.80

Shade No. B 6568½ Etched.

Number 2036

	Not Wired	Wired	Complete as shown No lamp
Rich Gilt	$1.20	$1.50	$2.40

Shade No. B 1412½ White Acid.

Number 2053

	Not Wired	Wired	Complete as shown No lamp
Rich Gilt	$1.00	$1.30	$2.20

Shade No. B 1412½ White Acid.

Number 2040

	Not Wired	Wired	Complete as shown No lamp
Rich Gilt	$1.50	$1.80	$2.75

Shade No. B 539½ C. R. I.

Number 2051

	Not Wired	Wired	Complete as shown No lamp
Rich Gilt	$1.50	$1.80	$2.75

Shade No. B 539½ C. R. I.

Number 2076
Arm ½-inch Tube.

	Not Wired	Wired	Complete as shown No lamp
Rich Gilt	$2.50	$2.80	$3.70

Shade No. B 1412½ White Acid.

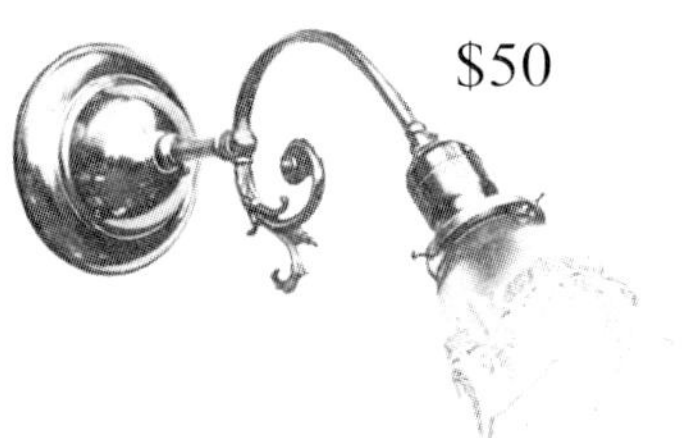

Number 2048

	Not Wired	Wired	Complete as shown No lamp
Rich Gilt	$1.40	$1.70	$2.95

Shade No. B 6568½ Etched.

Number 2038

	Not Wired	Wired	Complete as shown No lamp
Rich Gilt	$1.25	$1.55	$2.45

Shade No. B 1412½ White Acid.

Number 2037

	Not Wired	Wired	Complete as shown No lamp
Rich Gilt	$1.50	$1.80	$3.05

Shade No. B 6568½ Etched.

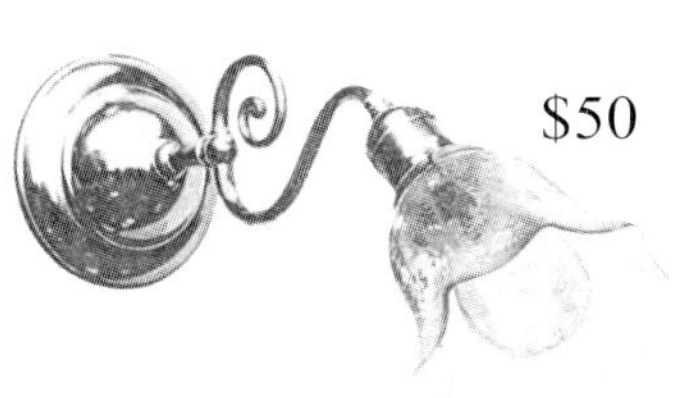

Number 2041

	Not Wired	Wired	Complete as shown No lamp
Rich Gilt	$1.25	$1.55	$2.45

Shade No. B 1412½ White Acid.

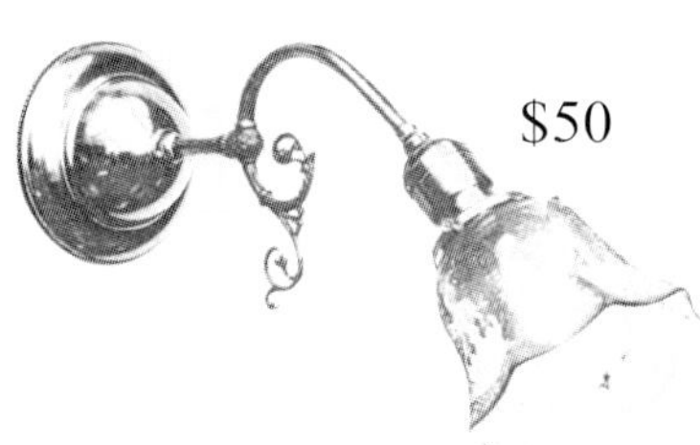

Number 2049

	Not Wired	Wired	Complete as shown No lamp
Rich Gilt	$1.20	$1.50	$2.40

Shade No. B 1412½ White Acid.

Number 2039

	Not Wired	Wired	Complete as shown No lamp
Rich Gilt	$1.25	$1.55	$2.45

Shade No. B 1906½ White Acid.

Price in right hand column always includes sockets; also holders and shades if shown, but no lamps.
Other prices include glassware, sockets, lamps or electric holders only where mentioned.

Number 1589
Socket Husk included.
Old Brass and Black

Not Wired	Wired	Complete as shown No lamp
$12.75	$13.25	$13.65

Number 1955
Brass Shade and Glass Bead Fringe included.
Brush Brass and Black.

Not Wired	Wired	Complete as shown No lamp
$6.25	$6.75	$7.45

Chain Pull Socket included in right hand column only.

Number 2045
Rich Gilt.

Not Wired	Wired	Complete as shown No lamp
$8.00	$8.50	$10.50

Shade No. G 439 Art Glass.
Select Glass Colors by Number.
See last page.

Number 1609
Socket Husk included.
Rich Gilt.

Not Wired	Wired	Complete as shown No lamp
$6.50	$7.00	$7.40

Number 2688
Candle, Miniature Socket and Lamp included.
Rich Gilt.

Not Wired	Wired	Complete as shown No lamp
$7.20	$7.70	$7.70

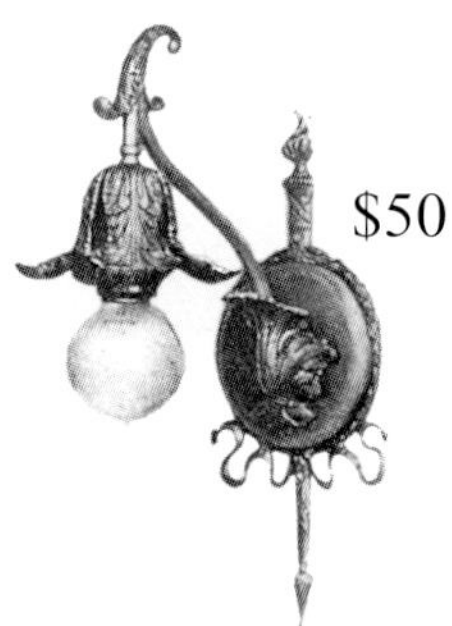

Number 1610
Socket Husk included.
Rich Gilt.

Not Wired	Wired	Complete as shown No lamp
$5.25	$5.75	$6.15

Number 1614
Socket Husks included.
Rich Gilt.

Not Wired	Wired	Complete as shown No lamps
$7.75	$8.75	$9.55

Number 2689
Candle, Miniature Socket and Lamp included.
Rich Gilt.

Not Wired	Wired	Complete as shown No lamp
$7.70	$8.20	$8.20

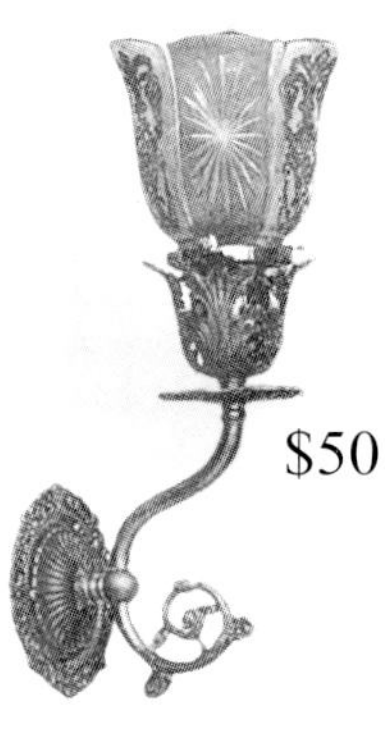

Number 1524
Socket Husk included.
Rich Gilt.

Not Wired	Wired	Complete as shown No lamp
$3.20	$3.50	$4.70

Shade No. B 602½ Etched and Imitation Cut.

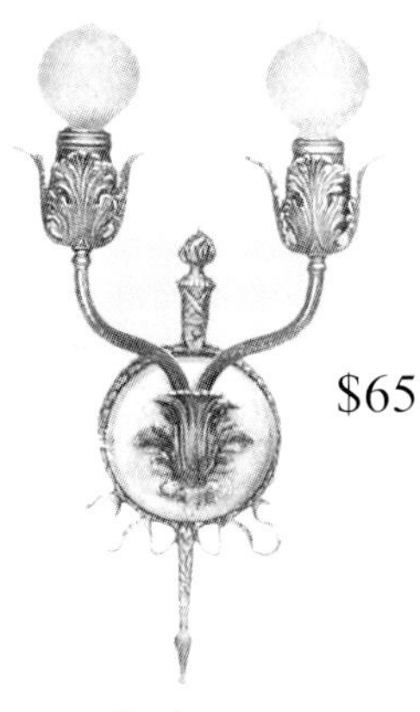

Number 1615
Socket Husks included.
1 Electric. Rich Gilt.

Not Wired	Wired	Complete as shown No lamps
$4.25	$4.75	$5.15
2 Electric. Rich Gilt.		
$5.50	$6.50	$7.30

Number 1526
Socket Husk included.
Rich Gilt.

Not Wired	Wired	Complete as shown No lamp
$6.50	$6.80	$7.20

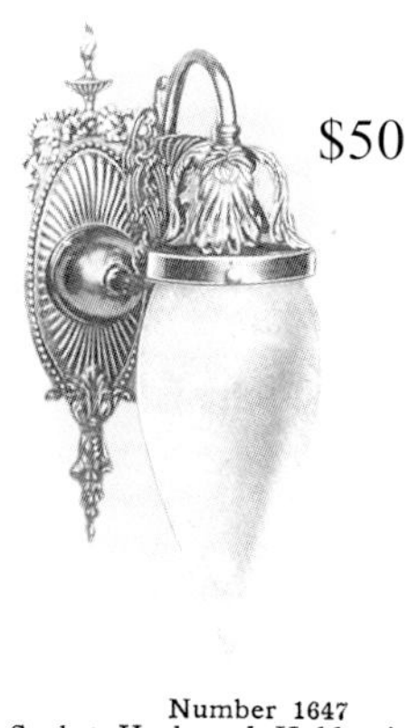

Number 1647
Socket Husk and Holder included.
1 Electric. Rich Gilt.

Not Wired	Wired	Complete as shown No lamps
$5.25	$5.55	$6.70
2 Electric. Rich Gilt.		
$7.25	$8.00	$10.30

No. B 6088 3¼x7-inch C. R. I. Stalactite.

If wanted with Chain Pull Sockets add 30 cents for each light to prices in right hand column.

Price in right hand column always includes sockets; also holders and shades if shown, but no lamps.
Other prices include glassware, sockets, lamps or electric holders only where mentioned.

$75

Number 2687
For Keyless Socket.
Rich Gilt.

Not Wired	Wired	Complete as shown No lamp
$16.50	$17.00	$18.00

3¼x6-inch C. R. I. Ball.

$50

Number 2644
Rich Gilt.

Not Wired	Wired	Complete as shown No lamp
$8.75	$9.25	$11.00

Shade No. B 3420 Alba.

$50

Number 1787
Candle, Miniature Socket and Lamp included.
Antique Brush Brass.

Not Wired	Wired	Complete as shown
$10.50	$11.00	$11.00

$50

Number 2704
3¼-inch Holder included.
Rich Gilt.

Not Wired	Wired	Complete as shown No lamp
$5.00	$5.50	$6.80

3¼x6-inch C. R. I. Ball.
Chain Pull Socket included in right hand column.

$100

Number 1596
Socket Husks included.
1 Electric. Old Brass.

Not Wired	Wired	Complete as shown No lamps
$15.50	$16.00	$16.40
2 Electric.	Old Brass.	
$17.50	$18.50	$19.30

$50

Number 2129
Rich Gilt.

Not Wired	Wired	Complete as shown No lamp
$3.00	$3.50	$4.45

Shade No. B 539½ C. R. I.

$50

Number 2705
3¼-inch Holder included.
Rich Gilt.

Not Wired	Wired	Complete as shown No lamp
$8.20	$8.70	$10.00

3¼x6-inch C. R. I. Ball.
Chain Pull Socket included in right hand column.

$50

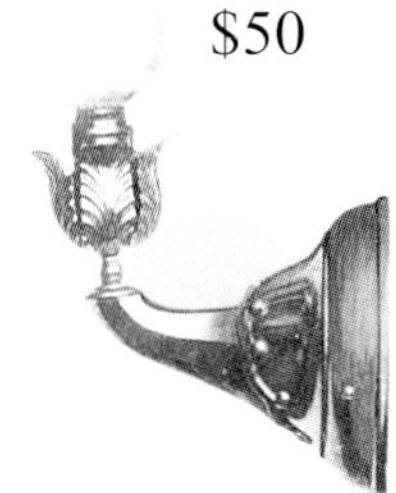

Number 1826
Socket Husk included.
Brush Brass and Black.

Not Wired	Wired	Complete as shown No lamp
$4.50	$5.00	$5.40

$60

Number 2393
4-inch Holder included.
Rich Gilt.

Not Wired	Wired	Complete as shown No lamp
$14.70	$15.20	$16.35

4x7-inch C. R. I. Ball.

$50

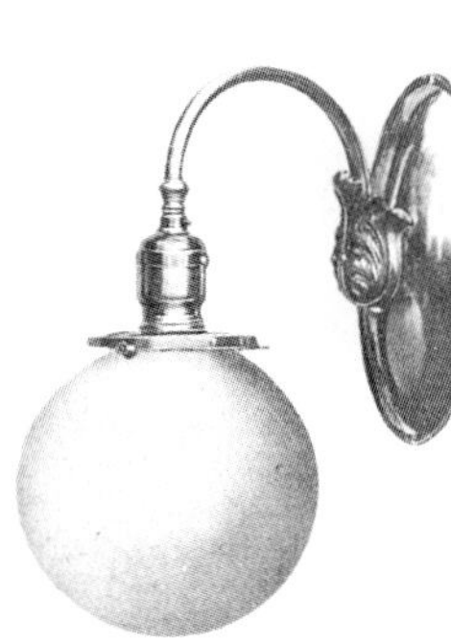

Number 2046
Rich Gilt.

Not Wired	Wired	Complete as shown No lamp
$4.70	$5.20	$6.40

3¼x6-inch C. R. I. Ball.

$50

Number 2044
Rich Gilt.

Not Wired	Wired	Complete as shown No lamp
$6.75	$7.25	$8.45

3¼x6-inch C. R. I. Ball.

$50

Number 2376
Brush Brass.

Not Wired	Wired	Complete as shown No lamp
$4.50	$5.00	$7.00

Holophane Shade No. 2 B.

If wanted with Chain Pull Sockets add 30 cents for each light to prices in right hand column.

Price in right hand column always includes sockets; also holders and shades if shown, but no lamps.
Other prices include glassware, sockets, lamps or electric holders only where mentioned.

$50

Number 2042

	Not Wired	Wired	Complete as shown No lamp
Rich Gilt	$1.40	$1.70	$2.60

Shade No. B 68½ C. R. I.

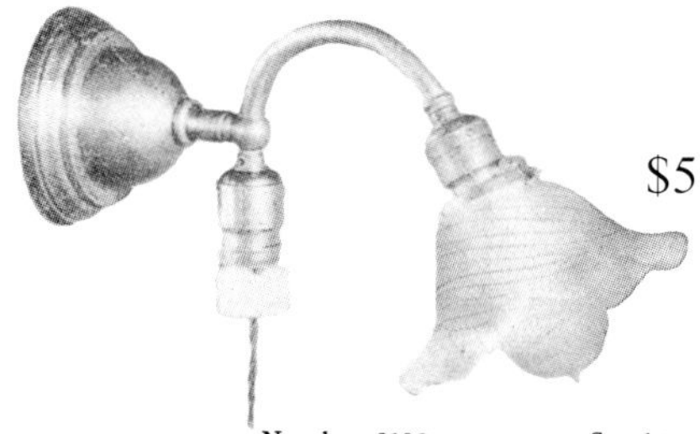

$50

Number 2198
Arm 7/16-inch Tube.

	Not Wired	Wired	Complete as shown No lamp
Rich Gilt	$1.75	$2.35	$4.00

Shade No. B 4920½ F. O. T.
Attachment Plug and Sockets included in right hand column only.

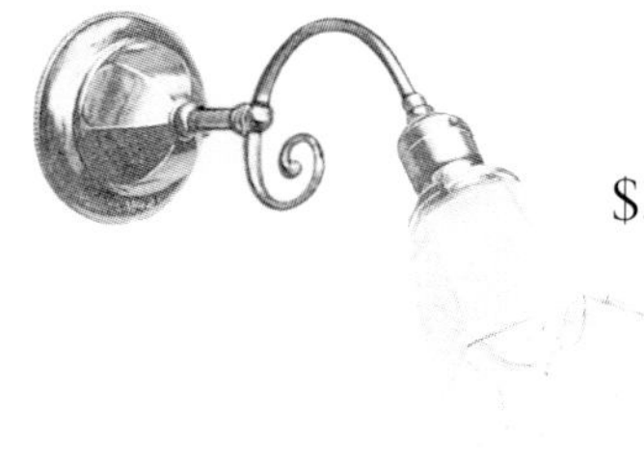

$50

Number 2064

	Not Wired	Wired	Complete as shown No lamp
Rich Gilt	$1.40	$1.70	$2.60

Shade No. B 68½ C. R. I.

$50

Number 2043

	Not Wired	Wired	Complete as shown No lamp
Rich Gilt	$1.35	$1.60	$2.50

Shade No. B 1906½ White Acid.

$75

Number 1606
Socket Husks and Holders included.

	Not Wired	Wired	Complete as shown No lamps
Rich Gilt	$13.00	$14.00	$16.00

3¼x6-inch C. R. I. Balls.

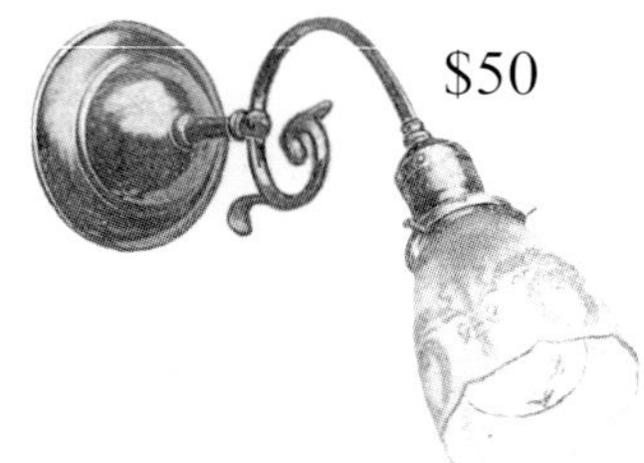

$50

Number 2056

	Not Wired	Wired	Complete as shown No lamp
Rich Gilt	$1.50	$1.80	$3.05

Shade No. B 6568½ Etched.

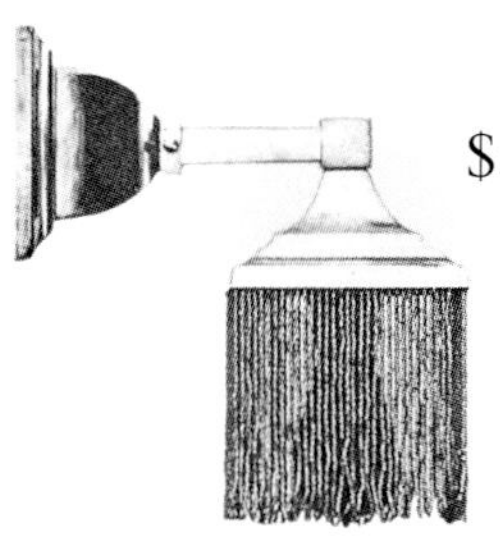

$50

Number 1786
Brass Shade and Glass Bead Fringe included.

	Not Wired	Wired	Complete as shown No lamp
Brush Brass	$5.45	$5.70	$6.40

Chain Pull Socket included in right hand column only.

$75

Number 1906
Socket Husks included.

	Not Wired	Wired	Complete as shown No lamps
Brush Brass and Black.	$10.00	$11.00	$11.80

$50

Number 2052
Arm 7/16-inch Tube.

	Not Wired	Wired	Complete as shown No lamp
Rich Gilt	$1.50	$1.80	$2.60

Shade No. 8983½ C. R. I.

$50

Number 2149
2¼-inch Socket Cover Holder included.
For Keyless Socket.

	Not Wired	Wired	Complete as shown No lamp
Brush Brass	$2.00	$2.25	$2.95

Shade No. B 8983½ C. R. I.

$50

Number 2310
3¼-inch Holder included.
For Keyless Socket.

	Not Wired	Wired	as shown Complete No lamp
Brush Brass	$5.50	$6.00	$7.45

3¼x7-inch C. R. I. Ball.

$50

Number 2406

	Not Wired	Wired	Complete as shown No lamp
Rich Gilt	$0.70	$0.85	$1.85

Shade No. B 249 C. R. I. Diameter, 6 inches.

If wanted with Chain Pull Sockets add 30 cents for each light to prices in right hand column.

Price in right hand column always includes sockets; also holders and shades if shown, but no lamps.
Other prices include glassware, sockets, lamps or electric holders only where mentioned.

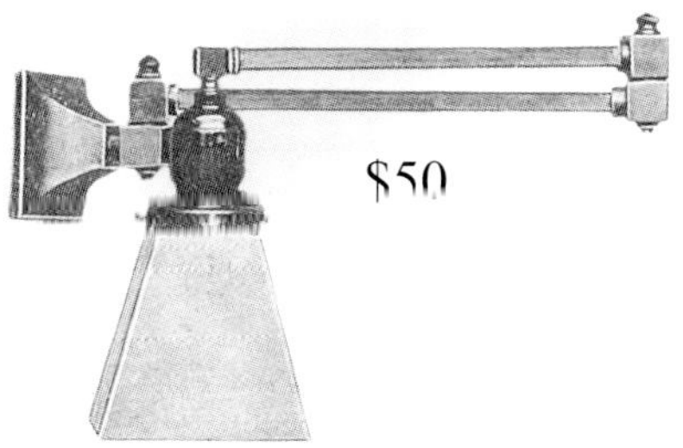

Number 1828
Double Swing.

	Not Wired	Wired	Complete as shown No lamp
Brush Brass	$3.00	$3.40	$4.40

Shade No. B 9547½ C. R. I.

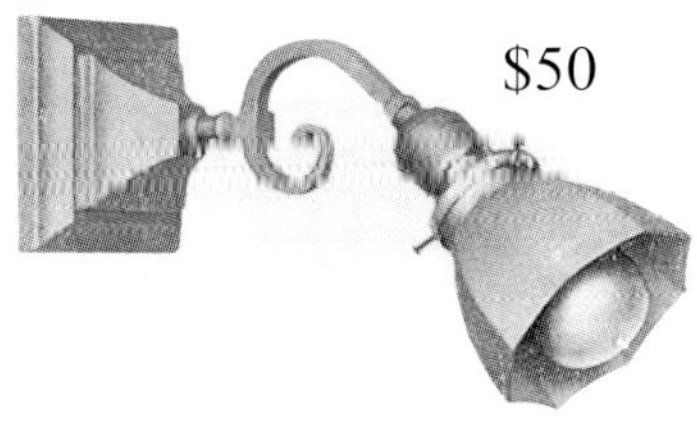

Number 2381

	Not Wired	Wired	Complete as shown No lamp
Brush Brass	$2.00	$2.30	$3.40

Shade No. B 4134½ C. R. I.

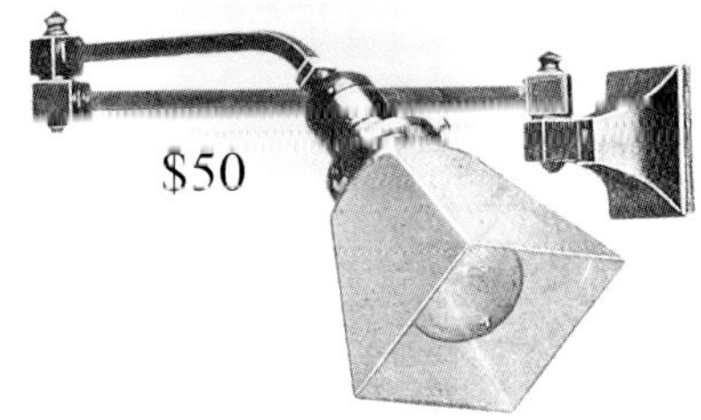

Number 1827
Double Swing.

	Not Wired	Wired	Complete as shown No lamp
Brush Brass	$3.00	$3.40	$4.40

Shade No. B 9547½ C. R. I.

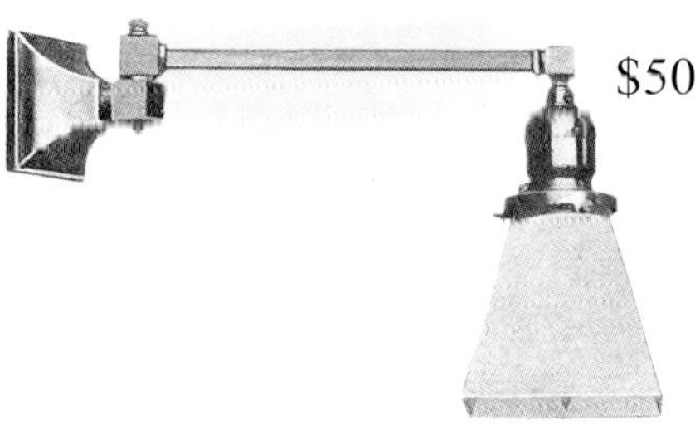

Number 1830
Single Swing.

	Not Wired	Wired	Complete as shown No lamp
Brush Brass	$1.70	$2.00	$3.00

Shade No. B 9547½ C. R. I.

Number 2055

	Not Wired	Wired	Complete as shown No lamp
Brush Brass	$4.00	$4.50	$6.50

Shade No. G 439 Art Glass.
Select Glass Colors by Number. See last page.

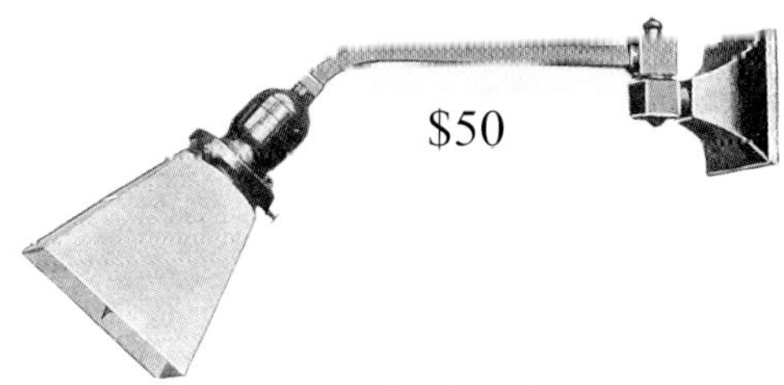

Number 1829
Single Swing.

	Not Wired	Wired	Complete as shown No lamp
Brush Brass	$1.70	$2.00	$3.00

Shade No. B 9547½ C. R. I.

Number 2383

	Not Wired	Wired	Complete as shown No lamp
Brush Brass	$1.50	$1.80	$2.90

Shade No. B 4134½ C. R. I.

Number 2060

	Not Wired	Wired	Complete as shown No lamp
Brush Brass	$1.75	$2.05	$3.05

Shade No. B 9547½ C. R. I.

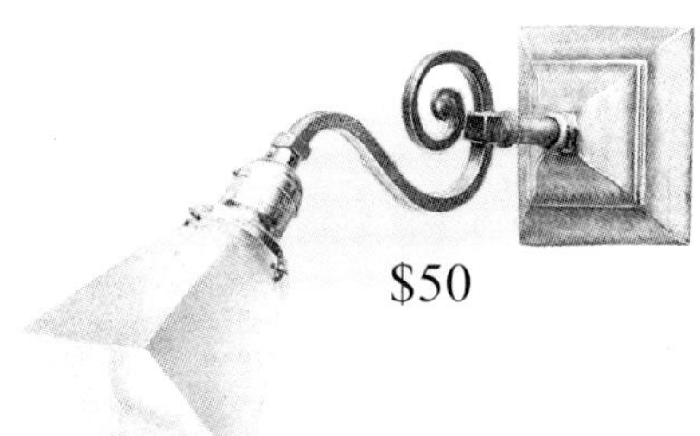

Number 1752

	Not Wired	Wired	Complete as shown No lamp
Brush Brass	$3.25	$3.55	$4.55

Shade No. B 9547½ C. R. I.

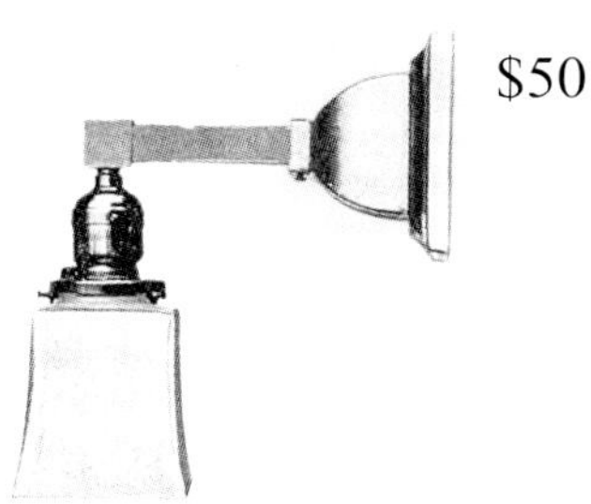

Number 1785

	Not Wired	Wired	Complete as shown No lamp
Brush Brass	$2.00	$2.25	$3.25

Shade No. B 9321½ C. R. I.

Number 2063

	Not Wired	Wired	Complete as shown No lamp
Brush Brass	$1.10	$1.35	$2.35

Shade No. B 9547½ C. R. I.

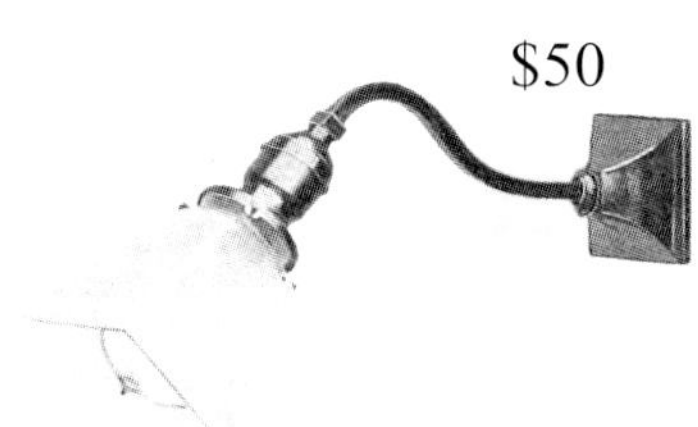

Number 2062

	Not Wired	Wired	Complete as shown No lamp
Brush Brass	$1.00	$1.25	$2.25

Shade No. B 9547½ C. R. I.

Price in right hand column always includes sockets; also holders and shades if shown, but no lamps.
Other prices include glassware, sockets, lamps or electric holders only where mentioned.

Number 2314
Art Glass included.
Select Glass Colors by Number. See last page.

	Not Wired	Wired	Complete as shown No lamp
Brush Brass	$13.25	$13.75	$14.45

Chain Pull Socket included in right hand column only.

Number 2182
No. G 415 Satin Finished Grapes included.

	Not Wired	Wired	Complete as shown No lamp
Verde Antique	$32.50	$33.00	$33.40

Number 2128

	Not Wired	Wired	Complete as shown No lamp
Antique Brush Brass...	$8.25	$8.75	$10.10

No. B 180 3¼x6-inch C. R. I. Square Ball.

Number 1800
Art Glass included.
Select Glass Colors by Number. See last page.

	Not Wired	Wired	Complete as shown No lamp
Brush Brass	$14.00	$14.50	$15.20

Chain Pull Socket included in right hand column only.

Number 2374

	Not Wired	Wired	Complete as shown No lamp
Brush Brass	$5.75	$6.25	$8.25

Holophane Shade No. 2 B.

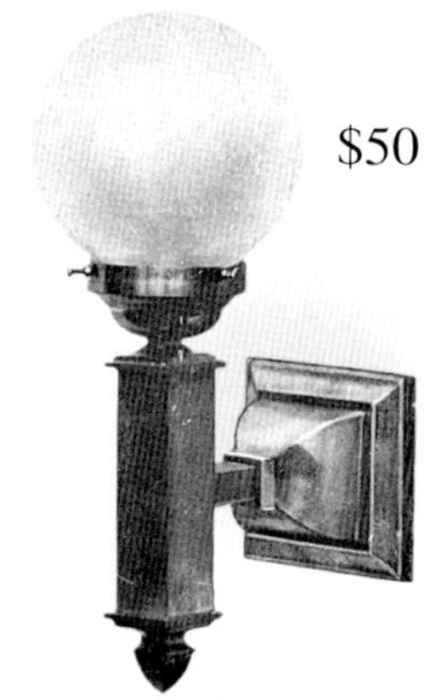

Number 2703
3¼-inch Holder included.

	Not Wired	Wired	Complete as shown No lamp
Brush Brass	$6.60	$7.10	$8.40

3¼x6-inch C. R. I. Ball.
Chain Pull Socket included in right hand column.

Number 2309

	Not Wired	Wired	Complete as shown No lamp
Brush Brass	$2.00	$2.25	$3.60

No. B 180 3¼x6-inch C. R. I. Square Ball.

Number 2377

	Not Wired	Wired	Complete as shown No lamp
Brush Brass	$2.00	$2.25	$4.25

Holophane Shade No. 2 B.

Number 2311

	Not Wired	Wired	Complete as shown No lamp
Brush Brass	$4.25	$4.75	$6.10

No. B 180 3¼x6-inch C. R. I. Square Ball.

If wanted with Chain Pull Sockets add 30 cents for each light to prices in right hand column.

Price in right hand column always includes sockets; also holders and shades if shown, but no lamps.
Other prices include glassware, sockets, lamps or electric holders only where mentioned.

$150

Number 2166
Art Glass included.
Select Glass Colors by Number. See last page.

	Not Wired	Wired	Complete as shown No lamp
Brush Brass	$16.25	$16.75	$17.45

Chain Pull Socket included in right hand column only.

$250

Number 2183
No. G 415 Satin Finished Grapes included.

	Not Wired	Wired	Complete as shown No lamp
Verde Antique	$49.00	$50.00	$50.80

$75

Number 2319
Art Glass included.
Select Glass Colors by Number. See last page.

	Not Wired	Wired	Complete as shown No lamp
Brush Brass	$11.75	$12.25	$12.95

Chain Pull Socket included in right hand column only.

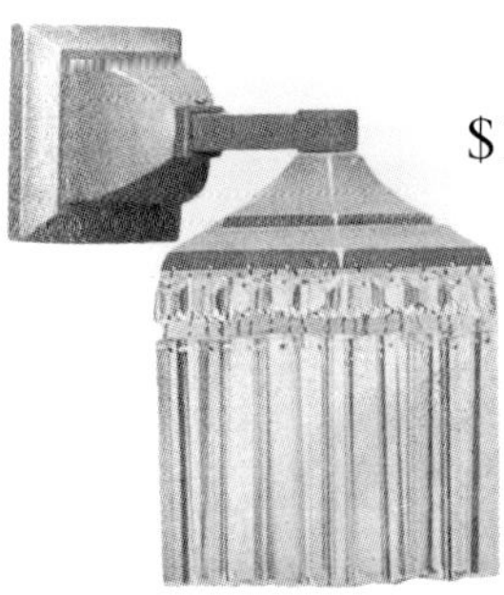

$100

Number 2315
Brass Shade and Colonial Prisms included.

	Not Wired	Wired	Complete as shown No lamp
Brush Brass	$6.75	$7.00	$7.70

Chain Pull Socket included in right hand column only.

$50

Number 2379

	Not Wired	Wired	Complete as shown No lamp
Brush Brass	$4.25	$4.75	$6.75

Holophane Shade No. 2 B.

$50

Number 2403

	Not Wired	Wired	Complete as shown No lamp
Brush Brass	$7.25	$7.75	$9.75

Holophane Shade No. 2 B. C.

$75

Number 1531
Socket Husk included.

	Not Wired	Wired	Complete as shown No lamp
Rich Gilt	$10.00	$10.50	$11.40

Shade No. B 4149 C. R. I.

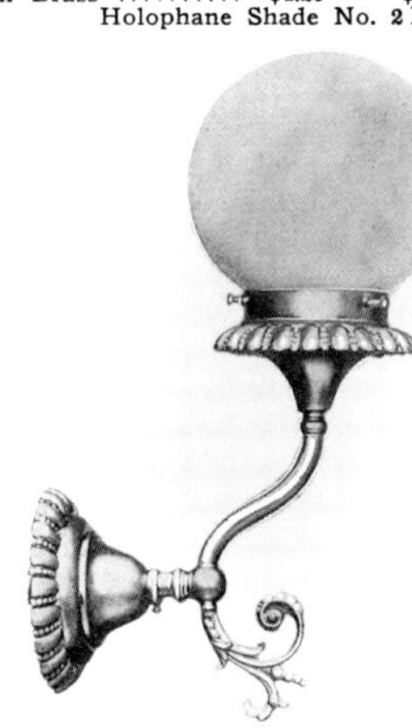

$75

Number 2702
3¼-inch Holder included.

	Not Wired	Wired	Complete as shown No lamp
Rich Gilt and Satin....	$6.00	$6.50	$7.80

3¼x6-inch C. R. I. Ball.
Chain Pull Socket included in right hand column.

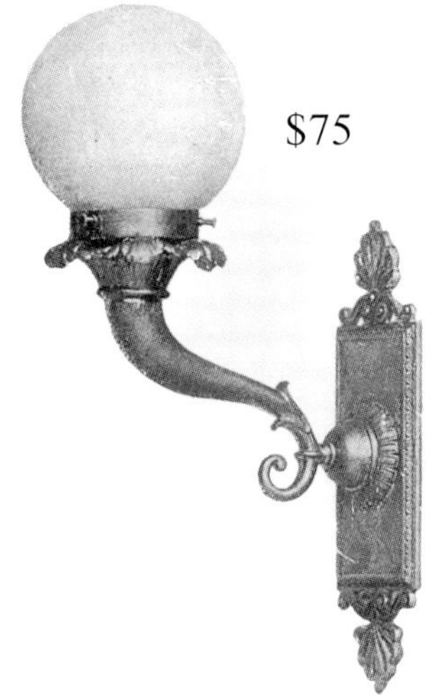

$75

Number 1529
3¼-inch Holder included.
For Keyless Socket.

	Not Wired	Wired	Complete as shown No lamp
Old Brass	$13.50	$14.00	$15.00

3¼x6-inch C. R. I. Ball.

If wanted with Chain Pull Sockets add 30 cents for each light to prices in right hand column.

Price in right hand column always includes sockets; also holders and shades if shown, but no lamps.
Other prices include glassware, sockets, lamps or electric holders only where mentioned.

Number 2404

	Not Wired	Wired	Complete as shown No lamps
Brush Brass	$2.30	$3.00	$5.00

Shades No. B 249 C. R. I. Diameter, 6 inches.

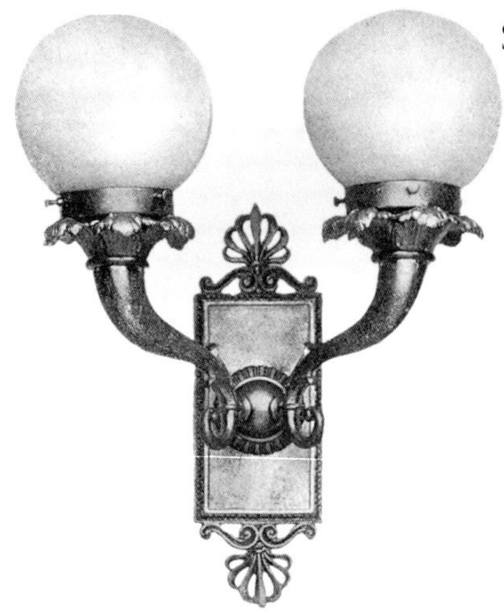

Number 1528
3¼-inch Holders included.
For Keyless Sockets.

	Not Wired	Wired	Complete as shown No lamps
Old Brass	$21.50	$22.50	$24.50

3¼x6-inch C. R. I. Balls.

Number 2127

	Not Wired	Wired	Complete as shown No lamps
Rich Gilt	$6.50	$7.50	$9.40

Shades No. B 539½ C. R. I.

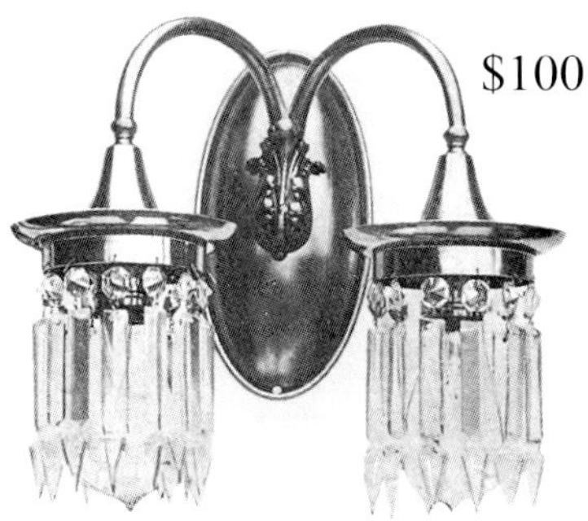

Number 1919
Prisms included.

	Not Wired	Wired	Complete as shown No lamps
Rich Gilt	$10.75	$11.75	$13.15

Chain Pull Sockets included in right hand column.

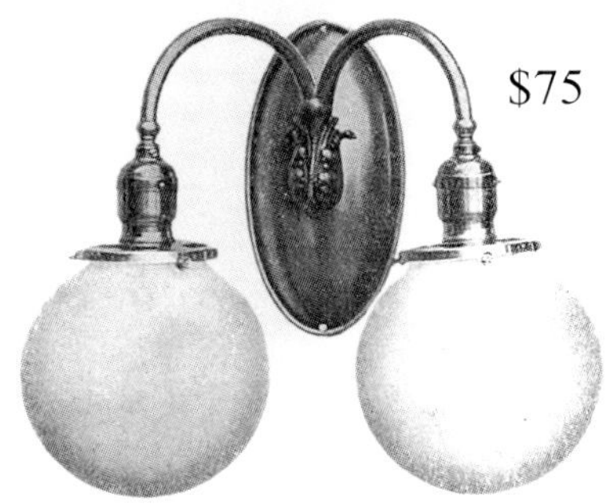

Number 2031

	Not Wired	Wired	Complete as shown No lamps
Rich Gilt	$5.40	$6.40	$8.80

3¼x6-inch C. R. I. Balls.

Number 2180
Colonial Cut Shade and Prisms included.

	Not Wired	Wired	Complete as shown No lamp
Rich Gilt	$15.00	$15.50	$16.20

Chain Pull Socket included in right hand column.

Number 2033

	Not Wired	Wired	Complete as shown No lamps
Rich Gilt	$2.50	$3.50	$5.40

Shades No. B 539½ C. R. I.

Number 1782

	Not Wired	Wired	Complete as shown No lamps
Brush Brass	$4.00	$5.00	$7.00

Shades No. B 9321½ C. R. I.

If wanted with Chain Pull Sockets add 30 cents for each light to prices in right hand column.

Price in right hand column always includes sockets; also holders and shades if shown, but no lamps.
Other prices include glassware, sockets, lamps or electric holders only where mentioned.

$200

Number 2698
Candles, Miniature Sockets and Lamps included.

	Not Wired	Wired	Complete as shown
Brush Brass and Black	$11.50	$13.00	$13.00

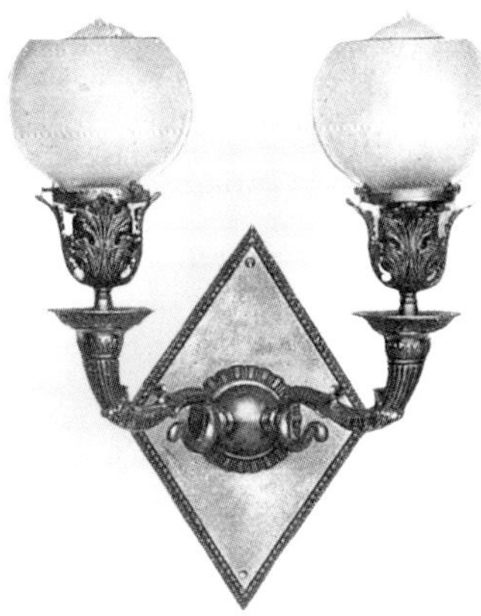

$150

Number 1530
Socket Husks included.

	Not Wired	Wired	Complete as shown No lamps
Rich Gilt	$15.25	$16.25	$18.05

Shades No. B 4149 C. R. I.

$100

Number 2035

	Not Wired	Wired	Complete as shown No lamps
Antique Brush Brass...	$5.75	$6.75	$10.75

Shades No. G 439 Art Glass.
Select Glass Colors by Number. See last page.

$200

Number 2701
Length, 24 inches (over all). Spread, 11 inches.
Candles and Special Sockets included.

	Not Wired	Wired	Complete as shown No lamps
Rich Gilt and Satin....	$35.00	$36.50	$36.50

$150

Number 1920
Colonial Cut Shades and 4-inch Prisms included.

	Not Wired	Wired	Complete as shown No lamps
Rich Gilt	$22.75	$23.75	$25.15

Chain Pull Sockets included in right hand column only.

$200

Number 2699
Candles, Miniature Sockets and Lamps included.

	Not Wired	Wired	Complete as shown
Rich Gilt and Satin....	$25.15	$26.65	$26.65

$200

Number 1678
Socket Husks included.

	Not Wired	Wired	Complete as shown No lamps
Antique Brush Brass...	$17.25	$18.25	$19.05

$250

Number 2700
Socket Husks included.

	Not Wired	Wired	Complete as shown No lamps
Rich Gilt and Satin....	$20.00	$21.50	$22.70

Price in right hand column always includes sockets; also holders and shades if shown but no lamps.
Other prices include glassware, sockets, lamps or electric holders only where mentioned.

$150

Number 2126

		Not Wired	Wired	Complete as shown No lamps
2 Electric	Antique Brush Brass.......	$11.50	$12.50	$15.20

No. B 180 3¼x6-inch C. R. I. Square Balls.

$150

Number 2030

		Not Wired	Wired	Complete as shown No lamps
2 Electric	Rich Gilt	$11.25	$12.25	$14.05

Shades No. B 68½ C. R. I.

$150

Number 2075

		Not Wired	Wired	Complete as shown No lamps
2 Electric	Polished Brass	$8.50	$9.50	$11.30
3 "	" "	10.75	12.25	14.95

Shades No. B 1412½ White Acid.

$150

Number 2034

		Not Wired	Wired	Complete as shown No lamps
3 Electric	Rich Gilt	$11.25	$12.75	$15.45

Shades No. B 68½ C. R. I.

$150

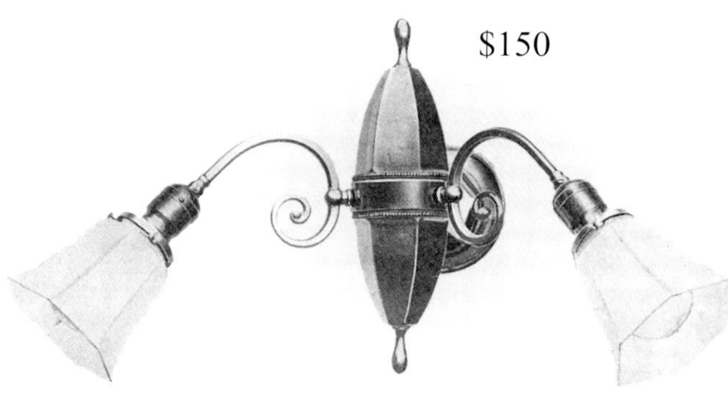

Number 2069

		Not Wired	Wired	Complete as shown No lamps
2 Electric	Rich Gilt	$4.75	$5.75	$7.55
3 "	" "	5.75	7.25	9.95

Shades No. B 68½ C. R. I.

$200

Number 2026

		Not Wired	Wired	Complete as shown No lamps
3 Electric	Rich Gilt	$5.50	$7.00	$9.70

Shades No. B 68½ C. R. I.

Price in right hand column always includes sockets; also holders and shades if shown but no lamps.
Other prices include glassware, sockets, lamps or electric holders only where mentioned.

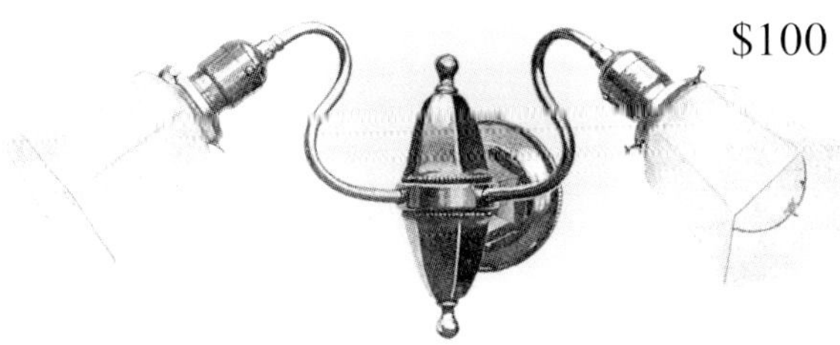

Number 2070

		Not Wired	Wired	Complete as shown No lamps
2 Electric	Rich Gilt	$3.00	$4.00	$5.80
3 "	" "	3.50	5.00	7.70

Shades No. B 68½ C. R. I.

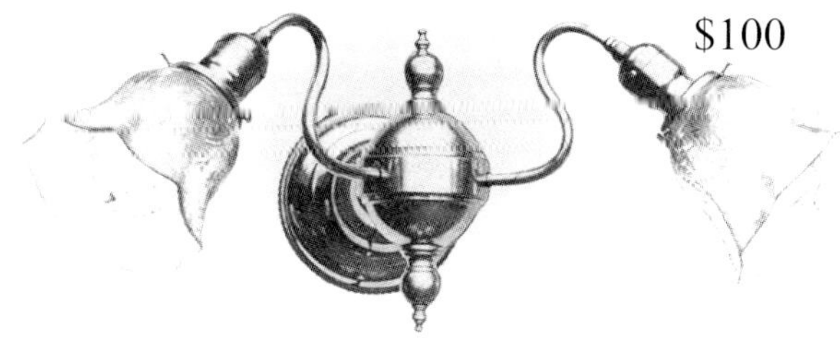

Number 2024

		Not Wired	Wired	Complete as shown No lamps
2 Electric	Polished Brass	$3.25	$4.25	$6.05
3 "	" "	3.75	5.25	7.95

Shades No. B 1412½ White Acid.

Number 2019

		Not Wired	Wired	Complete as shown No lamps
2 Electric	Polished Brass	$4.50	$5.50	$7.90
3 "	" "	5.25	6.75	10.35

3¼x6-inch C. R. I. Balls.

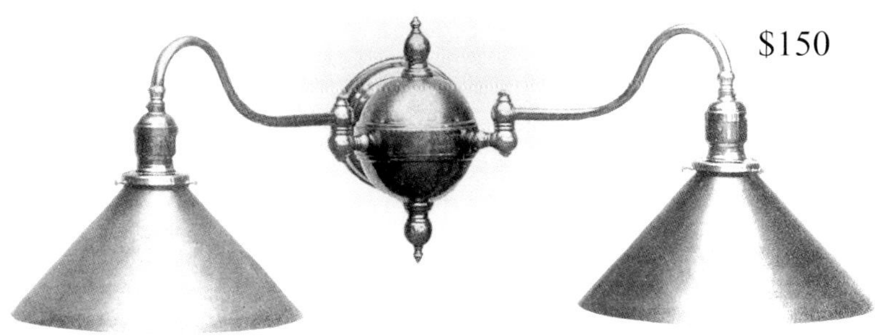

Number 2078

		Not Wired	Wired	Complete as shown No lamps
2 Electric	Polished Brass	$5.00	$6.00	$9.20

Shades No. B 999 Green Glass, White Inside. Diameter, 10 inches.

Number 2021

		Not Wired	Wired	Complete as shown No lamps
2 Electric	Polished Brass	$4.25	$5.25	$6.85
3 "	" "	5.00	6.50	8.90

Shades No. B 8983½ C. R. I.

Number 1802

		Not Wired	Wired	Complete as shown No lamps
2 Electric	Polished Brass	$4.00	$5.00	$6.50
3 "	" "	4.50	6.00	8.25
4 "	" "	5.00	7.00	10.00

Shades No. B 41½ Crystal.

Price in right hand column always includes sockets; also holders and shades if shown but no lamps.
Other prices include glassware, sockets, lamps or electric holders only where mentioned.

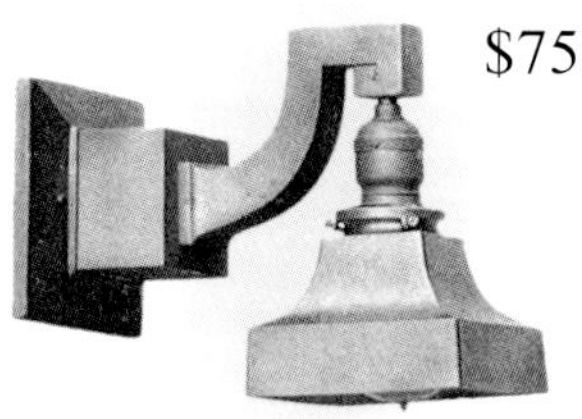

Number 2596

	Not Wired	Wired	Complete as shown No lamp
Brush Brass	$6.75	$7.25	$8.40

Shade No. B 4780½ C. R. I.

Number 2604
Socket Husks included.

	Not Wired	Wired	Complete as shown No lamps
Brush Brass	$23.00	$24.50	$25.70

Number 2597
3¼-inch Holder included.
For Keyless Socket.

	Not Wired	Wired	Complete as shown No lamp
Brush Brass and Black.	$11.75	$12.25	$15.65

No. B 397 3¼x6-inch Colonial Cut Ball.

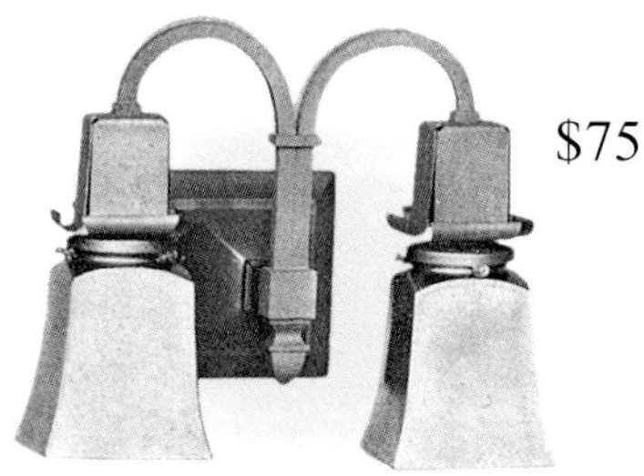

Number 2600
Socket Husks included.

	Not Wired	Wired	Complete as shown No lamps
Brush Brass	$6.00	$7.00	$9.00

Shades No. B 9321½ C. R. I.

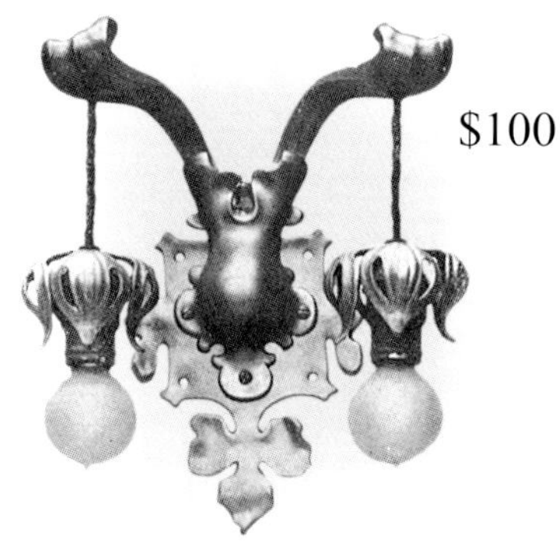

Number 2641
Cast Socket Husks included.

	Not Wired	Wired	Complete as shown No lamps
Brush Brass	$17.00	$18.00	$18.80

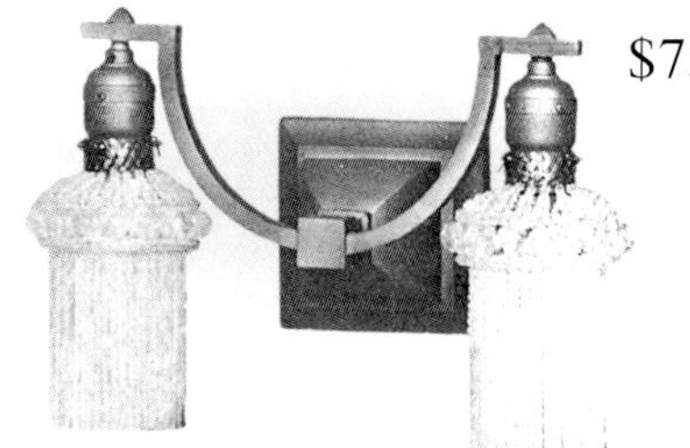

Number 2601

	Not Wired	Wired	Complete as shown No lamps
Brush Brass	$5.25	$6.25	$13.65

Shades No. B 1226½ Crystal Bead.

Number 2602

	Not Wired	Wired	Complete as shown No lamps
Brush Brass	$4.50	$5.10	$8.60

Shades No. B 3420 Alba.

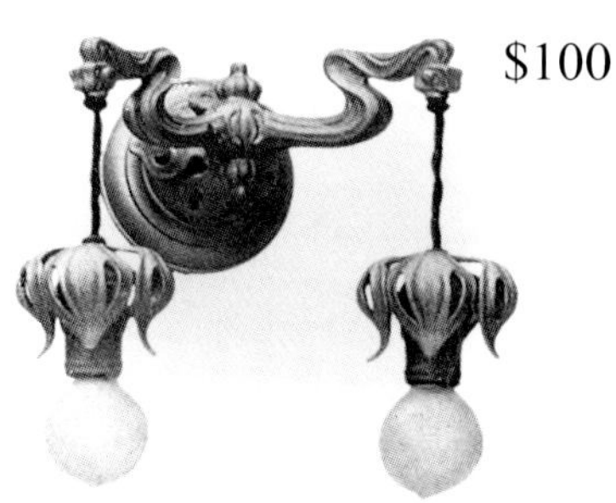

Number 2666
Cast Socket Husks included.

	Not Wired	Wired	Complete as shown No lamps
Brush Brass	$12.00	$13.00	$13.80

Number 2603
2¼-inch Socket Cover Holders included.
For Keyless Sockets.

	Not Wired	Wired	Complete as shown No lamps
Brush Brass	$3.75	$4.55	$11.85

Shades No. B 672 Amber Lustre.

Price in right hand column always includes sockets; also holders and shades if shown but no lamps.
Other prices include glassware, sockets, lamps or electric holders only where mentioned.

$50

Number 2577

	Not Wired	Wired	Complete as shown No lamp
Brush Brass	$1.50	$1.80	$2.85

Shade No. B 5014½ C. R. I.

$50

Number 2607

	Not Wired	Wired	Complete as shown No lamp
Brush Brass	$2.00	$2.30	$4.05

Shade No. B 3420 Alba.

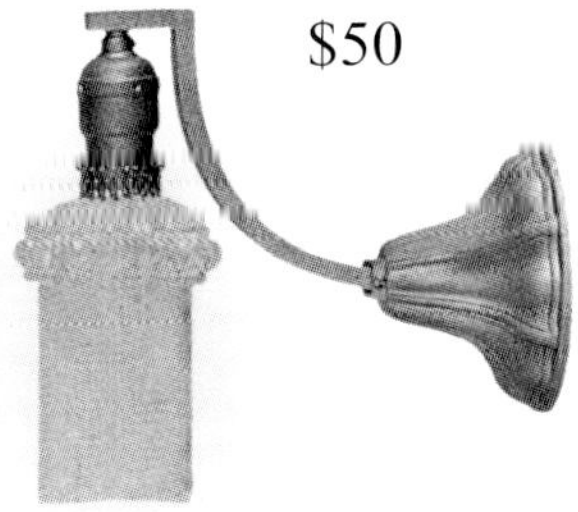

$50

Number 2582

	Not Wired	Wired	Complete as shown No lamp
Brush Brass	$2.75	$3.25	$6.95

Shade No. B 1226½ Crystal Bead.

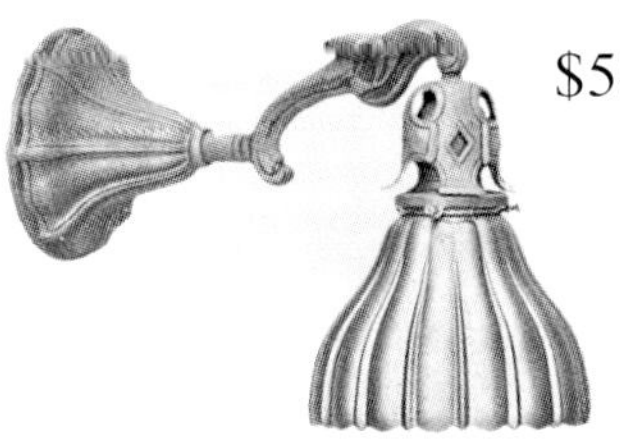

$50

Number 2606
Cast Socket Husk included.

	Not Wired	Wired	Complete as shown No lamp
Brush Brass and Black.	$5.75	$6.25	$8.00

Shade No. B 3420 Alba

$150

Number 2559
Candles, Miniature Sockets and Lamps included.

	Not Wired	Wired	Complete as shown
Brush Brass and Black.	$20.10	$21.10	$21.10

$50

Number 2561

	Not Wired	Wired	Complete as shown No lamp
Brush Brass and Black.	$4.50	$4.80	$5.85

Shade No. B 5014½ C. R. I.

$50

Number 2558

	Not Wired	Wired	Complete as shown No lamp
Brush Brass	$1.90	$2.20	$3.25

Shade No. B 5014½ C. R. I.

$50

Number 2557

	Not Wired	Wired	Complete as shown No lamp
Brush Brass	$8.25	$8.75	$9.75

Shade No. B 539½ C. R. I.

$50

Number 2560

	Not Wired	Wired	Complete as shown No lamp
Brush Brass	$1.85	$2.15	$3.20

Shade No. B 5014½ C. R. I.

Price in right hand column always includes sockets; also holders and shades if shown but no lamps.
Other prices include glassware, sockets, lamps or electric holders only where mentioned.

$300

Number 2029
Socket Husk and 3¼-inch Holder included.
Brush Brass and Black.

	Not Wired	Wired	Complete as shown No lamp
1 Electric	$15.75	$16.25	$17.55

Chain Pull Socket included in right hand column only.

$250

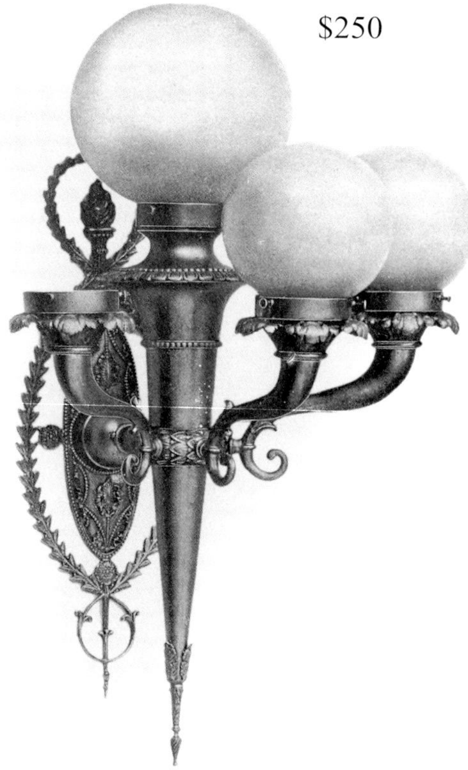

Number 1590
Length, 29 inches (over all).
3¼-inch Holders included.
Rich Gilt.

	Not Wired	Wired	Complete as shown No lamps
1 Electric	$26.50	$27.00	$28.30
3 "	42.50	44.00	47.30
4 "	50.50	52.50	56.80

3¼x8-inch C. R. I. Ball on center light.
3¼x6-inch " " side "

$100

Number 2706
3¼-inch Holder included.
Rich Gilt

	Not Wired	Wired	Complete as shown No lamp
1 Electric	$10.00	$10.50	$11.80

3¼x6-inch C. R. I. Ball.
Chain Pull Sockets included in right hand column only.

$300

Number 1909
Extends 7 inches.
3¼x6-inch C. R. I. Ball included.
Brush Brass and Black.

	Not Wired	Wired	Complete as shown No lamp
1 Electric	$26.00	$26.50	$27.10

$200

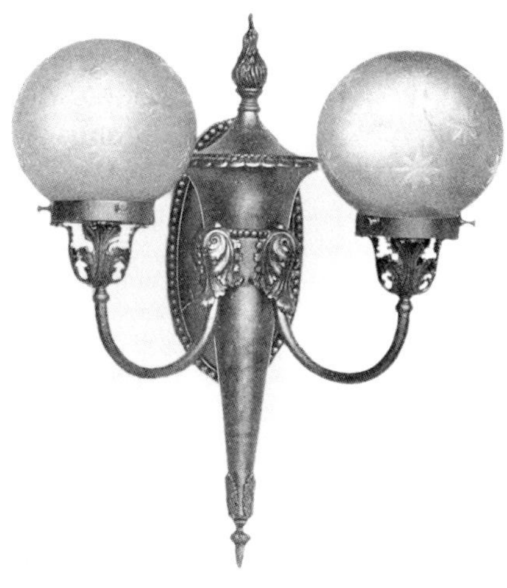

Number 1599
Length, 21 inches (over all).
Socket Husks and 3¼-inch Holders included.
Rich Gilt and Satin.

	Not Wired	Wired	Complete as shown No lamps
2 Electric	$19.50	$20.50	$24.30

No. B 5121 3¼x6-inch Ground and Cut Star Balls.

$300

Number 1904
Extends 7 inches.
Art Glass included.
Select Glass Colors by Number. See last page.
Brush Brass and Black.

	Not Wired	Wired	Complete as shown No lamp
1 Electric	$34.00	$34.50	$35.20

Chain Pull Socket included in right hand column only.

$75

Number 1661
3¼x6-inch C. R. I. Ball and Holder included.
For Keyless Socket.
Polished Brass and Black.

	Not Wired	Wired	Complete as shown No lamp
1 Electric	$15.25	$15.75	$16.15

$200

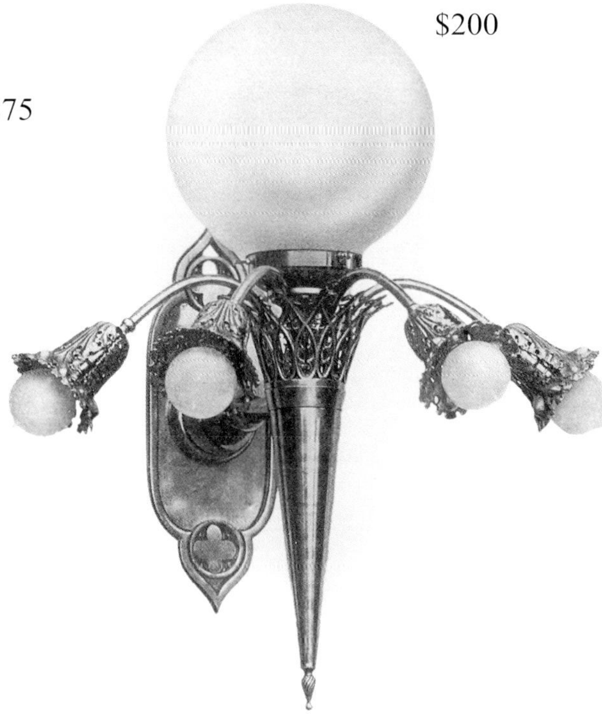

Number 2032
Length, 26 inches (over all).
Socket Husks and 4-inch Holder included.
Polished Brass and Black.

	Not Wired	Wired	Complete as shown No lamps
4 Electric	$28.25	$30.25	$33.65
5 "	32.00	34.50	38.30

4x10-inch C. R. I. Ball.

$75

Number 1751
Art Glass Shade and Socket Husk included.
Select Glass Colors by Number. See last page.
Brush Brass and Black.

	Not Wired	Wired	Complete as shown No lamps
2 Electric	$24.40	$25.40	$26.80

Chain Pull Sockets included in right hand column.

$100

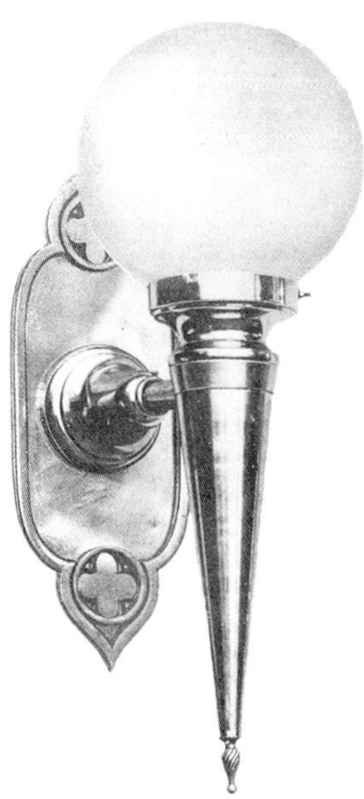

Number 2028
4-inch Holder included.
For Keyless Socket.
Polished Brass and Black.

	Not Wired	Wired	Complete as shown No lamp
1 Electric	$11.50	$12.00	$13.30

4x8-inch C. R. I. Ball.

$200

Number 1642
Length, 23 inches (over all).
Socket Husks and 3¼-inch Holders included.
Rich Gilt and Satin.

	Not Wired	Wired	Complete as shown No lamps
1 Electric	$21.00	$21.50	$22.80
3 "	29.00	30.50	34.40

3¼x8-inch C. R. I. Ball.
3¼x7-inch " Stalactites

$50

Number 1701
Socket Husks included.
Polished Brass and Black.

	Not Wired	Wired	Complete as shown No lamp
1 Electric	$7.50	$8.00	$8.90

Shade No. B4149 C. R. I.

$75

Number 2327
Spread, 14 inches.
3¼-inch Holders included.
For Keyless Sockets.

		Not Wired	Wired	Complete as shown No lamps
2 Electric	Brush Brass and Black	$17.00	$18.00	$20.00
3 "	" " " "	21.25	22.75	25.75

3¼x6-inch C. R. I. Balls.

$75

Number 2020
Spread, 15 inches.

		Not Wired	Wired	Complete as shown No lamps
2 Electric	Rich Gilt	$15.50	$16.50	$19.20
3 "	" "	21.50	23.00	27.05

3¼x6-inch C. R. I. Balls.

$75

Number 2631
Spread, 10½ inches.
3¼-inch Holders included.
For Keyless Sockets.

Brush Brass and Black.	Not Wired	Wired	Complete as shown No lamps
2 Electric	$58.00	$59.00	$62.80

No. B 5121 3¼x6-inch Ground and Cut Star Balls.

$60

$100

Number 2605
Spread, 11 inches.
3¼-inch Holders included.
For Keyless Sockets

Brush Brass and Black.	Not Wired	Wired	Complete as shown No lamps
3 Electric	$33.00	$34.50	$44.70

No. B 397 3¼x6-inch Colonial Cut Balls.

Number 2632
3¼-inch Holder included.
For Keyless Socket.

Brush Brass and Black.	Not Wired	Wired	Complete as shown No lamps
1 Electric	$30.00	$30.50	$32.40

No. B 5121 3¼x6-inch Ground and Cut Star Ball.

$75

Number 2599
Spread, 12 inches.

		Not Wired	Wired	Complete as shown No lamps
2 Electric	Brush Brass	$12.50	$13.50	$15.30

2¼x7-inch C. R. I. Domes.

$75

Number 2598
Spread, 11 inches.
3¼-inch Holders included.
For Keyless Sockets.

		Not Wired	Wired	Complete as shown No lamps
2 Electric	Brush Brass and Black	$24.75	$25.75	$32.55

No. B 397 3¼x6-inch Colonial Cut Balls.

Price in right hand column always includes sockets; also holders and shades if shown but no lamps.
Other prices include glassware, sockets, lamps or electric holders only where mentioned.

Number 2586
4x8-inch C. R. I. Ball included.

Black Iron only.	Not Wired	Wired	Complete as shown No lamp
1 Electric	$9.65	$10.15	$11.05

Number 2112
Art Glass Lantern included.
Select Glass Colors by Number. See last page.

Black Iron only.	Not Wired	Wired	Complete as shown No lamp
1 Electric	$10.00	$10.50	$11.20

Chain Pull Socket included in right hand column only.

Number 2325
Length, 30 inches (over all).
Extends, 14 inches (over all).
4x10-inch C. R. I. Ball included.

Black Iron only.	Not Wired	Wired	Complete as shown No lamp
1 Electric	$22.80	$23 30	$23.70

Number 1907
4x10-inch C. R. I. Ball and Holder included.

Black Iron only.	Not Wired	Wired	Complete as shown No lamp
1 Electric	$4.00	$4.30	$4.70

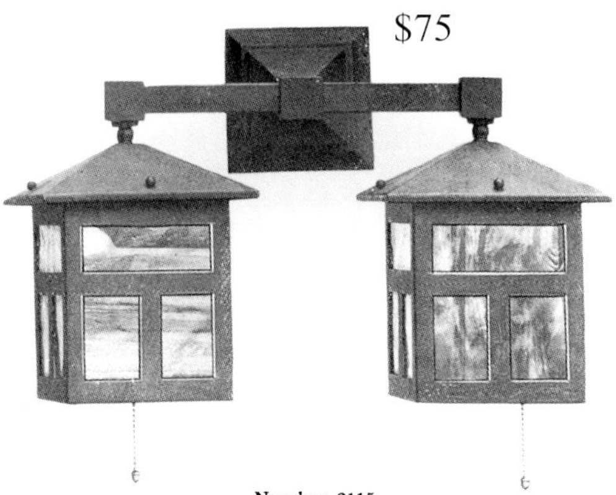

Number 2115
Spread, 10½ inches.
Art Glass Lanterns included.
Select Glass Colors by Number. See last page.

Black Iron only.	Not Wired	Wired	Complete as shown No lamps
2 Electric	$16.50	$17.50	$18.90

Chain Pull Sockets included in right hand column only.

Price in right hand column always includes sockets; also holders and shades if shown but no lamps.
Other prices include glassware, sockets, lamps or electric holders only where mentioned.

$100

Number 1593
8x5½x3 Beveled Glass included.

Black Iron only.	Not Wired	Wired	Complete as shown No lamp
1 Electric	$14.50	$15.00	$15.40

$100

Number 1440
6x12-inch C. R. I. Ball included.

Black Iron only.	Not Wired	Wired	Complete as shown No lamps
3 Electric	$45.00	$46.50	$47.70

$100

Number 2334
Length, 29 inches (over all).
Extends 17 inches (over all).
Crackeled Glass included.

Black Iron only.	Not Wired	Wired	Complete as shown No lamp
1 Electric	$26.00	$26.60	$27.00

$100

Number 1592
6x7½ Beveled Glass included.

Black Iron only.	Not Wired	Wired	Complete as shown No lamp
1 Electric	$14.50	$15.00	$15.40

$100

Number 1595
6x7 F. O. T. Cylinder included.

Black Iron only.	Not Wired	Wired	Complete as shown No lamp
1 Electric	$11.00	$11.50	$11.90

Price in right hand column always includes sockets; also holders and shades if shown but no lamps.
Other prices include glassware, sockets, lamps or electric holders only where mentioned.

$75

Number 2585
4x8 inch C. R. I. Ball included

Black Iron only.	Not Wired	Wired	Complete as shown No lamp
1 Electric	$11.50	$12.00	$12.90

$100

Number 2589
Length, 42 inches (over all).
Extends 21 inches (over all).
Crystal Roughed Glass included.

Black Iron only.	Not Wired	Wired	Complete as shown No lamps
2 Electric	$66.00	$67.00	$68.80

$75

Number 2593
4x10-inch C. R. I. Ball included.

Black Iron only.	Not Wired	Wired	Complete as shown No lamp
1 Electric	$19.30	$19.80	$20.70

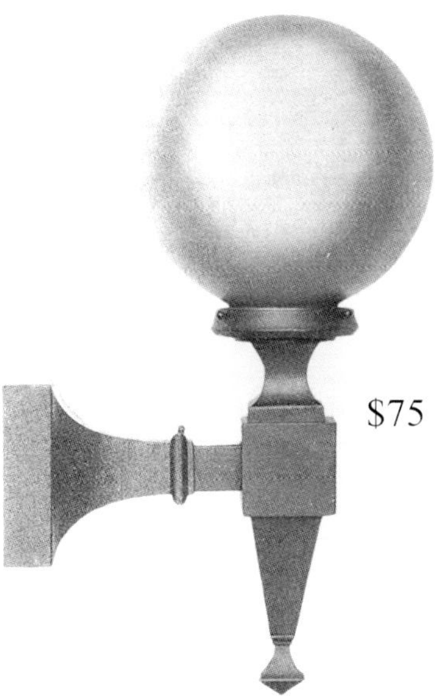

$75

Number 2588
4x10-inch C. R. I. Ball included.

Black Iron only.	Not Wired	Wired	Complete as shown No lamp
1 Electric	$15.80	$16.30	$17.20

$75

Number 2587
6x12-inch C. R. I. Ball included.

Black Iron only.	Not Wired	Wired	Complete as shown No lamp
1 Electric	$25.45	$25.95	$26.85

Price in right hand column always includes sockets; also holders and shades if shown but no lamps.
Other prices include glassware, sockets, lamps or electric holders only where mentioned.

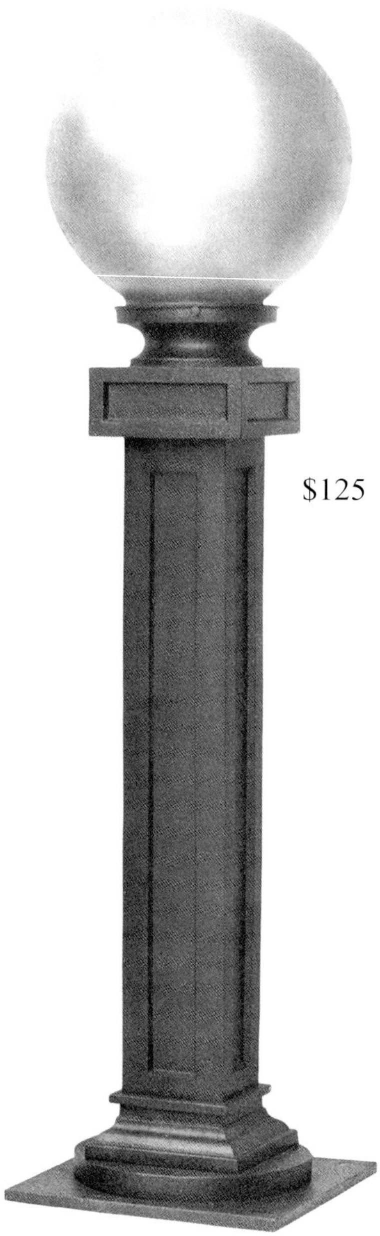

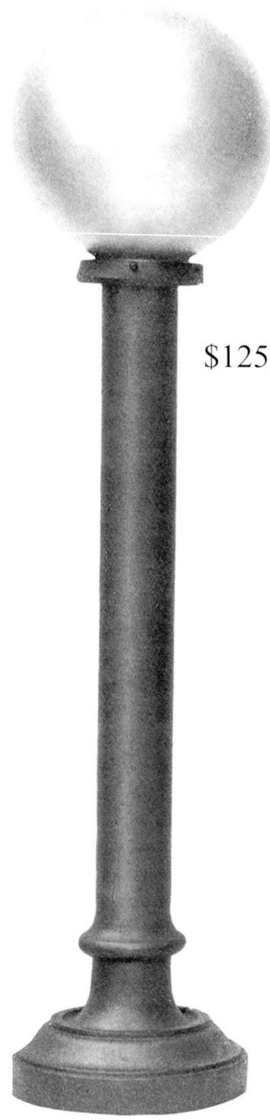

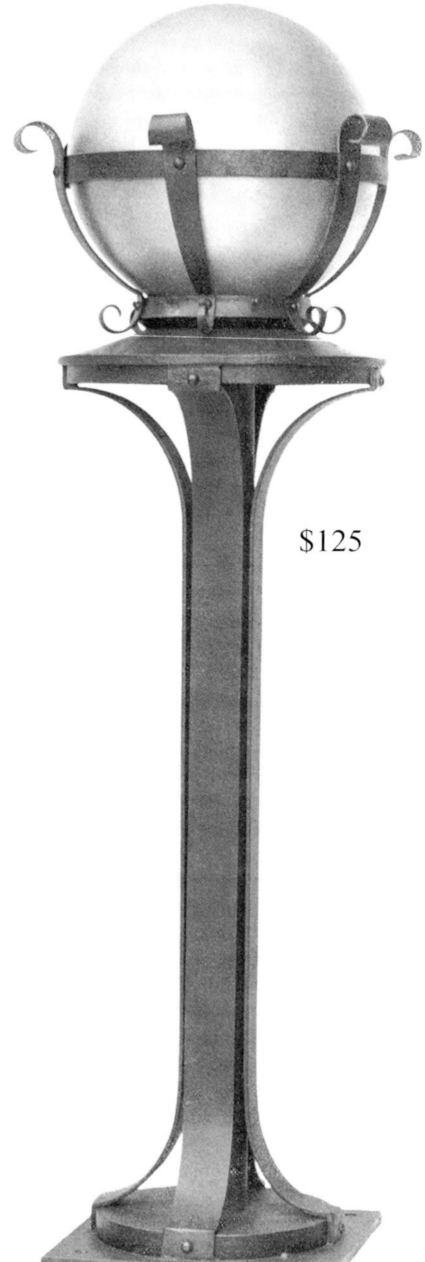

Number 2592
Height, 46 inches (over all). Base, 11 inches.
6x12-inch C. R. I. Ball included.

Black Iron only.	Not Wired	Wired	Complete as shown No lamps
2 Electric	$58.20	$59.20	$61.00

Number 2590
Height, 41 inches (over all). Base, 8 inches.
4x10-inch C. R. I. Ball included.

Black Iron only.	Not Wired	Wired	Complete as shown No lamp
1 Electric	$22.80	$23.30	$24.20

Number 2591
Height, 48 inches (over all). Base, 11 inches.
6x12-inch C. R. I. Ball included.

Black Iron only.	Not Wired	Wired	Complete as shown No lamps
2 Electric	$46.20	$47.20	$49.00

Price in right hand column always includes sockets; also holders and shades if shown but no lamps.
Other prices include glassware, sockets, lamps or electric holders only where mentioned.

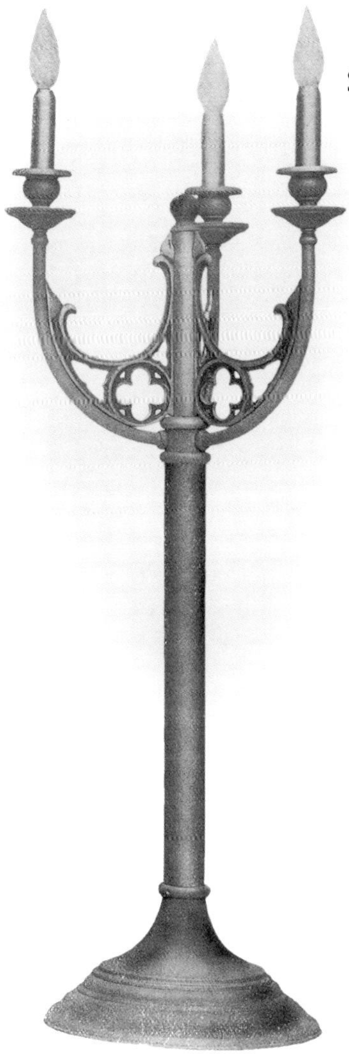

$175

$150

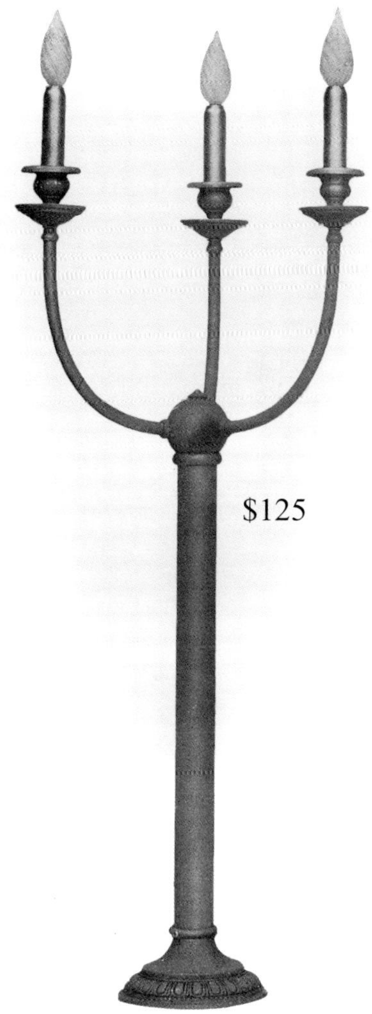

$125

Number 2486
Portable.
Height, 37 inches (over all). Spread, 10 inches.
Candles, Miniature Sockets and Lamps included.

Brush Brass.	Not Wired	Wired	Complete as shown
2 Electric	$16.55	$18.05	$18.40
3 "	20.70	22.70	23.05
4 "	24.85	27.35	27.70

Attachment Plug included in right hand column only.

Number 2615
Length, 35 inches (over all).
Colonial Cut Shade and 3¼-inch Holder included.

Brush Brass.	Not Wired	Wired	Complete as shown No lamp
1 Electric	$27.00	$28.00	$28.40

Number 2485
Portable.
Height, 37 inches (over all). Spread, 10 inches.
Candles, Miniature Sockets and Lamps included.

Brush Brass.	Not Wired	Wired	Complete as shown
3 Electric	$15.65	$17.65	$18.00
4 "	18.20	20.70	21.05

Attachment Plug included in right hand column only.

Price in right hand column always includes sockets; also holders and shades if shown but no lamps.
Other prices include glassware, sockets, lamps or electric holders only where mentioned.

$600

$700

Number 2525
Portable.
Height, 33 inches (over all).
Attachment Plug, Miniature Lamps and Sockets included.

Real Bronze Finish.	Not Wired	Wired	Complete as shown
Natural Vines and Leaves	$55.50	$55.50	$55.50

Number 2523
Portable.
Height, 38 inches (over all).
For standard base lamps.
Attachment Plug included.

Real Bronze Finish.	Not Wired	Wired	Complete as shown No lamps
Natural Leaves	$127.50	$127.50	$127.50

Price in right hand column always includes sockets; also holders and shades if shown but no lamps.
Other prices include glassware, sockets, lamps or electric holders only where mentioned.

$750

$600

$600

Number 2526
Portable.
Height, 21 inches (over all).
For standard base lamp.
Attachment Plug included.

	Not Wired	Wired	Complete as shown No lamp
Real Bronze Finish. Natural Leaves ...	$27.00	$27.00	$27.00

Number 2524
Portable.
Height, 41 inches (over all).
For standard base lamp.
Attachment Plug included.

	Not Wired	Wired	Complete as shown No lamps
Real Bronze Finish. Natural Leaves ...	$114.00	$114.00	$114.00

Number 2527
Portable.
Height, 23 inches (over all).
Attachment Plug, Miniature Lamp and Socket included.

	Not Wired	Wired	Complete as shown
Real Bronze Finish. Natural Vines and Leaves	$29.25	$29.25	$29.25

Price in right hand column always includes sockets; also holders and shades if shown but no lamps.
Other prices include glassware, sockets, lamps or electric holders only where mentioned.

$100

Number 1484
Newel.
Height, 18 inches (over all).
3¼x6-inch C. R. I. Ball and Holder included.

	Not Wired	Wired	Complete as shown No lamp
Rich Gilt	$4.75	$5.05	$5.45

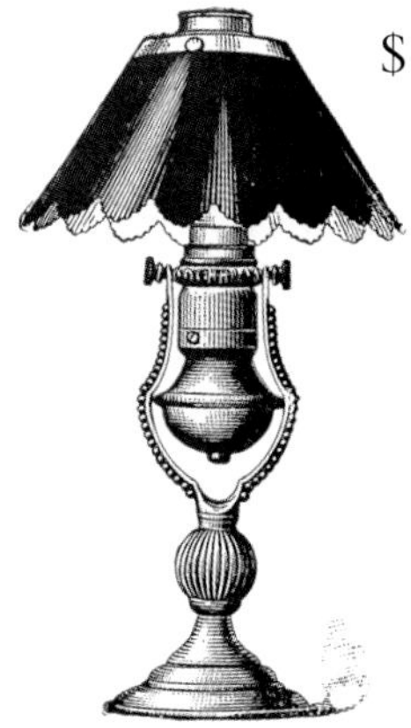

$100

Number 2118
Portable.
Celluloid Shade included.

	Not Wired	Wired	Complete as shown No lamp
Rich Gilt	$3.50	$4.10	$4.80

Attachment Plug included in right hand column only.

$100

Number 1486
Newel.
Height, 18 inches (over all).
3¼x6-inch C. R. I. Ball and Holder included.

	Not Wired	Wired	Complete as shown No lamp
Rich Gilt	$4.75	$5.05	$5.45

$130

Number 2186
Newel.
Height, 26 inches (over all).
3¼x7-inch C. R. I. Ball included.

	Not Wired	Wired	Complete as shown No lamp
Rich Gilt	$9.75	$10.00	$10.70

Chain Pull Socket included in right hand column only.

$150

Number 1600
Newel.
Height, 30 inches (over all).
3¼x8-inch C. R. I. Ball included.

	Not Wired	Wired	Complete as shown No lamp
Rich Gilt	$12.00	$12.50	$12.90

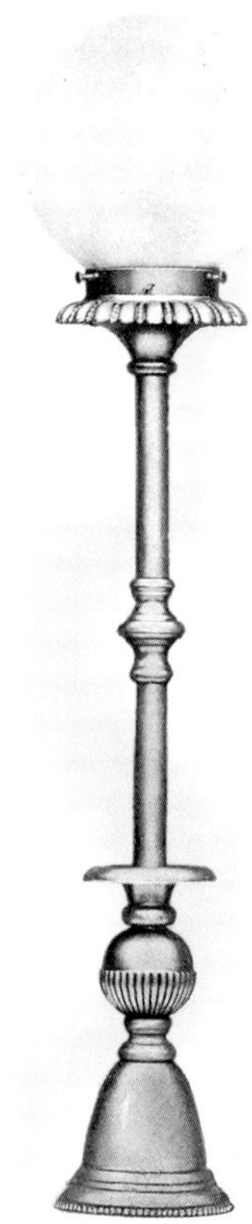

$150

Number 1485
Newel.
Height, 30 inches (over all).
3¼x7-inch C. R. I. Ball included.

	Not Wired	Wired	Complete as shown No lamp
Rich Gilt	$5.10	$5.40	$5.80

If wanted with Chain Pull Sockets add 30 cents for each light to prices in right hand column.

Price in right hand column always includes sockets; also holders and shades if shown but no lamps.
Other prices include glassware, sockets, lamps or electric holders only where mentioned.

$75

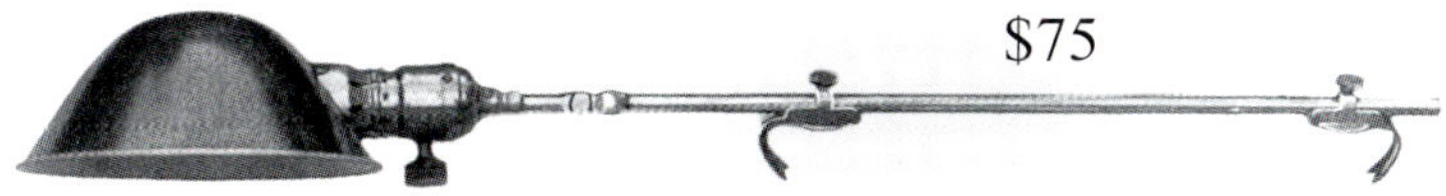

$75

$75

Number 2121
Adjustable Desk Clamp.

	Not Wired	Wired	Complete as shown No lamps
Rich Gilt	$1.75	$2.35	$3.65

No. B 27 7-inch Aluminum Frosted Shade.
Attachment Plug included in right hand column only.

Number 1536
Brass Shade included.

	Not Wired	Wired	Complete as shown No lamp
Rich Gilt	$2.25	$2.35	$2.75

Number 1835
3¼-inch Holder and Glass Bead Fringe included.

	Not Wired	Wired	Complete as shown No lamp
Rich Gilt	$1.85	$1.95	$2.35

$150

$150

Number 1537
Height, 35 inches (over all). Spread, 14 inches.
3¼-inch Holders included.

		Not Wired	Wired	Complete as shown No lamps
3 Electric	Rich Gilt	$29.50	$31.00	$34.15
4 "	" "	37.50	39.50	43.65
5 "	" "	45.50	48.00	53.15

3¼x7-inch C. R. I. Ball in center.
3¼x6-inch C. R. I. Balls on arms.

Number 1602
Height, 36 inches (over all). Spread, 13 inches.
3¼-inch Holders included.

		Not Wired	Wired	Complete as shown No lamps
3 Electric	Rich Gilt	$73.50	$75.00	$78.15
5 "	" "	97.50	100.00	105.15

3¼x7-inch C. R. I. Ball in center.
3¼x6-inch C. R. I. Balls on arms.

Price in right hand column always includes sockets; also holders and shades if shown but no lamps.
Other prices include glassware, sockets, lamps or electric holders only where mentioned.

$75

Number 1842
Rich Gilt.

Not Wired	Wired	Complete as shown No lamp
$0.75	$0.85	$1.60

Shade No. 41½ Crystal.

$75

Number 1598
Socket Husk included.
Rich Gilt.

Not Wired	Wired	as shown Complete No lamp
$1.50	$1.60	$2.00

$75

Number 1868
Socket Husk included.
Brush Brass.

Not Wired	Wired	Complete as shown No lamp
$1.60	$1.70	$2.10

$75

Number 1588
Socket Husk included.
Rich Gilt.

Not Wired	Wired	Complete as shown No lamp
$2.00	$2.10	$2.50

$700

$700

$600

Number 2169
Portable.
Height, 26 inches (over all).
Attachment Plug included.
Turinese Finish only.

	Not Wired	Wired	Complete as shown No lamps
2 Electric ..	$34.75	$34.75	$34.75

Number 2719
Newel.
Height, 35 inches (over all).
4-inch Holder included.
Statuary Bronze only.

	Not Wired	Wired	Complete as shown No lamps
1 Electric ..	$20.30	$21.05	$21.75

4x8-inch C. R. I. Ball.
Chain Pull Socket included in right hand column only.

Number 1470
Newel.
Height, 35 inches (over all).
Socket Husks included.
Statuary Bronze only.

	Not Wired	Wired	Complete as shown No lamps
3 Electric ..	$27.50	$29.00	$30.20
4 " ..	29.00	31.00	32.60
5 " ..	30.50	33.00	35.00

Price in right hand column always includes sockets; also holders and shades if shown but no lamps.
Other prices include glassware, sockets, lamps or electric holders only where mentioned.

Number 1833
Brass Shade and Prisms included.
Rich Gilt.

Not Wired	Wired	Complete as shown No lamp
$3.50	$3.60	$4.00

Number 1952
Brass Shade and Glass Bead Fringe included.
Rich Gilt.

Not Wired	Wired	Complete as shown No lamp
$6.00	$6.10	$6.50

Number 1953
Brass Shade and Glass Bead Fringe included.
Rich Gilt.

Not Wired	Wired	Complete as shown No lamp
$3.50	$3.60	$4.00

Number 1855
3¼-inch Holder and Glass Bead Fringe included.
Rich Gilt.

Not Wired	Wired	Complete as shown No lamp
$1.95	$2.05	$2.45

Number 1788
Newel.
Height, 26 inches (over all).
Art Glass included.
Select Glass Colors by Number. See last page.

		Not Wired	Wired	Complete as shown No lamps
1 Electric	Brush Brass	$14.50	$15.00	$15.70

Chain Pull Socket included in right hand column only.

Number 2011
Height, 24 inches. Spread, 23 inches.

		Not Wired	Wired	Complete as shown No lamps
1 Electric	Brush Brass	$6.50	$7.00	$8.60
2 "	" "	7.50	8.50	11.70

Shades No. B 999 Green Glass, White Inside. Diameter, 10 inches.

Price in right hand column always includes sockets; also holders and shades if shown but no lamps.
Other prices include glassware, sockets, lamps or electric holders only where mentioned.

Number 1976
Brass Shade and Glass Bead Fringe included.
Brush Brass.

Not Wired	Wired	Complete as shown No lamp
$3.90	**$4.00**	**$4.40**

Number 2000
Brush Brass.

Not Wired	Wired	Complete as shown No lamp
$1.15	**$1.25**	**$2.25**

Shade No. B 9547½ C. R. I.

Number 1534
Brass Shade included.
Rich Gilt.

Not Wired	Wired	Complete as shown No lamp
$3.75	**$3.85**	**$4.25**

Number 1587
Socket Husk included.
Rich Gilt.

Not Wired	Wired	Complete as shown No lamp
$2.10	**$2.20**	**$2.60**

Number 1601
Portable.

	Not Wired	Wired	Complete as shown No lamp
Polished Brass	**$2.25**	**$2.85**	**$4.65**

Shade No. B 990 Green Glass, White Inside.
Attachment Plug included in right hand column.

Number 1993
Height, 26 inches.

		Not Wired	Wired	Complete as shown No lamps
1 Electric (1 Swing Arm)	Polished Brass	**$4.25**	**$4.75**	**$6.35**
2 " (2 " ")		6.00	7.00	10.20

Shades No. B 999 Green Glass, White Inside. Diameter, 10 inches.

Number 1992
Height, 26 inches.

	Not Wired	Wired	Complete as shown No lamps
1 Electric (1 Arm) Polished Brass....	**$3.50**	**$4.00**	**$5.60**
2 " (2 ") " "	5.00	6.00	9.20

Shades No. B 999 Green Glass, White Inside. Diameter, 10 inches.

Price in right hand column always includes sockets; also holders and shades if shown but no lamps.
Other prices include glassware, sockets, lamps or electric holders only where mentioned.

$125

$125

$100

Number 2555

Brush Brass.	Not Wired	Wired	Complete as shown No lamps
3 Electric	$3.50	$3.95	$6.95
5 "	4.00	4.75	9.75

Shades No. B 539½ C. R. I.

Number 1626
3¼x6-inch C. R. I. Ball included.

Rich Gilt.	Not Wired	Wired	Complete as shown No lamps
3 Electric	$2.50	$3.00	$5.40
4 "	2.65	3.30	6.70
5 "	2.80	3.60	8.00

Shades No. B 4190½ Crystal Roughed inside.

Number 1629

Rich Gilt.	Not Wired	Wired	Complete as shown No lamps
2 Electric	$3.70	$4.00	$5.80
3 "	3.85	4.30	7.00
4 "	4.00	4.00	8.20

Shades No. B 1582½ Etched and Cut.

$150

$175

$125

Number 2713
Portable.
Miniature Socket and Lamp included.

	Not Wired	Wired	Complete as shown
Antique Brush Brass...	$11.05	$11.65	$12.00

Attachment Plug included in right hand column.

Number 2002
Height, 24 inches. Spread, 18 inches.

		Not Wired	Wired	Complete as shown No lamps
1 Electric (1 Swing Arm)	Polished	$3.00	$3.50	$4.70
2 " (2 " ")	Brass	4.50	5.50	7.90

Shades No. B 999 Green Glass, White Inside. Diameter, 7 inches.

Number 1996
Height, 24 inches.

		Not Wired	Wired	Complete as shown No lamps
1 Electric (1 Swing Arm)	Polished	$2.75	$3.25	$4.45
2 " (2 " ")	Brass	4.25	5.25	7.65

Shades No. B 999 Green Glass, White Inside. Diameter, 7 inches.

Price in right hand column always includes sockets; also holders and shades if shown but no lamps.
Other prices include glassware, sockets, lamps or electric holders only where mentioned.

$125

Number 1627

Rich Gilt.	Not Wired	Wired	Complete as shown No lamps
2 Electric	$0.85	$1.15	$2.95
3 "	1.00	1.45	4.15
4 "	1.15	1.70	5.30

Shades No. B 418½ Etched.

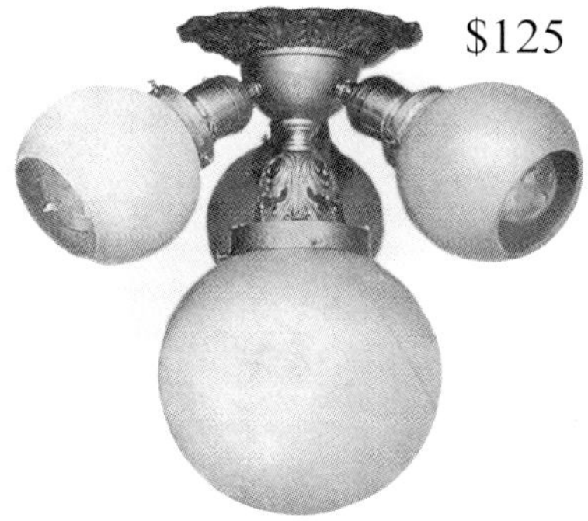

$125

Number 1624

3¼x6-inch C. R. I. Bottom Ball included.

Rich Gilt.	Not Wired	Wired	Complete as shown No lamps
3 Electric	$5.75	$6.25	$8.45
4 "	5.90	6.60	9.70
5 "	6.05	6.85	10.85

Shades No. B4190½ C. R. I.

$125

Number 1631

Rich Gilt.	Not Wired	Wired	Complete as shown No lamps
2 Electric	$1.10	$1.40	$3.20
3 "	1.25	1.70	4.40
6 "	1.70	2.60	8.00

Shades No. B 68½ C. R. I.

$250

Number 2665

Height, 22 inches (over all).

No. G 409 14-inch Art Glass Shade included.

Select Glass Colors by Number. See last page.

Brush Brass and Black.	Not Wired	Wired	Complete as shown No lamps
2 Electric	$18.00	$18.85	$20.60

Price in right hand column includes Pull Sockets and Attachment Plug.

$250

Number 2659

Height, 25½ inches (over all).

14-inch Art Glass Shade with Glass Bead Fringe included.

Select Glass Colors by Number. See last page.

Brush Brass.	Not Wired	Wired	Complete as shown No lamps
2 Electric	$19.50	$20.35	$22.10

Price in right hand column includes Pull Sockets and Attachment Plug.

$250

Number 2660

Height, 23½ inches (over all).

No. G 449 12-inch Art Glass Shade included.

Select Glass Colors by Number. See last page.

Brush Brass.	Not Wired	Wired	Complete as shown No lamps
2 Electric	$19.50	$20.35	$22.10

Price in right hand column includes Pull Sockets and Attachment Plug.

Price in right hand column always includes sockets; also holders and shades if shown but no lamps.
Other prices include glassware, sockets, lamps or electric holders only where mentioned.

Number 2114
3¼x8-inch C. R. I. Ball included.
Black Iron only.

Not Wired	Wired	Complete as shown No lamp
$5.60	$5.80	$6.20

Number 2113
4x8-inch C. R. I. Ball included.
Black Iron only.

Not Wired	Wired	Complete as shown No lamp
$7.50	$7.70	$8.10

Number 1636
3¼x8-inch C. R. I. Ball included.
Rich Gilt.

Not Wired	Wired	Complete as shown No lamp
$5.45	$5.65	$6.05

Number 1634
3¼x8-inch C. R. I. Ball included.
Rich Gilt.

Not Wired	Wired	Complete as shown No lamp
$8.75	$8.95	$9.35

Number 2710
Height, 19½ inches (over all).
Portable Stand only.

Statuary Bronze and Green only.

	Not Wired	Wired	Complete as shown No lamp
1 Electric	$3.00	$3.60	$7.40

Price in right hand column includes Pull Socket, Attachment Plug, Shade Holder and No. B 210 10-inch Straw Roughed Inside Shade.

No. B 212 Plain Green Mushroom Shade at same price if ordered that way.

Number 2697
Portable.
Height, 23 inches (over all).
Candles, Miniature Sockets and Lamps included.

Rich Gilt.	Not Wired	Wired	Complete as shown No lamps
3 Electric	$20.65	$22.15	$22.15
4 "	25.20	27.20	27.20

Number 2148½
Height, 20¾ inches (over all).
Portable Stand only.

Nubian Bronze only.

	Not Wired	Wired	Complete as shown No lamp
1 Electric	$4.25	$4.85	$9.40

Price in right hand column includes Pull Socket, Attachment Plug, Shade Holder and No. B 164 10-inch Decorated Shade.

Price in right hand column always includes sockets; also holders and shades if shown but no lamps.
Other prices include glassware, sockets, lamps or electric holders only where mentioned.

$100

Number 1640
3¼x8-inch C. R. I. Ball included.
Rich Gilt.

Not Wired	Wired	Complete as shown No lamp
$3.50	$3.70	$4.10

$100

Number 1481
3¼x6-inch C. R. I. Ball included.
Rich Gilt.

Not Wired	Wired	Complete as shown No lamp
$3.10	$3.30	$3.70

$100

Number 1479
3¼x6-inch C. R. I. Ball included.
Rich Gilt.

Not Wired	Wired	Complete as shown No lamp
$4.60	$4.80	$5.20

$100

Number 1480
3¼x8-inch C. R. I. Ball included.
Rich Gilt.

Not Wired	Wired	Complete as shown No lamp
$6.15	$6.35	$6.75

$600

$100

Number 1638
3¼x8-inch C. R. I. Ball included.

	Not Wired	Wired	Complete as shown No lamp
Rich Gilt	$4.75	$4.85	$5.25

$500

Number 2147
Height, 21¾ inches (over all).
Portable Stand only.

	Not Wired	Wired	Complete as shown No lamps
1 Electric Oxidized Copper only......	$4.50	$5.10	$8.15

Price in right hand column includes Pull Socket, Attachment Plug, Shade Holder and No. B 963 10-inch Green Shade.

Number 2711
Height, 22 inches (over all).
Portable Stand only.

	Not Wired	Wired	Complete as shown No lamps
1 Electric Brush Brass and Black....	$20.25	$20.85	$40.15

Price in right hand column includes Pull Socket, Attachment Plug, Holder and No. G 400 16-inch Art Glass Shade with Fringe.
Select Glass Colors by Number. See last page.

Price in right hand column always includes sockets; also holders and shades if shown but no lamps.
Other prices include glassware, sockets, lamps or electric holders only where mentioned.

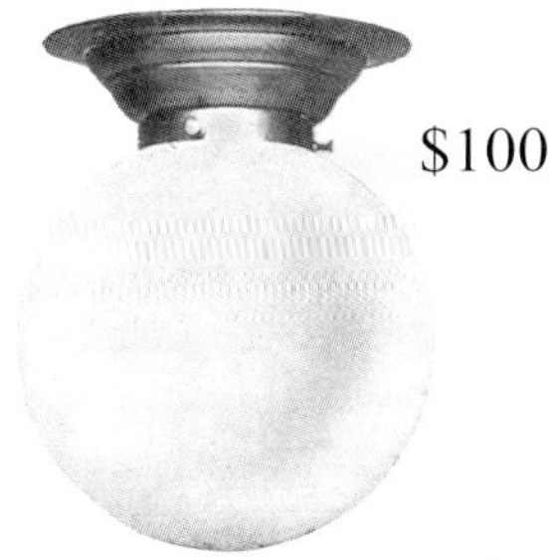

Finishes.

Number	
2714	Rich Gilt. Price given below.
2714½	Oxidized Copper ten per cent extra.
2715	Black, made of heavy cast iron for out door use. Price below.
2716	Black, made of copper for out door use. Price below.

Size of Metal 4x7 inches.
4x8 inch C. R. I. Ball included.

	Not Wired	Complete as shown No lamps
Number 2714	$2.25	$2.75
" 2715	2.25	2.75
" 2716	2.50	3.00

Number 2208
3¼x6-inch C. R. I. Ball included.

	Not Wired	Complete as shown No lamps
Polished Brass	$1.25	$1.75

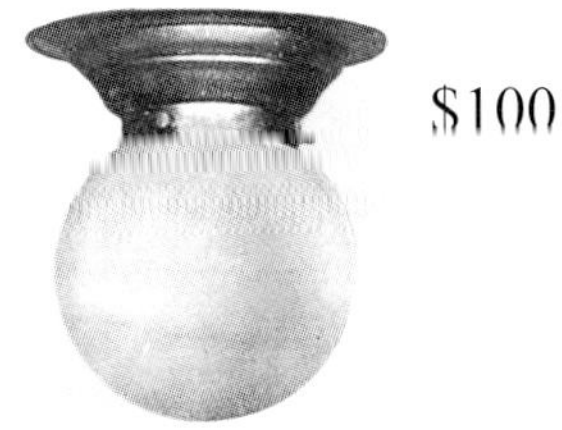

Finishes.

Number	
2204	Polished Brass. Price below.
2204½	Oxidized Copper at ten per cent extra.
2205	Black, made of zinc for out door use. Price below.
2206	Black, made of heavy cast iron for out door use. Price below.

Size of Metal 6¼x7 inches.
3¾x6-inch C. R. I. Ball included.

	Not Wired	Complete as shown No lamps
Number 2204	$1.40	$1.80
" 2205	1.30	1.70
" 2206	1.40	1.80

Number 1442
Size of Metal 4x7 inches.
4x10-inch F. O. T. Ball included.

	Not Wired	Complete as shown No lamps
Rich Gilt	$3.25	$3.75

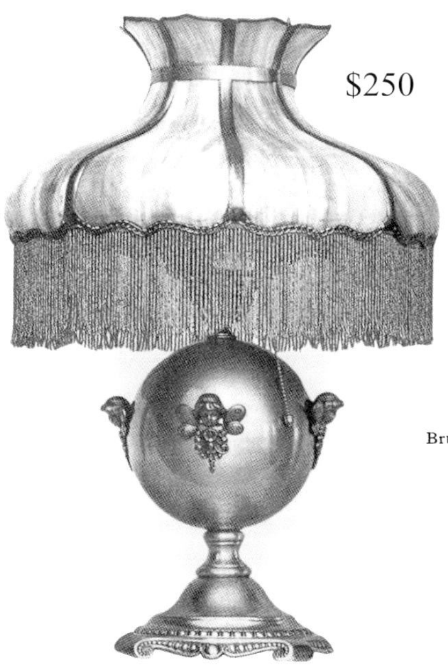

Number 1716
3¼x8-inch C. R. I. Ball included.

	Not Wired	Wired	Complete as shown No lamp
Brush Brass and Black	$3.00	$3.10	$3.50

Number 2708
Height, 23 inches (over all).
Portable Stand only.

		Not Wired	Wired	Complete as shown No lamps
1 Electric	Brush Brass and Black	$15.00	$15.60	$34.90

Price in right hand column includes Pull Socket, Attachment Plug, Shade Holder and No. G 400 16-inch Art Glass Shade with Fringe.
Select Glass Colors by Number. See last page.

Number 2709
Height, 23 inches (over all).
Portable Stand only.

		Not Wired	Wired	Complete as shown No lamps
1 Electric	Brush Brass and Black	$16.00	$16.60	$35.90

Price in right hand column includes Pull Socket, Attachment Plug, Holder and No. G 417 Art Glass Shade. Pond Lily, White and Green.

Price in right hand column always includes sockets; also holders and shades if shown but no lamps.
Other prices include glassware, sockets, lamps or electric holders only where mentioned.

$100

$100

$100

$100

Number 2484 Black Iron
Number 2484½ Brush Brass
Length, 16 inches (over all).
For use as Bracket or Ceiling Light.
Number 2484

Not Wired	Wired	Complete as shown No lamp
$2.00	**$2.50**	**$3.70**

Number 2484½

Not Wired	Wired	Complete as shown No lamp
$2.00	**$2.50**	**$3.70**

Shade No. B 250 C. R. I.
Diameter, 8 inches.

Number 2674
Length, 19 inches (over all).
Brush Brass.

Not Wired	Wired	Complete as shown No lamp
$1.25	**$1.55**	**$5.20**

Shade No. B 10168 Colonial Cut.
Diameter, 8 inches.

Number 2676
Length, 19 inches (over all).
Brush Brass.

Not Wired	Wired	Complete as shown No lamp
$1.25	**$1.55**	**$3.55**

Holophane Shade No. 2 B. C.

Number 2675
Length, 19 inches (over all).
Brush Brass.

Not Wired	Wired	Complete as shown No lamp
$1.25	**$1.55**	**$2.75**

Shade No. B 250 C. R. I.
Diameter, 8 inches.

$300

$350

$250

Number 2661
Height, 18¾ inches (over all).
Portable Stand only.

	Not Wired	Wired	Complete as shown No lamp
Brush Brass and Black..	$8.50	$9.10	$13.15

Price in right hand column includes Pull Socket, Attachment Plug, Shade Holder and 10-inch Decorated Shade.

Number 2712
Height, 21 inches (over all).
Portable Stand only.

	Not Wired	Wired	Complete as shown No lamp
Oxidized Copper only...	$4.50	$5.10	$14.45

Price in right hand column includes Pull Socket, Attachment Plug, and No. G 409 12-inch Art Glass Shade.
Select Glass Colors by Number. See last page.

Number 2132
Height, 19½ inches (over all).
Portable Stand only.

	Not Wired	Wired	Complete as shown No lamp
Antique Brush Brass only	$10.00	$10.60	$15.15

Price in right hand column includes Pull Socket, Attachment Plug, Shade Holder and 10-inch Decorated Shade.

Price in right hand column always includes sockets; also holders and shades if shown but no lamps.
Other prices include glassware, sockets, lamps or electric holders only where mentioned.

Number 2433
Length, 16 inches (over all).
For use as Bracket or Ceiling Light.
Brush Brass.

Not Wired	Wired	Complete as shown No lamp
$1.00	$1.30	$2.50

Shade No. B 250 C. R. I.
Diameter, 8 inches.

Number 2316
Length, 17 inches.
Lantern and 4x6-inch C. R. I. Cylinder included.
Brush Brass.

Not Wired	Wired	Complete as shown No lamp
$5.30	$5.80	$6.20

Number 2373
Length, 19 inches (over all).
3¼x9-inch C. R. I. D. Stalactite included.
Antique Brush Brass.

Not Wired	Wired	Complete as shown No lamp
$13.25	$13.75	$14.15

Number 2372
Length, 19 inches (over all).
No. B 180 3¼x8-inch C. R. I. Square Ball included.
Antique Brush Brass.

Not Wired	Wired	Complete as shown No lamp
$13.50	$14.00	$14.40

Number 2707
Height, 17¾ inches (over all).
Portable Stand only.

	Not Wired	Wired	Complete as shown No lamp
Antique Brush Brass only	$9.10	$9.70	$12.75

Price in right hand column includes Pull Socket, Attachment Plug, Shade Holder and No. B 963 10-inch Green Shade.

Number 2340
Portable.
Height, 19 inches (over all).
Colonial Cut Shade and Prisms included.

	Not Wired	Wired	Complete as shown No lamp
Brush Brass	$12.60	$13.20	$14.25

Chain Pull Socket and Attachment Plug included in right hand column only.

Number 1650
Height, 23 inches (over all).
Portable Stand only.

	Not Wired	Wired	Complete as shown No lamp
Brush Brass and Black.	$16.00	$16.60	$19.65

Price in right hand column includes Pull Socket, Attachment Plug, Shade Holder and No. B 963 10-inch Green Shade.

Price in right hand column always includes sockets; also holders and shades if shown but no lamps.
Other prices include glassware, sockets, lamps or electric holders only where mentioned.

Number 2678
Length, 19 inches (over all).
Brush Brass.

Not Wired	Wired	Complete as shown No lamp
$1.25	$1.55	$3.70

Shade No. B 3424 Alba.

Number 2680
Length, 20 inches (over all).
Brush Brass.

Not Wired	Wired	Complete as shown No lamp
$1.25	$1.55	$4.35

Shade No. B 3429 Alba.

Number 2679
Length, 19 inches (over all).
Brush Brass.

Not Wired	Wired	Complete as shown No lamp
$1.25	$1.55	$3.70

Shade No. B 3432 Alba.

Number 2673
Length, 19 inches (over all).
Brush Brass.

Not Wired	Wired	Complete as shown No lamp
$1.25	$1.55	$2.80

Shade No. B 007½ Frosted, with Crystal Stars and Bars. Diameter, 7 inches.

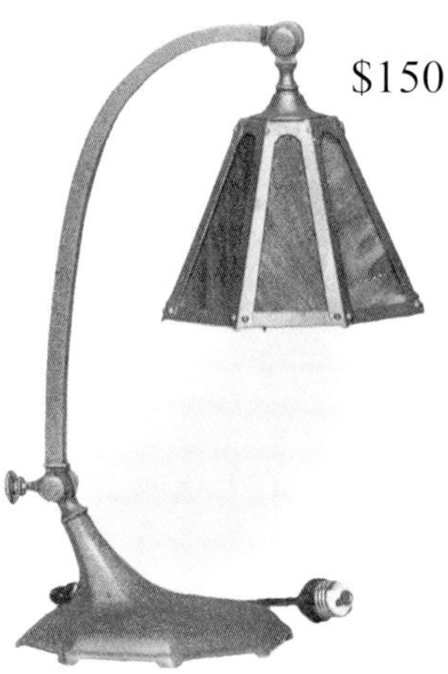

Number 2664
Adjustable Piano or Desk Lamp.
Height, 18 inches.
Art Glass Shade and Attachment Plug included.
Colors for Art Glass are Green and Red Blended, also Green and White Blended.
Brush Brass.

Not Wired	Wired	Complete as shown No lamp
$21.50	$21.50	$21.50

Number 2720
Portable.
Height, 15 inches (over all).
Silk Shade, Holder, Glass Bead Fringe, Candle, Miniature Pull Socket and Lamp included.
Brush Brass.

Not Wired	Wired	Complete as shown
$10.05	$10.65	$11.00

Attachment Plug included in right hand column.

Number 2339
Portable.
Height, 15 inches (over all).
6½-inch Art Glass Shade, Glass Bead Fringe and Holder included.
Select Glass Colors by Number. See last page.
Brush Brass.

Not Wired	Wired	Complete as shown No lamp
$10.35	$10.95	$12.00

Chain Pull Socket and Attachment Plug included in right hand column only.

Number 2344
Portable.
Height, 15 inches (over all).
6½-inch Art Glass Shade, Glass Bead Fringe and Holder included.
Select Glass Colors by Number. See last page.
Brush Brass.

Not Wired	Wired	Complete as shown No lamp
$8.35	$8.95	$10.00

Chain Pull Socket and Attachment Plug included inright hand column only.

Price in right hand column always includes sockets; also holders and shades if shown but no lamps.
Other prices include glassware, sockets, lamps or electric holders only where mentioned.

$150

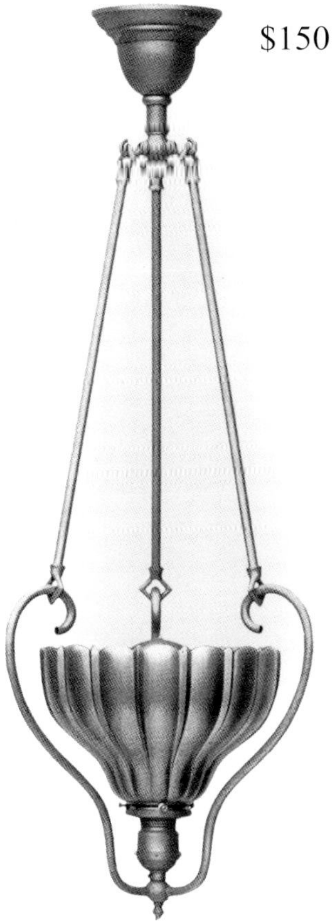

$175

Number 2574
Length, 13 inches (over all).

	Not Wired	Wired	Complete as shown No lamp
Brush Brass	$4.10	$1.05	$5.30

No. B 1039 4x7-inch Colonial Cut Squat Ball.

$150

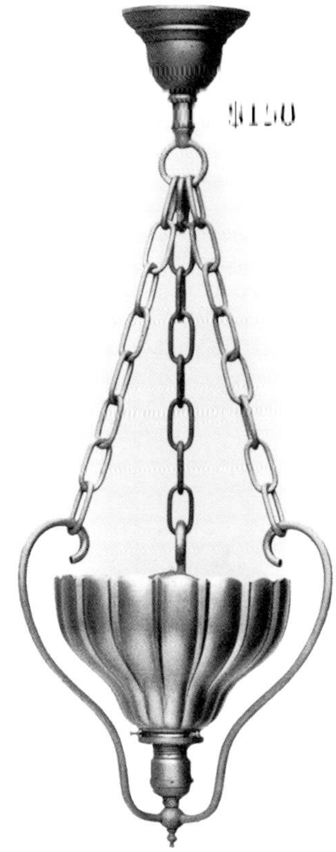

Number 2685
Length, 32 inches.
Alba Shade No. B 3429 included.

	Not Wired	Wired	Complete as shown No lamp
Brush Brass	$7.40	$8.40	$8.90

Semi-direct, Semi-indirect Unit has the advantages of both direct and indirect lighting without the disadvantages. Made for 60 or 100 watt Tungsten lamps upright, with Alba Glass Shade, the most perfect diffusing glass made, eliminates the glare and reflects the light.

Number 2686
Length, 30 inches.
Alba Shade No. B 3429 included.

	Not Wired	Wired	Complete as shown No lamp
Brush Brass	$8.50	$9.50	$10.00

Semi-direct, Semi-indirect Unit has the advantages of both direct and indirect lighting without the disadvantages. Made for 60 or 100 watt Tungsten lamps upright, with Alba Glass Shade, the most perfect diffusing glass made, eliminates the glare and reflects the light.

$400

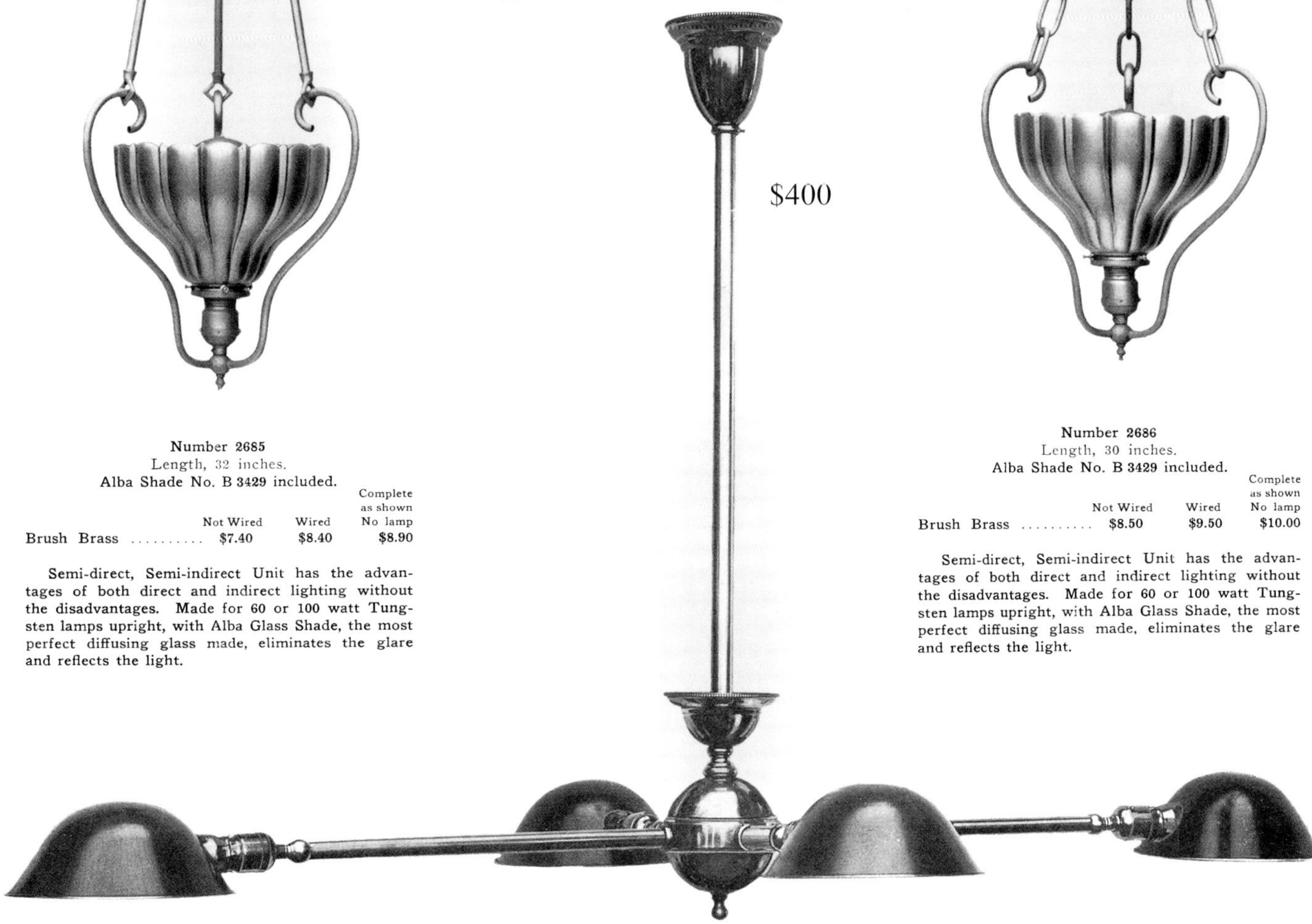

Number 2130
Length, 36 inches. Spread, 24x48 inches.
No. B 28 8-inch Aluminum Frosted Shades included.

		Not Wired	Wired	Complete as shown No lamps
2 Electric	Rich Gilt	$4.50	$5.50	$8.30
4 "	" "	5.50	7.50	13.10

Price in right hand column always includes sockets; also holders and shades if shown but no lamps.
Other prices include glassware, sockets, lamps or electric holders only where mentioned.

Number 2212
No. B 180 3¼x7-inch C. R. I. Square Ball included.

	Not Wired	Complete as shown No lamps
Brush Brass	$2.30	$2.80

Number 2474
Special Socket included.

	Not Wired	Complete as shown No lamps
Brush Brass	$1.75	$2.45

Shade No. B 007½ Frosted, with Crystal Stars and Bars. Diameter, 7 inches.

Number 2718
Special Socket included.

	Not Wired	Complete as shown No lamps
Brush Brass	$1.75	$2.45

Shade No. B 007½ Frosted, with Crystal Stars and Bars. Diameter, 7 inches.

Number 2717
Special Socket included.

	Not Wired	Complete as shown No lamps
Rich Gilt	$1.75	$3.20

Holophane Shade No. 2 B. C.

Number 2111
12 inches square at top.
Socket Husks, 3¼-inch Holders and Opal Glass Panels included.

Black Iron only.	Not Wired	Wired	Complete as shown No lamps
6 Electric (2 lights inside)	$25.50	$28.50	$33.90

No. B 180 3¼x6-inch C. R. I. Square Balls.

Number 2501
Length, 13 inches. Spread, 10 inches.
Art Glass Shade and Socket Husks included.

		Not Wired	Wired	Complete as shown No lamps
5 Electric	Brush Brass	$39.75	$42.25	$44.25

Number 2268
Length, 13 inches (over all). Spread, 20 inches.

		Not Wired	Wired	Complete as shown No lamps
2 Electric	Brush Brass	$8.00	$9.50	$12.20
4 "	" "	12.20	15.20	20.60

No. B 180 3¼x6-inch C. R. I. Square Balls.

Number 1860
Length, 13 inches. Spread, 17 inches.

		Not Wired	Wired	Complete as shown No lamps
2 Electric	Brush Brass	$12.50	$13.50	$15.50
4 "	" "	16.50	18.50	22.50

Shades No. B 9547½ C. R. I.

Price in right hand column always includes sockets; also holders and shades if shown but no lamps.
Other prices include glassware, sockets, lamps or electric holders only where mentioned.

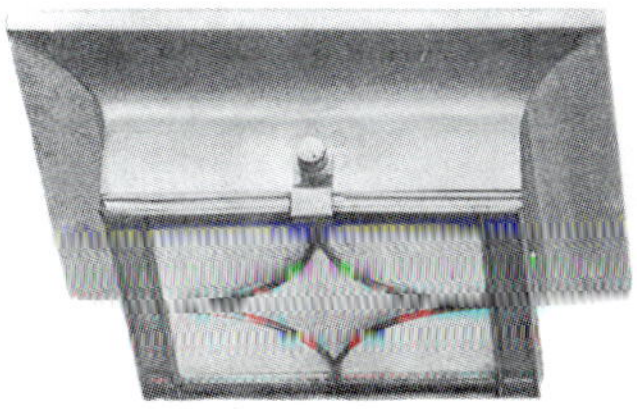

$300

Number 2096
11 inches square at top.
Crystal Cathedral Glass included.
If Colored Glass is desired, Select Glass Colors by Number. See last page.

Old Brass.	Not Wired	Wired	Complete as shown No lamps
2 Electric	$16.60	$17.10	$17.90

$400

Number 2640
Length, 14 inches (over all). Spread, 10 inches.
3¼-inch Holders included.

Brush Brass and Black.	Not Wired	Wired	Complete as shown No lamps
2 Electric	$39.00	$40.00	$43.80
4 "	60.00	71.00	78.60

No. B5121 3¼x6-inch Ground and Cut Star Balls.

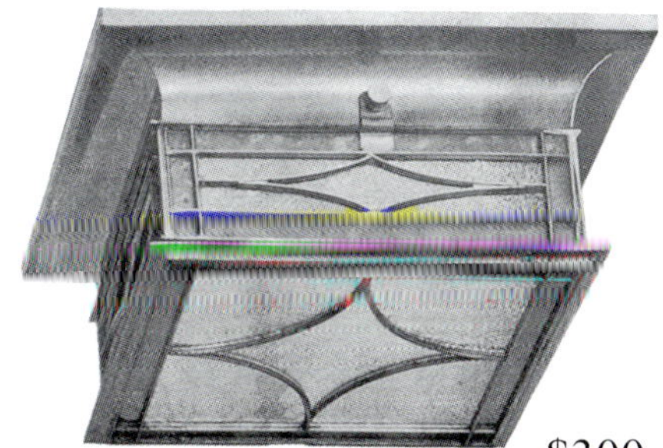

$300

Number 2095
13½ inches square at top.
Crystal Cathedral Glass included.
If Colored Glass is desired, Select Glass Colors by Number. See last page.

Old Brass.	Not Wired	Wired	Complete as shown No lamps
2 Electric	$29.00	$29.50	$30.30
4 "	29.50	30.50	32.10

$200

Number 2488
Length, 13 inches (over all).
Iridescent Prisms and Special Socket included.

Brush Brass and Black.	Not Wired	Wired	Complete as shown No lamp
1 Electric	$21.25	$21.35	$21.35

$350

Number 2622
Length, 14 inches. Spread, 12 inches.

Brush Brass.	Not Wired	Wired	Complete as shown No lamps
2 Electric	$17.50	$18.50	$22.00
4 "	26.00	28.00	35.00

Shades No. B 3431 Alba.

$250

Number 1834
Prisms included.

Rich Gilt.	Not Wired	Wired	Complete as shown No lamp
1 Electric	$10.25	$10.35	$10.75

$300

Number 2489
Length, 14 inches (over all).
Decorated Shade included.

Brush Brass.	Not Wired	Wired	Complete as shown No lamp
1 Electric	$11.25	$11.75	$12.15

$300

Number 2620
Length, 14 inches (over all). Spread, 12 inches.

Brush Brass.	Not Wired	Wired	Complete as shown No lamps
2 Electric	$17.75	$18.75	$20.55
4 "	26.25	28.25	31.85

2¼x7-inch C. R. I. Domes.

$125

Number 2329
Length, 15 inches.
Art Glass included.
Select Glass Colors by Number. See last page.

Brush Brass.	Not Wired	Wired	Complete as shown No lamp
1 Electric	$9.00	$9.50	$9.90

Price in right hand column always includes sockets; also holders and shades if shown but no lamps.
Other prices include glassware, sockets, lamps or electric holders only where mentioned.

$75

Number 1582
Made with Hinge.
12-inch Holophane Bowl included.

Polished Brass.	Not Wired	Wired	Complete as shown No lamps
2 Electric	$13.25	$13.75	$14.55
3 "	13.50	14.25	15.45
4 "	13.75	14.75	16.35

$75

Number 2553
Length, 14 inches.
Crystal Roughed Glass included.

Brush Brass.	Not Wired	Wired	Complete as shown No lamp
1 Electric	$14.00	$14.50	$14.90

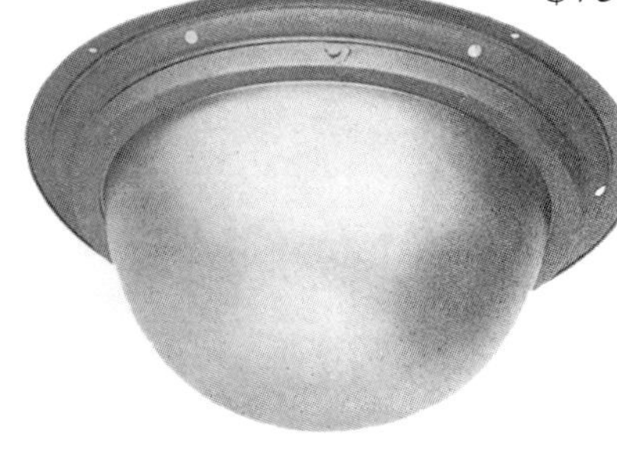

$75

Number 2627
Made with Hinge.
12-inch C. R. I. Bowl included.

Brush Brass.	Not Wired	Wired	Complete as shown No lamps
3 Electric	$9.30	$10.05	$11.25

$300

Number 2003
Length, 14 inches. Spread, 24 inches.

		Not Wired	Wired	Complete as shown No lamps
2 Electric	Rich Gilt	$3.25	$4.00	$5.90
3 "	" "	3.75	4.75	7.60
4 "	" "	4.25	5.50	9.30
5 "	" "	4.75	6.25	11.00
6 "	" "	5.25	7.00	12.70

Shades No. B 539½ C. R. I.

$250

Number 1900
Length, 12 inches (over all). Spread, 23 inches.

		Not Wired	Wired	Complete as shown No lamps
2 Electric	Rich Gilt	$3.20	$4.20	$5.70
3 "	" "	3.80	5.30	7.55
4 "	" "	4.40	6.40	9.40
5 "	" "	5.00	7.50	11.25

Shades No. B 41½ Crystal.

$300

Number 1893
Length, 13 inches (over all). Spread, 24 inches.

		Not Wired	Wired	Complete as shown No lamps
2 Electric	Rich Gilt	$4.00	$4.75	$6.25
3 "	" "	4.75	5.75	8.00
4 "	" "	5.50	6.75	9.75
5 "	" "	6.25	7.75	11.50

Shades No. B 41½ Crystal.

$300

Number 1894
Length, 14 inches (over all). Spread, 15 inches.

		Not Wired	Wired	Complete as shown No lamps
2 Electric	Rich Gilt	$4.00	$4.75	$7.15
3 "	" "	4.75	5.75	9.35
4 "	" "	5.50	6.75	11.55

3¼x6-inch C. R. I. Balls.

Price in right hand column always includes sockets; also holders and shades if shown but no lamps.
Other prices include glassware, sockets, lamps or electric holders only where mentioned.

$150

Number 1885

Length, 11 inches (over all). Spread, 23 inches.

		Not Wired	Wired	Complete as shown No lamps
2 Electric	Rich Gilt	$4.75	$5.75	$7.55
3 "	" "	5.75	7.25	9.95
4 "	" "	6.75	8.75	12.35

Shades No. B 1412½ White Acid.

$150

Number 1888

Length, 14 inches (over all). Spread, 23 inches.

		Not Wired	Wired	Complete as shown No lamps
2 Electric	Rich Gilt	$4.45	$6.15	$6.95
3 "	" "	5.05	6.55	8.80
4 "	" "	5.65	7.65	10.65

Shades No. B 41½ Crystal.

$200

Number 1899

Length, 12 inches (over all). Spread, 15 inches.

		Not Wired	Wired	Complete as shown No lamps
2 Electric	Rich Gilt	$3.00	$3.75	$5.35
3 "	" "	3.50	4.50	6.90
4 "	" "	4.00	5.25	8.45
5 "	" "	4.50	6.00	10.00

Shades No. B 8983½ C. R. I.

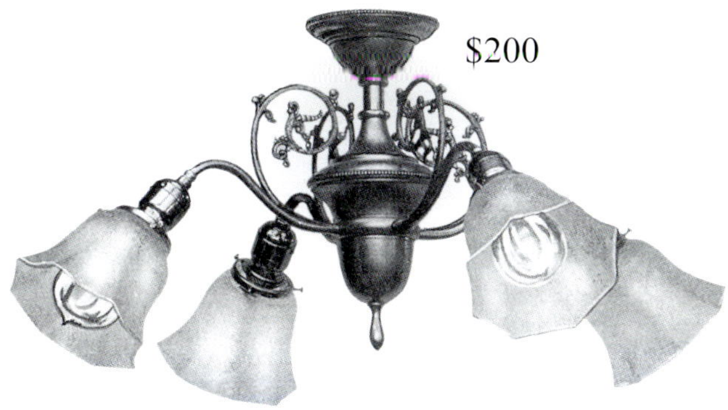

$200

Number 1897

Length, 12 inches (over all). Spread, 24 inches.

		Not Wired	Wired	Complete as shown No lamps
2 Electric	Rich Gilt	$4.40	$5.15	$6.95
3 "	" "	5.60	6.60	9.30
4 "	" "	6.80	8.05	11.65

Shades No. B 1412½ White Acid.

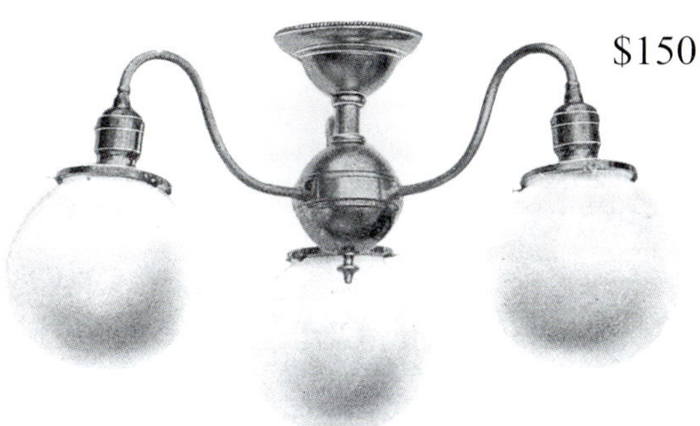

$150

Number 1891

Length, 11 inches (over all). Spread, 15 inches.

		Not Wired	Wired	Complete as shown No lamps
2 Electric	Rich Gilt	$2.50	$3.25	$5.65
3 "	" "	3.00	4.00	7.60
4 "	" "	3.50	4.75	9.55

3¼x6-inch C. R. I. Balls.

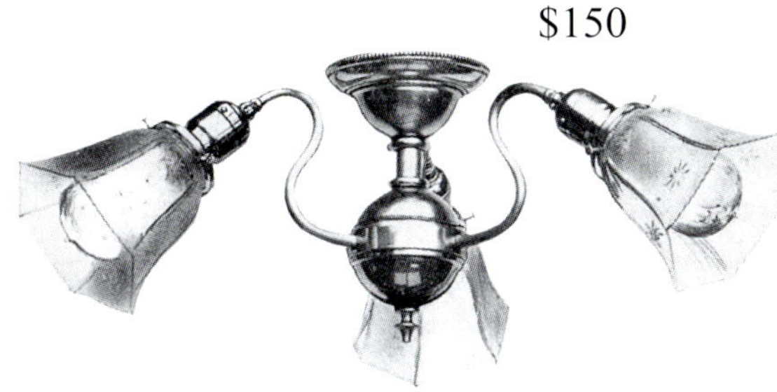

$150

Number 1843

Length, 8 inches (over all). Spread, 20 inches.

		Not Wired	Wired	Complete as shown No lamps
2 Electric	Rich Gilt	$2.50	$3.25	$4.75
3 "	" "	3.00	4.00	6.25
4 "	" "	3.50	4.75	7.75
5 "	" "	4.00	5.50	9.25

Shades No. B 41½ Crystal.

Price in right hand column always includes sockets; also holders and shades if shown, but no lamps.
Other prices include glassware, sockets, lamps or electric holders only where mentioned.

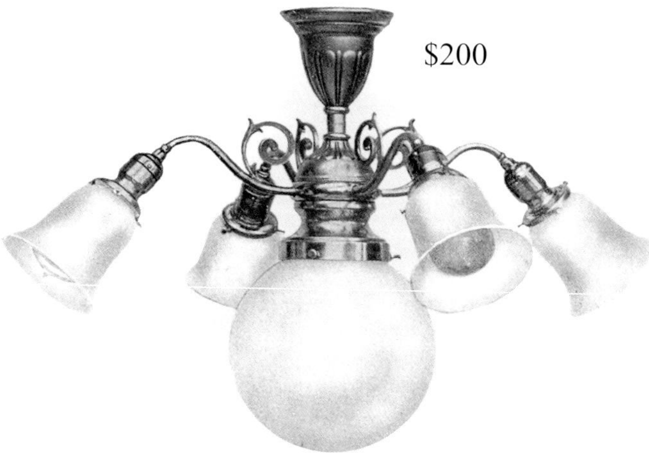

Number 1896
Length, 19 inches (over all). Spread, 24 inches.
4x8-inch C. R. I. Bottom Ball included.

		Not Wired	Wired	Complete as shown No lamps
3 Electric	Rich Gilt	$5.25	$6.25	$8.25
4 "	" "	6.00	7.25	10.05
5 "	" "	6.75	8.25	11.85

Shades No. B 8983½ C. R. I.

Number 2005
Length, 19 inches (over all). Spread, 15 inches.
4x8-inch C. R. I. Bottom Ball included.

		Not Wired	Wired	Complete as shown No lamps
3 Electric	Rich Gilt	$5.25	$6.25	$8.45
4 "	" "	6.00	7.25	10.35
5 "	" "	6.75	8.25	12.25

2¼x7-inch C. R. I. Domes.

Number 1990
Length, 11 inches. Spread, 23 inches.

		Not Wired	Wired	Complete as shown No lamps
2 Electric	Rich Gilt	$4.25	$5.25	$7.05
3 "	" "	5.25	6.75	9.45
4 "	" "	6.25	8.25	11.85
5 "	" "	7.25	9.75	14.25

Shades No. B 68½ C. R. I.

Number 1890
Length, 11 inches (over all). Spread, 15 inches.

		Not Wired	Wired	Complete as shown No lamps
2 Electric	Rich Gilt	$3.25	$4.00	$7.00
3 "	" "	3.75	4.75	9.25
4 "	" "	4.25	5.50	11.50
5 "	" "	4.75	6.25	13.75

3¼x7-inch C. R. I. Stalactites.

Price in right hand column always includes sockets; also holders and shades if shown, but no lamps.
Other prices include glassware, sockets, lamps or electric holders only where mentioned.

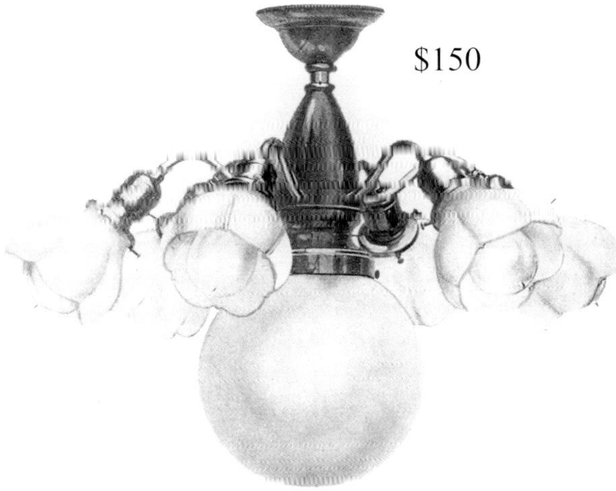

$150

Number 1995

Length, 19 inches (over all). Spread, 24 inches.

4x8-inch C. R. I. Bottom Ball included.

		Not Wired	Wired	Complete as shown No lamps
3 Electric	Rich Gilt	$4.50	$5.50	$7.80
4 "	" "	5.00	6.25	9.50
5 "	" "	5.50	7.00	11.20
6 "	" "	6.00	7.75	12.90
7 "	" "	6.50	8.50	14.60

Shades No. B 539½ C. R. I.

$125

Number 1886

Length, 16 inches (over all). Spread, 15 inches.

4x8-inch C. R. I. Bottom Ball included.

		Not Wired	Wired	Complete as shown No lamps
3 Electric	Rich Gilt	$4.25	$5.25	$8.65
4 "	" "	4.75	6.00	10.90
5 "	" "	5.25	6.75	13.15

No. B 6088 3¼x7-inch C. R. I. Stalactites.

$150

Number 1853

Length, 16 inches (over all). Spread, 15 inches.

4x8-inch C. R. I. Bottom Ball included.

		Not Wired	Wired	Complete as shown No lamps
3 Electric	Rich Gilt	$4.50	$5.50	$7.70
4 "	" "	5.00	6.25	9.35
5 "	" "	5.50	7.00	11.00

Shades No. B 68½ C. R. I.

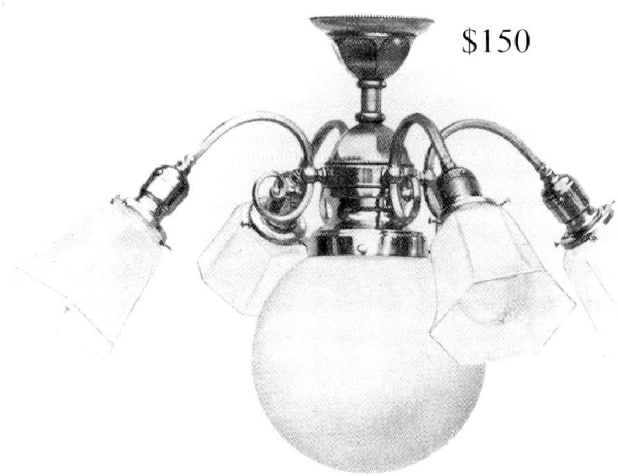

$150

Number 2009

Length, 16 inches (over all). Spread, 23 inches.

4x8-inch C. R. I. Bottom Ball included.

		Not Wired	Wired	Complete as shown No lamps
3 Electric	Rich Gilt	$5.50	$7.00	$9.20
4 "	" "	6.50	8.50	11.60
5 "	" "	7.50	10.00	14.00
6 "	" "	8.50	11.50	16.40

Shades No. B 68½ C. R. I.

Price in right hand column always includes sockets; also holders and shades if shown, but no lamps. Other prices include glassware, sockets, lamps or electric holders only where mentioned.

Number 1895
Length, 17 inches (over all). Spread, 12 inches.

		Not Wired	Wired	Complete as shown No lamps
2 Electric	Rich Gilt	$4.50	$5.50	$8.50
3 "	" "	5.50	7.00	11.50
4 "	" "	6.50	8.50	14.50

No. G 446 3¼-inch Holders with Glass Bead Fringe.

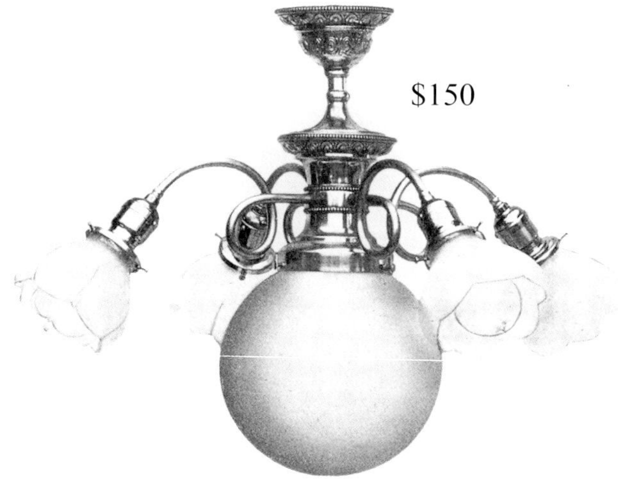

Number 1986
Length, 17 inches (over all). Spread, 23 inches.
4x8-inch C. R. I. Bottom Ball included.

		Not Wired	Wired	Complete as shown No lamps
3 Electric	Rich Gilt	$4.95	$6.45	$8.75
4 "	" "	5.55	7.55	10.80
5 "	" "	6.15	8.65	12.85

Shades No. B 539½ C. R. I.

Number 1848
Length, 17 inches (over all). Spread, 15 inches.

		Not Wired	Wired	Complete as shown No lamps
2 Electric	Brush Brass	$6.75	$7.75	$9.75
4 "	" "	8.25	10.25	14.25

Shades No. B 9547½ C. R. I.

Number 1892
Length, 17 inches (over all). Spread, 24 inches.
4x8-inch C. R. I. Bottom Ball included.

		Not Wired	Wired	Complete as shown No lamps
3 Electric	Rich Gilt	$4.50	$5.50	$7.50
4 "	" "	5.00	6.25	9.05
5 "	" "	5.50	7.00	10.60

Shades No. B 8983½ C. R. I.

Price in right hand column always includes sockets; also holders and shades if shown, but no lamps.
Other prices include glassware, sockets, lamps or electric holders only where mentioned.

Number 2645
Length, 15 inches. Spread, 20 inches.
Holders included.

		Not Wired	Wired	Complete as shown No lamps
2 Electric	Brush Brass	$26.75	$27.75	$36.05
3 "	" "	32.25	33.75	46.20
4 "	" "	37.75	39.75	56.35

No. B 1039 4x7-inch Colonial Cut Squat Balls.

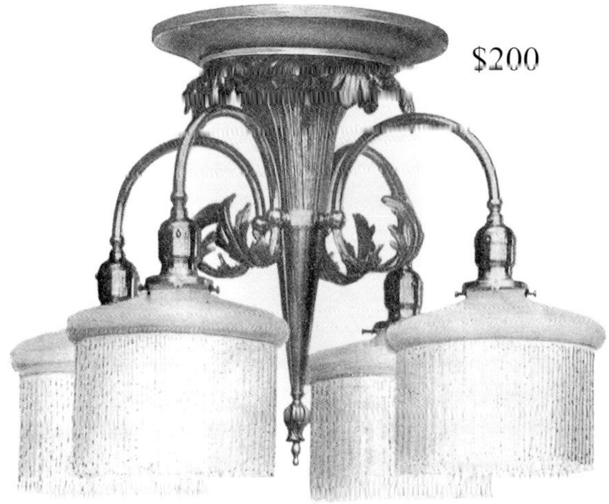

Number 1847
Length, 15 inches (over all). Spread, 15 inches.

		Not Wired	Wired	Complete as shown No lamps
2 Electric	Rich Gilt and Satin.........	$16.50	$17.50	$21.50
3 "	" " " "	18.25	19.75	25.75
4 "	" " " "	20.00	22.00	30.00

Shades No. G 448 Crystal Roughed Inside with Glass Bead Fringe.

Number 2378
Length, 13 inches (over all). Spread, 14 inches.

		Not Wired	Wired	Complete as shown No lamps
2 Electric	Brush Brass	$9.20	$10.20	$12.60
4 "	" "	14.20	16.20	21.00

Shades No. B 250 C. R. I. Diameter, 8 inches.

Number 2368
Length, 13 inches (over all). Spread, 20 inches.

		Not Wired	Wired	Complete as shown No lamps
2 Electric	Brush Brass	$7.50	$8.50	$12.50
4 "	" "	11.00	13.00	21.00

Holophane Shades No. 2 B. C.

Price in right hand column always includes sockets; also holders and shades if shown, but no lamps.
Other prices include glassware. sockets, lamps or electric holders only where mentioned.

$200

$275

Number 2576
Length, 13 inches (over all). Spread, 12 inches.

		Not Wired	Wired	Complete as shown No lamps
2 Electric	Brush Brass	$5.25	$6.25	$8.35
3 "	" "	6.00	7.50	10.65
4 "	" "	6.75	8.75	12.95

Shades No. B 5014½ C. R. I.

Number 2583
Length, 19 inches. Spread, 21 inches.

		Not Wired	Wired	Complete as shown No lamps
2 Electric	Brush Brass	$21.00	$22.00	$27.30
3 "	" "	23.25	24.75	32.70
4 "	" "	25.50	27.50	38.10
5 "	" "	27.75	30.25	43.50
6 "	" "	30.00	33.00	48.90

Shades No. B 10167 Colonial Cut. Diameter, 6 inches.

$300

$300

Number 2573
Length, 18 inches. Spread, 18 inches.

		Not Wired	Wired	Complete as shown No lamps
2 Electric	Brush Brass	$8.50	$9.50	$17.00
3 "	" "	9.75	11.25	22.50
4 "	" "	11.00	13.00	28.00
5 "	" "	12.25	14.75	33.50
6 "	" "	13.50	16.50	39.00

Shades No. B 672 Amber Lustre.

Number 2570
Length, 15 inches (over all). Spread, 14 inches.

		Not Wired	Wired	Complete as shown No lamps
2 Electric	Brush Brass	$6.25	$7.25	$9.35
3 "	" "	7.50	9.00	12.15
4 "	" "	8.75	10.75	14.95
5 "	" "	10.00	12.50	17.75
6 "	" "	11.25	14.25	20.55

Shades No. B 5014½ C. R. I.

Price in right hand column always includes sockets; also holders and shades if shown but no lamps.
Other prices include glassware, sockets, lamps or electric holders only where mentioned.

$300

Number 2535

Length, 18 inches (over all). Spread, 14 inches.

				Not Wired	Wired	Complete as shown No lamps
3	Electric	Brush	Brass	$8.00	$9.50	$13.25
4	"	"	"	8.50	10.50	15.50
5	"	"	"	9.00	11.50	17.75

Shades No. B 007½ Frosted, with Crystal Stars and Bars. Diameter, 7 inches.

$300

Number 2571

Length, 16 inches. Spread, 20 inches.

				Not Wired	Wired	Complete as shown No lamps
2	Electric	Brush	Brass	$9.25	$10.25	$12.35
3	"	"	"	10.25	11.75	14.90
4	"	"	"	11.25	13.25	17.45
5	"	"	"	12.25	14.75	20.00
6	"	"	"	13.25	16.25	22.55
8	"	"	"	15.25	19.25	27.65

Shades No. B 5014½ C. R. I.

$200

Number 2569

Length, 18 inches. Spread, 15 inches.

				Not Wired	Wired	Complete as shown No lamps
2	Electric	Brush	Brass	$8.50	$9.50	$16.90
3	"	"	"	9.75	11.25	22.35
4	"	"	"	11.00	13.00	27.80
5	"	"	"	12.25	14.75	33.25
6	"	"	"	13.50	16.50	38.70

Shades No. B 1226½ Crystal Bead.

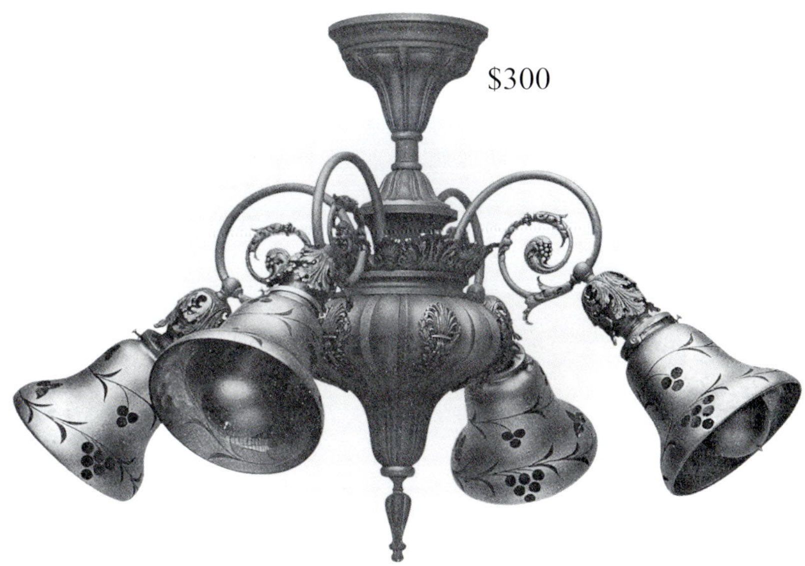

$300

Number 2581

Length, 20 inches. Spread, 27 inches.

				Not Wired	Wired	Complete as shown No lamps
2	Electric	Brush	Brass	$25.50	$26.50	$31.50
3	"	"	"	28.75	30.25	37.75
4	"	"	"	32.00	34.00	44.00
5	"	"	"	35.25	37.75	50.25
6	"	"	"	38.50	41.50	56.50

Shades No. B 10167 Colonial Cut. Diameter, 6 inches.

Price in right hand column always includes sockets; also holders and shades if shown but no lamps.
Other prices include glassware, sockets, lamps or electric holders only where mentioned.

$175

Number 1941
Length, 18 inches (over all). Spread, 12 inches.
Socket Husks included.

		Not Wired	Wired	Complete as shown No lamps
4 Electric	Rich Gilt	$17.50	$19.50	$21.10
5 "	" "	20.00	22.50	24.50

$275

Number 2690
Length, 18 inches (over all). Spread, 12 inches.
Art Glass included.
Select Glass Colors by Number. See last page.

		Not Wired	Wired	Complete as shown No lamps
5 Electric	Brush Brass and Black....	$57.75	$60.25	$62.25

$75

Number 1617
6x12-inch C. R. I. Ball included.

		Not Wired	Wired	Complete as shown No lamps
1 Electric	Rich Gilt	$5.00	$5.25	$5.65
2 "	" "	5.50	6.00	6.80
3 "	" "	5.75	6.50	7.70
4 "	" "	6.00	7.00	8.60

$300

Number 1608
Length, 16 inches. Spread, 22 inches.

		Not Wired	Wired	Complete as shown No lamps
2 Electric	Rich Gilt and Satin	$21.00	$22.00	$24.40
3 "	" " " "	23.75	25.25	28.85
4 "	" " " "	26.50	28.50	33.30
5 "	" " " "	29.25	31.75	37.75

3¼x6-inch C. R. I. Balls.

Price in right hand column always includes sockets; also holders and shades if shown but no lamps.
Other prices include glassware, sockets, lamps or electric holders only where mentioned.

Number 2207

Length, 20 inches (over all). Spread, 18 inches.

Holders and No. B 90 3¼x8-inch Roughed and Cut Star Bottom Ball included.

		Not Wired	Wired	Complete as shown No lamps
3 Electric	Rich Gilt and Satin	$32.25	$33.75	$37.45
4 "	" " " "	37.25	39.25	44.60
5 "	" " " "	42.25	44.75	51.75
6 "	" " " "	47.25	50.25	58.90
7 "	" " " "	52.25	55.75	66.05

No. B 90 3¼x6-inch Roughed and Cut Star Balls.

Number 1942

Length, 19 inches (over all). Spread, 12 inches.

Brass Shades and Glass Bead Fringe included.

		Not Wired	Wired	Complete as shown No lamps
4 Electric	Brush Brass	$22.50	$24.50	$26.10
5 "	" "	26.25	28.75	30.75

Number 2313

Length, 13 inches (over all). Spread, 14 inches.

		Not Wired	Wired	Complete as shown No lamps
2 Electric	Brush Brass	$9.25	$10.25	$12.95
4 "	" "	14.25	16.25	21.65

No. B 180 3¼x6-inch C. R. I. Square Balls.

Number 2200

Length, 13 inches (over all). Spread, 12 inches.

Holders and 3¼x7-inch C. R. I. Bottom Ball included.

		Not Wired	Wired	Complete as shown No lamps
3 Electric	Rich Gilt and Satin........	$22.50	$24.00	$26.40
4 "	" " " "	27.50	29.50	32.90
5 "	" " " "	32.50	35.00	39.40

3¼x6-inch C. R. I. Balls.

Price in right hand column always includes sockets; also holders and shades if shown but no lamps.
Other prices include glassware, sockets, lamps or electric holders only where mentioned.

$250

$250

Number 1866
Length, 16 inches (over all). Spread, 12 inches.
4x8-inch C. R. I. Bottom Ball included.

		Not Wired	Wired	Complete as shown No lamps
4 Electric	Rich Gilt	$8.75	$9.75	$13.75
5 "	" "	9.00	10.25	15.45

3¼x6-inch C. R. I. Balls.

Number 2502
Length, 11 inches. Spread, 18 inches.

		Not Wired	Wired	Complete as shown No lamps
3 Electric	Brush Brass	$7.50	$9.00	$12.75
4 "	" "	8.25	10.25	15.25
5 "	" "	9.00	11.50	17.75
6 "	" "	9.75	12.75	20.25

Shades No. B 007½ Frosted, with Crystal Stars and Bars. Diameter, 7 inches.

$275

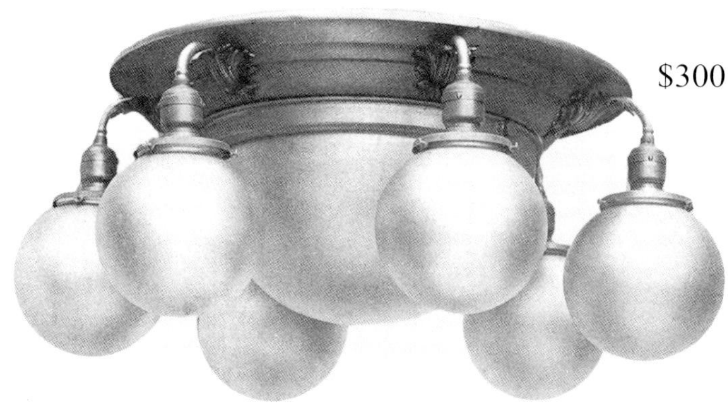

$300

Number 1687
Length, 12 inches (over all). Spread, 15 inches.

		Not Wired	Wired	Complete as shown No lamps
2 Electric	Brush Brass	$9.40	$10.40	$13.40
4 "	" "	11.90	13.90	19.90

No. G 446 3¼-inch Holders with Glass Bead Fringe.

Number 2295
Spread, 20 inches.
12-inch C. R. I. Bowl included.

			Not Wired	Wired	Complete as shown No lamps
5 Electric	(3 lights outside)	Rich Gilt..	$14.25	$15.50	$19.90
6 "	(4 " ")	" " ..	15.50	17.00	22.60
7 "	(5 " ")	" " ..	16.75	18.50	25.30
8 "	(6 " ")	" " ..	18.00	20.00	28.00

3¼x6-inch C. R. I. Balls.

Price in right hand column always includes sockets; also holders and shades if shown but no lamps.
Other prices include glassware, sockets, lamps or electric holders only where mentioned.

$400

Number 2109

Length, 16 inches (over all). Spread, 20 inches.

Made of Iron.

3¼-inch Holders and 14-inch C. R. I. Bowl included.

		Not Wired	Wired	Complete as shown No lamps
7 Electric (3 lights inside)	Antique Old / Brass only	$70.80	$74.30	$79.50

3¼x6-inch C. R. I. Balls.

$300

Number 2534

Length, 17 inches (over all). Spread, 16 inches.

		Not Wired	Wired	Complete as shown No lamps
3 Electric	Brush Brass and Black....	$9.00	$10.50	$16.50
4 "	" " " " "	11.00	13.00	21.00
5 "	" " " " "	13.00	15.50	25.50

Shades No. G 448 Crystal Roughed Inside with Glass Bead Fringe.

$300

Number 2266

Length, 13 inches (over all). Spread, 20 inches.

Brass Shades and Colonial Prisms included.

		Not Wired	Wired	Complete as shown No lamps
2 Electric	Brush Brass	$17.00	$18.00	$18.80
4 "	" "	30.00	32.00	33.60

$325

Number 2201

Length, 16 inches. Spread, 20 inches.

3¼x8-inch C. R. I. Bottom Ball included.

		Not Wired	Wired	Complete as shown No lamps
3 Electric	Rich Gilt	$18.25	$19.75	$22.55
4 "	" "	20.50	22.50	26.50
5 "	" "	22.75	25.25	30.45
6 "	" "	25.00	28.00	34.40

3¼x6-inch C. R. I. Balls.

Price in right hand column always includes sockets; also holders and shades if shown but no lamps.
Other prices include glassware, sockets, lamps or electric holders only where mentioned.

$150

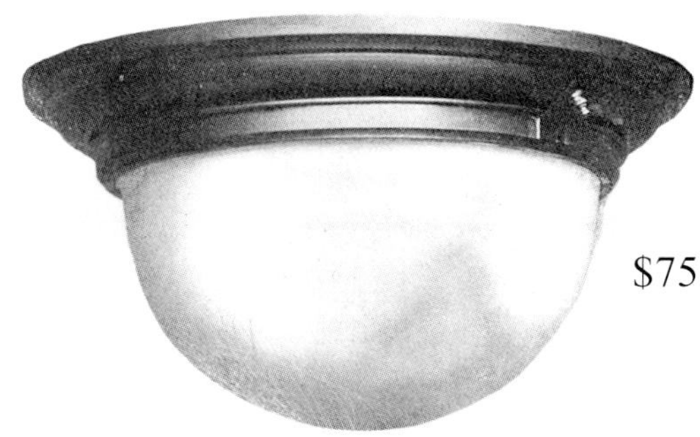

$75

Number 2296

Diameter, 20 inches. (over all).

12-inch Colonial Cut Bowl and Colonial Prisms included.

		Not Wired	Wired	Complete as shown No lamps
2 Electric	Rich Gilt	$34.10	$34.60	$35.40
3 "	" "	34.35	35.10	36.30
4 "	" "	34.60	35.60	37.20

Number 2199

Diameter, 18 inches. (over all).

14-inch C. R. I. Bowl and Hinge included.

		Not Wired	Wired	Complete as shown No lamps
2 Electric	Polished Brass	$11.70	$12.20	$13.00
3 "	" "	11.95	12.70	13.90
4 "	" "	12.20	13.20	14.80
5 "	" "	12.45	13.70	15.70
6 "	" "	12.70	14.20	16.60

$125

$400

Number 2550

Length, 29 inches (over all). Spread, 10 inches.

Lanterns and 4x6-inch C. R. I. Cylinders included.

		Not Wired	Wired	Complete as shown No lamps
2 Electric	Brush Brass	$22.55	$24.05	$24.85
3 "	" "	27.70	29.95	31.15
4 "	" "	32.85	35.85	37.45

Number 2633

Length, 31 inches (over all). Spread, 17 inches.

3¼-inch Holders included.

		Not Wired	Wired	Complete as shown No lamps
4 Electric	Brush Brass and Black.....	$112.00	$114.00	$121.60

No. B 5121 3¼x6-inch Ground and Cut Star Balls.

Price in right hand column always includes sockets; also holders and shades if shown but no lamps.
Other prices include glassware, sockets, lamps or electric holders only where mentioned.

$275

$300

Number 2655
Diameter, 18 inches
16-inch C. R. I. Bowl included.

		Not Wired	Wired	Complete as shown No lamps
4 Electric	Brush Brass and Black....	$79.75	$80.75	$82.35

Number 2658
Diameter, 20 inches.
16-inch C. R. I. Bowl and 4 only Special Sockets in Band included.

		Not Wired	Wired	Complete as shown No lamps
8 Electric (4 lights outside)	Brush Brass and Black	$87.75	$88.75	$90.35

$350

$350

Number 2636
Length, 33 inches. Diameter, 18 inches.
16-inch C. R. I. Bowl included.

		Not Wired	Wired	Complete as shown No lamps
4 Electric	Brush Brass and Black....	$116.75	$118.75	$120.35

Number 2657
Length, 31 inches. Diameter, 20 inches.
16-inch C. R. I. Bowl and 4 only Special Sockets in Band included.

		Not Wired	Wired	Complete as shown No lamps
8 Electric (4 lights outside)	Brush Brass and Black	$143.75	$147.75	$149.35

Price in right hand column always includes sockets; also holders and shades if shown but no lamps.
Other prices include glassware, sockets, lamps or electric holders only where mentioned.

Number 2176
14-inch Beaded Crystal Bowl included.

		Not Wired	Wired	Complete as shown No lamps
2 Electric	Rich Gilt	$48.60	$49.10	$49.90
3 "	" "	48.85	49.60	50.80
4 "	" "	49.10	50.10	51.70

Number 2178
Length, 18 inches (over all). Spread, 22 inches.
14-inch Beaded Crystal Bowl and Brass Shades with Prisms included.

		Not Wired	Wired	Complete as shown No lamps
8 Electric (4 lights outside)	Rich Gilt	$69.80	$72.80	$76.00
9 " (5 " ")	" "	74.10	77.60	81.20
10 " (6 " ")	" "	78.40	82.40	86.40

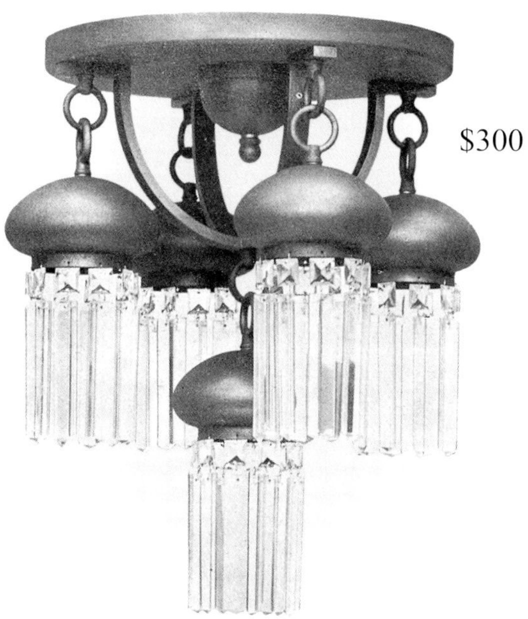

Number 2509
Length, 21 inches (over all). Spread, 13 inches.
Colonial Prisms included.

		Not Wired	Wired	Complete as shown No lamps
3 Electric	Brush Brass	$22.00	$23.50	$24.70
4 "	" "	27.00	29.00	30.60
5 "	" "	32.00	34.50	36.50

Number 2565
Length, 22 inches (over all). Spread, 18 inches.
14-inch Colonial Cut Bowl, 6-inch Prisms and Holders included.

		Not Wired	Wired	Complete as shown No lamps
6 Electric (4 lights outside)	Brush Brass	$76.40	$79.40	$81.30
7 " (5 " ")		83.45	86.95	89.25
8 " (6 " ")		90.50	94.50	97.20

Price in right hand column always includes sockets; also holders and shades if shown but no lamps.
Other prices include glassware, sockets, lamps or electric holders only where mentioned.

$350

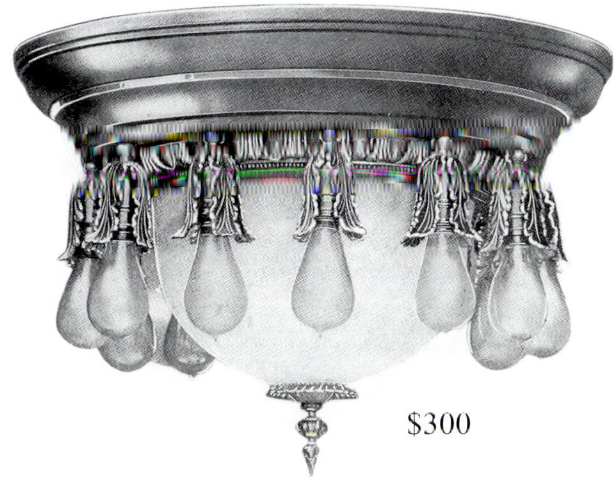

$300

Number 2567
Length, 20 inches (over all). Spread, 18 inches.
14-inch Colonial Cut Bowl and Holders included.

		Not Wired	Wired	Complete as shown No lamps
6 Electric (4 lights outside)	Brush Brass	$60.30	$62.80	$79.70
7 " (5 " ")		63.40	66.40	87.45
8 " (6 " ")		66.50	70.00	95.20

No. B 1039 4x7-inch Colonial Cut Squat Balls.

Number 1472
Socket Husks and 14-inch C. R. I. Bowl included.

		Not Wired	Wired	Complete as shown No lamps
8 Electric (6 lights outside)	Rich Gilt	$53.75	$57.75	$60.95
11 " (8 " ")	" "	58.25	63.75	68.15
14 " (10 " ")	" "	62.75	69.75	75.35
16 " (12 " ")	" "	66.75	74.75	81.15

$400

$275

Number 2564
Length, 23 inches (over all). Spread, 21 inches.
10-inch Iridescent Prisms, C. R. I. Bottom Plate, Glass Bottom Ball, and Holders included.

		Not Wired	Wired	Complete as shown No lamps
6 Electric (4 lights outside)	Brush Brass	$64.85	$68.35	$83.75
7 " (5 " ")		67.95	72.20	91.25
8 " (6 " ")		71.05	76.05	98.75

Shades No. B 672 Amber Lustre.

Number 2566
Length, 24 inches (over all).
10 and 6-inch Iridescent Prisms included.

	Not Wired	Wired	Complete as shown No lamps
4 Electric Brush Brass	$63.30	$65.30	$66.90

Price in right hand column always includes sockets; also holders and shades if shown but no lamps.
Other prices include glassware, sockets, lamps or electric holders only where mentioned.

$350

Number 2626
Length, 13 inches (over all). Spread, 23 inches.
14-inch Colonial Cut Bowl and Holders included.

		Not Wired	Wired	Complete as shown No lamps
4 Electric (2 lights outside)	Brush Brass	$31.75	$33.75	$42.85
5 " (3 " ")		34.25	36.75	50.00
6 " (4 " ")		36.75	39.75	57.15

No. B 1039 4x7-inch Colonial Cut Squat Balls.

$250

Number 1861
Length, 15 inches (over all). Spread, 12 inches.
Brass Shades and Prisms included.

		Not Wired	Wired	Complete as shown No lamps
4 Electric	Rich Gilt	$19.25	$20.25	$21.85
5 "	" "	22.00	23.25	25.25

$275

Number 2317
Length, 13 inches (over all). Spread, 14 inches.
Art Glass included.
Select Glass Colors by Number. **See last page.**

		Not Wired	Wired	Complete as shown No lamps
2 Electric	Brush Brass	$23.55	$24.55	$25.35
4 "	" "	42.85	44.85	46.45

$250

Number 1685
Length, 16 inches. Spread, 24 inches.
2¼-inch Socket Cover Holders included.

		Not Wired	Wired	Complete as shown No lamps
2 Electric	Brush Brass	$16.50	$17.50	19.30
4 "	" "	22.00	24.00	27.60

Shades No. B 9321½ C. R. I.

Price in right hand column always includes sockets; also holders and shades if shown but no lamps.
Other prices include glassware, sockets, lamps or electric holders only where mentioned.

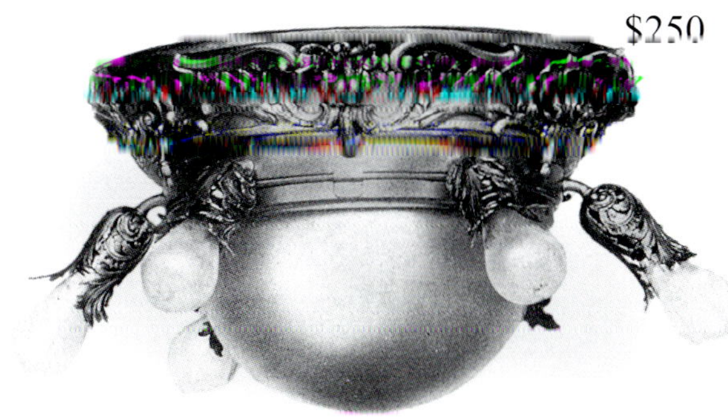

Number 1616
12-inch C. R. I. Bowl included.

		Not Wired	Wired	Complete as shown No lamps
2 Electric	Rich Gilt	$37.60	$38.10	$38.90
3 "	" "	37.85	38.60	39.80
4 "	" "	38.10	39.10	40.70
5 "	" "	38.35	39.60	41.60
6 "	" "	38.60	40.10	42.50

Number 1611
Socket Husks and 12-inch C. R. I. Bowl included.

		Not Wired	Wired	Complete as shown No lamps
6 Electric (3 outside, 3 inside)	Rich Gilt	$42.35	$44.60	$47.00
8 " (4 " 4 ")	" "	44.10	47.10	50.30
10 " (5 " 5 ")	" "	15.85	49.60	53.60
12 " (6 " 6 ")	" "	47.60	52.10	56.90

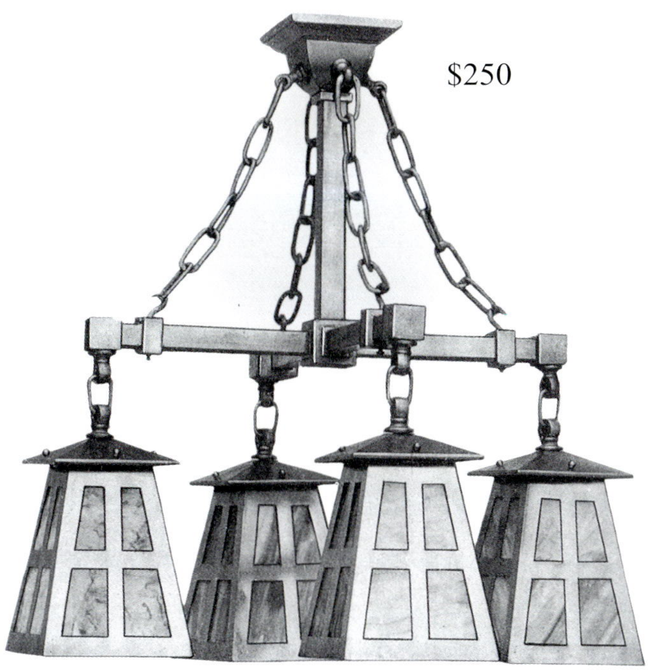

Number 2155
Length, 24 inches (over all). Spread, 18 inches.
Made of Iron.
Art Glass included.
Select Glass Colors by Number. See last page.

		Not Wired	Wired	Complete as shown No lamps
4 Electric	Antique Brush Brass only.	$36.75	$38.75	$40.35

Quotation for above fixture made of Brass, furnished upon application.

Number 2681
Length, 23 inches (over all). Spread, 19 inches.
4x10-inch C. R. I. Bottom Ball included.

		Not Wired	Wired	Complete as shown No lamps
3 Electric	Rich Gilt	$24.60	$26.10	$29.20
4 "	" "	30.60	32.60	37.05
5 "	" "	36.60	39.10	44.90
6 "	" "	42.60	45.60	52.75

3¼x7-inch Crystal Roughed Inside Balls.

Price in right hand column always includes sockets; also holders and shades if shown but no lamps.
Other prices include glassware, sockets, lamps or electric holders only where mentioned.

$100

$400

Number 1635
6x12-inch C. R. I. Ball included.

		Not Wired	Wired	Complete as shown No lamps
2 Electric	Rich Gilt ...	$15.70	$16.20	$17.00
3 "	" " ...	16.20	16.95	18.15
4 "	" " ...	16.70	17.70	19.30

Number 2179
Length, 18 inches. Spread, 32 inches.

		Not Wired	Wired	Complete as shown No lamps
4 Electric	Polished Brass and Black..............................	$69.00	$71.00	$72.60
5 "	" " " "	79.25	81.75	83.75
6 "	" " " "	89.50	92.50	94.90
7 "	" " " "	99.75	103.25	106.05
8 "	" " " "	110.00	114.00	117.20

$100

$400

Number 2682
Length, 19 inches (over all).
6x12-inch C. R. I. Ball included.

		Not Wired	Wired	Complete as shown No lamps
2 Electric	Antique Brush Brass	$35.00	$36.00	$36.80
3 "	" " "	35.50	37.00	38.20
4 "	" " "	36.00	38.00	39.60

Number 2185
Length, 21 inches. Spread, 34 inches.
12-inch C. R. I. Bowl included.

			Not Wired	Wired	Complete as shown No lamps
7 Electric	(4 lights in bowl)	Polished Brass and Black	$72.75	$76.25	$79.05
8 "	(4 " ")	" " " "	83.00	87.00	90.20
9 "	(4 " ")	" " " "	93.25	97.75	101.35
10 "	(4 " ")	" " " "	103.50	108.50	112.50
12 "	(4 " ")	" " " "	124.00	130.00	134.80

Price in right hand column always includes sockets; also holders and shades if shown but no lamps. Other prices include glassware, sockets, lamps or electric holders only where mentioned.

$300

Number 2493
Length, 20 inches.
Spread, 32 inches (over all).
Special Sockets included.

		Not Wired	Wired	Complete as shown No lamps
12 Electric (9 lights on upper, 3 lights on lower tier)	Brush Brass and Black	$123.00	$126.00	$126.00
16 " (12 " " " 4 " " " ")	" " " "	125.00	129.00	129.00
20 " (15 " " " 5 " " " ")	" " " "	127.00	132.00	132.00

$250

Number 2491
Length, 20 inches.
Spread, 32 inches (over all).
Special Sockets included.

		Not Wired	Wired	Complete as shown No lamps
12 Electric (9 lights on upper, 3 lights on lower tier)	Brush Brass	$86.00	$89.00	$89.00
16 " (12 " " " 4 " " " ")	" "	88.00	92.00	92.00
20 " (15 " " " 5 " " " ")	" "	90.00	95.00	95.00

Price in right hand column always includes sockets; also holders and shades if shown but no lamps.
Other prices include glassware, sockets, lamps or electric holders only where mentioned.

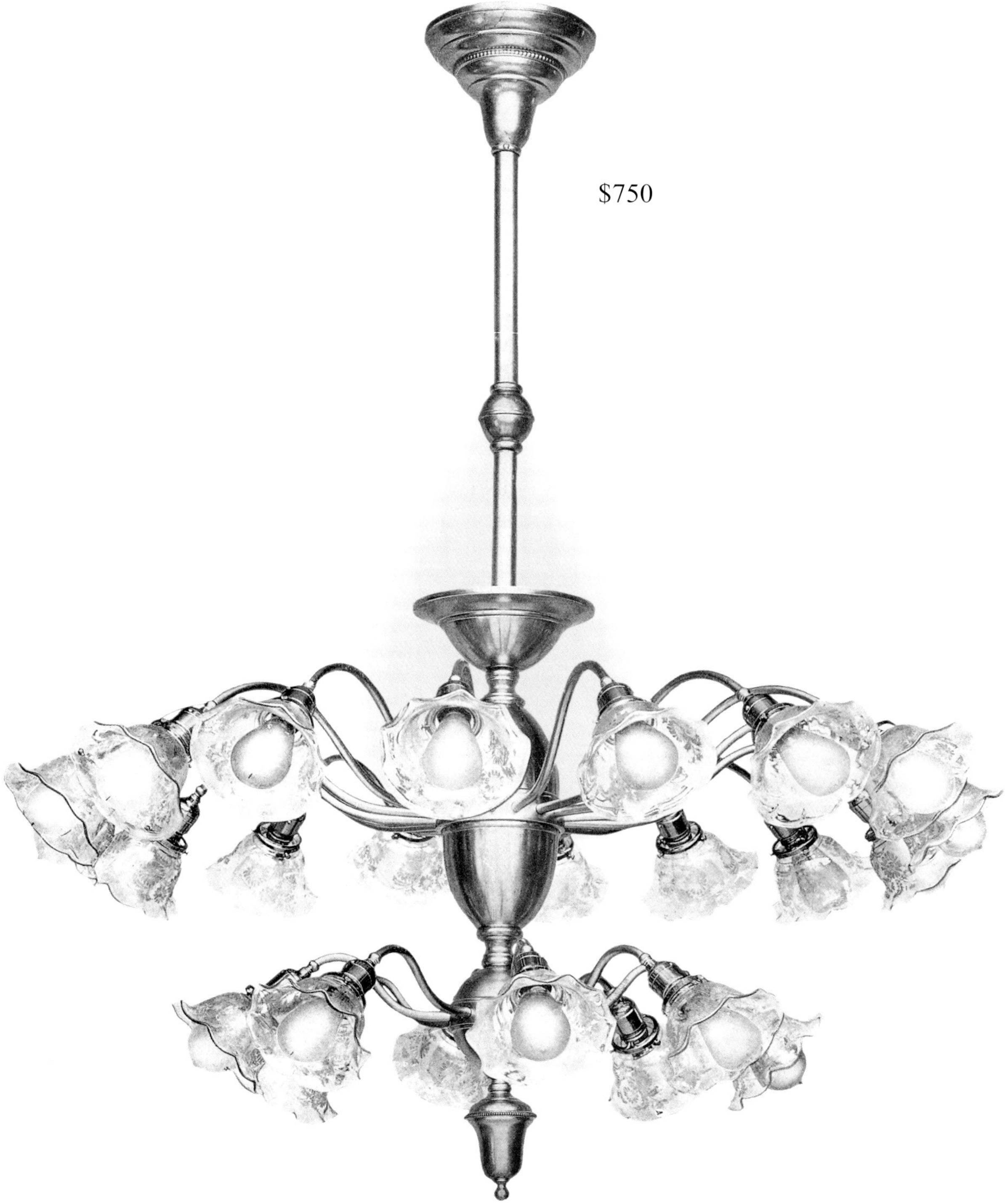

$750

Number 1929

Length, 57 inches. Spread, 44 inches.

			Not Wired	Wired	Complete as shown No lamps
12	Electric	Polished Brass	**$31.00**	**$37.00**	**$47.80**
15	"	" "	**33.75**	**41.25**	**54.75**
18	"	" "	**36.50**	**45.50**	**61.70**
21	"	" "	**39.25**	**49.75**	**68.65**
24	"	" "	**42.00**	**54.00**	**75.60**

Shades No. B 1906½ White Acid.

Price in right hand column always includes sockets; also holders and shades if shown but no lamps. Other prices include glassware, sockets, lamps or electric holders only where mentioned.

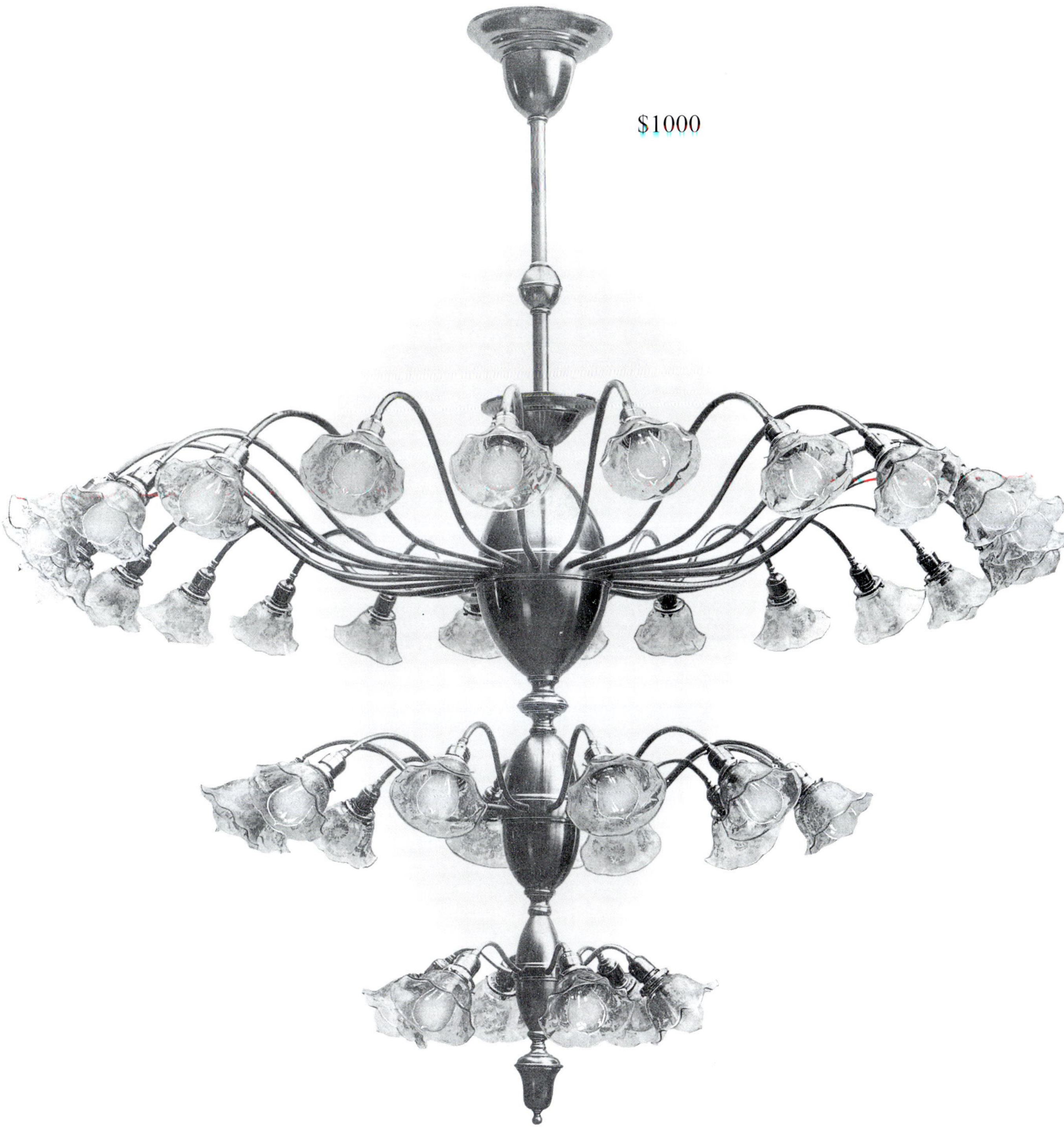

Number 1970

Length, 84 inches. Spread, 68 inches.

			Not Wired	Wired	Complete as shown No lamps
28	Electric	Polished Brass	$70.00	$84.00	$109.20
35	"	" "	77.00	94.50	126.00
42	"	" "	84.00	105.00	142.80

Shades No. B 1906½ White Acid.

Price in right hand column always includes sockets; also holders and shades if shown but no lamps. Other prices include glassware, sockets, lamps or electric holders only where mentioned.

$650

Number 1931
Length, 44 inches. Spread, 36 inches.

		Not Wired	Wired	Complete as shown No lamps
4 Electric	Rich Gilt	$33.00	$35.00	$38.60
6 "	" "	39.00	42.00	47.40
8 "	" "	45.00	49.00	56.20
10 "	" "	51.00	56.00	65.00

Shades No. B 1906½ White Acid.

Price in right hand column always includes sockets; also holders and shades if shown but no lamps.
Other prices include glassware, sockets, lamps or electric holders only where mentioned.

Number 1928

Length, 54 inches. Spread, 36 inches.

			Not Wired	Wired	Complete as shown No lamps
12	Electric	Rich Gilt	$56.50	$62.50	$73.30
14	"	" "	61.75	68.75	81.35
16	"	" "	67.00	75.00	89.40
18	"	" "	72.25	81.25	97.45

Shades No. B 1906½ White Acid.

Price in right hand column always includes sockets; also holders and shades if shown but no lamps. Other prices include glassware, sockets, lamps or electric holders only where mentioned.

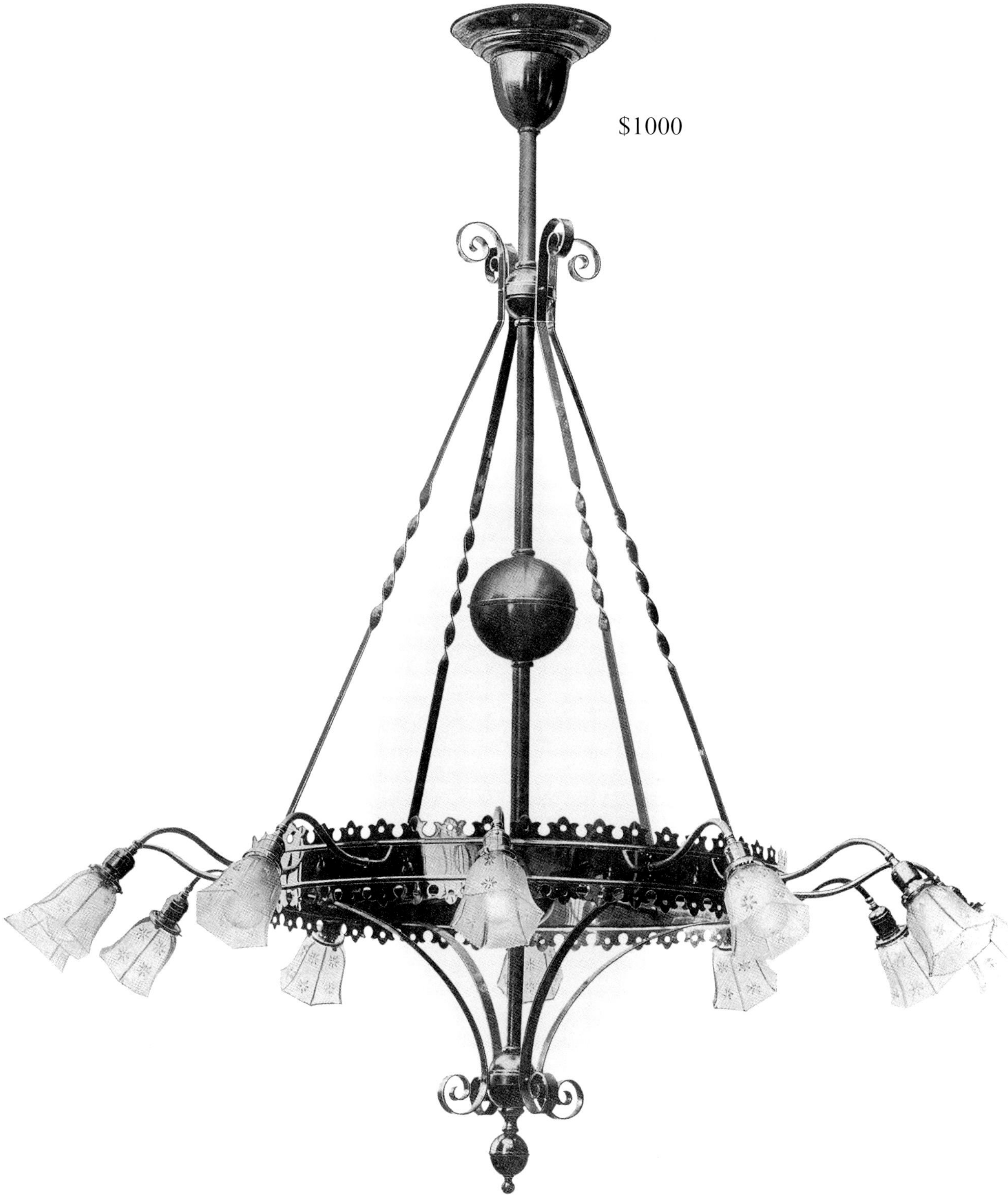

Number 1804

Length, 72 inches. Spread, 58 inches.

		Not Wired	Wired	Complete as shown No lamps
12 Electric	Polished Brass	$64.00	$70.00	$79.00
16 "	" "	68.00	76.00	88.00
20 "	" "	72.00	82.00	97.00
24 "	" "	76.00	88.00	106.00

Shades No. B 41½ Crystal.

Price in right hand column always includes sockets; also holders and shades if shown but no lamps. Other prices include glassware, sockets, lamps or electric holders only where mentioned.

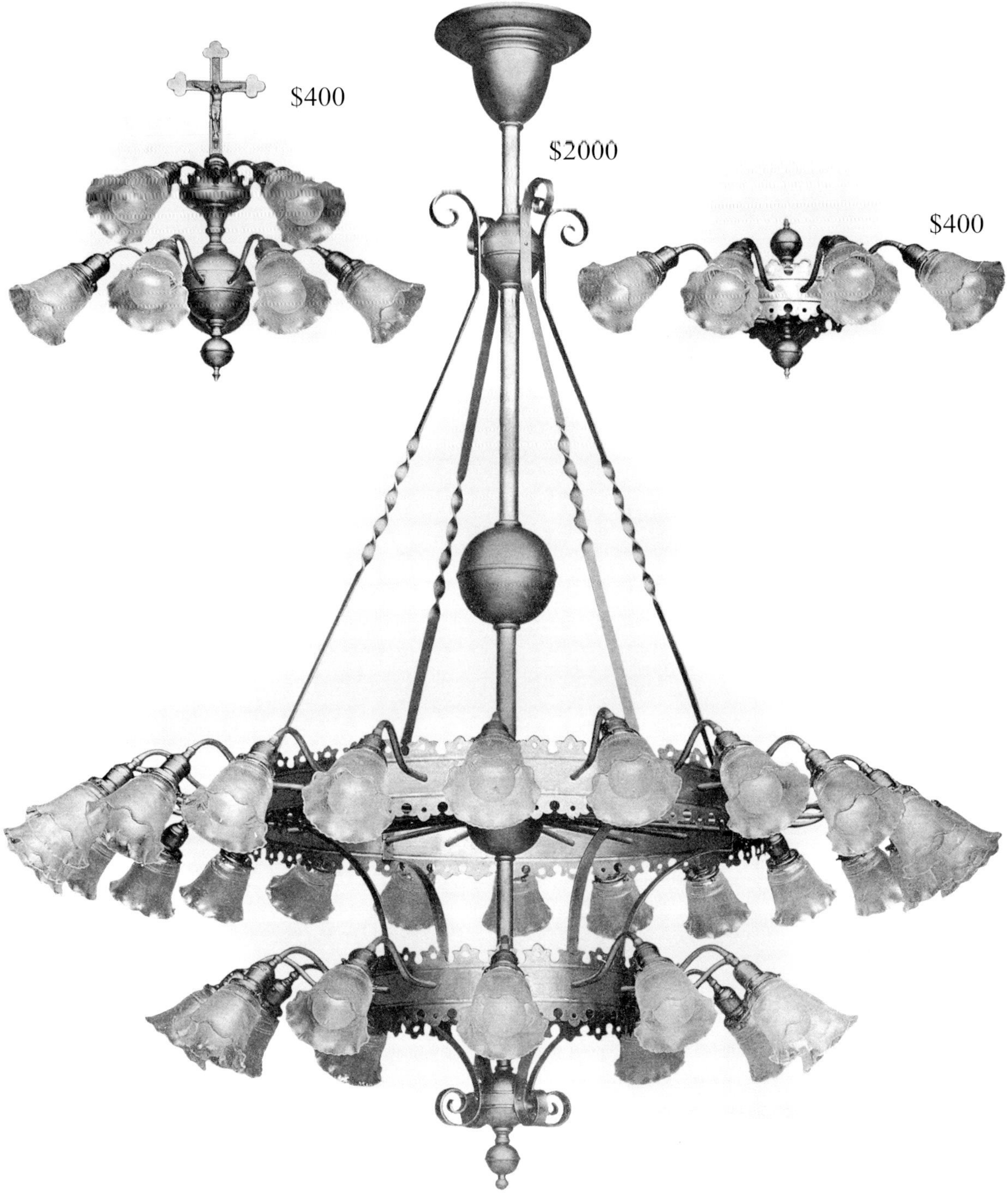

Number 1620

Length, 78 inches. Spread, 60 inches.

		Not Wired	Wired	Complete as shown No lamps
30 Electric	Polished Brass	$99.50	$114.50	$138.50
36 "	" "	105.00	123.00	151.80
42 "	" "	110.50	131.50	165.10

Shades No. B 973½ Crystal.

Price in right hand column always includes sockets; also holders and shades if shown but no lamps. Other prices include glassware, sockets, lamps or electric holders only where mentioned.

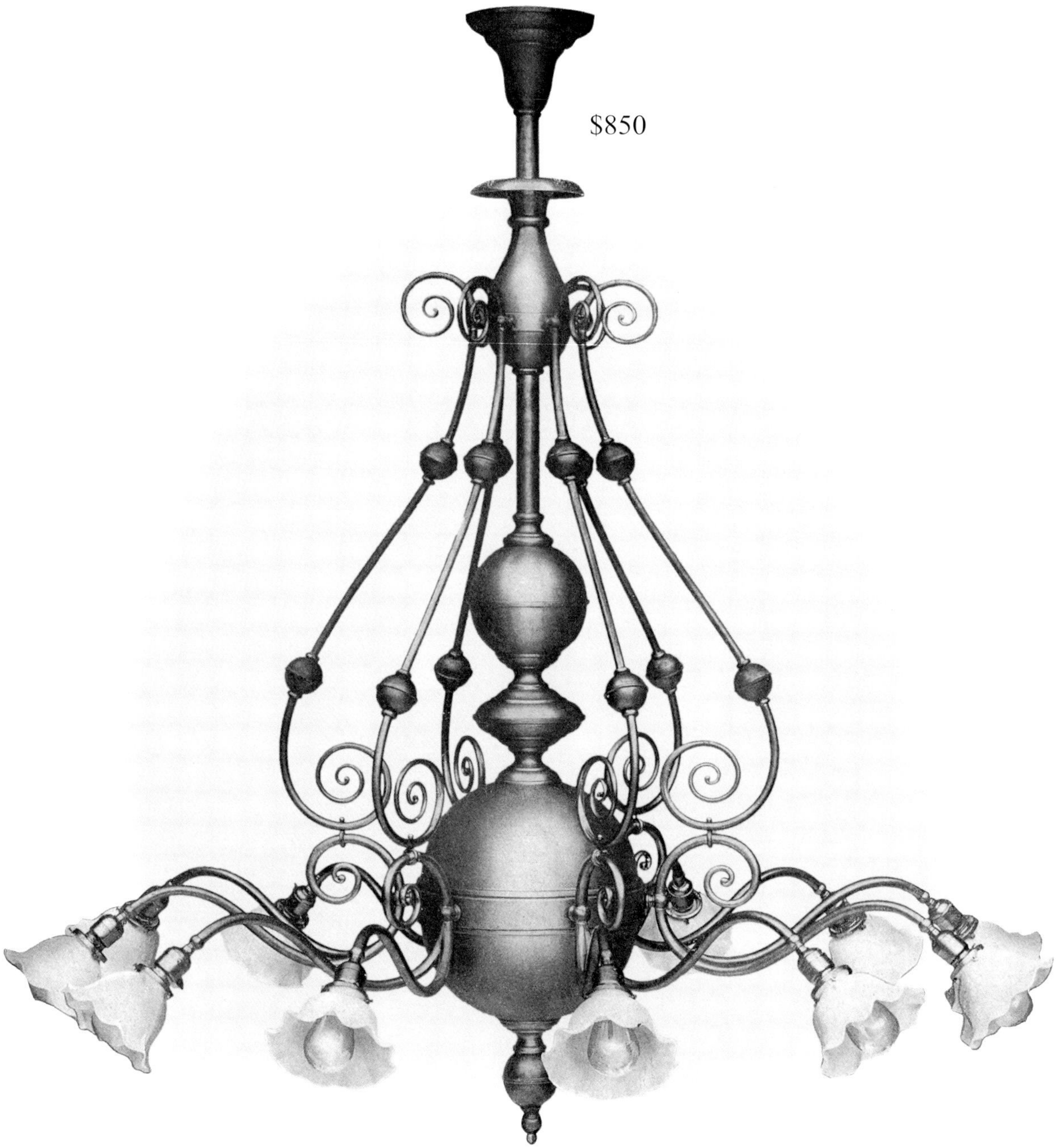

$850

Number 1645

Length, 72 inches. Spread, 54 inches.

		Not Wired	Wired	Complete as shown No lamps
8 Electric	Polished Brass	$62.50	$66.50	$72.10
10 "	" "	70.00	75.00	82.00
12 "	" "	77.50	83.50	91.90
Same fixture as above, made with two tiers of lights:				
15 Electric (10 arms on lower, 5 arms on upper tier)	Polished Brass	85.50	93.00	103.50
18 " (12 " " " 6 " " " ")	" "	96.00	105.00	117.60
21 " (14 " " " 7 " " " ")	" "	106.50	117.00	131.70
24 " (16 " " " 8 " " " ")	" "	117.00	129.00	145.80

Shades No B 256½ Opal.

Price in right hand column always includes sockets; also holders and shades if shown but no lamps. Other prices include glassware, sockets, lamps or electric holders only where mentioned.

$2000

			Not Wired	Wired	Complete as shown No lamps
28	Electric	Rich Gilt	$115.50	$129.50	$154.70
31	"	" "	124.25	139.75	167.65
35	"	" "	133.50	151.00	182.50
38	"	" "	135.50	154.50	188.70

Shades No. B 1906½ White Acid.

Price in right hand column always includes sockets; also holders and shades if shown but no lamps.

Other prices include glassware, sockets, lamps or electric holders only where mentioned.

Number 2305
Length, 72 inches (over all). Spread, 50 inches.
Holders included.

$1750

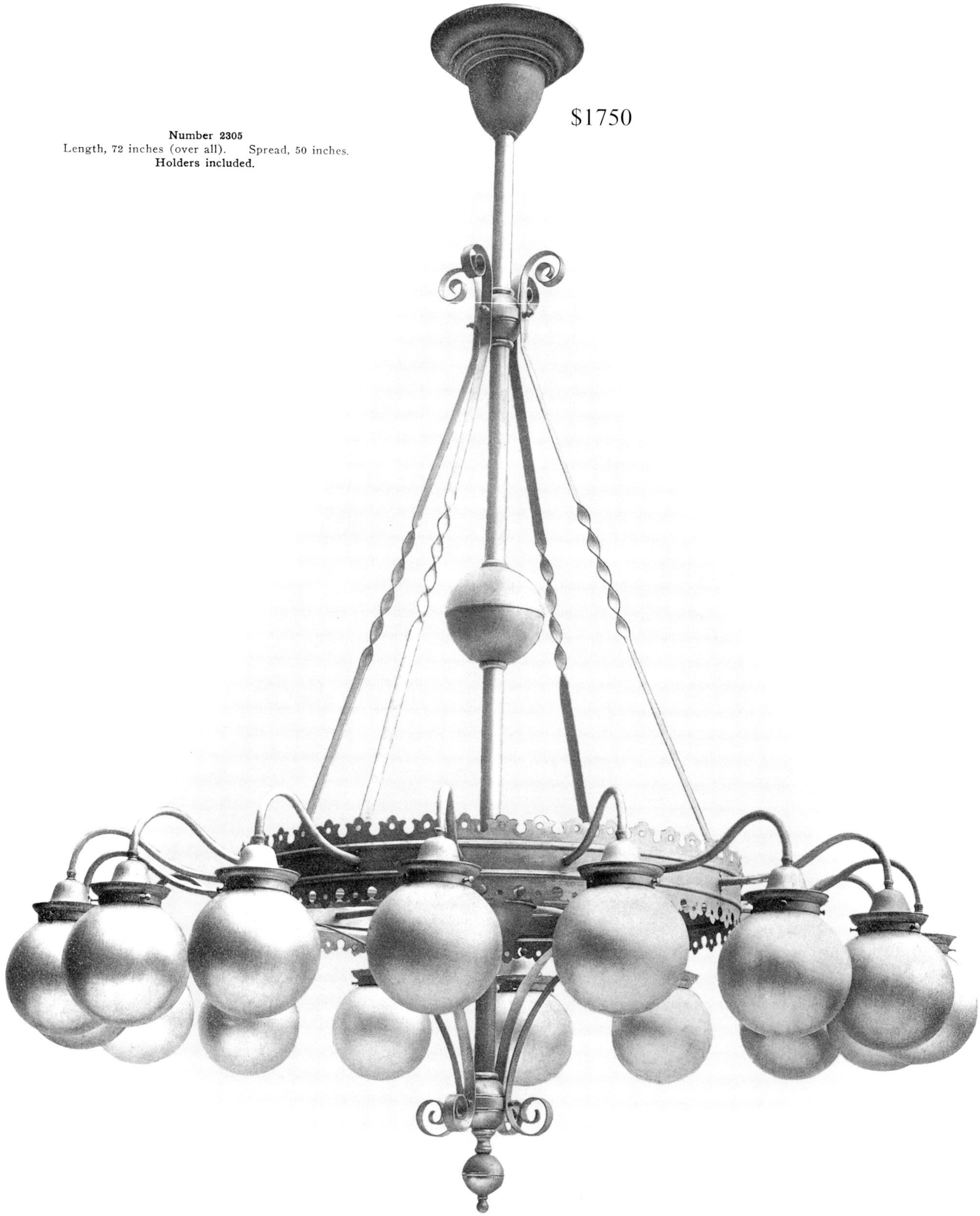

		Not Wired	Wired	Complete as shown No lamps
12 Electric	Rich Gilt	$76.00	$82.00	$95.80
14 "	" "	80.00	87.00	103.10
16 "	" "	84.00	92.00	110.40

3¼x7-inch Crystal Roughed Inside Balls.

Price in right hand column always includes sockets; also holders and shades if shown but no lamps.
Other prices include glassware, sockets, lamps or electric holders only where mentioned.

$2000

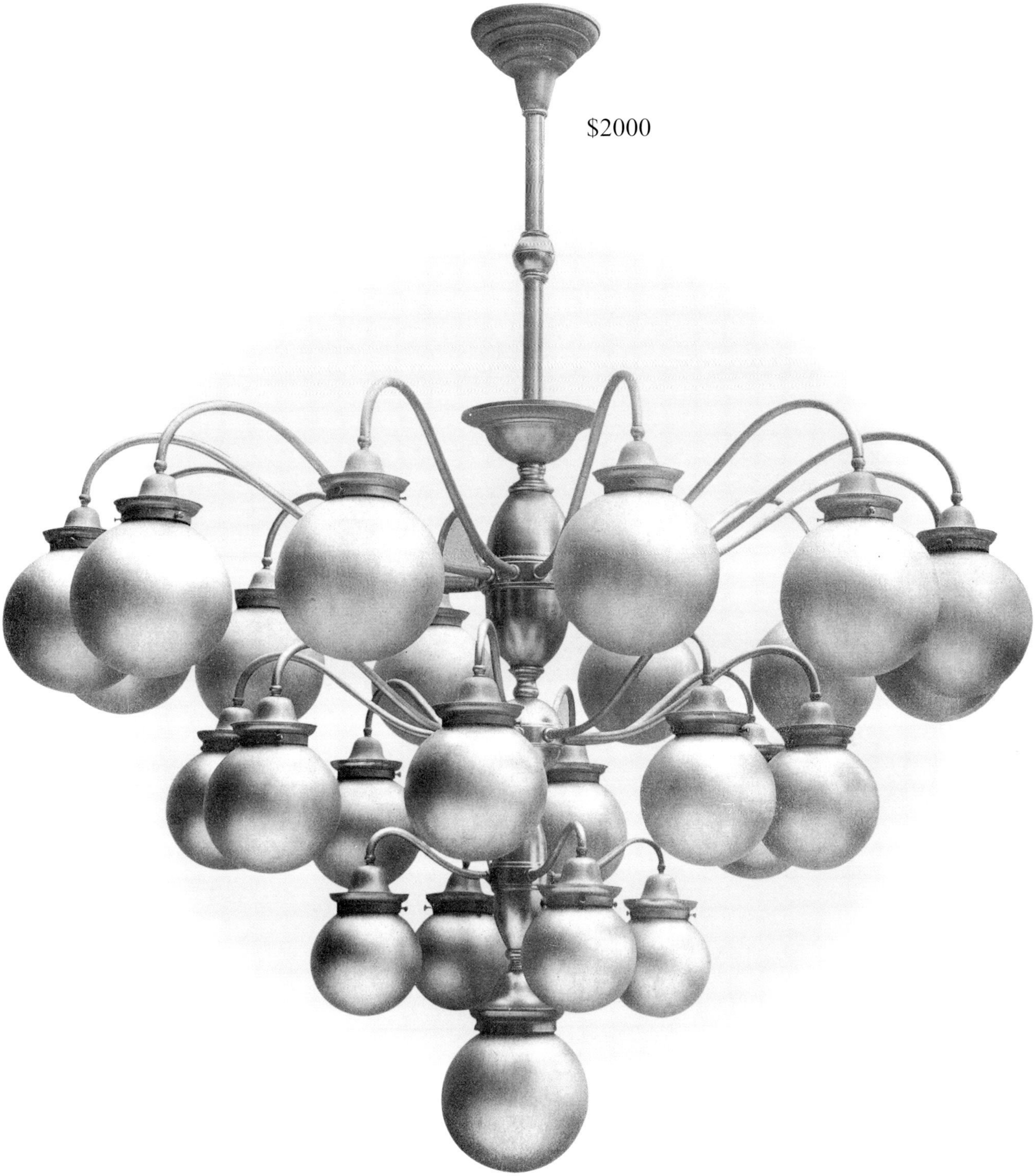

Number 2683

Length, 82 inches (over all). Spread, 48 inches.

4x8-inch C. R. I. Bottom Ball and Holder, and Holders on Arms included.

	Not Wired	Wired	Complete as shown No lamps
20 Electric Rich Gilt	$62.50	$72.50	$95.80
25 " " "	73.00	85.50	114.70

3¼x6, 3¼x7 and 3¼x8-inch Crystal Roughed Inside Balls.

Price in right hand column always includes sockets; also holders and shades if shown but no lamps. Other prices include glassware, sockets, lamps or electric holders only where mentioned.

Number 2505
Length, 92 inches. Spread, 48 inches (over all).

Price in right hand column always includes sockets; also holders and shades if shown but no lamps.
Other prices include glassware, sockets, lamps or electric holders only where mentioned.

$1500

	Not Wired	Wired	Complete as shown No lamps
12 Electric (8 lights on upper, 4 lights on lower tier) Brush Brass	**$256.45**	**$265.45**	**$280.45**
15 " (10 " " " 5 " " " ") " "	**257.20**	**268.45**	**287.20**
18 " (12 " " " 6 " " " ") " "	**257.95**	**271.45**	**293.95**

Shades No. B 007½ Frosted, with Crystal Stars and Bars. Diameter, 7 inches.
Extra lengthening, Brass Plated Steel Chain used, per foot, **$1.10**.

Number 2466
Length, 68 inches. Spread, 45 inches (over all).
Candles included.

Price in right hand column always includes sockets; also holders and shades if shown but no lamps.
Other prices include glassware, sockets, lamps or electric holders only where mentioned.

$1250

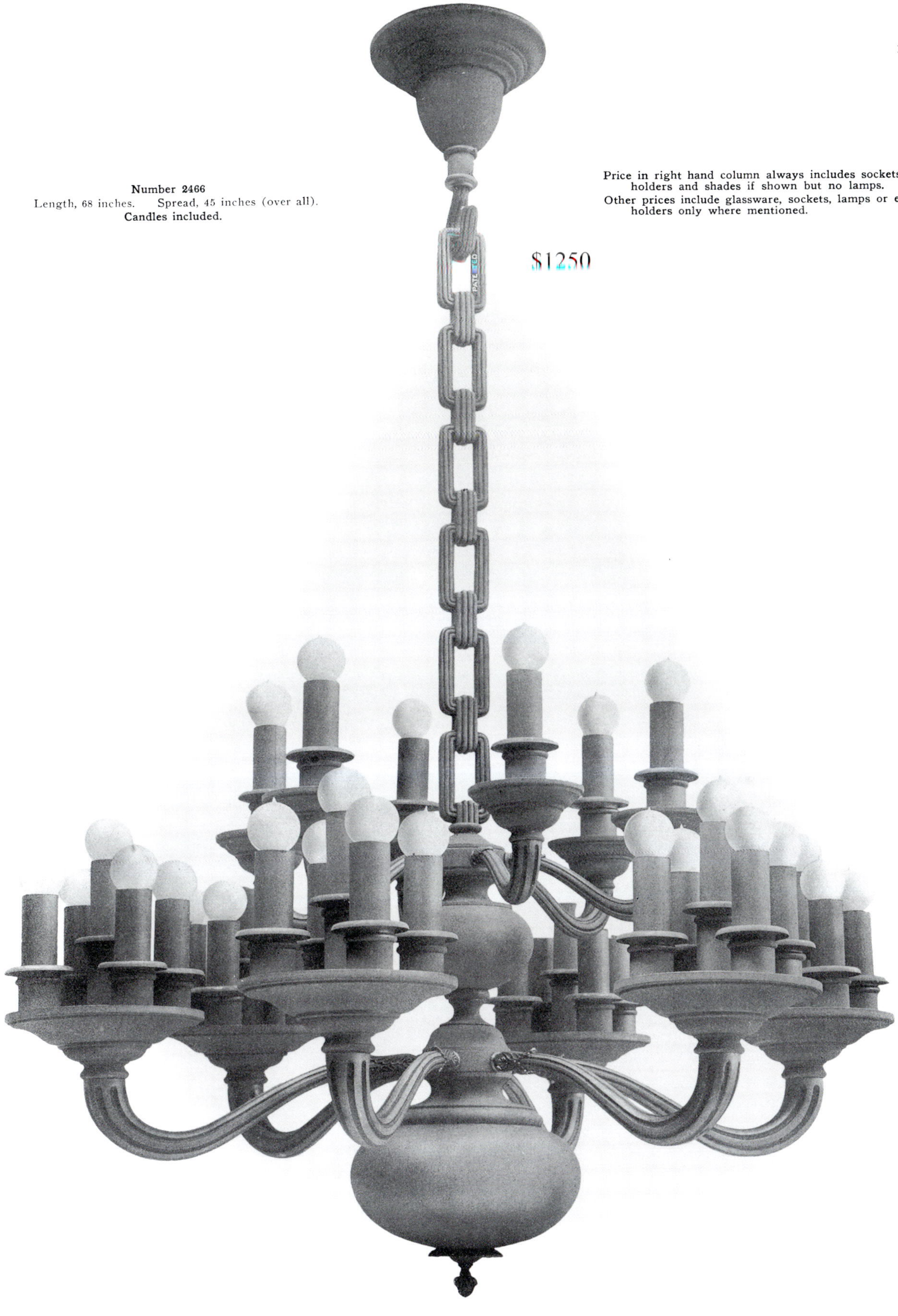

		Not Wired	Wired	Complete as shown No lamps
24 Electric (4 upper, 4 lower arms)	Brush Brass with Black Relief	$159.00	$167.25	$176.85
30 " (5 " 5 " ")	" " " " "	185.00	195.00	207.00
36 " (6 " 6 " ")	" " " " "	211.00	222.75	237.15

One light on upper arms, five lights on lower arms. Beardslee Patent Chandelier Stem Concealing Wires used in Stem. Extra lengthening per foot, $7.50.

$1750

Number 2143
Length, 78 inches (over all.) Spread, 53 inches.
4x10-inch C. R. I. Bottom Ball included.

Price in right hand column always includes sockets; also holders and shades if shown but no lamps.
Other prices include glassware, sockets, lamps or electric holders only where mentioned.

			Not Wired	Wired	Complete as shown No lamps
9	Electric	Polished Brass and Black..	$122.80	$127.30	$134.10
13	"	" " " " ..	126.80	133.30	143.30
17	"	" " " " ..	130.80	139.30	152.50
21	"	" " " " ..	134.80	145.30	161.70

Shades No. B 8983½ Crystal Roughed Inside.

$2500

Number 2144
Length, 84 inches (over all). Spread, 60 inches.

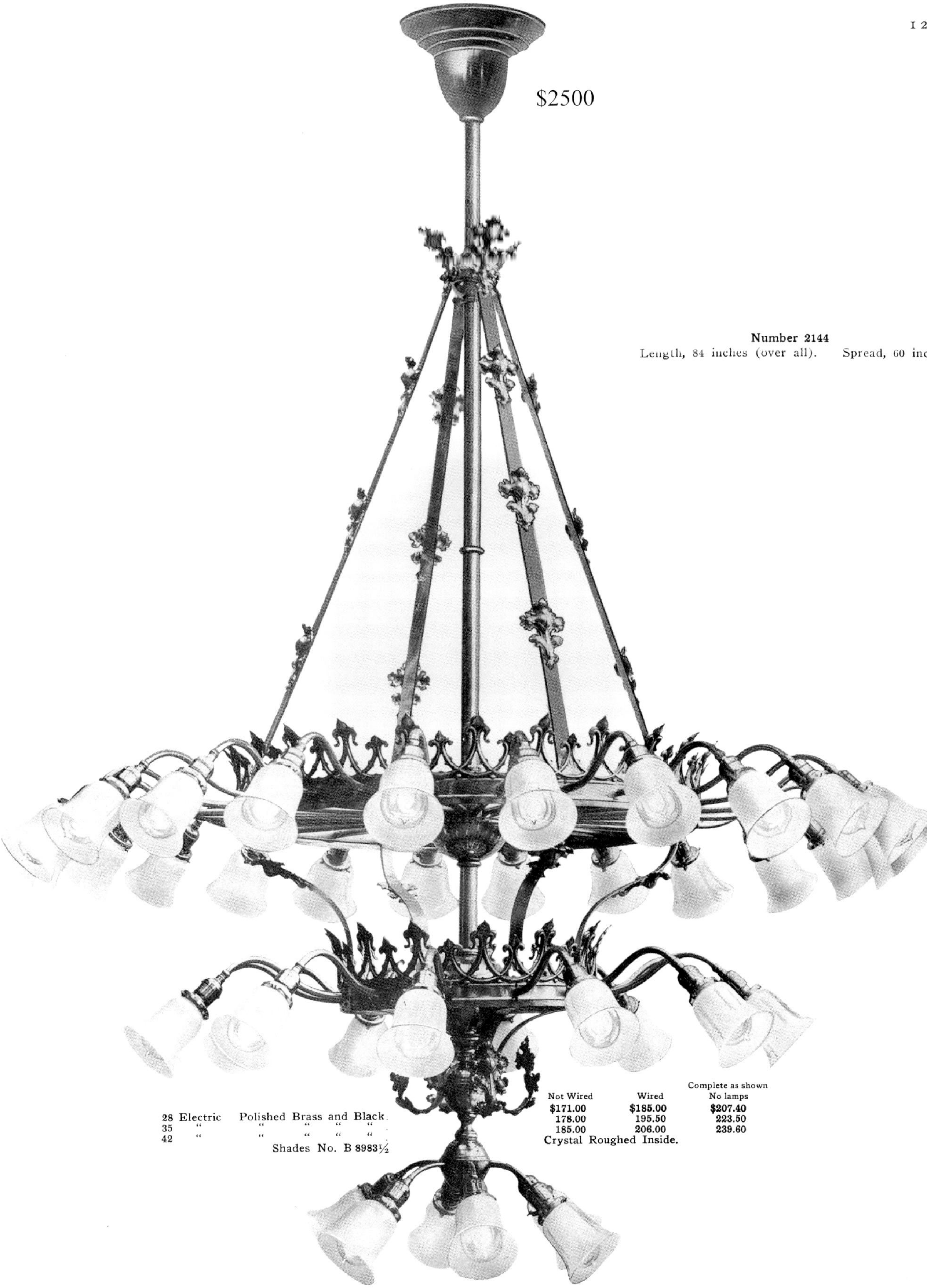

		Not Wired	Wired	Complete as shown No lamps
28 Electric	Polished Brass and Black.	**$171.00**	**$185.00**	**$207.40**
35 "	" " " "	178.00	195.50	223.50
42 "	" " " "	185.00	206.00	239.60

Shades No. B 8983½ Crystal Roughed Inside.

Price in right hand column always includes sockets; also holders and shades if shown but no lamps.
Other prices include glassware, sockets, lamps or electric holders only where mentioned.

$850

Number 1927
Length, 56 inches (over all). Spread, 30 inches.
4x10-inch C. R. I. Bottom Ball included.

		Not Wired	Wired	Complete as shown No lamps
7 Electric	Black Iron only	$26.30	$29.80	$37.40
9 "	" " "	28.30	32.80	42.80
11 "	" " "	30.30	35.80	48.20
13 "	" " "	32.30	38.80	53.60

3¼x6-inch Crystal Roughed Inside Balls.
Extra lengthening per foot, 50 cents.
Quotation for above fixture made of Brass, furnished upon application.

Price in right hand column always includes sockets; also holders and shades if shown but no lamps.
Other prices include glassware, sockets, lamps or electric holders only where mentioned.

Number 2546
Length, 66 inches. Spread, 32 inches (over all).
Special Sockets included.

	Not Wired	Wired	Complete as shown No lamps
12 Electric Brush Brass	$111.00	$117.00	$117.00
16 " " "	113.00	121.00	121.00
20 " " "	115.00	125.00	125.00

Extra lengthening, Brass Plated Steel Chain used, per foot, $1.10.

Number 2547
Length, 73 inches (over all). Spread, 35 inches (over all).
6-Light Clusters included.

	Not Wired	Wired	Complete as shown No lamps
36 Electric Brush Brass and Black....	$223.10	$226.10	$226.10

Extra lengthening, Brass Plated Steel Chain used, per foot $1.10.

Price in right hand column always includes sockets; also holders and shades if shown but no lamps.
Other prices include glassware, sockets, lamps or electric holders only where mentioned.

$850

Number 2497

Length, 92 inches. Spread, 48 inches (over all).

Special Sockets included.

	Not Wired	Wired	Complete as shown No lamps
27 Electric (18 lights on upper, 6 lights on middle, 3 lights on lower tier) Brush Brass	$282.00	$295.50	$295.50
40 " (24 " " " 12 " " " 4 " " " ") " "	288.50	308.50	308.50
50 " (30 " " " 15 " " " 5 " " " ") " "	293.50	318.50	318.50

Extra lengthening, Brass Plated Steel Chain used, per foot, $1.10.

Price in right hand column always includes sockets; also holders and shades if shown but no lamps.
Other prices include glassware, sockets, lamps or electric holders only where mentioned.

$700

Number 2496

Length, 92 inches. Spread, 48 inches (over all).

Special Sockets included.

		Not Wired	Wired	Complete as shown No lamps
27 Electric (18 lights on upper, 6 lights on middle, 3 lights on lower tier)	Brush Brass and Black	$350.00	$363.50	$363.50
40 " (24 " " " 12 " " " 4 " " " ")	" " " "	356.50	376.50	376.50
50 " (30 " " " 15 " " " 5 " " " ")	" " " "	361.50	386.50	386.50

Extra lengthening, Brass Plated Steel Chain used, per foot, $1.10.

Price in right hand column always includes sockets; also holders and shades if shown but no lamps.
Other prices include glassware, sockets, lamps or electric holders only where mentioned.

$1000

Number 2516
Length, 100 inches (over all). Spread, 51 inches (over all).
6-Light Clusters included.

	Not Wired	Wired	Complete as shown No lamps
96 Electric Brush Brass and Black....	$501.10	$513.10	$513.10

Extra lengthening, Brass Plated Steel Chain used, per foot $1.10.

Price in right hand column always includes sockets; also holders and shades if shown but no lamps.
Other prices include glassware, sockets, lamps or electric holders only where mentioned.

$1100

Number 1932
Length, 96 inches (over all). Spread, 60 inches.
4x10-inch C. R. I. Bottom Ball included.

	Not Wired	Wired	Complete as shown No lamps
40 Electric Rich Gilt	$152.75	$172.75	$219.95
53 " " "	170.00	196.50	259.30

3¼x6-inch Crystal Roughed Inside Balls.

Prices in right hand column always includes sockets; also holders and shades if shown but no lamps. Other prices include glassware sockets, lamps and electric holders only where mentioned.

Beardslee Patent Chandelier Stem.

Made for Electric, Gas or Combination fixtures, concealing wires and gas tubes, simulating a chain; can be applied to any chandelier or can be used to suspend an arc light. Also used on dining room domes.

Patented October 19th 1909

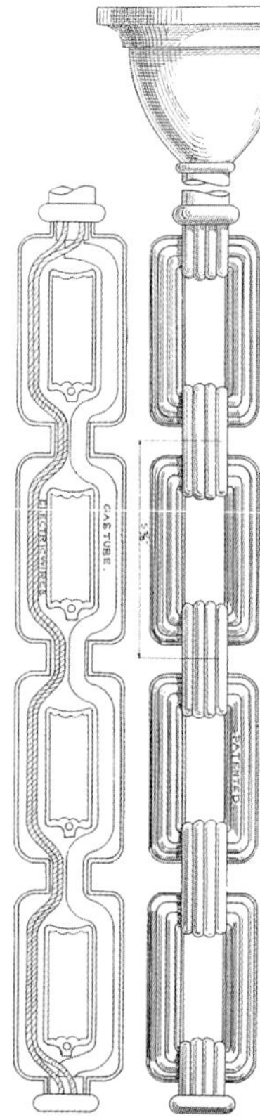

Number A2
Length, 30 inches (over all)
Brush Brass and Black.
Large Size.
1¼-inch Casing. ¼-inch Iron Pipe.

Number		Complete as shown
A1	Large size Electric Stem	$20.50
	Extra lengthening per foot	7.50
A2	Large size Combination Stem	21.25
	Extra lengthening per foot	8.50
A3	Large Size Gas Stem	21.25
	Extra lengthening per foot	8.50
	Gas tube will supply 8 lights.	
	Medium Size. 7/8-inch Casing. ¼-inch Iron Pipe.	
A4	Medium size Electric Stem	$11.50
	Extra lengthening per foot	3.50
A5	Medium Size Combination Stem	12.40
	Extra lengthening per foot	3.90
A6	Medium size Gas Stem	12.40
	Extra lengthening per foot	3.90
	Gas tube will supply 4 lights.	
	Small Size. ¾-inch Casing. ¼-inch Iron Pipe.	
A7	Small size Electric Stem	$6.70
	Extra lengthening per foot	2.25
A8	Small size Gas Stem	7.65
	Extra lengthening per foot	2.65
	Gas tube will supply 1 or 2 lights.	

Number 052
Polished Brass. Length, 12 inches.
Wireless Cluster. No Sockets Required.

With Holder and 14-in. opal shade shown		With Holder but without shade	
2 light	$3.15	2 light	$2.55
3 light	3.40	3 light	2.80
4 light	3.65	4 light	3.05
5 light	3.90	5 light	3.30
6 light	4.15	6 light	3.55

Made for Edison Base only.
For wiring above, add 50 cents.

Standard Sockets.

Number 970 Polished Brass. Number 971

Number		Each
970	Edison Key Socket	$0.33
971	Edison Keyless Socket	.30

Old Brass, Brush Brass, Black Iron, Rich Gilt, two cents each list extra.
All other brass finishes except Sand Blast, all copper finishes except Sand Blast, Nickel and Acid Bronze, four cents each list extra.
All Sand Blast and other finishes not specified, six cents each list extra.

Hubbell Pull Socket.

Number		Each
951	Edison Base	$0.60

Old Brass, Brush Brass, Black Iron, Rich Gilt, three cents each list extra.
All other brass finishes except Sand Blast, all copper finishes except Sand Blast, Nickel, Acid Bronze, six cents each list extra.
All Sand Blast and other finishes not specified, ten cents each list extra.

Number 216
1-piece Cluster Shade Holder.
3¼-inch. Slips ¾-inch Casing.
Polished Brass, each $0.30

Number 05339
Hubbell Shade Holder.

		Each	Per Doz.	Per Gross
05339	Polished Brass, 2¼-in.	$0.10	$1.00	$10.00
05340	" " 3¼-in.	.20	2.00	20.00

For other finishes add three cents each to list price.

Heavy Electric Shade Holders.

Number		Each	Per Doz.	Per Gross
07943	Polished Brass, 2¼-in.	$0.10	$1.00	$10.00
987½	" " 3¼-in.	.20	1.50	13.00
486	" " 4 -in.	.30	2.00	

For other finishes add two cents each to list price.

Light Competitive Electric Shade Holders.

Number		Per Doz.	Per Gro.
986½	Polished Brass, 2¼-in.	$0.80	$7.00

For other finishes add two cents each list.

Number 092

Number 952
Adjustable Socket Cluster Plug. Polished Brass.
No. 952 2 light with Plug, wired $1.25
No. 953 3 " " " " 1.55
No. 954 4 " " " " 1.85
Benjamin Adjustable Plug and Socket Clusters are designed for use with dome fixtures and stand lamps where more than one light is wanted. The socket may be turned to any position between two points 180 degrees apart and locked by means of a screw.

Wall Sockets.

Number 976 Number 977
Polished Brass.

Number		Each
976	Edison Key Wall Socket	$0.44
977	Edison Keyless Wall Socket	.40

Old Brass, Brush Brass, Black Iron, Rich Gilt, two cents each list extra.
All other brass finishes except Sand Blast, all copper finishes except Sand Blast, Nickel and Acid Bronze, four cents each list extra.
All Sand Blast and other finishes not specified, six cents each list extra.

Number 951
Hubbell Pull Socket.
Polished Brass.

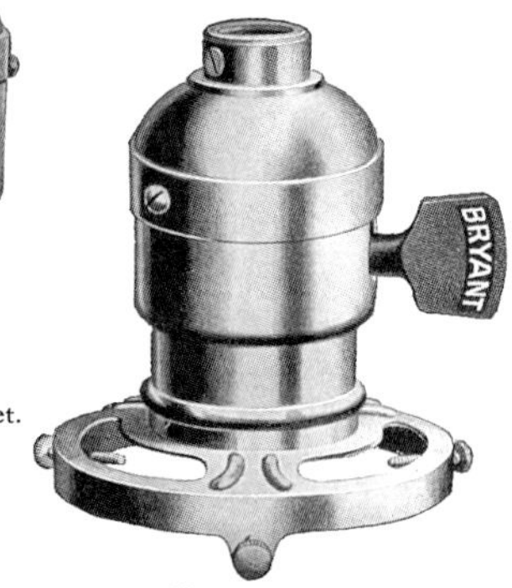

Number 948
Socket with Holder Attached.
Polished Brass.

Number			Each
948	Edison Key	2¼-in. Shade Holder	$0.39
947	Edison Keyless	2¼-in. " "	.36
948½	Edison Key	3¼-in. " "	.47
947½	Edison Keyless	3¼-in. " "	.44

The Shade Holder that DON'T come off. Holder attached rigidly and permanently to shell of socket.
Old Brass, Brush Brass, Black Iron, Rich Gilt, four cents each list extra.
All other brass finishes except Sand Blast, all copper finishes except Sand Blast, Nickel, Acid Bronze, six cents each list extra.
All Sand Blast and other finishes not specified, eight cents each list extra.

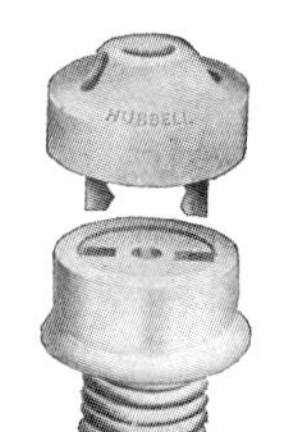

Number 05406
Hubbell Attachment Plug
Edison.
Porcelain Cap, each .. $0.30

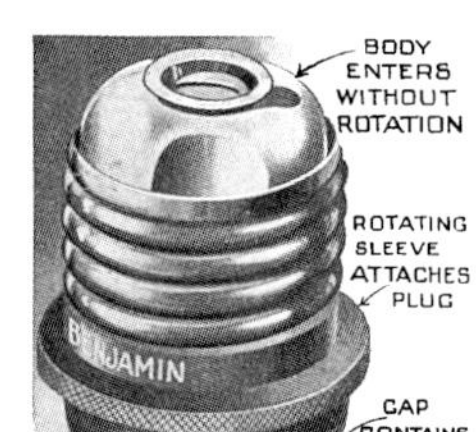

Number 903
Attachment Plug.
Each $0.25

Number 092
Polished Brass.
Edison Receptacle Plug. Wireless.
Just the thing for a fan motor connection, also for using 2, 3 or 4 lights from one socket.
No. 092 2 light $1.00
No. 093 3 " 1.30
No. 094 4 " 1.60
Made for Edison Base only.

Number 099

TUNGSTEN ADAPTER.

Number		List Price
099	1-light Brush Brass	$0.70

For Nickel Plated Finish add 5 cents to list.
Enables you to use Tungsten Lamps on any fixture. Changes the position of your lamps to the vertical. Rotating sleeve permits attachment without turning device.

In Ordering Always Give Number of Article and Plate Number.

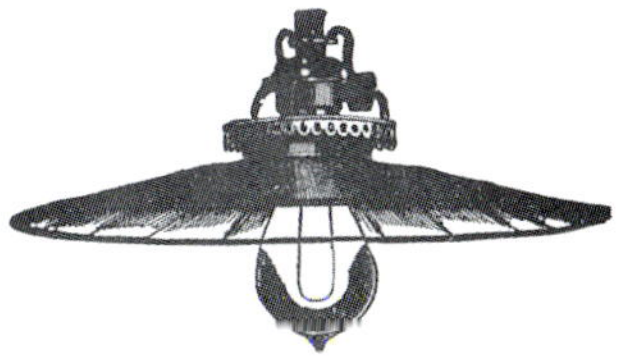

Number B997
Mirror Reflector.

		Reflector only
10-in.,	each	$0.85
12-in.,	"	1.00
14-in.,	"	1.20
16-in.,	"	1.50
18-in.,	"	2.00

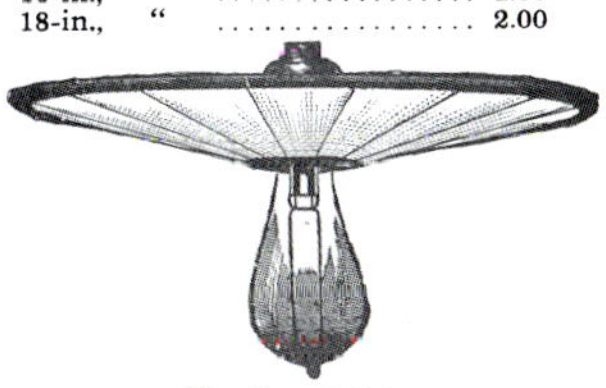

Number B998
Mirror Reflector.

		Reflector only
10-in.,	each	$0.85
12-in.,	"	1.00
14-in.,	"	1.20
16-in.,	"	1.50
18-in.,	"	2.00

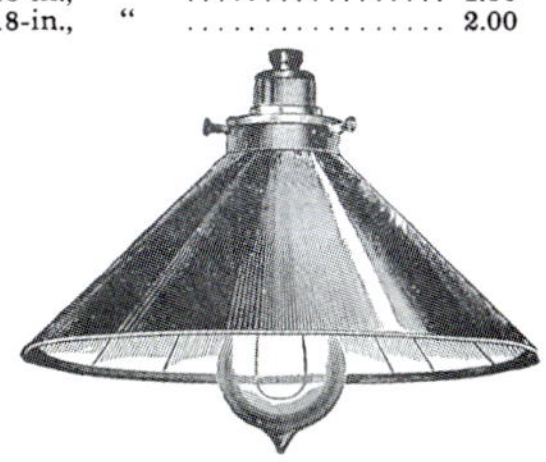

Number B996
Mirror Reflector.

		Reflector only
7-in.,	each	$0.90
10-in.,	"	1.00
12-in.,	"	1.20

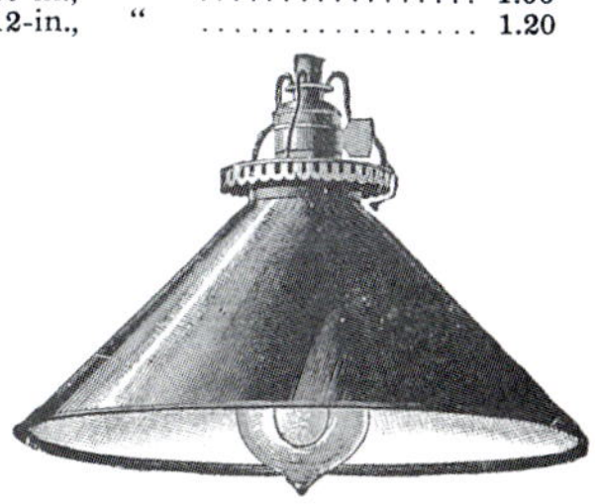

Number B995
Tin Green. White Enamel Lined.

		Shade only
7-in.,	each	$0.25
8-in.,	"	.30
10-in.,	"	.35
12-in.,	"	.45

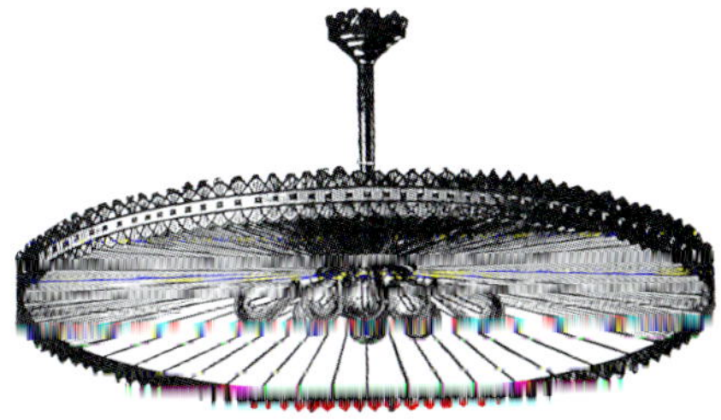

Number 1102
Silver Glass Mirror Reflectors. Length, 36 inches.

	Wired		Wired
20-in. 3-light	$9.75	30-in. 6-light	$15.25
24-in. 4-light	11.75	35-in. 8-light	20.00

Sockets and Lamps not included. If wanted with more lights than mentioned above, add 25 cents for each additional light.

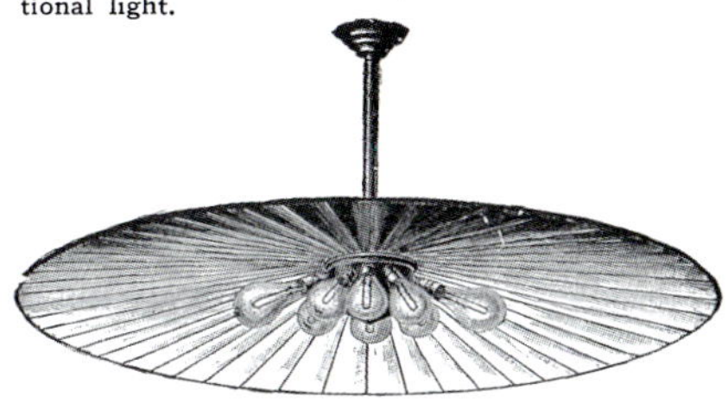

Number 1103
Silver Glass Mirror Reflectors. Length, 36 inches.

	Wired		Wired
20-in. 3-light	$6.75	30-in. 6-light	$11.75
24-in. 4-light	8.50	35-in. 8-light	16.00

Sockets and Lamps not included. If wanted with more lights than mentioned above, add 25 cents for each additional light.

Number 1104
Silver Glass Reflector for Incandescent Clusters with Prisms. Length, 36 inches.

	Wired		Wired
20-in. 3-light	$16.50	30-in. 6-light	$26.50
24-in. 4-light	20.50	35-in. 8-light	32.00

Sockets and Lamps not included. If wanted with more lights than mentioned above, add 25 cents for each additional light.

Number 1
Economical
Pull String Lamp.

Number 2
Economical
Turn Base Lamp.

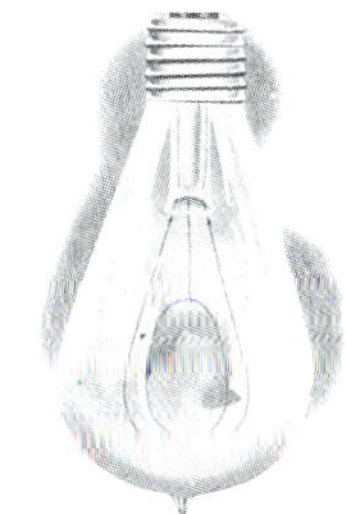

Number 3
Electric Lamps.

	Candle Power	Voltage	Each	Lots 100	Lots 250
No. 1	8 to 1	50 to 130	$0.90	$0.85	$0.80
	16 to 1	50 to 130	.90	.85	.80
No. 2	8 to 1	50 to 130	.90	.85	.80
	16 to 1	50 to 130	.90	.85	.80
					Lots 200
No. 3	2 to 16	45 to 130	.40	....	.36
	20 to 50	45 to 130	.60	....	.54

Frosted Lamps add 10% to above prices.
Round Bulb Lamps, 2 to 16 C. P. add to regular prices 10 cents per lamp.
Tubular Lamps, 2 to 16 C. P. add to regular prices 20 cents per lamp.
Always state Voltage and Candle Power wanted.

No. E-405
Price $14.40

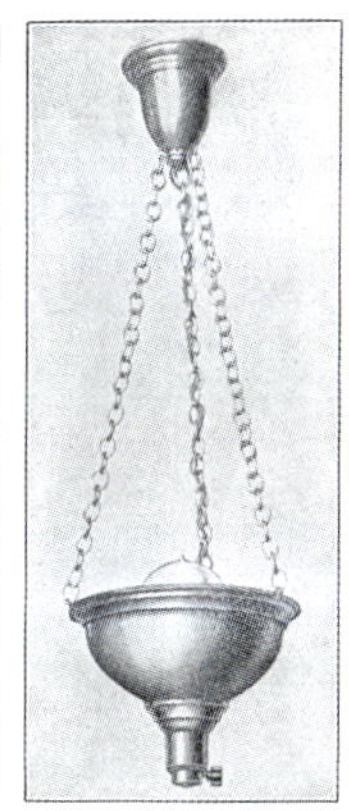

No. E-401
Price $13.20

Single Unit I-Comfort Fixtures used in center of rooms up to 14x14 feet, with 60 or 100-watt Tungsten lamps.

They are furnished complete, wired with key or keyless socket as desired and with blind insulating joint for ⅜-inch gas pipe.

The stems are so arranged that fixtures can be readily attached whether the pipe comes even with the ceiling or extends 1½ to 1¾ inches.

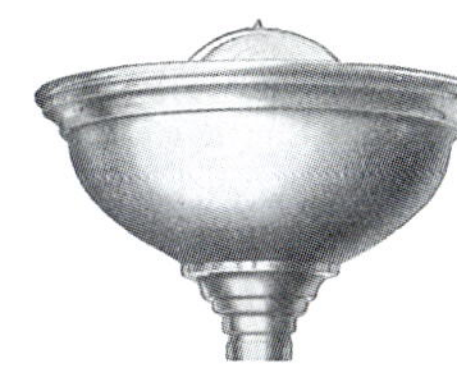

Eye-Comfort Unit.
No. E305 "I-Comfort."

Diameter, 9¾ inches, each $4.80

For use on combination or electric fixtures already in use or where the sockets stand perpendicular. Fits all standard sockets.

The "I-Comfort" (eye-comfort) system is a combination of the highly efficient 60 or 100-watt Tungsten lamp upright, and a specially designed one-piece glass reflector with spiral and vertical corrugations, plated with pure silver, giving the most perfect reflecting surface known to Science.

By placing under the brilliant source of light this reflector the light is reflected to the ceiling, the diffused light is then reflected from the ceiling evenly distributed throughout the room, giving results that are surprising in efficiency, aesthetic effect, and eye-comfort.

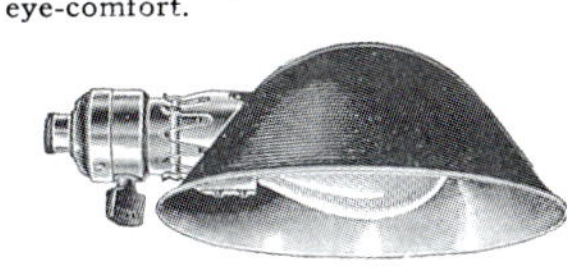

Number B27
Aluminum Shade only.

Number		Each
B25	7-in., polished	$0.80
B26	8-in., polished	1.20
B27	7-in., frosted	.60
B28	8-in., frosted	1.00

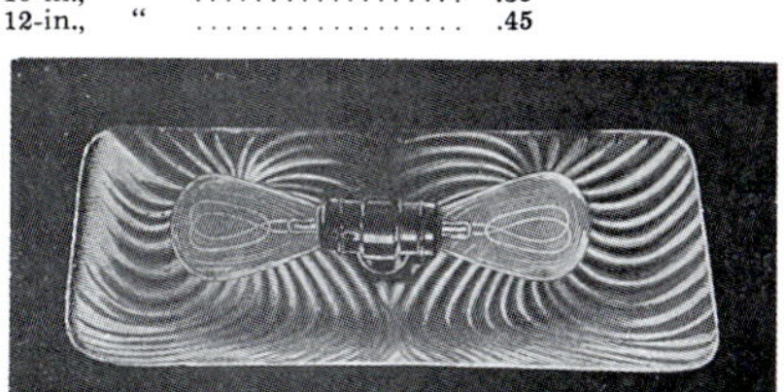

Figure C
Showing interior of Trough.

Number D750
Trough with 12-inch stem.

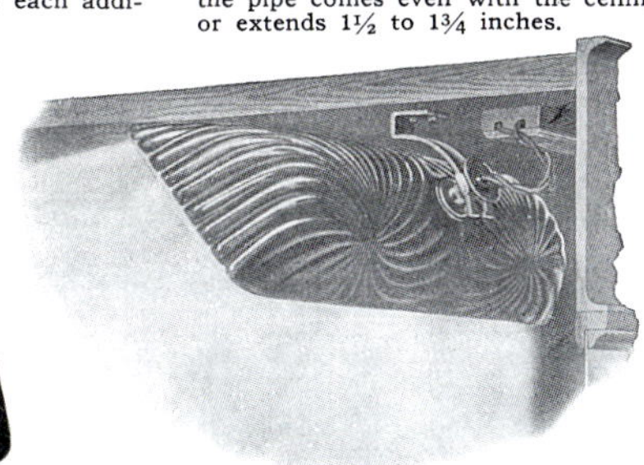

Number B750
Trough supported from ceiling.

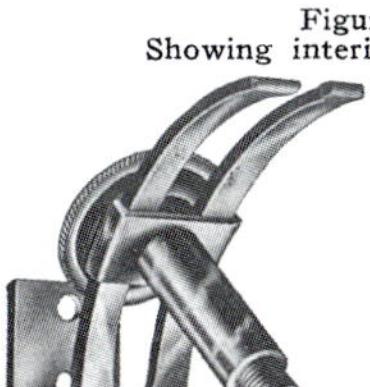

Figure A
Detail of Adjuster.

No. B 750 Poke Bonnet Reflector, 2 lights, wired with twin socket complete	$9.75
No. D 750 Poke Bonnet Reflector, 2 lights, wired with twin socket and 12-inch stem	10.88
Extra lengthening stem, per ft.	.50

The "Poke Bonnet" Trough Reflector is a window reflector 14 inches long, made of one piece of crystal glass blown into perfect shape for reflecting and concentrating the rays of light.

The entire reflecting surface is plated with pure sterling silver and the spiral corrugations so diffuse the rays that the light is evenly distributed.

The shape combines the efficiency of the old style trough and cone reflector without their disadvantages. The adjuster is so designed that the trough can be suspended from wall or ceiling.

Number B53
Half Cone Aluminum Shade only.

Number		Each
B52	8-in., polished	$1.10
B53	8-in., frosted	.90

Glassware Packed Carefully. No Allowance for Breakage in Transportation.

Mica Insulating Joints.

Number 983
Combination Bracket.

3/8 x 1/8-in.	$0.45
3/8 x 1/8-in.	.45
3/8 x 3/8-in.	.45
1/2 x 1/4-in.	.60

Number 984
Combination Fixture.

3/8 x 1/8-in.	$0.55
3/8 x 1/4-in.	.55
3/8 x 3/8-in.	.55
1/2 x 1/8-in.	.75
1/2 x 1/4-in.	.75
1/2 x 3/8-in.	.75
1/2 x 1/2-in.	.75

Number 982
Electrolier.

3/8 x 1/8-in.	$0.60
3/8 x 1/4-in.	.60
3/8 x 3/8-in.	.60
1/2 x 1/8-in.	.75
1/2 x 1/4-in.	.75
1/2 x 3/8 in.	.75
1/2 x 1/2-in.	.75

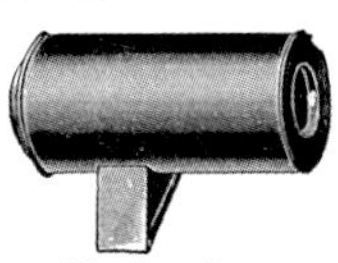

Number B985
Orchestra Shade.
Electric only, each $1.50

Number 933
Polished Brass.
Turned Angle Nozzle.

	Per Doz.
1/8 x 1/8 iron	$1.75
1/4 x 1/8 "	2.75

Number 934
Polished Brass.
Turned Side Nozzle.

	Per Doz.
1/8 x 1/8 iron	$1.50
1/4 x 1/8 "	2.25

Number 935
Polished Brass.
Turned Straight Nozzle

	Per Doz.
1/8 x 1/8 iron	$1.25
1/4 x 1/8 "	2.00

Number 932
3-inch Cast Back.
1/8 Polished Brass.

		Each
No. 931	Female	$0.40
No. 932	Male	.40

Number 930
2-inch Stamped Back.
1/8 Polished Brass.

		Per Doz.
No. 929	Female	$1.50
No. 930	Male	1.50

Number 586
Electrolier Body Iron.

	Each
2-light, 1/4 x 1/8	$0.20
3-light, 1/4 x 1/8	.30
4-light, 1/4 x 1/8	.40

With Binding Screws.

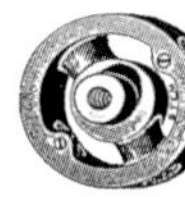

Number 587
Combination Chand Body Iron.

	Each
2-light, 1/4 x 1/8	$0.30
3-light, 1/4 x 1/8	.40
4-light, 1/4 x 1/8	.50

With Binding Screws.

Number 1244 1/2
Polished Brass.

	Each
2-light, not wired	$0.24
3-light, " "	.30
4-light, " "	.36

Number 545

Number		Each	Doz.	Gross
545	Finishers or Seating Rings, 5/8-in., slips 1/8-in. pipe	$0.05	$0.35	$3.50
546	Finishers or Seating Rings, 3/4-in., slips 1/8-in. pipe	.05	.35	3.50
547	Finishers or Seating Rings, 3/4-in., slips 1/4-in. pipe	.05	.35	3.50
548	Finishers or Seating Rings, 7/8-in., slips 1/4-in. pipe	.06	.45	4.50
549	Finishers or Seating Rings, 1-in., slips 1/4-in. pipe	.07	.55	5.50
550	Finishers or Seating Rings, 1-in., slips 3/8-in. pipe	.07	.55	5.50
551	Finishers or Seating Rings, 1 1/4-in., slips 1/2-in. pipe	.10	.75	7.00

Special Finishes Furnished at 1 cent each list, extra.

Number 590
Iron Chand Body.

	Each
2-light, 1/4 x 1/8	$0.12
3-light, 1/4 x 1/8	.14
4-light, 1/4 x 1/8	.18
5-light, 1/4 x 1/8	.25
6-light, 1/4 x 1/8	.35

Number 589 1/2
Iron Tripod.
2 3/4-in. diameter.

	Each
1/8-in., iron	$0.06
1/4-in., "	.06
3/8-in., "	.06
Any of above sizes per 100	5.00

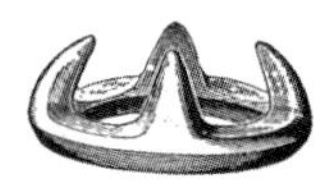

Number 588
Iron Top Finisher.

	Per Doz.
1/4 x 3/4-in.	$0.50
1/4 x 7/8-in.	.50
1/4 x 1-in.	.50
1/8 x 3/4-in.	.50

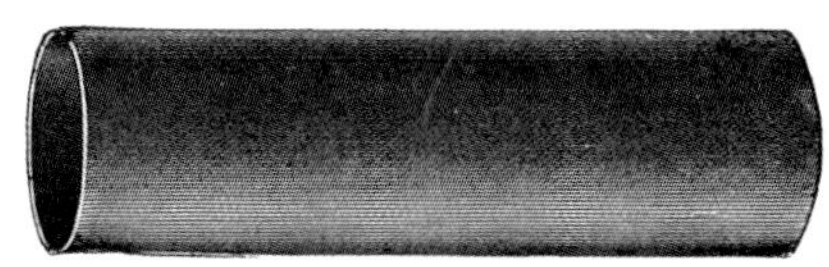

Number 500

Polished Brass Casing.

500 Brass Casing, 1/2-in., slips 1/8-in. iron pipe, polished brass or rich gilt, 6-ft. lengths, per length......$1.20
501 Brass Casing, 5/8-in., slips 1/4-in. iron pipe, polished brass or rich gilt, 6-ft. lengths, per length......$1.30
502 Brass Casing, 3/4-in., slips 3/8-in. iron pipe, polished brass or rich gilt, 6-ft. lengths, per length......$1.40
503 Brass Casing, 7/8-in., slips 3/8-in. iron pipe, polished brass or rich gilt, 6-ft. lengths, per length......$1.65
504 Brass Casing, 1-in., slips 1/2-in. iron pipe, polished brass or rich gilt, 6-ft. lengths, per length......$1.85
505 Brass Casing, 1 1/8-in., slips 1/2-in. iron pipe, polished brass or rich gilt, 6-ft. lengths, per length......$2.40
506 Brass Casing, 1 1/4-in., slips 1/2-in. iron pipe, polished brass or rich gilt, 6-ft. lengths, per length......$2.60

Polished Brass Square Casing.

480 Brass Casing, 3/4-in., slips 3/8-in. iron pipe, polished brass or rich gilt, 6-ft. lengths, per length......$2.10
481 Brass Casing, 7/8-in., slips 3/8-in. iron pipe, polished brass or rich gilt, 6-ft. lengths, per length......$2.50
482 Brass Casing, 1-in., slips 1/2-in. iron pipe, polished brass or rich gilt, 6-ft. lengths, per length......$2.85

Polished Brass Hexagon Casing.

483 Brass Casing, 3/4-in., slips 3/8-in. iron pipe, polished brass or rich gilt, 6-ft. lengths, per length......$1.70
484 Brass Casing, 7/8-in., slips 3/8-in. iron pipe, polished brass or rich gilt, 6-ft. lengths, per length......$2.00
485 Brass Casing, 1-in., slips 1/2-in. iron pipe, polished brass or rich gilt, 6-ft. lengths, per length......$2.20

For Oxidized Copper add 15 per cent; for Silver, 30 per cent extra. Special prices in quantities.

Number 904
4 1/2-in. wide, 3 in. deep.
Brush Brass.

		Each	Per Doz.
Slip 3/4-in.	Brass	$1.25	$12.75
" 7/8-in.	"	1.25	12.75
" 1-in.	"	1.25	12.75

Number 905
4 1/2-in. wide, 4 in. deep.
Brush Brass.

		Each	Per Doz.
Slip 3/4-in.	Brass	$1.50	$15.30
" 7/8-in.	"	1.50	15.30
" 1-in.	"	1.50	15.30

Number 906
4 1/2-in. wide, 3 in. deep.
Polished Brass.

		Each	Per Doz.
Slip 3/8-in.	Brass	$0.40	$4.25
" 5/8-in.	"	.40	4.25
" 3/4-in.	"	.40	4.25
" 7/8-in.	"	.40	4.25

Number 955
4 1/2-in. wide, 4 in. deep.
Polished Brass.

		Each	Per Doz.
Slip 5/8-in.	Brass	$0.45	$4.80
" 3/4-in.	"	.45	4.80
" 7/8-in.	"	.45	4.80
" 1-in.	"	.45	4.80

Canopies, finished Oxidized Copper, add 5 cents each or 50 cents per dozen

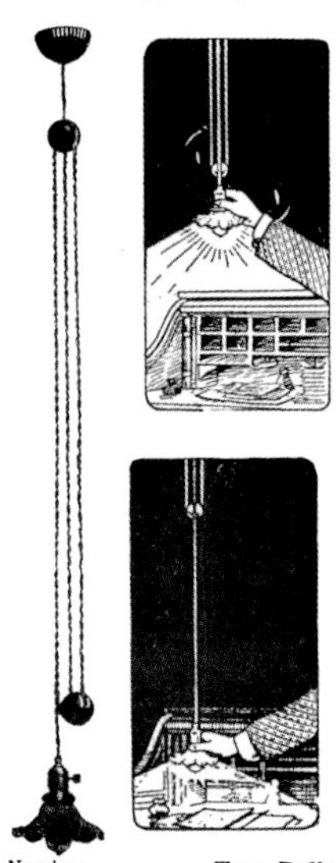

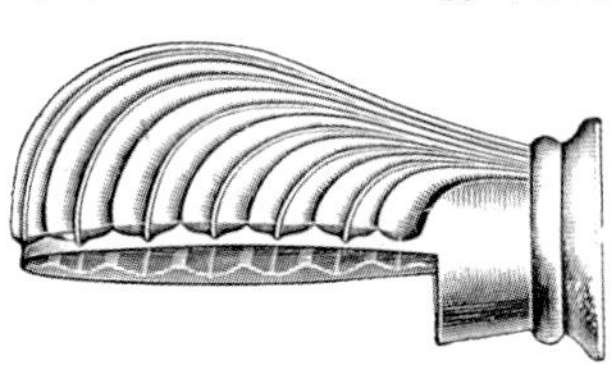

Number B990
Half Shade.
Green Glass, white lining, each..$1.00
" " " " doz... 9.00

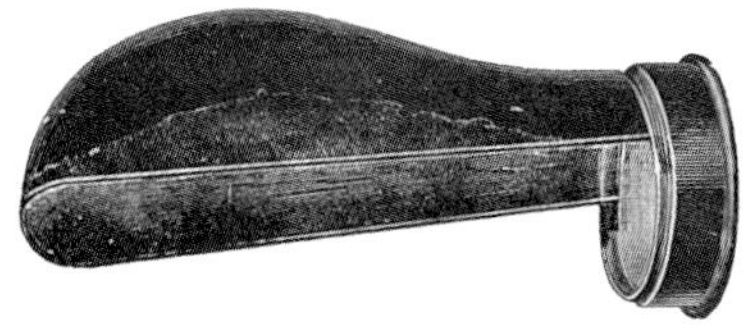

Number B991 1/2
Tin Half Shade.
Green Outside, White Inside.
Per doz. $4.50

Number B969
Pulpit Hood.
French Bronze Finish.
For Electric Light, each........$3.00

Two Balls Adjuster.

Number		Each
35	Two Balls only, black or aluminum	$1.40
36	Two Balls only, polished brass or nickel	2.20

In Ordering Always Give Number of Article and Plate Number.

$50

Number B5121
Ground and Cut Star.
3¼x6 inches, each $1.50
3¼x8 " " 2.25

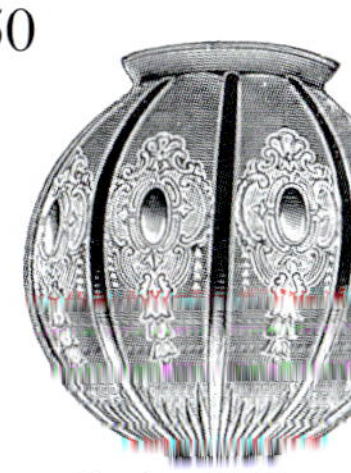

$75

Number B906
Needle Etched and Cut,
Clear Pillar.
3¼x6 inches, each $3.00

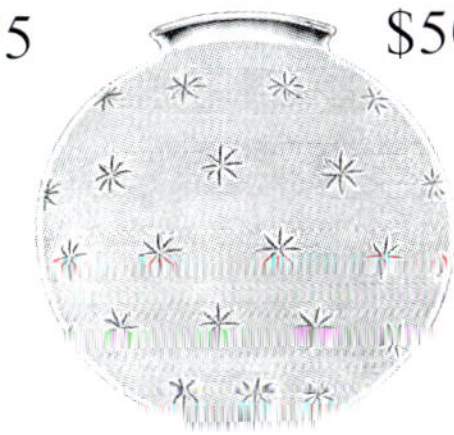

$50

Number B90
Roughed and Cut Star.
3¼x6 inches, each $1.25
3¼x8 " " 2.25

$50

Crystal Roughed Inside Ball.

		Each	Per Doz.
B505	3¼x 5	$0.45	$4.50
B506	3¼x 6	.50	5.00
B507	3¼x 7	.65	6.50
B507½	4 x 7	.65	6.50
B508	3¼x 8	.80	8.00
B508½	4 x 8	.80	8.00
B551	4 x10	1.80	18.00
B552	6 x12	2.70	27.00

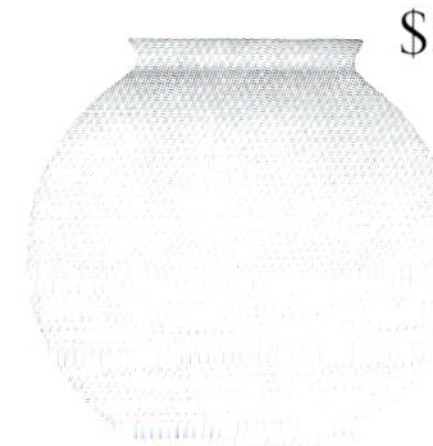

$50

Number B2169

	Plain Straw Opalescent	Straw Opalescent Roughed Inside
3¼x6 inches, each	$0.75	$0.80
3¼x7 " "	.90	1.00
3¼x8 " "	1.00	1.15
4 x8 " "	1.00	1.15

Number B2169½
Plain Flint Opalescent.
3¼x6 inches, each $0.65
3¼x7 " " .75
3¼x8 " " .... .90

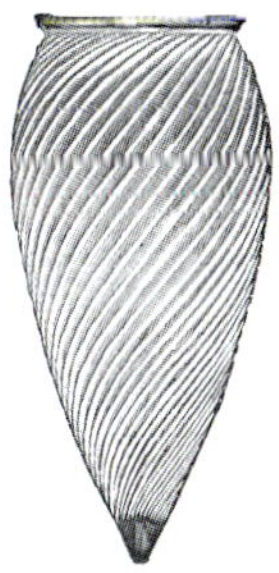

$50

Number B5622½
Flint Opalescent Twist.
3¼x7 inches, each $0.75
3¼x9 " " 1.00

Number B5622
Ruby Twist.
3¼x7 inches, each $1.50
3¼x9 " " 2.00

$50

Number B521
Grecian Design.
Etched, with Cut Star on bottom.
3¼x6 inches, each $1.80

$75

Number B2032½
Silver Etching.
3¼x6 inches, each $1.50
3¼x8 " " 2.00

$50

Number B5204½
Flint Opalescent Twist.
3¼x6 inches, each $0.75
3¼x8 " " 1.00

Number B5204
Ruby Twist.
3¼x6 inches, each $1.50
3¼x8 " " 2.00

$50

Holophane.
Class B for Pendant.

Number	Diameter	Holder	Each
B3155½	6½ in.	3¼ in.	$2.00
B3550½	8 in.	4 in.	4.00

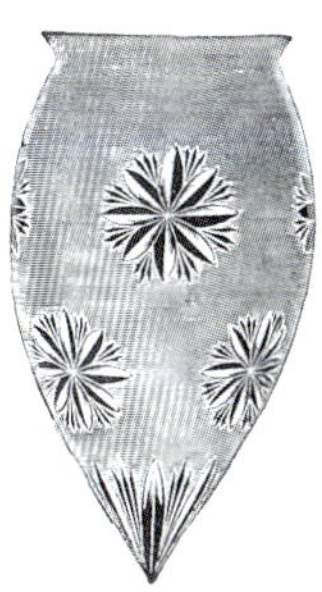

$50

Number B5122
Ground and Cut Star.
3¼x8 inches, each......$1.50

$50

Number B90½
Roughed and Cut Star.
3¼x8 inches, each......$1.25

$50

Number B906½
Needle Etched and Cut,
Clear Pillar.
3¼x8 inches, each......$2.75

$75

Number B2030½
Silver Etching.
3¼x8 inches, each......$1.25

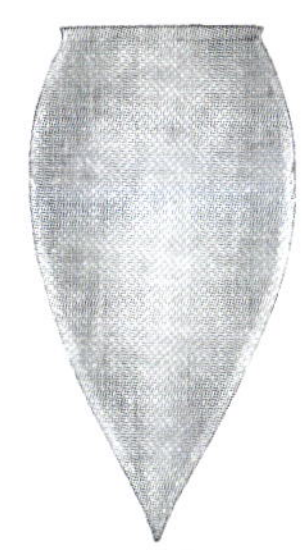

Number B6088½
Plain Straw Opalescent.
3¼x7 inches, each......$0.90
3¼x9 " " 1.25

Number B6088
Crystal Roughed Inside.
3¼x7 inches, each......$0.90
3¼x9 " " 1.25

$50

Number B180½
Crystal Roughed Inside.
3¼x7½ inches, each $1.00

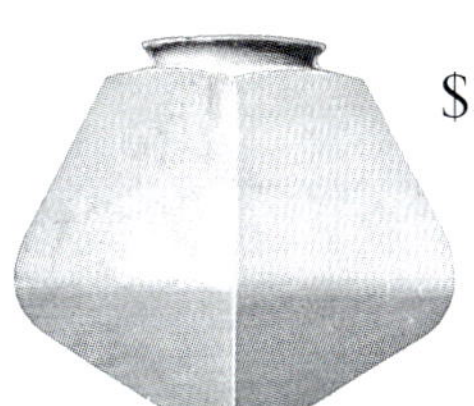

$50

Number B180
Crystal Roughed Inside.
3¼x6 inches, each $0.70
3¼x7 " " .... .80
3¼x8 " " 1.20

$100

Number G415

	Each
Light Green, Satin Finish	$12.00
Purple, Satin Finish	12.50

$100

Number B586
Grape Stalactite 3¼x7½ inches.

	Each
Purple Roughed Outside	$1.75
Red Roughed Outside	1.50
Opalescent Roughed Outside	1.50
Crystal Roughed Outside	1.00

Glassware Packed Carefully. No Allowance for Breakage in Transportation.

$50

Number B1582½
White Acid Etching and Imitation Cut.
2¼-inch Holder, each $0.40

$75

Number B1570½
White Acid Etching.
2¼-inch Holder, each $0.30

$75

Number B1319½
White Acid Etching.
2¼-inch Holder, each $0.40

$50

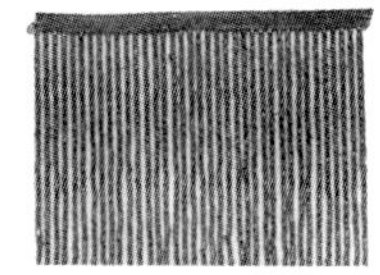

Number G447
Glass Bead Fringe.
Colors: Opal, Green, Red, Crystal, Gold and Mixed.

4-inch, per yard	$1.10
5-inch "	1.35
6-inch "	1.60

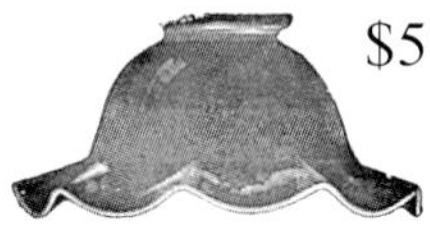

$50

Number B5213½
Plain Straw Opalescent.
2¼-inch Holder, each $0.50

Number B2013½
Same shape as above.
Crystal Roughed Inside.
2¼-inch Holder, each $0.40

$75

Number B1538½
White Etching.
2¼-inch Holder, each $0.40

$75

Number B1906½
White Acid Etching.
2¼-inch Holder, each $0.40

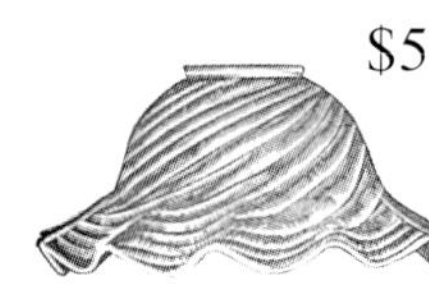

$50

Number B4920½
Flint Opalescent.
2¼-inch Holder, each $0.40

$50

Number B4780½
Crystal Roughed Inside.
2¼-inch Holder, each...........$0.65

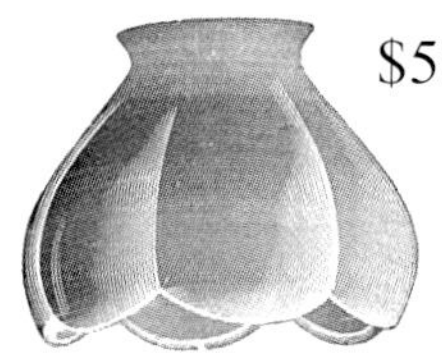

$50

Number B539½
Crystal Roughed Inside.
2¼-inch Holder, each $0.50

$50

Number B8983½
Crystal Roughed Inside.
2¼-inch Holder, each...........$0.35

$75

Number B973½
Crystal.
2¼-inch Holder, each...........$0.30

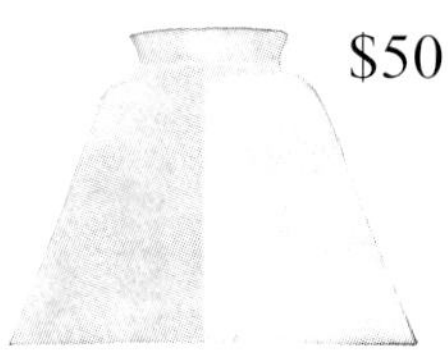

$50

Number B9547½
Crystal Roughed Inside.
2¼-inch Holder, each $0.50

$50

Number B68½
Crystal Roughed Inside.
2¼-inch Holder, each $0.40

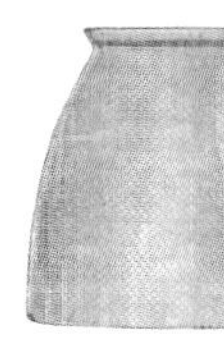

$50

Number B3446½
Crystal Roughed Inside.
2¼-inch Holder, each $0.35

$50

Number B4190½
Crystal Roughed Inside.
2¼-inch Holder, each $0.50

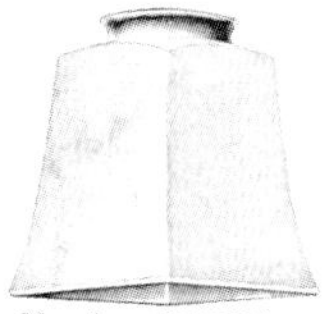

$50

Number B9321½
Crystal Roughed Inside.
2¼-inch Holder, each $0.50

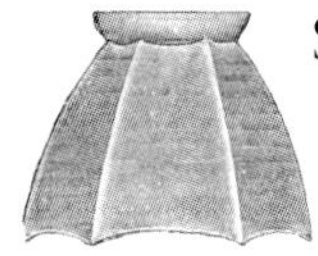

$50

Number B4134½
Crystal Roughed Inside.
2¼-inch Holder, each $0.60

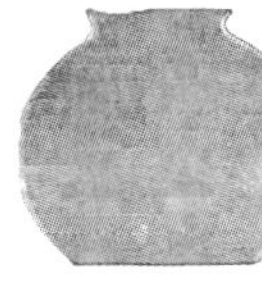

$50

Number B4149
Crystal Roughed Inside.
2¼x4½ inches, each $0.40

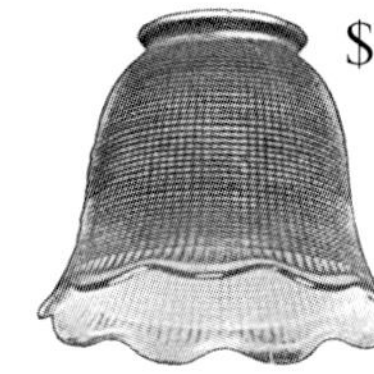

$50

Number B33½
Crystal Prism.
2¼-inch Holder, each $0.25

$50

Number B5014½
Crystal Roughed Inside.
2¼-inch Holder, each $0.55

$50

Number B418½
Light Etched.
2¼-inch Holder, each $0.40

$50

Number B41½
Crystal Glass.
2¼-inch Holder, each $0.25

$50

Number B4284½
Crystal.
2¼-inch Holder, each $0.25

Glassware Packed Carefully. No Allowance for Breakage in Transportation.

Number B1345½
Silver Etching.
2¼-inch Holder, each $0.70

Number B1532½
Metallic Etching.
2¼-inch Holder, each $0.85

Number B1467½
Metallic Etching and Cut.
2¼-inch Holder, each $1.10

Number B1407½
Silver Etching and Cut.
2¼-inch Holder, each $1.10

Number B8057½
White Acid Etching.
2¼-inch Holder, each $0.45

Number B6568½
Etched.
2¼-inch Holder, each $0.75

Number B6075½
Electro Etching.
2¼-inch Holder, each $0.70

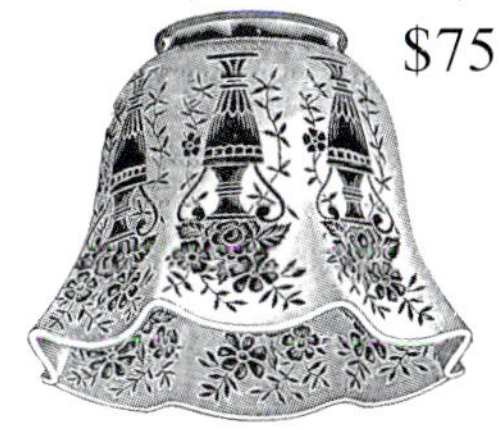

Number B1412½
White Acid Etching.
2¼-inch Holder, each $0.40

Number B602½
Etched and Imitation Cut.
2¼-inch Holder, each $0.70

Number B615½
Etched.
2¼-inch Holder, each $0.55

Number B6043½
Etched.
2¼-inch Holder, each $0.65

Number B5589½ Etched.
2¼-inch Holder, each $0.50
Number B2986½ White Acid.
2¼-inch Holder, each $0.40

Number B807½
Ground and Cut Star.
2¼-inch Holder, each $1.00

Number B870½
Ground and Cut Star.
2¼-inch Holder, each $1.00

Number B2906½
Needle Etched and Cut Clear Pillar.
2½-inch Holder, each $1.65

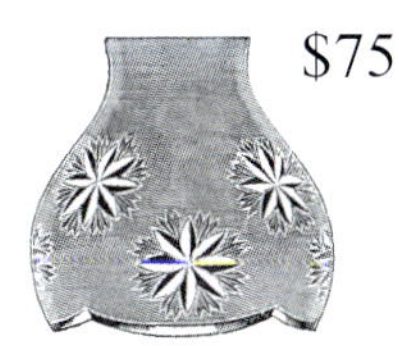

Number B416½
Ground and Large Cut Star.
2¼-inch Holder, each $1.75

Number B5990½
White Acid Etching.
2¼-inch Holder, each $0.45
Ruby or Blue.
2¼-inch Holder, each $0.80

Number B939½
Rose Tint.
2¼-inch Holder, each $1.00

Number G448
Crystal Roughed Inside.
2¼x5½ inches, with Glass Bead Fringe, each $1.50

Number G446
3¼-inch Holder, with Glass Bead Fringe $1.10
4-inch Holder, with Glass Bead Fringe 1.25

Number B118½
Satin Finish Pink.
2¼-inch Holder, each $0.90

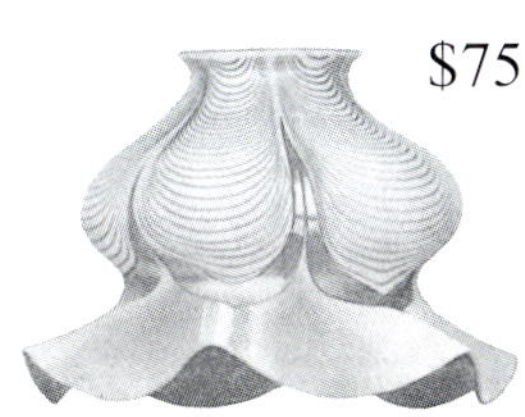

Number B820
Ivory, with gold lustre and green decoration.
2¼-inch Holder, each $4.25

Number B831
Amber Lustre.
2¼-inch Holder, each $9.00

Number B672
Amber Lustre.
2¼-inch Holder, each $3.25

Glassware Packed Carefully. No Allowance for Breakage in Transportation.

$75

Number B 007
Frosted, with Crystal Stars and Bars.
2¼x7 inches, each $0.60

Many eye trobules and headaches are caused by exposing the delicate organs of sight to the direct rays of brilliant modern light sources.

A shade, frosted on the outside, for indirect lighting when used in an upright position, that has a decorative effect and excellent reflecting qualities, giving a soft flood of light through the shade and also reflecting to the ceiling, diffusing the light, and giving excellent results with 40 and 60 watt Tungsten lamps, upright.

$75

Colonial Cut Bowls.

No. B 10112	12-inch Fitter, each	$14.00
No. B 10114	14-inch " "	20.00

$75

Crystal Roughed Inside Bowls.

No. B 2160	10-inch Fitter, each	$1.85
No. B 2162	12-inch " "	2.25
No. B 2164	14-inch " "	3.00
No. B 2166	16-inch " "	6.75

$75

Electric Dome Shades.

Number		Each
B 555	Crystal Roughed Inside, 3¼x10	$1.00
B 556	" " " 4 x12	1.50
B 55½	Plain Straw, Opalesc't, 3¼x10	1.50
B 556½	" " " 4 x12	1.50
B 557½	Green outside, White inside, 3¼x10	1.25
B 9402	Etched Dome as on No. 1710, 3¼x10	2.00

$75

Number B9633
Colonial Cut.
3¼-inch Holder, each $5.00

$75

Number B1039
Colonial Cut.
4x7 inches, each $3.75

$75

Number B397
Colonial Cut.
3¼x6 inches, each $3.00

$75

Number B398½
Colonial Cut.
2¼-inch Holder, each $1.80

$75

Electric Dome Shades.
10-inch Fitter.

Number		Each
B 210	Plain Straw Opalescent R. I.	$2.25
B 212	Green outside, White Inside	2.25

$75

Number B164
Decorated Electric Dome Shade.
10-inch Fitter, each $3.00

$50

Number B256½
Opal.
2¼x6 inches, each $0.18

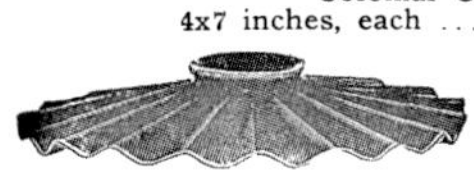

$75

Number B4251½
Opal.
6-in., each $0.18
8-in., " .... .22

$75

Number B255½
Opal.

6-in., each	$0.18	16-in., each	$1.00
8-in., "	.22	18-in., "	1.30
10-in., "	.30	20-in., "	1.70
12-in., "	.50	22-in., "	2.20
14-in., "	.60	24-in., "	2.80

$75

Number B4184½
Opal.
2¼x6 inches, each $0.20

$75

Number B007½
Frosted, with Crystal Stars and Bars.
2¼x7 inches, each $0.60
For 40 and 60-watt lamp.

$50

Number B999
Green Glass. White Inside.

	Each	Per Doz.
2¼x 7 inches	$0.70	$7.00
2¼x10 inches	1.10	11.00

$75

Number		Each
B702	Crystal Roughed Inside Dome	$0.40
B702½	Plain Straw Opalescent Dome	.50

For 40 and 60 watt lamp.

$75

(E 7) Number H106250
For 60-watt lamp.
Full line of Holophane Shades at manufacturer's established prices.

$75

Number B3452
Crystal Roughed Inside.
2¼x8 inches, each $0.90
For 60 and 100-watt lamp.
Opal Glass at same price.
Can be used with our No. 07943 Holder.

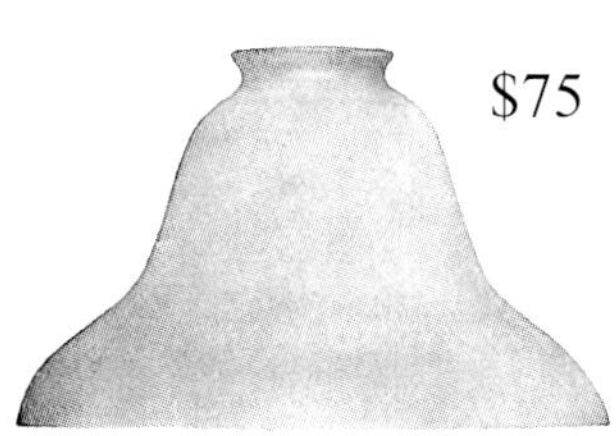

$75

Crystal Roughed Inside.

Number		Each
B 249	2¼x6 inches	$0.35
	For 40-watt lamp.	
B 250	2¼x8 inches	$0.55
	For 60 and 100-watt lamp.	

$75

Colonial Cut.

Number		Each
B 10167	2¼x6 inches	$2.00
	For 40-watt lamp.	
B 10168	2¼x8 inches	3.00
	For 60 and 100-watt lamp.	

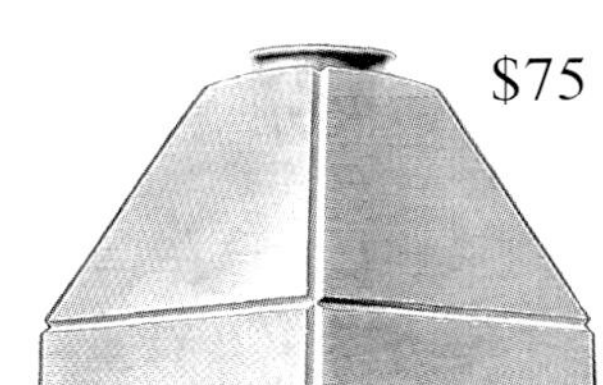

$75

Number B4033
Crystal Roughed Inside.
2¼x6 inches, each.............. $0.85
For 60 and 100-watt lamp.

Glassware Packed Carefully. No Allowance for Breakage in Transportation.

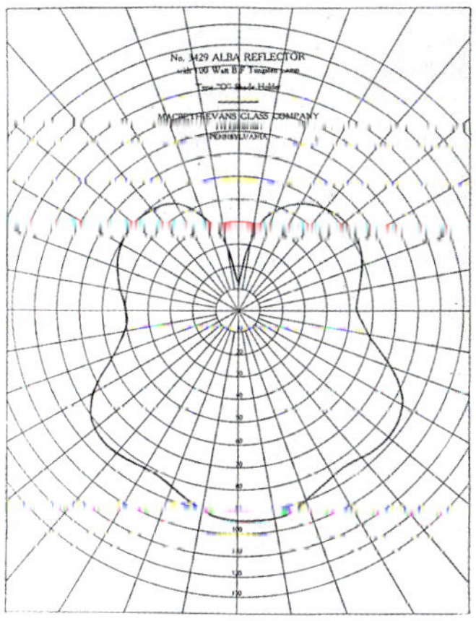

Alba Reflector No. B3429
With 100-watt B. F. Tungsten lamp.

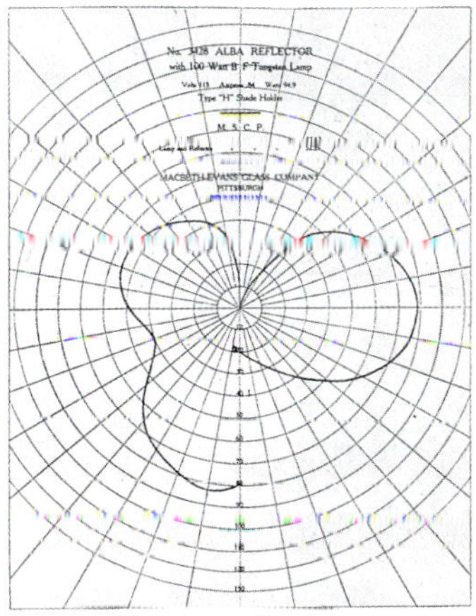

Alba Reflector No. B3428
With 100-watt B. F. Tungsten lamp.

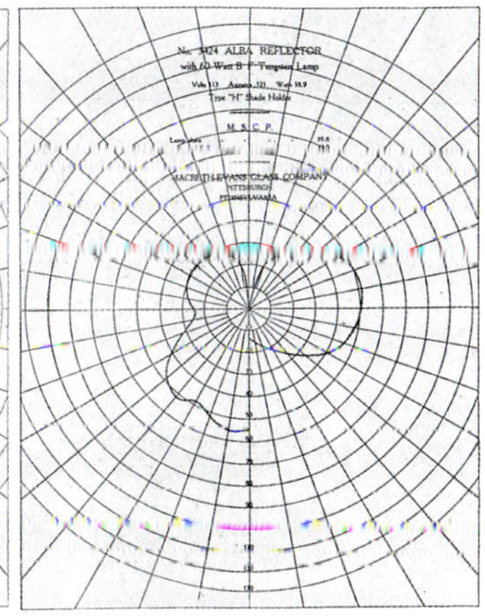

Alba Reflector No. B3424
With 60-watt B. F. Tungsten lamp.

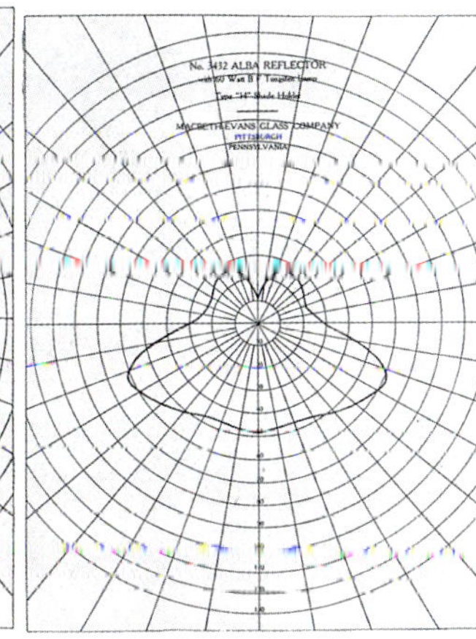

Alba Reflector No. B3432
With 60-watt B. F. Tungsten lamp.

Alba Glass in its present form is the product of some three years of experimentation and development. At the present time it has all the requirements of the ideal reflector for high efficiency lamps, among which are reflective power, maximum of diffusion, color of light transmitted, structure and decorative effect.

Alba Glass is a crystal base filled with microscopic opaque, white particles which produce the above mentioned effect. As there is no color to Alba glass other than pure white, it is incomparable in use with the Tungsten lamp, especially as the remarkable diffusion does away with the constant glare so objectionable in some other kinds of reflectors.

Alba Glass reflectors have no frosted surfaces whatsoever and no sharp prisms, for this reason they are easily cleaned. This is important as they do not have to be removed and scrubbed with the resulting breakage of lamps.

The decorative effect of Alba Glass can be compared only to Alabaster Marble, except that there are no discolorations, being of perfect whiteness throughout. It is now not only used for all commercial purposes but very generally in residential lighting.

Further information gladly furnished on request.

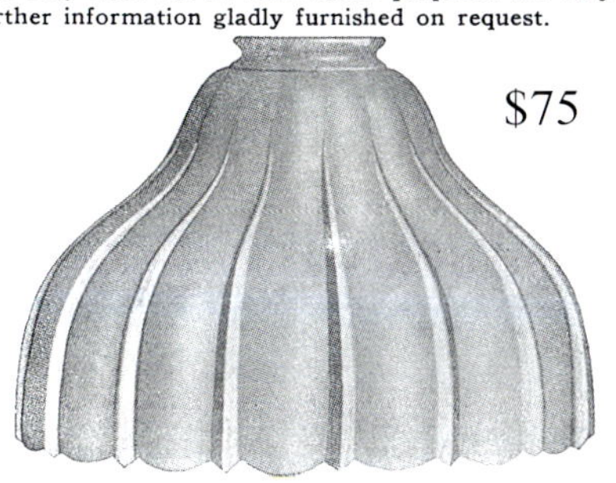

Number B3429 Alba Glass
For 100-watt lamp.
2¼x8¼ inches, per dozen.......$25.75

Number B3424 Alba Glass
For 60-watt lamp.
2¼x7¼ inches, per dozen.......$18.00

Number B3419 Alba Glass
For 25-watt lamp.
2¼x5 inches, per dozen.........$15.00

Number B3428 Alba Glass.
For 100-watt lamp.
2¼x6½ inches, per dozen.......$25.75

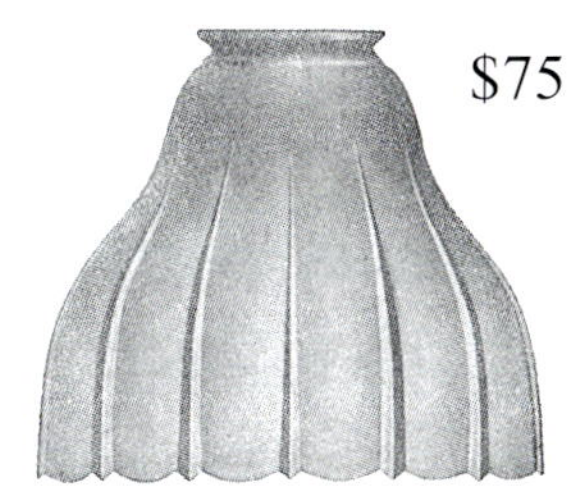

Number B3421 Alba Glass.
For 60-watt lamp.
2¼x6 inches, per dozen.........$16.50

Number B3420 Alba Glass.
For 40-watt lamp.
2¼x5¾ inches, per dozen.......$15.00

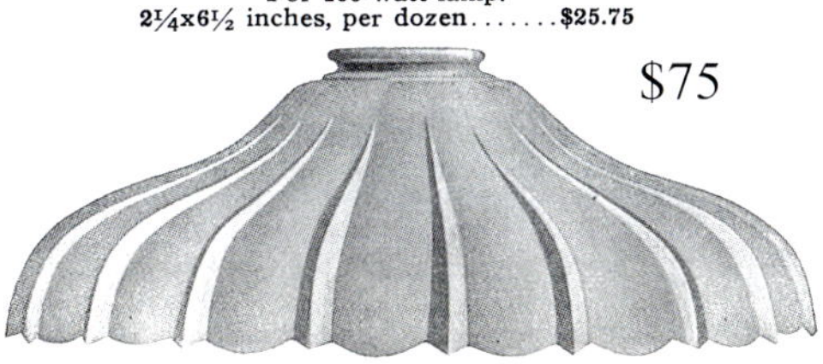

Number B3438 Alba Glass.
For 100-watt lamp.
2¼x11 inches, per dozen........$25.75

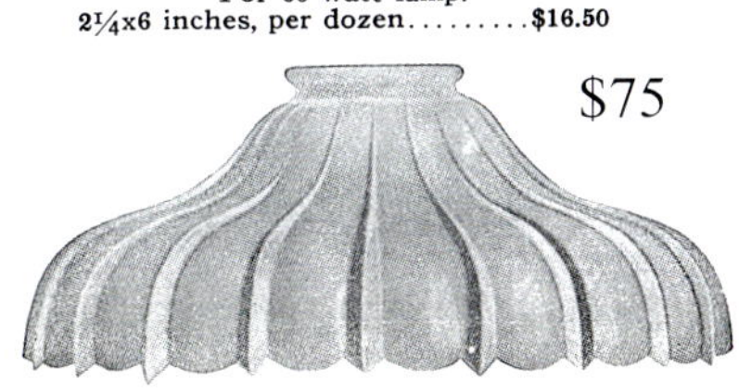

Number B3432 Alba Glass.
For 60-watt lamp.
2¼x9 inches, per dozen.........$18.00

Number B3431 Alba Glass.
For 40-watt lamp.
2¼x7 inches, per dozen.........$15.00

The tables above show that the reflective power of Alba Reflectors is sufficient for all general purposes.

Glassware Packed Carefully. No Allowance for Breakage in Transportation.

$75

Number G441
2¼x6 in., each....$7.50
Pond Lily, White and Green.

$75

Number G439
Will Ship Color 5 unless otherwise ordered.
2¼x4¾ in., each..$1.50

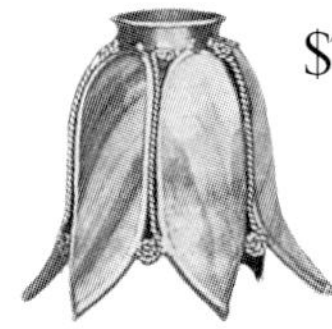
$75

Number G436
Will Ship Color 1 unless otherwise ordered.
2¼x4¾ in., each..$4.00

$75

Number G424
Will Ship Colors 5 and 4 unless otherwise ordered.
2¼x6 inches, each..............$5.10

$75

Number G423
Will Ship Color 7 unless otherwise ordered.
2¼x5 inches, each..............$2.50

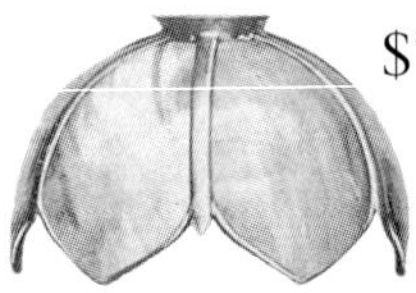
$75

Number G432
Will Ship Color 9 unless otherwise ordered.
2¼x7 in., each....$4.25

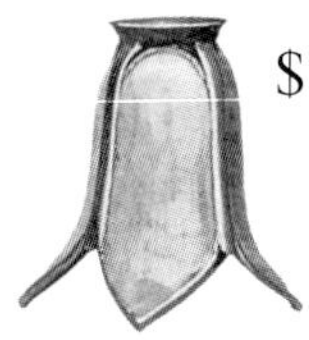
$75

Number G438
Will Ship Color 7 unless otherwise ordered.
2¼x5 in., each....$2.00

$75

Number G437
Will Ship Color 7 unless otherwise ordered.
2¼x4½ in., each..$2.50

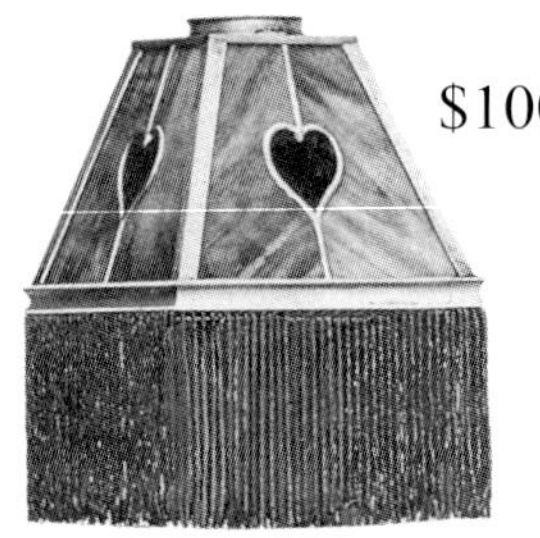
$100

Number G427
Will Ship Colors 5 and 4 unless otherwise ordered.
2¼x6 inches, with Glass Bead Fringe, each $6.00

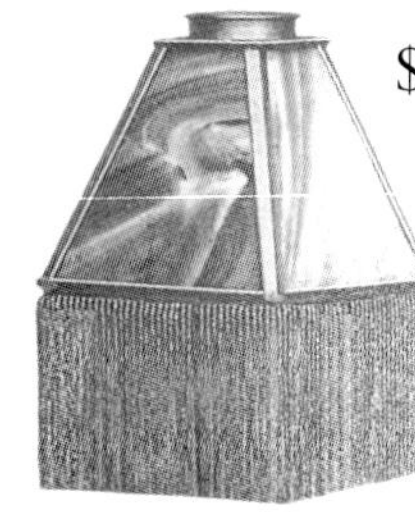
$75

Number G435
Will Ship Color 7 unless otherwise ordered.
2¼x5 inches, with Glass Bead Fringe, each $3.25

$75

Number G445
Will Ship Color 7 unless otherwise ordered.
3¼x6 in., each....$5.75

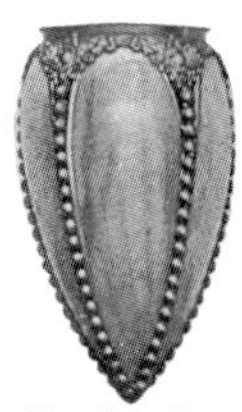
$75

Number G401
Will Ship Color 7 unless otherwise ordered.
3¼x7 in., each....$5.00
3¼x9 " 7.00

$75

Number G417
4-inch Holder, 9 inches High, 12 inches Diameter.
For Gas or Electric, each.......$18.25
Pond Lily, White and Green.

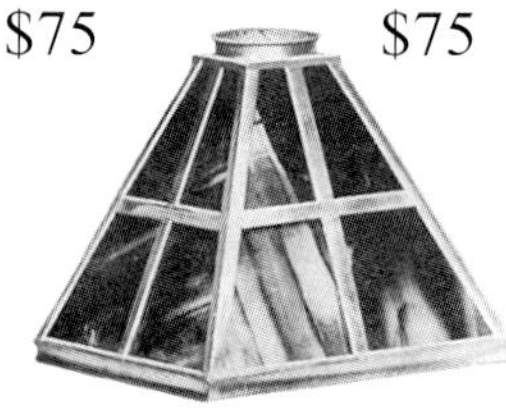
$75

Number G421
Will Ship Color 7 unless otherwise ordered.
2¼x6¾ inches, each.......$5.00

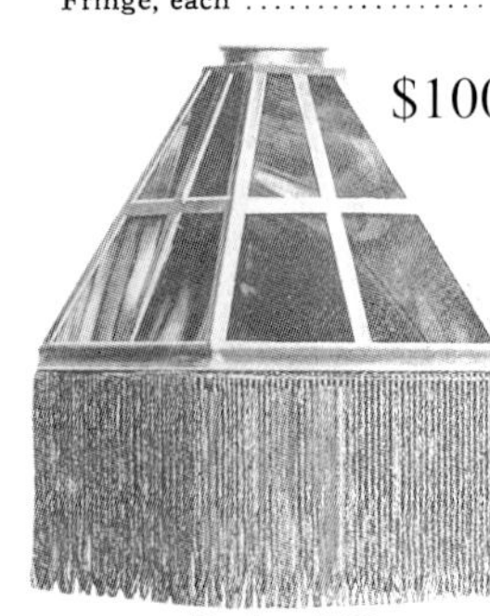
$100

Number G428
Will Ship Color 7 unless otherwise ordered.
2¼x6¾ inches, with Glass Bead Fringe, each $6.00

$75

Number G409
Will Ship Color 1 unless otherwise ordered.
3¼x10 inches, each $5.00
4 x12 " " 6.00
4 x14 " " 7.00
4 x16 " " 9.00
4 x18 " " 12.50

$125

Number G414
Will Ship Color 5 unless otherwise ordered.
3¼x10 inches with Glass Bead Fringe.........$7.50
4 x12 " " " " " 8.50
4 x14 " " " " " 9.50
4 x16 " " " " " 13.50
4 x18 " " " " " 16.00

$125

Number G429
Will Ship Color 7 unless otherwise ordered.
3¼x12 inches, with Glass Bead Fringe...............$7.00
3¼x14 " " " " " 8.00
3¼x16 " " " " " 10.00
3¼x18 " " " " " 12.50

$125

Number G400
Will Ship Color 7 unless otherwise ordered.
Diameter 16 inches No Fringe..............$14.25
" 16 " With " 17.25
" 22 " No " 20.00
" 22 " With " 24.00

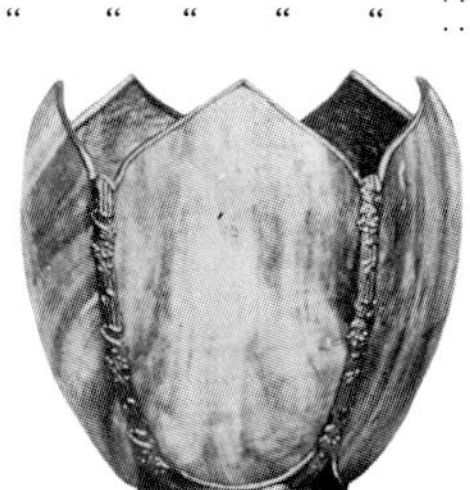
$75

Number G431
Will Ship Color 7 unless otherwise ordered.
4-in. Holder, 8-in. high, Gas or Electric, each....$4.50

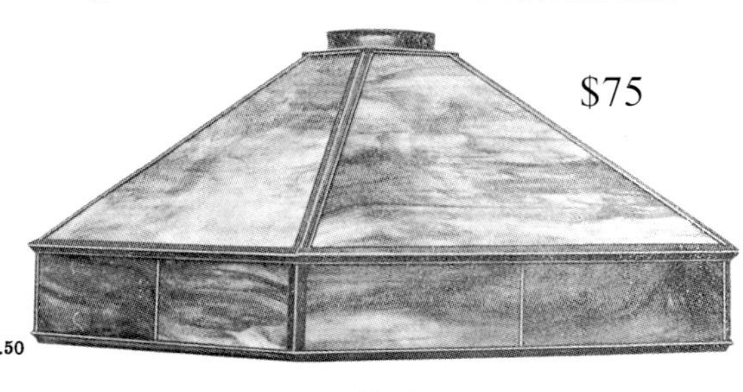
$75

Number G449
Will Ship Color 7 unless otherwise ordered.
3¼x12 inches ....$8.00 3¼x16 inches ...$11.00
3¼x14 " .... 9.00 3¼x18 " 13.50

Select Art Glass Shades by Color Numbers. See last page.

Glassware Packed Carefully. No Allowance for Breakage in Transportation.